Humboldt and the modern German university

An intellectual history

JOHAN ÖSTLING

Translation: Lena Olsson

Lund University Press

Copyright © Johan Östling 2018

The right of Johan Östling to be identified as the author of this work has been asserted by him in accordance with the UK Copyright, Designs and Patents Act 1988.

Lund University Press
The Joint Faculties of Humanities and Theology

LUND
UNIVERSITY
PRESS

P.O. Box 117
SE-221 00 LUND
Sweden
http://lunduniversitypress.lu.se

Lund University Press books are published in collaboration with Manchester University Press

Lund University Press gratefully acknowledges the generous financial assistance of Riksbankens Jubileumsfond, which funded the translation and most of the production costs of this volume.

First published by Atlantis, Stockholm, in 2016, as *Humboldts universitet: Bildning och vetenskap i det moderna Tyskland*
ISBN 978-91-7353-856-5

ISBN 978-91-983768-0-7 hardback
ISBN 978-91-983768-1-4 open access

First published 2018

An electronic version of this book is also available under a Creative Commons (CC-BY-NC-ND) licence

The publisher has no responsibility for the persistence or accuracy of URLs for any external or third-party internet websites referred to in this book, and does not guarantee that any content on such websites is, or will remain, accurate or appropriate.

Typeset
by Toppan Best-set Premedia Limited
Printed in Great Britain
by Lightning Source

Contents

List of images	*page* vii
Acknowledgements	viii
Preface: Unter den Linden 6	xii

1	**The history of the university**	**1**
	The university and historiography	1
	University history as intellectual history and history of knowledge	5
	The history of the Humboldtian tradition	8
	The form and content of the Humboldtian tradition	14
2	**Wilhelm von Humboldt and his idea**	**23**
	A modern university	23
	Humboldt's idea	35
	Humboldt's nineteenth century	43
3	**The discovery of Humboldt**	**50**
	Discovering Humboldt	55
	The Weimar Republic	64
	The Third Reich	72
	Humboldt's shifting guises	80
4	**The rebirth of the university**	**84**
	Humboldt during the years of occupation	88
	Karl Jaspers and the rebirth of the university	98
	Towards a vitalisation	103
	Karl Jaspers and the Humboldtian tradition	108
	Gerhard Ritter and the liberal university	110
	Ideals under review	117
	The mandarins and the Humboldtian tradition	122
	The wider stage	127
	The university reborn	135

5	**Tradition under debate**	140
	A Humboldt for the post-war world	148
	The idea of the Berlin university	152
	The theoretical university	158
	Schelsky and the Humboldtian tradition	162
	Ralf Dahrendorf and the liberal university	170
	'Hochschule in der Demokratie'	179
	Debating tradition	192
6	**From Berlin to Bologna**	207
	The morphology of the Bologna process	214
	The ubiquity of Humboldt	220
	The Humboldtian tradition's intellectual history and history of knowledge	223
	The Humboldtian tradition and the modern university	236
	Humboldt's topicality	245
Bibliography		250
Index		285

Images

1 The University of Bologna (© Buena Vista Images/Getty Images)	*page* xviii
2 The Hong Kong University of Science and Technology (© ImageRite/Alamy Stock Photo)	xviii
3 A picture from the 1930 film *Der blaue Engel* (© Moviestore Collection Ltd/Alamy Stock Photo)	19
4 Wilhelm von Humboldt (© Ullstein Bild/Getty Images)	33
5 Carl Heinrich Becker (© Ullstein Bild/Getty Images)	66
6 German students in 1933 (© Ullstein Bild)	75
7 The war-damaged Berlin university in 1945 (© Ullstein Bild)	86
8 Karl Jaspers (© Ullstein Bild/Getty Images)	100
9 Oxford students around 1950 (© Trinity Mirror/Mirrorpix/Alamy Stock Photo)	128
10 Protesting students in Munich in 1968 (© INTERFOTO/Alamy Stock Photo)	142
11 Helmut Schelsky (© Ullstein Bild – Hellgoth)	163
12 Humboldt University anniversary celebrations in 1960, in the GDR period (© Keystone Pictures USA/Alamy Stock Photo)	193
13 Student protests in Magdeburg in 2010 (© Dpa Picture Alliance Archive/Alamy Stock Photo)	214
14 A photo from present-day Berlin (© Dpa Picture Alliance Archive/Alamy Stock Photo)	246

Acknowledgements

This book was written during my postdoctoral itinerant years. The topic, however, I realise now, has followed me longer than that. Already as a student, I spent time in Tübingen, where I encountered an academic culture which seemed both alien and fascinating with its old-fashioned traits and the eccentric personalities of its professors. A few years later I was a visiting doctoral student at Humboldt-Universität zu Berlin, following, at close quarters, the public trial of strength regarding the university that the Bologna process had engendered. I was struck by the seriousness and historical depth of the German debate. Here, issues that in Sweden were mostly treated as if they were technicalities – the structure of the studies, the conditions for research, the nature of knowledge – became the subject of original contemplation and intense controversy.

Since then, I have had the privilege of exploring the Humboldtian tradition in several scholarly environments. A first foundation was laid at the Research Policy Institute at Lund University, where I had a postdoctoral appointment financed by the Swedish Research Council. Here, as a historian, I came into contact with a multifaceted study of the institutions of knowledge and research. I attached special value to my exchanges with Mats Benner, Olof Hallonsten, Gustav Holmberg, and Anna Tunlid.

Most of the work on this book has been conducted within the framework of my position as a Pro Futura Scientia Fellow, generously financed by Riksbankens Jubileumsfond. For a total of two terms, in 2013 and 2014, I was a fellow in residence at the Swedish Collegium for Advanced Study (SCAS) in Uppsala. The social and intellectual atmosphere that permeates SCAS enriched me in an exceptional manner. I owe a special debt of gratitude to Björn Wittrock, whose knowledge of university history and enthusiasm for my topic has been of inestimable value. My two mentors in the Pro Futura programme, Hans Joas and Jürgen Kocka, have conveyed

Acknowledgements ix

important insights about modern German history and opened doors for me in Berlin. During countless lunches and meetings at SCAS I have been able to discuss the theory and practice of academic life, not least with Kimmo Alho, Anders Andrén, Gustaf Arrhenius, Gian Vittorio Caprara, Rodney Edvinsson, Gunnel Engwall, Anandi Hattiangadi, Paula Henrikson, Petter Johansson, Barbro Klein, Virginia Langum, Dirk Meyer, Stephen Mitchell, Christer Nordlund, Jonas Olofsson, Michael Puett, Wlodek Rabinowicz, Sandra Rekanovic, H. Otto Sibum, Krishnan Srinivasan, and Kristin Zeiler.

During an invaluable academic year, 2013–2014, I was able to deepen my understanding of the history of the Humboldtian tradition and the modern university on German soil. The first term was spent at the Zentrum für Zeithistorische Forschung (ZZF) in Potsdam, where I gained fruitful insights into the dynamic research on contemporary history that is conducted there. Frank Bösch, Maren Möhring, and Martin Sabrow were my kind hosts in Brandenburg. During the second term I was attached to the Max-Planck-Institut für Wissenschaftsgeschichte (MPIWG) in Berlin, that extraordinary institution for the history of science at Boltzmannstraße in Dahlem. I am grateful to Lorraine Daston for her hospitality and inspirational leadership.

Throughout the terms of travel and temporary anchorages, the Department of History at Lund was the fixed point in my professional existence. Here I briefly held a post as a postdoctoral research fellow, and it was here I completed this study in 2016. It is a generous environment with many good friends and proficient colleagues. It has been especially inspiring to introduce the history of knowledge as a new field at the Department in happy partnership with David Larsson Heidenblad, Anna Nilsson Hammar, and others. Our Norwegian comrades have been indispensable in these efforts: Kari Hernæs Nordberg and the incomparable Erling Sandmo, with whom good fortune brought me together at the MPIWG in Berlin.

I share my interest in Wilhelm von Humboldt and his university with Peter Josephson and Thomas Karlsohn. Together, we have organised a conference in Uppsala and edited a book. It has always been very educational and rewarding to discuss the university with them, the historical university as well as the contemporary one. The distinctive features and unused potential of university history I have, in addition, discussed with Anders Ahlbäck, Henrik Björck, John Peter Collett, Pieter Dhondt, Ylva Hasselberg, Laura Hollsten, Thomas Kaiserfeld, Tamson Pietsch, Sverker Sörlin, Fredrik W. Thue, and Sven Widmalm. On a more local level, it has been as useful as it has been enjoyable to be a part of the group that worked with the history of the university on the eve of the Lund University 350-year anniversary under the leadership of Gunnar Broberg and David Dunér. Here I was able to convert thoughts about university history into concrete practice. With Martin Wiklund I have had continuing conversations about the premises of the writing of history, and with Charlotta Seiler Brylla, Kristian Gerner, Kay Glans, Barbro Landén, and Johanna Ringarp I have discussed German matters.

During the years I have devoted to the fundamental issues of the university, I have come into contact with a number of experienced academics who have supported me and my research. Many of them have shared their insights about the conditions and transformational power of the academic world. For encouragement and stimulation, I direct my thanks to Carl-Gustaf Andrén, Jenny Björkman, Göran Blomqvist, Lars Edgren, Sverker Gustavsson, Alf W. Johansson, Klas-Göran Karlsson, Britta Lövgren, Kjell Å. Modéer, Thorsten Nybom, Hans Ruin, Kerstin Sahlin, Kim Salomon, Bo Stråth, Birgitta Svensson, Marianne Thormählen, Anette Warring, and Lynn Åkesson.

Several people have read and commented on sections from this book. A few of them have tackled the whole of it. For critical and extraordinarily constructive viewpoints I thank Peter Josephson, Thomas Kaiserfeld, Thomas Karlsohn, Kim Salomon, and Erling Sandmo.

And then, finally, my beloved family. Mia has subjected my texts to perceptive scrutiny, been my best conversational partner, and given me her unconditional support, most of all during my many stays in Uppsala. Together with her, I have endured the trials of the recent years but also shared all the good things they offered. During this period our sons, Malkolm and Viktor, have begun to find their places in the world. As they continue to grow, I can only wish that they will be allowed to retain their joy in knowledge, and in life.

* * *

This book is a translation of *Humboldts universitet: Bildning och vetenskap i det moderna Tyskland*, which appeared from the Swedish publisher Atlantis in September 2016. In all essential respects, it constitutes a translation of that work, although certain additions and adaptations have been made. When I decided to have my book published in English, I contacted Marianne Thormählen at Lund University Press. She instantly showed an enthusiastic interest in the

Acknowledgements

project, and her sincere commitment to it has never faltered. Like my translator Lena Olsson, she tackled the job with meticulous care and a sense of style; the two of them together have managed to change one book into another. I am deeply indebted to them, and the same applies to the two anonymous peer reviewers for Lund University Press, who scrutinised the Swedish version of the book and offered a number of valuable suggestions.

The publication of the book has come about with the generous support of Riksbankens Jubileumsfond, which also funded the Swedish version in 2016. At an early stage of my work I was awarded the Nils Klim Prize, which encouraged me to continue my research about the idea of the university. Early on, I also received valuable grants from the Fahlbeck Foundation (*Fahlbeckska stiftelsen*), the Helge Ax:son Johnson Foundation (*Helge Ax:son Johnsons stiftelse*), and the Inga and John Hain Foundation (*Inga och John Hains stiftelse*). For all this I am very grateful.

Johan Östling
Lund, in May 2017

Preface: Unter den Linden 6

Berlin's well-filled tourist buses tend to slow down on the grand boulevard Unter den Linden. The reason is that the multilingual city guides have much information to impart soon after leaving 'Museum Island', *Museumsinsel*. On the left, the Berlin State Opera and the Bebelplatz appear; and opposite them, in quick succession, follow the German Historical Museum, the Neue Wache memorial, and the Berlin State Library. This can be seen, for those who wish to do so, as a German national nexus, a focus for historical monuments and events. In a city replete with a ubiquitous past, the concentrations of history here are especially tangible.

In this part of the city, more precisely at Unter den Linden 6, you also find the main building of Humboldt-Universität zu Berlin. Those who leave the main thoroughfare and move closer to the imposing entrance of the building will pass students, bookstalls, and statues of Prussian nineteenth-century figures. Inside the entrance hall the visitor encounters a quotation from Karl Marx, an alumnus of the University. Moving up the stairs to the first floor, a visitor finds photographs of German Nobel Prize winners who were affiliated, at one time or another, with the German capital's university. Albert Einstein, Werner Heisenberg, Robert Koch, Theodor Mommsen, Max Planck, Erwin Schrödinger, and another twenty-odd prominent scientists belong to this group. Almost all of them worked here during the early decades of the twentieth century. As impressive as this list is, the lacunae after 1933 are disheartening in equal measure. The history of the Berlin university reflects the *splendeurs et misères* of modern Germany.

The university on Unter den Linden is at the same time part of a more comprehensive history of the development of science, scholarship, and higher education. When the Berlin Universität opened in October 1810, it inaugurated a new era in the history of the university. The man behind its creation was the Prussian official, linguist, and educational reformer Wilhelm von Humboldt.

In a famous manifesto, he drew up the guidelines for the new institution. Here, *Bildung* and scholarship were more important than mechanically teaching long-established material; here was a dynamic connection between the production and the dissemination of knowledge; here academic freedom was given a broader and firmer meaning. The first modern university had been born.

This is one way of summarising the historiography surrounding the Berlin university. During the twenty-first century, it has been reproduced in surveys, encyclopaedias, and scholarly descriptions. In the twenty-first edition of the time-honoured encyclopaedia *Brockhaus*, attention is paid to the importance of the new university in Berlin as a model for 'a reform based on the combination of research and education', a combination which became a structural principle of academic activities, initially in Central Europe and then in the rest of Europe and in the USA.[1] The *Encyclopædia Britannica* also attributes a paradigmatic importance to the new Prussian university. 'The school was dedicated to the scientific approach to knowledge, to the combination of research and teaching', it says. During the third quarter of the nineteenth century, its principles of *Lernfreiheit* ('freedom to learn') and *Lehrfreiheit* ('freedom to teach') spread 'throughout the academic world'. The Swedish national encyclopaedia *Nationalencyklopedin* also considers the Berlin university a new type of institution, established on the basis of the principles of Wilhelm von Humboldt, and maintains that it 'became a model outside Germany as well'.[2]

---

1 'Universität', *Brockhaus*, 30 vols (Leipzig and Mannheim, 2006), xxviii, 369. All quotations in this book taken from sources other than those written in the English and Scandinavian languages are translations of the author's original translations into Swedish, unless explicitly stated otherwise. The translations of German concepts into English were made by Marianne Thormählen.
2 'Education', *Encyclopædia Britannica: Britannica Academic*, http://academic.eb.com/EBchecked/topic/179408/education (accessed 15 February 2016); 'University', *Wikipedia*, https://en.wikipedia.org/wiki/University (accessed 15 February 2016); Tore Frängsmyr, 'Universitet', in *Nationalencyklopedin*, ed. by Kari Marklund and others, 20 vols (Höganäs, 1989–1996), xix (1996). A similar historiography can be found in articles in the more extensive language versions of *Wikipedia*, for instance 'History of European research universities', *Wikipedia*, https://en.wikipedia.org/wiki/History_of_European_research_universities (accessed 15 February 2016), 'Humboldtian model of higher education', *Wikipedia*, https://en.wikipedia.org/wiki/Humboldtian_model_of_higher_education (accessed 15 February 2016) and 'Humboldtsches Bildungsideal', *Wikipedia*, https://de.wikipedia.org/wiki/Humboldtsches_Bildungsideal (accessed 15 February 2016).

In a broader perspective, this story forms the basis for an academic self-understanding; ultimately, it supports an intellectual identity. To this day, perhaps even especially today, Humboldt's name is invoked in laudatory speeches and in debates about the university. When examined more closely, however, the actual history turns out to be more complex. Over the last two decades, researchers have completed a thorough historicisation of the birth of the modern university, including the efforts of Wilhelm von Humboldt and the academic ideals with which he is associated. Those who wish to present well-founded reflections on the foundations of the university must incorporate these new insights.[3]

In spite of this belated historicisation, it is indisputable that the Humboldtian tradition has represented the central academic ideals in many significant struggles over research and higher education. During the previous century, this tradition continuously inspired criticism, reform, and the glorification of former greatness. The new historical research in no way implies a refutation of this tradition, and still less a reduction of its importance. Instead, it opens up the way to a deeper understanding of the role that has been – and still is – played by this tradition in the clashes over the goals and meaning of the university.

In the twenty-first century, intense debates concerning the university have flared up in Germany. An underlying factor is the general feeling that the country's once so excellent universities have been irredeemably left behind. It has been noticeably difficult for German universities to compete with the most prominent American or British universities, even though Germany possesses vital research environments which combine domestic intellectual traditions with new impulses. When Germany ends up far down in the academic ranking tables in survey after survey, this gives rise to feelings of crisis and

---

3 Wilhelm von Humboldt is commonly mistaken for his younger brother, the natural scientist Alexander von Humboldt – in laudatory speeches, political debates, and scholarly presentations. To give an example: In *The University: An Illustrated History* (New York, 2011), ed. by Fernando Tejerina – a magnificent volume on the history of the university – the chapter on the Enlightenment and liberalism (pp. 112–13) opens with an illustration of Humboldt-Universität zu Berlin and an accompanying caption that is connected to an established historiography: 'Wilhelm von Humboldt (1767–1835) founded the University of Berlin in 1810. It was created as the first wholly modern university. Education was based on teaching and research combined, and the humanities provided an overarching context. It has carried his name since 1949.' The mishap in this context is that the image is of Alexander von Humboldt.

frustration. A second, directly triggering factor is the Bologna Process. The purpose of that process, which set up a uniform educational system based on the Anglo-Saxon model, was to promote mobility, employability, and European competitiveness. In Germany, this reform of the structure of the university has given rise to sophisticated reflection on the very nature of higher education as well as to intense polemics against adaptation to the market. Since the turn of the millennium, countless contributions have been published – from fact-based memorandums to critical pamphlets – that together make up a multifaceted discussion. When it comes to conducting basic research on cardinal academic issues, Germany remains a scholarly nation in a class by itself. Those who wish to ponder the idea of the university cannot disregard the German tradition of scrutiny and reflection.

In this book, I anchor the current debate about the university in the past by exploring the history and varying meanings of the Humboldtian tradition. My research is not intended as a thought-provoking background for contributions of a more unreservedly contemporary orientation. On the contrary, I am convinced that an understanding of history is necessary for anyone who wishes to form an accurate opinion on the characteristics of the academic debate that is taking place in the political and economic power centres of Europe. Indeed, the current German discussions also acquire their special vigour and tone from a historical sounding-board. Those among today's academics who seek an answer to the specifically German question of the idea of the university are still turning to the past. It is not least the classic German university tradition, a tradition more or less associated with Wilhelm von Humboldt, that forms their point of departure. With a series of historical examples, each of which is characteristic of its time, I will demonstrate what this classic German line of thought has meant during the modern period, and what it might mean to us.

In our time, the university is the bearer of many promises. It is expected to provide education for today and tomorrow, engender knowledge and learning, stimulate regional and national economies, serve as a critical authority, and be a forum for fresh ideas. All over the world – for a long time in Europe and North America, but increasingly also in Asia and on other continents – enormous sums are invested in universities and research institutes every year. Since the year 2000, the number of students taking academic degrees in China has almost octupled, and the annual figure now stands at more than 7.5 million. Fifteen years ago, Ethiopia had two universities;

today there are about thirty. In Europe, too, huge expansion is a reality. In Great Britain, there were 46 universities in the early 1990s; now there are over 140.[4] Consequently, the wealth and welfare of nations, businesses, and individuals are tied to the university in a way that was not the case a mere couple of decades ago. There is another aspect to consider as well: for the ever-increasing numbers of young people who go into tertiary education, the university becomes an environment that shapes their norms and attitudes for the rest of their lives.

The idea of the university – the ideals on which education and research are based – is a concern for more people than those who have already realised that.

---

4 See, for instance, *The Transnational Politics of Higher Education: Contesting the Global/Transforming the Local*, ed. by Meng-Hsuan Chou, Isaac Kamola, and Tamson Pietsch (New York, 2016); Hans Peter Hertig, *Universities, Rankings and the Dynamics of Global Higher Education* (London, 2016); and Stefan Collini, *Speaking of Universities* (London, 2017).

1 The University of Bologna

2 The Hong Kong University of Science and Technology

1
The history of the university

The university and historiography

The university has a grand and extensive past. On ceremonial occasions it tends to be presented as the European societal institution with the longest unbroken tradition, alongside the monarchy, the judicial system, and the Catholic Church. It ought to be possible to write the rich history of the university employing dissimilar focal points; it should be possible to vary its theme. Nevertheless, it is remarkable how limited the historiography of the university has been – and still is.[1]

As a genre, university history is an old phenomenon. During the sixteenth and seventeenth centuries, Europe's learned community was inspired by the anniversary celebrations of the church to create a secular commemorative culture of its own. The earliest writings of university history were produced against this background, their principal task being to celebrate the *alma mater*. At the end of the eighteenth century, when historiography gradually developed into a form of professional scholarship, academic publications on the history of universities began to appear. Behind these lay a growing need for scholarly self-reflection; but it was the academic anniversaries that continued to give rise to the great majority of works of university history. This situation remained unchanged during the nineteenth and twentieth centuries.[2]

---

1 This chapter is mainly based on Johan Östling, 'Bortom konventionens gränser: Universitetshistoria som idé- och kunskapshistoria', in *Universitetets gränser*, ed. by Peter Josephson & Thomas Karlsohn (Göteborg, forthcoming).
2 The historiography and general character of university histories are discussed in Sheldon Rothblatt, 'The Writing of University History at the End of Another Century', *Oxford Review of Education*, 23:2 (1997); Rainer A. Müller, 'Genese, Methoden und Tendenzen der allgemeinen deutschen Universitätsgeschichte: Zur Entwicklung einer historischen Spezialdisziplin', *Mitteilungen der Österreichischen Gesellschaft für Wissenschaftsgeschichte*,

Thus there has been, since the very beginning, a close relationship between university history and the historical jubilees of the academy. Modern historians have pointed out that while this symbiosis has resulted in a large number of publications of university history, the historiography itself has left much to be desired. Sivert Langholm has suggested that the history of universities must be emancipated from the 'jubilee syndrome' and needs to contain a critical dimension. He writes, 'Laudatory speeches should be held at jubilees, but the one genre should not be confused with the other'.[3]

---

20 (2000); Robert M. Friedman, *Integration and Visibility: Historiographic Challenges to University History* (Oslo, 2000); Sylvia Paletschek, *Die permanente Erfindung einer Tradition: Die Universität Tübingen im Kaiserreich und in der Weimarer Republik* (Stuttgart, 2001), pp. 1–8; Rüdiger vom Bruch, 'Methoden und Schwerpunkte der neueren Universitätsgeschichtsforschung', in *Die Universität Greifswald und die deutsche Hochschullandschaft im 19. und 20. Jahrhundert*, ed. by Werner Buchholz (Stuttgart, 2004); Matthias Asche & Stefan Gerber, 'Neuzeitliche Universitätsgeschichte in Deutschland: Entwicklungslinien und Forschungsfelder', *Archiv für Kulturgeschichte*, 90:1 (2008); Anne Rohstock, 'The History of Higher Education: Some Conceptual Remarks on the Future of a Research Field', in *Education Systems in Historical, Cultural, and Sociological Perspectives*, ed. by Daniel Tröhler & Ragnhild Barbu (Rotterdam, 2011); Sylvia Paletschek, 'Stand und Perspektiven der neueren Universitätsgeschichte', *N.T.M.*, 19:2 (2011); Sylvia Paletschek, 'The Writing of University History and University Jubilees: German Examples', *Studium: Tijdschrift voor Wetenschaps- en Universiteitsgeschiedenis / Revue d'Histoire des Sciences et des Universités*, 5:3 (2012); Anders Ahlbäck & Laura Hollsten, 'Changing the Narratives of University History', *Kasvatus & Aika*, 9:3 (2015); and Pieter Dhondt, 'University History Writing: More Than A History of Jubilees?', in *University Jubilees and University History Writing: A Challenging Relationship*, ed. by Pieter Dhondt (Leiden and Boston, 2015).

3 Sivert Langholm, *Helheten och delene: Hvordan skrive en 200 års historie for Universitetet i Oslo?* (Oslo, 1996), pp. 2–3. See also Paletschek, 'Stand und Perspektiven'; *National, Nordic or European? Nineteenth-Century University Jubilees and Nordic Cooperation*, ed. by Pieter Dhondt (Leiden and Boston, 2011); and *University Jubilees and University History Writing: A Challenging Relationship*, ed. by Pieter Dhondt (Leiden and Boston, 2015). Gunnar Broberg has pointed out that few 'genres are as tightly bound to jubilees' as traditional university history; it belongs to 'the same world as medals, fireworks, and laudatory speeches'. In addition, he continues, few genres seem to 'contain as little self-reflection'. See Gunnar Broberg, 'Från jubileumshistoria till komparativ universitetshistoria', in *Nordiska universitetskulturer*, ed. by Sten Högnäs (Lund, 1998), p. 15.

However, the criticism does not stop with the fact that a good deal of such university history has consisted of self-justification. A significant majority of all works published during the twentieth century dealt with individual universities, works that were almost without exception written by academics with strong connections to the universities in question. Sheldon Rothblatt speaks of 'the house history, the general biography of a single university'. Far from all of these writers were historians, and they were far from always linked to newer currents within historical research. In spite of the fact that many books were sound and based on solid empirical investigations, too many writers neglected to put their respective universities into wider social, political, or intellectual contexts. These authors were limited by their own complacency.[4]

In addition to the jubilee syndrome and the focus on an author's own university, another characteristic can be distinguished in the historiography of the university. Based on German evidence, Matthias Asche and Stefan Gerber argue that university history as a genre has flourished in periods of academic crisis and rapid change. They highlight the decades around the year 1800 and the period from the founding of the German Empire to the First World War as illustrative examples. During these periods the university and its understanding of itself was rocked to its foundations, and this seems to have given rise to a need for examining the historical development of the institution. It is a noteworthy observation. Asche and Gerber see a limitation here, because that connection makes the field of university history over-sensitive to temporal phenomena: not only is it influenced by the recurring academic jubilees, it also tends to flourish whenever the university system goes through rapid change. The first aspect is certainly true, and it has hampered research in the history of the university. However, I find it difficult to see that the second circumstance is a significant problem. Important historical writing feeds off of contemporary issues; it takes hold of and reflects the predicaments of its own time. If anything, the fact that university history is brought to the fore whenever the academic world is being restructured is a testimony to the importance of the topic.[5]

The scholarly history of the university that was written during the past century had varying emphases, but broadly speaking four

---

4 Rothblatt, 'The Writing of University History', 154.
5 Asche & Gerber, 'Neuzeitliche Universitätsgeschichte', 159–67; vom Bruch, 'Methoden und Schwerpunkte'.

specific trends dominated. In the beginning of the twentieth century, scholars engaged in a form of *Geistesgeschichte* in which history was described as a series of consecutive ideas about the nature of the university where the distinction between ideal and reality was not always obvious. Another important approach focused on the university as an institution. Its organisation, administration, financing, and so on were analysed from the perspective of structural history. In the 1960s and 1970s a current of social history emerged, and the social conditions and recruitment mechanisms of the academic system came under scrutiny. The fourth trend, derived from the history of science, regarded the university as primarily an arena of science and scholarship. This approach dealt with disciplines and research environments, but also with individual researchers and over-arching paradigms.[6]

Since the mid-1990s, the history of the university has had something of a renaissance: the field has been vitalised, not least in the German-speaking world. Like the subject of history per se, university history has been transformed through the influence of linguistic and cultural theories. The rituals, myths, and conceptual worlds of the academy have become central areas of research. Other catalysts have been gender history, media history, and studies of systems of power and organisational systems. The chronological focus has shifted, and the modern era has been brought into focus. Several analysts, among them Sylvia Paletschek, have connected this reawakening within university history to the radical changes in academic reality around the year 2000. In Germany, in addition, the experiences of two dictatorships have led to a need for a historical reckoning, a kind of academic *Vergangenheitsbewältigung* (approx. 'coming to terms with the past'). The many studies of the universities under the Nazi and Communist regimes have raised burning issues concerning the relationship between politics and science/scholarship and the responsibility of the individual researcher.[7]

Despite the existence of important impulses for renewal, much of the university history that is being written is still embarrassingly conventional, as if the historiography is shackled by generic demands and jubilatory expectations. This is unfortunate; the subject contains

---

6 Asche & Gerber, 'Neuzeitliche Universitätsgeschichte', 186 and 191.
7 Asche & Gerber, 'Neuzeitliche Universitätsgeschichte'; Paletschek, 'Stand und Perspektiven'; Paletschek, 'The Writing of University History'; Rohstock, 'The History of Higher Education'; Johan Östling, 'Universitetshistoria: Friska vindar över gammalt fält', *Respons*, 2015:2.

too many potential insights to be left to collectors of anecdotes and writers of chronicles. For this reason, I will present a framework drawn from intellectual history and the history of knowledge which may provide university history with relevant themes and methods.

University history as intellectual history and history of knowledge

Writing university history as intellectual history may seem puzzling, almost tautological in fact, because the history of ideas as an academic field has traditionally included the history of universities. In this case the history of ideas should primarily be understood as an equivalent of what is known in English as 'intellectual history'. Peter E. Gordon has discussed what distinguishes this field from others in an instructive manner. Defining the field as 'the study of intellectuals, ideas, and intellectual patterns over time' is factually correct; but in order to create a clearer focus, he compares intellectual history to the 'history of ideas'. In the latter case, researchers have traditionally concentrated on key ideas and how these have changed over the course of history. 'An historian of ideas', writes Gordon, 'will tend to organize the historical narrative around one major idea and will then follow the development or metamorphosis of that idea as it manifests itself in different contexts and times.'[8]

---

8 Peter E. Gordon, 'What is Intellectual History? A Frankly Partisan Introduction to a Frequently Misunderstood Field' (2013), p. 2, http://scholar.harvard.edu/files/pgordon/files/what_is_intell_history_pgordon_mar2012.pdf (accessed 15 February 2016). For general discussions regarding the history of ideas, intellectual history, *Geistesgeschichte, Ideengeschichte*, etc., see Donald R. Kelley, *The Descent of Ideas: The History of Intellectual History* (Aldershot, 2002); Anthony Grafton, 'The History of Ideas: Precept and Practice, 1950–2000 and Beyond', *Journal of the History of Ideas*, 67:1 (2006); and Riccardo Bavaj, 'Intellectual History, Version 1.0', in *Docupedia-Zeitgeschichte*, http://docupedia.de/zg/Intellectual_History?oldid=106434 (accessed 15 February 2016). Several publications testify to a renewed interest in the history of ideas and intellectual history in the twenty-first century, in both North America and Germany; see, e.g., Ulrich Raulff, Helwig Schmidt-Glintzer, & Hellmut Th. Seemann, 'Einen Anfang machen: Warum wir eine Zeitschrift für Ideengeschichte gründen', *Zeitschrift für Ideengeschichte*, 1 (2007); Alexander Gallus, '"Intellectual History" mit Intellektuellen und ohne sie: Facetten neuerer geistesgeschichtlicher Forschung', *Historische Zeitschrift*, 288:1 (2009); *Global Intellectual History*, ed. by Samuel Moyn & Andrew Sartori (New York, 2013); and *Rethinking Modern European Intellectual History*, ed. by Darrin M. McMahon & Samuel Moyn (Oxford, 2014).

One advantage of this approach is that it is possible to discern intellectual similarities and continuities even when the chronological distance between two phenomena is very great. The classic representative of this type of history of ideas was Arthur O. Lovejoy and his *The Great Chain of Being* (1936). Although Lovejoy's own arguments were more complex than many later scholars have been willing to admit, he was accused of espousing a kind of Platonic view of ideas, where major thoughts and concepts were fundamentally the same throughout history and different manifestations of them were simply variations on eternal themes.[9]

A radical alternative to this older form of history of ideas was expressed by Quentin Skinner and what would become known as the Cambridge School. In a famous essay from 1969, Skinner attacked a context-free, diachronic history of ideas à la Lovejoy. Instead Skinner argued for the notion that ideas can only be understood in specific historical contexts, as responses to contemporary questions or as interventions in ongoing debates. In a large number of studies on the history of political thinking, he and his successors analysed how so-called speech acts worked in both well-known and not so well-known texts. The Cambridge School has, in its turn, been criticised for, among other things, limiting the concept of context and reducing history to a kind of rhetorical struggle.[10]

Peter E. Gordon's version of intellectual history represents a fruitful attempt to bridge the gap between Lovejoy's and Skinner's extreme positions. Gordon considers ideas to be 'historically conditioned features of the world which are best understood within some larger context'. The crucial point is the context of the ideas in question – whether this consists of institutions, social environments, economic factors, or broader cultural and linguistic patterns. Sometimes the context is toned down in favour of a more internalist analysis, but in general the aim with this approach to intellectual history is to

---

9 Arthur O. Lovejoy, *The Great Chain of Being: A Study of the History of an Idea* (Cambridge, MA, 1936); Grafton, 'The History of Ideas'.
10 Quentin Skinner, 'Meaning and Understanding in the History of Ideas', *History and Theory*, 8:1 (1969). There are a large number of works on Skinner. See, e.g., *Meaning and Context: Quentin Skinner and His Critics*, ed. by James Tully (Cambridge, 1988); Emile Perreau-Saussine, 'Quentin Skinner in Context', *The Review of Politics*, 69:1 (2007); Joseph M. Levine, 'Intellectual History as History', *Journal of the History of Ideas*, 66:2 (2005); and Martin Jay, 'Historical Explanation and the Event: Reflections on the Limits of Contextualization', *New Literary History*, 42:4 (2011).

The history of the university

introduce the ideas into larger structures or locate them in relation to other contemporary forces.[11]

This is the spirit in which I write the history of the university as intellectual history. At the centre is an intellectual reflection on basic academic issues, but not in isolation from the surrounding world. Throughout, I combine analyses of distinct periods with changes over the longer course of history. In order to fill this framework from intellectual history with specific content from university history, I turn to the emerging field designated as the history of knowledge.

The history of knowledge (*Wissensgeschichte*) deals, at least as the field has developed in German-speaking countries during the twenty-first century, with the forms of more or less rational knowledge, more precisely the social production and circulation of knowledge. So far, however, there is no consensus about what the history of knowledge comprises; and according to Daniel Speich Chassé and David Gugerli in their attempt at articulating a position, the word *Wissensgeschichte* is used without any precise meaning. There are no normative handbooks; there is no established canon.[12]

The Zentrum Geschichte des Wissens ('The Centre for the History of Knowledge') in Zürich has been of major importance for the establishment of the history of knowledge as a field of research. According to the Swiss historians, when working with the history of knowledge 'our common starting point is ... an assumption: We assume that the historical development of knowledge – with all its epistemic, technological, and cultural premises as well as its consequences – has to be understood as an open-ended process'. The important thing is that knowledge – not scholarship, not culture, not ideas – is foregrounded, and that it is placed in relation to a larger societal context.[13]

Philipp Sarasin, one of the leading theoreticians among the Zürich scholars, has emphasised that knowledge is always developing,

---

11 Gordon, 'What is Intellectual History?', p. 2.
12 Daniel Speich Chassé & David Gugerli, 'Wissensgeschichte: Eine Standortbestimmung', *Traverse: Zeitschrift für Geschichte*, 1 (2012).
13 Philipp Sarasin, 'Was ist Wissensgeschichte?', *Internationales Archiv für Sozialgeschichte der deutschen Literatur (IASL)*, 36:1 (2011); Speich Chassé & Gugerli, 'Wissensgeschichte'; Johan Östling, 'Vad är kunskapshistoria?', *Historisk tidskrift*, 135:1 (2015); Peter Burke, *What Is the History of Knowledge?* (Cambridge, 2016). Presentation of the Center 'History of Knowledge' at its website, https://www.zgw.ethz.ch/en/portrait.html (accessed 15 February 2016).

changing, and being realised anew through its movement among various social spheres. He highlights the fact that knowledge circulates among people and groups because sign systems and discourses can, in principle, cross institutional, social, political, and geographical borders. This is not to say that knowledge is freely disseminated and evenly distributed. But it does mean that knowledge can, intrinsically, be mediated and circulated, and that it can interact with other fields of knowledge. Through these processes, knowledge is simultaneously transformed.[14]

In this respect, knowledge is considered a genuinely historical phenomenon. The central issues have nothing to do with certain forms of knowledge being good or bad, useful or useless, but simply with how, when, and why a certain type of knowledge appears and possibly vanishes, and, ultimately, what effects it has, in what contexts it appears, who are its bearers, in what forms it is manifested, and so forth. In studying the history of knowledge, one must therefore take into account what was considered to be knowledge at a given time and in a given context – and what was not.[15]

Writing a history of the university as a history of knowledge implies an important clarification: discussions about the idea of the university are not just part of a public debate on ideas or a national tradition. They represent an aspect of the changing nature and institutional foundations of knowledge: the kind of knowledge that is worth achieving, the way in which it is generated and mediated, what its organisation and structure look like, and so on.

Together, recent intellectual history and *Wissensgeschichte* provide a general direction for my investigation into the history of the university. Within both these fields there are, in addition, a number of concepts and methods that can lend stringency and stability to the analysis. However, before I explain in greater detail what this means, the subject matter of my research needs to be introduced.

The history of the Humboldtian tradition

The aim of this study is to create a historical understanding of the Humboldtian tradition and its varying meanings during the modern era. One key task is to investigate the significance of the classic university model (more or less associated with Wilhelm von Humboldt) and how this model has changed over time. At the same

---

14 Sarasin, 'Wissensgeschichte', 165–66.
15 Ibid., 165.

time, the analysis must be expanded and the debates about the idea of the university must be put in relation to broader patterns of thought. It is especially important to consider the intellectual groupings that interpreted the mission and the basic ideals of the German university. All in all, this provides a basis for reflecting on the place of the Humboldtian tradition in modern German history and its relevance today. This way, the rich German university history is used in order to provide a perspective on the academic self-understanding of our own time.

All attempts to reform a cultural or social institution rest on a set of ideas about the mission and function of this institution. This is especially true of research and higher education. As has been emphasised by Björn Wittrock, the idea of the university cannot be seen as 'a free-floating abstraction but a guiding conception, rooted in the experiences, traditions, and life-worlds of individuals'. Since the Enlightenment, these ideals have been tested and retested as society has changed. However, none of the major university reforms can be seen solely as a response to the emergence of modernity. 'They occurred because leaders, thinkers, scholars, and scientists continually questioned the basic nature and meaning of higher learning', argues Wittrock.[16]

One of the most important of these 'guiding conceptions', at least today, is the one associated with Wilhelm von Humboldt (1767–1835). This is true not only in Germany but also in the many countries that have been influenced by the German academic model. In the twenty-first century, the main features of the Humboldtian university programme are often summarised through a set of concepts or slogans: the combination of research and teaching; academic freedom (often expressed as *Lehr-* and *Lernfreiheit*); education rather than training; the idea of the unity of science and scholarship; and the community of students and teachers.[17] Coupled to these academic ideals is a historiography in which the Berlin university emerges as the first modern research university, an institution that

---

16 Björn Wittrock, 'The Modern University: The Three Transformations', in *The European and American University since 1800: Historical and Sociological Essays*, ed. by Sheldon Rothblatt & Björn Wittrock (Cambridge, 1993), p. 347. See also Jens Erik Kristensen, 'Gamle og nye ideer med et universitet', in *Ideer om et universitet: Det moderne universitets idehistorie fra 1800 til i dag*, ed. by Jens Erik Kristensen and others (Århus, 2007), p. 19.
17 The specific ideals that are associated with Wilhelm von Humboldt or the Humboldtian university model vary somewhat, but in all essentials the same things recur. On this issue, compare texts as different as *German Universities*

was to provide the model for how research and higher education would be conducted both in and outside Germany.[18] What is customarily presented as an unbroken line of ideas – the Humboldtian tradition – is, however, a much more complex affair. Recent research has problematised both its origins and its development. First, researchers have asked just how original Wilhelm von Humboldt was while emphasising the importance of other German New Humanist philosophers.[19] Second, it became clear that it was a long time before the model had any impact outside of Berlin. And when it was exported, it was always transformed when encountering foreign university cultures.[20]

Last but not least, a more radical historicisation of the Humboldtian tradition has begun. Somewhat simplified, it may be said that the leading idea in the new research is that Humboldt was

---

Past and Future: Crisis or Renewal?, ed. by Mitchell G. Ash (Providence, RI, 1997); Marc Schalenberg, *Humboldt auf Reisen? Die Rezeption des 'deutschen Universitätsmodells' in den französischen und britischen Reformdiskursen (1810–1870)* (Basel, 2002), pp. 59–62; Sylvia Paletschek, 'Die Erfindung der Humboldtschen Universität: Die Konstruktion der deutschen Universitätsidee in der ersten Hälfte des 20. Jahrhunderts', *Historische Anthropologie*, 10 (2002), 184; Robert D. Anderson, *European Universities from the Enlightenment to 1914* (Oxford, 2004), p. 51; 'Humboldtsches Bildungsideal', *Wikipedia*, https://de.wikipedia.org/wiki/Humboldtsches_Bildungsideal (accessed 15 February 2016); Mitchell G. Ash, 'Bachelor of What, Master of Whom? The Humboldt Myth and Transformations of Higher Education in Germany and the US', *European Journal of Education*, 41:2 (2006), 246; and Anne Rohstock, '"Some Things Never Change": The (Re)Invention of Humboldt in Western Higher Education Systems', in *Theories of Bildung and Growth: Connections and Controversies between Continental European Educational Thinking and American Pragmatism*, ed. by Pauli Siljander & Arno Kivelä (Rotterdam, 2012), pp. 172–73.

18 Paletschek, 'The Writing of University History', pp. 151–52.
19 Rüdiger vom Bruch, 'Abschied von Humboldt? Die deutsche Universität vor dem Ersten Weltkrieg', in *Die deutsche Universität im 20. Jahrhundert*, ed. by Karl Strobel (Vierow, 1994); *A History of the University in Europe: Universities in the Nineteenth and Early Twentieth Centuries (1800–1945)*, ed. by Walter Rüegg (Cambridge, 2004). In a way, this insight has been present long before now, for instance in *Die Idee der deutschen Universität: Die fünf Grundschriften aus der Zeit ihrer Neubegründung durch klassischen Idealismus und romantischen Realismus*, ed. by Ernst Anrich (Darmstadt, 1956).
20 *Humboldt international: Der Export des deutschen Universitätsmodells im 19. und 20. Jahrhundert*, ed. by Rainer Christoph Schwinges (Basel, 2001); Schalenberg, *Humboldt auf Reisen?*

born not in 1810, but in 1910. Underlying this drastic statement is the realisation that Humboldt was never particularly present in the nineteenth-century debate about the university. His writings were unknown, his ideas were not widely disseminated, and it was the reform universities in Halle and Göttingen rather than the one in Berlin that formed the points of reference. But at the turn of the twentieth century, Humboldt was suddenly discovered. His manifesto about the university was published and became famous when the Berlin university celebrated its centenary in 1910. At the same time, influential educational politicians and pedagogues such as Adolf von Harnack and Eduard Spranger disseminated his ideas.[21]

Mitchell G. Ash, Rüdiger vom Bruch, Sylvia Paletschek, Walter Rüegg, and other leading representatives of the new research agree:

---

21 The most important contributions to this new research are Walter Rüegg, 'Der Mythos der Humboldtschen Universität', in *Universitas in theologia–theologia in universitate: Festschrift für Hans Heinrich Schmid*, ed. by Mathias Krieg & Martin Rose (Zürich, 1997); *German Universities*, ed. by Ash; Rüdiger vom Bruch, 'A Slow Farewell to Humboldt? Stages in the History of German Universities, 1810–1945', in *German Universities Past and Future*, ed. by Ash; Paletschek, *Die permanente Erfindung*; Sylvia Paletschek, 'Verbreitete sich ein "Humboldt'sches Modell" an den deutschen Universitäten im 19. Jahrhundert?', in *Humboldt international*, ed. by Schwinges; Sylvia Paletschek, 'The Invention of Humboldt and the Impact of National Socialism: The German University Idea in the First Half of the Twentieth Century', in *Science in the Third Reich*, ed. by Margit Szöllösi-Janze (Oxford, 2001); Paletschek, 'Die Erfindung'; Schalenberg, *Humboldt auf Reisen?*; Dieter Langewiesche, 'Die "Humboldtsche Universität" als nationaler Mythos: Zum Selbstbild der deutschen Universitäten im Kaiserreich und in der Weimarer Republik', *Historische Zeitschrift*, 290:1 (2010); Heinz-Elmar Tenorth, 'Wilhelm von Humboldts (1776–1835) Universitätskonzept und die Reform in Berlin – eine Tradition jenseits des Mythos', *Zeitschrift für Germanistik*, N.F. XX:1 (2010); and Dieter Langewiesche, 'Humboldt als Leitbild? Die deutsche Universität in den Berliner Rektoratsreden seit dem 19. Jahrhundert', *Jahrbuch für Universitätsgeschichte*, 14 (2011). Critiques of this field of research can be found in Thomas Albert Howard, *Protestant Theology and the Making of the Modern German University* (Oxford, 2006), pp. 4–5, Martin Eichler, 'Die Wahrheit des Mythos Humboldt', *Historische Zeitschrift*, 294:1 (2012), and Heinz-Elmar Tenorth, 'Wilhelm von Humboldt, ein Philosoph als Bildungspolitiker: Zuschreibungen, historische Praxis, fortdauernde Herausforderung', *Zeitschrift für Religions- und Geistesgeschichte*, 69:2 (2017). See also the contributions in *The Humboldtian Tradition: Origins and Legacies*, ed. by Peter Josephson, Thomas Karlsohn, & Johan Östling (Leiden and Boston, 2014), in particular the discussion in Peter Josephson, Thomas Karlsohn, & Johan Östling, 'The Humboldtian Tradition and Its Transformations'.

the discovery of Humboldt during the early twentieth century must be linked with the general development of the German Empire in the decades preceding the First World War. This was a dynamic phase in which science and scholarship, education, and historiography became essential components of the cultural identity that was being shaped in the young German nation state. In addition, Humboldt's principles legitimised trends in the scholarly/scientific community, in particular the increasing importance given to research during these decades.[22] This new historicising research – which I have reason to discuss in greater detail in Chapters 2 and 3 – contains key insights: what was presented as a meta-historical idea, the Humboldtian tradition, in fact became entangled in the predicaments of various periods, by turns inspiring criticism, reform, and glorification of former greatness.

Almost all research about the Humboldtian tradition has dealt with the nineteenth and early twentieth centuries, whereas the most recent hundred years have been unevenly illuminated. In a way this is a paradox, because there seems to be a consensus that it was during the twentieth century, and in particular during the years after the Second World War, that the university was radically transformed and many time-honoured ideals were fundamentally challenged.[23] For this reason, the chronological focus of this study is the period after 1945. For a long time there was no research-based historical knowledge concerning this period, especially with respect to the transformation of the basic ideals of the university. Many opinions were based on general assumptions or personal memories.[24] In the course of the

---

22 Paletschek, 'Die Erfindung'. See also Chapters 2 and 3 below.
23 See, for instance, Konrad H. Jarausch, 'The Humboldt Syndrome: West German Universities, 1945–1989', in *German Universities Past and Future*, ed. by Ash, and Hans-Albrecht Koch, *Die Universität: Geschichte einer europäischen Institution* (Darmstadt, 2008).
24 This became apparent in the fourth and final volume of the substantial historical account of the universities of Europe, *A History of the University in Europe: Universities since 1945*, ed. by Walter Rüegg (Cambridge, 2011). This work contains many interesting facts about post-war universities, but in countless areas it was impossible to conceal the lack of well-founded knowledge to build on. As a result, several chapters mainly consist of statistical summaries and official reports. The larger historical picture becomes blurred, and the deeper contexts remain unexplained. See Johan Östling, 'Universiteten hämmas av krav på effektivitet', *Svenska Dagbladet*, 17 October 2011, and Anne Rohstock, 'Walter Rüegg (Hg.): Geschichte der Universität in Europa', *sehepunkte*, 12:1 (2012).

The history of the university

last few years, however, more detailed research has been conducted about the post-war period, in Germany and in other countries. For example, thanks to studies by Olaf Bartz, Anne Rohstock, Nikolai Wehrs, Barbara Wolbring, and others, the reform debates, research policy, and academic culture of the old Federal Republic have begun to assume firmer outlines.[25] In a wider perspective, their works are also a sign that broad themes in the intellectual history of the post-war era are gradually being subjected to historical analysis. I have every reason to revisit this newer research on university history in the ensuing chapters.[26]

---

25 Olaf Bartz, *Der Wissenschaftsrat: Entwicklungslinien der Wissenschaftspolitik in der Bundesrepublik Deutschland 1957–2007* (Stuttgart, 2007); Boris Spix, *Abschied vom Elfenbeinturm? Politisches Verhalten Studierender 1957–1967: Berlin und Nordrhein-Westfalen im Vergleich* (Essen, 2008); Anne Rohstock, *Von der 'Ordinarienuniversität' zur 'Revolutionszentrale'? Hochschulreform und Hochschulrevolte in Bayern und Hessen 1957–1976* (Munich, 2010); Stefan Paulus, *Vorbild USA? Amerikanisierung von Universität und Wissenschaft in Westdeutschland 1945–1976* (Munich, 2010); Konstantin von Freytag-Loringhoven, *Erziehung im Kollegienhaus: Reformbestrebungen an den deutschen Universitäten der amerikanischen Besatzungszone 1945–1960* (Stuttgart, 2012); Uwe Rohwedder, *Kalter Krieg und Hochschulreform: Der Verband Deutscher Studentenschaften in der frühen Bundesrepublik (1949–1969)* (Essen, 2012); Barbara Wolbring, *Trümmerfeld der bürgerlichen Welt: Universität in den gesellschaftlichen Reformdiskursen der westlichen Besatzungszonen (1945–1949)* (Göttingen, 2014); Nikolai Wehrs, *Protest der Professoren: Der 'Bund Freiheit der Wissenschaft' in den 1970er Jahren* (Göttingen, 2014); *Universität, Wissenschaft und Öffentlichkeit in Westdeutschland: (1945 bis ca. 1970)*, ed. by Sebastian Brandt et al. (Stuttgart, 2014); and Moritz Mälzer, *Auf der Suche nach der neuen Universität: Die Entstehung der 'Reformuniversitäten': Konstanz und Bielefeld in den 1960er Jahren* (Göttingen, 2016). See, in addition, two of the most important studies on the university in East Germany: Ralph Jessen, *Akademische Elite und kommunistische Diktatur: Die ostdeutsche Hochschullehrerschaft in der Ulbricht-Ära* (Göttingen, 1999) and John Connelly, *Captive University: The Sovietization of East German, Czech and Polish Higher Education, 1945–1956* (Chapel Hill, NC, 2000).

26 A. Dirk Moses, 'Intellectual History in and of the Federal Republic of Germany', *Modern Intellectual History*, 9:3 (2012). For significant, more recent contributions, see, e.g., Jens Hacke, *Philosophie der Bürgerlichkeit: Die liberalkonservative Begründung der Bundesrepublik* (Göttingen, 2006); A. Dirk Moses, *German Intellectuals and the Nazi Past* (Cambridge, 2007); Marcus Payk, *Der Geist der Demokratie: Intellektuelle Orientierungsversuche im Feuilleton der frühen Bundesrepublik: Karl Korn und Peter de Mendelssohn* (Munich, 2008); and Philipp Felsch, *Der lange Sommer der*

The form and content of the Humboldtian tradition

My aim is thus to explore the history of the Humboldtian tradition during the modern era: how it has been interpreted and transformed, and how it has provided direction to the debate on the idea of the university. The twin approaches of intellectual history and the history of knowledge supply a general framework for my examination, as well as providing me with concrete categories and methodological tools.

A key methodological question within intellectual history is whether it is possible to combine a *longue durée* of ideas with analyses of central political, ethical, and scholarly scientific concepts. David Armitage has argued that it would be fruitful to follow a complex of ideas over a long period while simultaneously dealing with its manifestations during a specific stage. For him it is not a matter of returning to Lovejoy, but of extending the chronological horizon.[27]

Armitage emphasises three methodological strategies for producing studies of intellectual history covering longer stretches of time. First, he advocates *transtemporal history*. Transnational history is about connections and comparisons among geographical units without for that reason discounting nations. Similarly, transtemporal history brings contexts, events, and periods together and makes them subjects of analysis without the specific contexts being suppressed or denied. 'Transtemporal history is not transhistorical', emphasises Armitage, 'it is time-*bound* not timeless'. In contradistinction to the older history of ideas, actors are of major importance, as are questions regarding how ideas are actually transferred, passed on, and received.[28]

Second, transtemporal history should be done using what Armitage calls *serial contextualism*. By this he means that a historian

---

Theorie: Geschichte einer Revolte 1960–1990 (Munich, 2015); and also a number of anthologies, such as *Streit um den Staat: Intellektuelle Debatten in der Bundesrepublik 1960–1980*, ed. by Dominik Geppert & Jens Hacke (Göttingen, 2008); *Was war Bielefeld? Eine ideengeschichtliche Nachfrage*, ed. by Sonja Asal & Stephan Schlak (Göttingen, 2009); and *Rückblickend in die Zukunft: Politische Öffentlichkeit und intellektuelle Positionen in Deutschland um 1950 und um 1930*, ed. by Alexander Gallus & Axel Schildt (Göttingen, 2011).

27 David Armitage, 'What's the Big Idea? Intellectual History and the *Longue Durée*', *History of European Ideas*, 38:4 (2012). In *The History Manifesto* (Cambridge, 2014), David Armitage and Jo Guldi also argue enthusiastically for the necessity of long chronological periods in historical studies.

28 Armitage, 'Big Idea', 498.

reconstructs a series of synchronous contexts within which clearly distinguishable actors use language in a strategic manner in order to realise their goals. This procedure bears the unmistakable imprint of Skinner, but according to Armitage there is nothing to prevent several distinct contexts from being linked in a larger analytic chain. In this way it is possible to write a transtemporal history that is neither based on artificial units nor on deceptive continuities.[29]

The combination of transtemporal history and linked contexts ultimately gives rise to what Armitage calls a *history in ideas*. Writing the history of specific ideas becomes a transtemporal narrative encompassing several decades or even centuries. The ideas that form the structure of the account cannot, however, be seen as independent phenomena with an existence of their own, but as 'focal points of arguments shaped and debated episodically across time with a conscious – or at least a provable – connection with both earlier and later instances of such struggles'. The idea at the centre of a given study is linked to both earlier and later counterparts, and dialogues across time are brought to the fore.[30]

David Armitage's methodological programme is couched in general terms, but it is well suited as a point of departure for anyone wishing to write university history as intellectual history. It is particularly applicable to a study of the idea of the university in which it is possible to follow how a configuration of ideas is given different meanings and serves different purposes in distinct periods of time. In the specific case under discussion, this means that the most significant periods of reform from the past century will be foregrounded. For, as has been emphasised by Peter Lundgreen, it is precisely the periods of reform in the history of the university that are especially interesting to study. This is when the intellectual heritage of the institution is brought to life and old ideals are highlighted and placed in contrast to new visions for the future.[31]

Within each period, an analysis drawn from intellectual history is combined with an approach taken from the history of knowledge. In the version of the latter that has been evolved by the Zürich School, genealogies and structural orders of knowledge play a preponderant

---

29 Ibid.
30 Ibid., 499.
31 Peter Lundgreen, 'Mythos Humboldt Today: Teaching, Research, and Administration', in *German Universities Past and Future*, ed. by Ash. See also *Jahrbuch für Universitätsgeschichte*, 13 (2010), which deals with university reforms.

role. This is not the case here. It is true that I wish to understand the origins of the Humboldtian tradition, but not by being genealogical in Michel Foucault's sense of the term. Rather, I follow an intellectual line of thought found in German pedagogical and institutional thinking in order to investigate how the Humboldtian tradition has been reinterpreted in different periods of history. But there are a number of other analytical concepts, drawn directly from the arsenal provided by the history of knowledge, which lend structure to my study: the media forms, actors, concepts, and spaces of knowledge.

The media forms of knowledge takes as its premise the idea that knowledge is in some sense always formatted. That is to say, it does not exist as a pure substance, but entails the need for media for storage, transport, or reproduction. Media conventions simultaneously enable and constrain the creation and transformation of knowledge.[32] For me, this becomes primarily a matter of paying attention to those genre conventions that shaped the form of presentation with regard to different historical contexts. In concrete terms, I will identify a number of theoretical core texts concerning the university from each era. Since the end of the eighteenth century in Germany, it is possible to identify a set of texts that have had the 'idea of the university' as their theme. Renowned philosophers and authors, such as Kant, Schiller, Fichte, Schelling, and Schleiermacher, were responsible for several of the earlier ones, and during the twentieth century several of the leading thinkers in Germany contributed to this body of texts as well. The publication of such texts seems to have been particularly frequent during periods when the university was undergoing a crisis or was on the eve of a major transformation. These texts constitute the foundational empirical sources for this study.[33]

These theoretical texts about the university can be considered a genre of their own.[34] This does not mean that they constitute a type of

---

32 Sarasin, 'Wissensgeschichte', 168–69.
33 For the 'idea of the university' in general in the German and the English traditions, see Sheldon Rothblatt, *The Modern University and Its Discontents: The Fate of Newman's Legacies in Britain and America* (London, 1997), pp. 1–49.
34 Heinz-Elmar Tenorth has argued that from the end of the nineteenth century there was 'a distinct genre of a literature of reflection' that dealt with the idea of the university. He does not, however, specify what characterises this genre. Heinz-Elmar Tenorth, 'Genese der Disziplinen – Die Konstitution der Universität', in *Geschichte der Universität Unter den Linden: Genese der Disziplinen: Die Konstitution der Universität*, ed. by Heinz-Elmar Tenorth (Berlin, 2010), p. 10.

text that exhibits conventions and stylistic features that are eternally valid. Rather, I count myself among those who see genre as a kind of manifestation of an abstract structure. Tzvetan Todorov belongs to this group. He regards a genre as a theoretical unit constructed by an observer after the fact. According to Todorov, these units are both prescriptive (like a grammar) and changeable (because of recurring creative innovations).[35] It is only posterity that can bring together the philosophical tracts concerning the university to form a genre, even though these are united by a common topic. This is not to say that the texts lacked a reciprocal relationship with one another in their own time. Not everyone who wrote a contribution was aware of the longer tradition, but they conspicuously often made references to older contributions. For instance, when Helmut Schelsky, one of the true protagonists of this book, published his writings about the university in the 1960s, he not only entered into a dialogue with Wilhelm von Humboldt, but also with Max Scheler and Carl Heinrich Becker. The ideological and intellectual arguments about the university took the form of intertextual exchanges of opinions across several generations.[36]

Within the framework of a common, genre-unifying theme – the idea of the university – approaches, focuses, and tones could vary considerably over time. Clarifying what these variations looked like is a significant aspect of my analysis of the history of the Humboldtian tradition. From the perspective of the history of knowledge, it is also important to take note of the concrete variations in the genre's media context, though this is not one of my main concerns. For example, during the early post-war period the basic issues of the university were mostly discussed in the form of written speeches that were subsequently printed, while debate books, often of a more voluminous type, were common two decades later. These texts in their turn generated articles in newspapers and journals.

If genre is one of the basic analytical categories, *knowledge actors* is another. Ultimately, this has to do with characterising the personages

---

35 Chapter 1, 'Literary Genres', in Tzvetan Todorov, *The Fantastic: A Structural Approach to a Literary Genre*, trans. by Richard Howard (Ithaca, NY, 1975).
36 Helmut Schelsky, *Einsamkeit und Freiheit: Idee und Gestalt der deutschen Universität und ihrer Reformen* (Reinbek bei Hamburg, 1963). In some cases the intertextual connection is completely clear: in *Theorie der Unbildung: Die Irrtümer der Wissensgesellschaft* (Vienna, 2006), Konrad Paul Liessmann expressly attempts to update Theodor W. Adorno's theses from 'Theorie der Halbbildung' (1959) and apply them to the Bologna process. See Chapter 6.

who interpreted the Humboldtian tradition and placing them in their respective contexts. My point of departure is that in each historical period, there was a specific group of people who shaped the view of the cardinal academic issues. They were not in sole control of the debate, but they did leave their unmistakable imprint upon it. The German mandarins appear to have played an especially important role. According to Fritz K. Ringer's influential *The Decline of the German Mandarins* (1969), the mandarins made up a social and intellectual class which, by virtue of their education and academic status, held a special position in German society. Their golden age was the decades around the year 1900; but during the Weimar Republic they were still powerful, and their legacy survived far longer than that. In their perceptions of themselves, the mandarins were bearers of culture (*Kulturträger*), and they felt that they had a special calling to direct the spiritual progress of the nation. In Nazi Germany many of them gave passive or active support to the regime; but there were also those who stayed away from political power and who, after the end of the war, were able to step forward on to the academic stage again. In historical research the concept of the mandarin has been a contested one, and it has often, for Ringer but even more so for other scholars, had simultaneously descriptive and polemical dimensions.[37]

I, however, use the concept of the mandarin in a purely analytic manner in order to determine whether there were biographical and intellectual aspects that united the major players in the debate on the university during a particular period. It is equally important to assess whether there were common generational experiences that formed the basis for their attitude to the classic German university model. In addition, when the mandarins are seen as a kind of knowledge actors, it is important to understand the significance of the Humboldtian tradition to their identities as academics and scholars or scientists.[38]

---

37 Fritz K. Ringer, *The Decline of the German Mandarins: The German Academic Community, 1890–1933* (Cambridge, MA, 1969). A discussion of Ringer and the criticism levelled at him can be found in James C. Albisetti, 'The Decline of the German Mandarins After Twenty-Five Years', *History of Education Quarterly*, 34:4 (1994). See also Claus-Dieter Krohn, 'Intellektuelle und Mandarine in Deutschland um 1930 und 1950', in *Rückblickend in die Zukunft*, ed. by Gallus & Schildt (Göttingen, 2011), pp. 64–69, and my discussion in the subsequent chapters of the present work.
38 Sarasin, 'Wissensgeschichte', 169–71.

The history of the university

3 A picture from the 1930 film *Der blaue Engel*, based on Heinrich Mann's novel *Professor Unrat* (1905)

Even at this point, though, it should be said that there was only a limited class of people in each period who delved deeply into the basic issues of the university. Professors, and to some extent senior academic administrators, clearly dominated, while students and younger scholars were only gradually able to make their voices heard in the post-war period. Throughout the entire twentieth century an overwhelming majority of these knowledge actors were men, a circumstance that reflected the fact that the university was a male bastion. Only after the year 2000 did the percentage of female professors at German universities exceed ten per cent.[39]

---

39 *Bildung und Kultur: Personal an Hochschulen – Vorläufige Ergebnisse*, Statistisches Bundesamt (Wiesbaden, 2015). On female German academics and intellectuals and their place both within and outside the university, see Christine von Oertzen, *Strategie Verständigung: Zur transnationalen Vernetzung von Akademikerinnen 1917–1955* (Göttingen, 2012); *Beyond the Academy: Histories of Gender and Knowledge*, ed. by Christine von Oertzen, Maria Rentetzi, & Elizabeth Watkins Siegel (New York, 2013); and *Eingreifende Denkerinnen: Weibliche Intellektuelle im 20. und 21. Jahrhundert*, ed. by Ingrid Gilcher-Holtey (Tübingen, 2015). At a more

Yet another analytic category is made up of *the concepts of knowledge*. This category can be developed with reference to Reinhart Koselleck's programme of conceptual history. Two of his assumptions are particularly important: on the one hand, that human experience is conditioned by language; and on the other, that there are certain basic political-social concepts which are absolutely essential for a person to be able to orientate him- or herself in the modern world. Both of these assumptions can be transferred to other central areas – politics, science, aesthetics – where there are a more or less limited number of basic concepts. Precisely because these concepts are fundamental, debates are largely about engaging in a kind of struggle over their definitions.[40]

In this study, I assume a stance that might be called a state of heightened awareness in relation to the history of concepts. I am interested in the conceptual world of the Humboldtian tradition and how it has changed since the nineteenth century. It is hence important to pay attention to the meaning of the key history-of-knowledge concepts that have, to varying degrees, been associated with a classic German idea about the university: *Einheit von Forschung und Lehre, Lern- und Lehrfreiheit, Bildung, Einheit der Wissenschaften*, and so on (see further Chapter 2).[41]

---

fundamental level one may ask if the German concept of education from the period around the year 1800 was modelled on a male subject, and if so, what the consequences of this have been. See the discussion in Claudia Lindén, 'It Takes a Real Man to Show True Femininity: Gender Transgression in Goethe's and Humboldt's Concept of *Bildung*', in *The Humboldtian Tradition*, ed. by Josephson, Karlsohn, & Östling.

40 Reinhart Koselleck outlined his programme in 'Einleitung' in *Geschichtliche Grundbegriffe: Historisches Lexikon zur politisch-sozialen Sprache in Deutschland*, ed. by Otto Brunner, Werner Conze, & Reinhart Koselleck, 8 vols (Stuttgart, 1972–1997), vol. I (1972). For discussions of his history of concepts, see Melvin Richter, *The History of Political and Social Concepts: A Critical Introduction* (New York, 1995), pp. 9–57; Helge Jordheim, *Läsningens vetenskap: Utkast till en ny filologi*, transl. Sten Andersson (Gråbo, 2003), pp. 154–70; *Begriffene Geschichte: Beiträge zum Werk Reinhart Kosellecks*, ed. by Hans Joas & Peter Vogt (Berlin, 2011); and Niklas Olsen, *History in the Plural: An Introduction to the Work of Reinhart Koselleck* (New York, 2012).

41 For methodological discussions on the history of concepts and contemporary history, see Kathrin Kollmeier & Stefan-Ludwig Hoffmann, 'Zeitgeschichte der Begriffe? Perspektiven einer Historischen Semantik des 20. Jahrhunderts: Einleitung', *Zeithistorische Forschungen/Studies in Contemporary History*,

Knowledge always exists in a particular space, and in this case the space is Germany. Like much other research on the university – including recent work on Humboldt – the present research is thus conducted within a national framework. In this lies a potential limitation. The university system is never a result of exclusively endogenous processes, but forms an alloy of native traditions and international influences.[42] More generally, historians focusing on a single country or a single culture risk falling into methodological nationalism, where the nation is seen as the indisputable object of knowledge, both that which is being explained and that which supplies all the explanations. In order to avoid this type of narrow-mindedness, I will place Germany in relation to other relevant countries through intermittent geographical comparisons, above all in the general discussions of my empirical investigations.[43]

At the same time, the exploration of the Humboldtian tradition provides a point of entry to an entire intellectual culture, namely that of Germany. The German university model originated in experiences at the national level, and the differences of opinion about the idea of the university were aspects of wider controversies. Consequently, a person who studies the debate about the basic academic principles is able to discern the broader currents of ideas. Having this comprehensive picture clear in one's mind is, in its turn, a prerequisite for being able to understand the nature of the modern research university. In popular as well as in scholarly and scientific contexts, there is a widespread notion to the effect that the German model became an example for others in the nineteenth century, and that it ultimately formed a kind of intellectual foundation for the university of the twentieth century. In its general features this appears to be an accurate description, even if the process – which

---

7:1 (2010); Christian Geulen, 'Plädoyer für eine Geschichte der Grundbegriffe des 20. Jahrhunderts', *Zeithistorische Forschungen/Studies in Contemporary History*, 7:1 (2010); Theresa Wobbe, 'Für eine Historische Semantik des 19. und 20. Jahrhunderts: Kommentar zu Christian Geulen', *Zeithistorische Forschungen/Studies in Contemporary History*, 7:1 (2010); and Jan-Werner Müller, 'European Intellectual History as Contemporary History', *Journal of Contemporary History*, 46:3 (2011).

42 *Humboldt international*, ed. by Schwinges; Schalenberg, *Humboldt auf Reisen?*
43 Andreas Wimmer & Nina Glick Schiller, 'Methodological Nationalism and Beyond: Nation-State Building, Migration and the Social Sciences', *Global Networks*, 4:2 (2002); Sebastian Conrad, *Globalgeschichte: Eine Einführung* (Munich, 2013).

is still incompletely analysed – was never a linear one. But in order to determine what characterises the modern university, knowledge about its origins is required. For this reason Germany, the birthplace of the Humboldtian tradition, should be given special attention.

In what follows I will initially, in two chapters, outline the formation of a classic German university tradition and its subsequent fortunes up to the Second World War. The first of these, Chapter 2, is devoted to the ideas of Wilhelm von Humboldt and the establishment of the Berlin university. Following this, there is a survey of the Humboldt renaissance in the period around the year 1900 and the reform proposals of the subsequent decades. The purpose of these two chapters is to supply a basic historical understanding of the Humboldtian tradition, but also to clarify the principal issues and themes of this study. Two chapters that constitute the empirical essence of the book ensue, each of them dealing with a specific period: the years of occupation after the Second World War, when the debate was characterised by a desire to examine and vitalise the academic heritage (Chapter 4), and the first half of the 1960s, when a new generation of intellectuals discussed how the emerging mass university was related to older German ideals (Chapter 5). In conclusion, the early twenty-first-century Bologna process is linked to the Humboldtian tradition and to the overarching importance of that tradition in modern-day Germany. In this final chapter, where I again refer to my points of departure with respect to intellectual history and the history of knowledge, I summarise my insights while expanding the range of my observations.

2
Wilhelm von Humboldt and his idea

A modern university

In many depictions of the German eighteenth century, the university is in a state of decay. The eighteenth-century university was intellectually dormant, it was constrained by nepotism and class privileges, and it provided an education that was scholastic and pedantic, at best encyclopaedic.[1] During the second half of the century, increasingly vociferous demands were raised for genuine reform. A growing opinion demanded that teaching should be reorganised and aimed at meeting the needs of the professions rather than dispensing old learning. Changing the university was, however, a slow and drawn-out process, and instead a number of special schools were established within, among other things, veterinary medicine, mining, and commerce in order to fulfil the requirements of the new age. It was at these educational establishments, as well as at the science

---

1 Thomas Nipperdey, *Deutsche Geschichte 1800–1866: Bürgerwelt und starker Staat* (Munich, 1983), p. 57; Christopher Clark, *Iron Kingdom: The Rise and Downfall of Prussia, 1600–1947* (Cambridge, 2006), pp. 331–33; Howard, *Protestant Theology*, pp. 80–81. See also the discussion in Josephson, Karlsohn, & Östling, 'Humboldtian Tradition', pp. 3–7. Sections of this chapter have previously been published as Johan Östling, 'Humboldts idé: Bildning och universitet i det moderna Tyskland', in *Humaniora i kunskapssamhället: En nordisk debattbok*, ed. by Jesper Eckhart Larsen & Martin Wiklund (Malmö, 2012); Johan Östling, 'The Humboldtian Tradition: The German University Transformed, 1800–1945', in *University Jubilees and University History at the Beginning of the 21st Century*, ed. by Dhondt; Johan Östling, 'What Is a University? Answers to a Very German Question', in *Thinking Ahead: Research, Funding and the Future: RJ Yearbook 2015/2016*, ed. by Jenny Björkman & Björn Fjæstad (Göteborg, 2015); and Johan Östling, 'Vad är ett universitet? Svar på en mycket tysk fråga', in *Tänka vidare: Forskning, finansiering, framtid: RJ:s årsbok 2015/2016*, ed. by Jenny Björkman & Björn Fjæstad (Göteborg, 2015).

academies, that most of the practical and theoretical research was to be conducted. Towards the end of the eighteenth century, the university as an institution was thus not held in great repute either among utilitarian natural scientists, rationalist Enlightenment philosophers, or the emergent bourgeoisie. Along with the church, the university, with its mediaeval character and religious overtones, became the symbol of *l'ancien régime*.[2]

More recently researchers have, from different perspectives, tested this idea about the eighteenth century – and ultimately relativised the significance of the establishment of the Berlin university and the year 1810 as an academic *annus mirabilis*. Some of them have claimed that the enlightened rulers of the time were well aware of the stagnation and launched reforms in order to revitalise higher education. Seen from this perspective, the continued development during the nineteenth century mainly becomes the completion of a transformation that was already under way.[3] Others have promoted the idea that the creation of the modern university must be understood as a stage in the development of the bureaucratic state. For instance, in an innovative work William Clark has argued that the growing state administration tried to limit the old academic freedom and increase political control.[4] At the same time he claims – as do others – that the rise of the modern university must be seen in relation to an emergent book market and changes in the public sphere. Books became more easily accessible, more and more people began to take up their pens in order to express their opinions, and literacy increased significantly. All this led to professors being exposed to competition as authorities of knowledge. Ultimately, their role was transformed. The writing, pioneering researcher became an ideal.[5]

---

2 *A History of the University in Europe: Universities in Early Modern Europe (1500–1800)*, ed. by Hilde de Ridder-Symoens (Cambridge, 1996), pp. 52–80.
3 Anderson, *European Universities*, pp. 4, 20–38, and 51–52.
4 William Clark, *Academic Charisma and the Origins of the Research University* (Chicago, 2006).
5 Clark, *Academic Charisma*; Thomas H. Broman, *The Transformation of German Academic Medicine, 1750–1820* (Cambridge, 1996); Peter Josephson, 'Böcker eller universitet? Om ett tema i tysk utbildningspolitisk debatt kring 1800', *Lychnos*, 2009; Peter Josephson, 'The Publication Mill: The Beginnings of Publication History as an Academic Merit in German Universities, 1750–1810', in *The Humboldtian Tradition*, ed. by Josephson, Karlsohn & Östling; Thomas Karlsohn, *Originalitetens former: Essäer om bildning och universitet* (Göteborg, 2012), pp. 30–35 and 37–61; Peter Josephson, 'Publicitetens politiska ekonomi: Introduktion av skriftställarskap som merit

What connects Clark to other scholars is his emphasis on the fact that a new and supporting foundation for the modern university was laid down already during the eighteenth century. There is much to recommend these interpretations. At the same time, it is difficult to deny that the upheavals in European societies in the decades around the year 1800 – the Enlightenment, the French Revolution and all that followed – had a profound effect on the academic system. In hindsight it seems as if two new main academic models, the French and the Prussian one, emerged in the wake of the Napoleonic Wars. In many parts of Europe, not least in the north, south, and in the British Isles, much would long remain as before; but in two large areas of the continent, things developed in a different direction.[6] In France the autonomy of the universities was completely circumscribed, and they were subordinated to the power of the political regime. *Collèges* and traditional faculties were replaced by a series of professional and special schools. Nevertheless, some older institutions, such as Collège de France, survived both the Revolution and Napoleon; and it was

---

vid tyska universitet 1750–1810', *Lychnos*, 2014; Chad Wellmon, *Organizing Enlightenment: Information Overload and the Invention of the Modern Research University* (Baltimore, 2015). The transformation of German political and intellectual culture during the latter half of the eighteenth century is discussed in a number of foundational studies from the time after the Second World War, among them Reinhart Koselleck, *Kritik und Krise: Eine Studie zur Pathogenese der bürgerlichen Welt* (Munich, 1959); Jürgen Habermas, *Strukturwandel der Öffentlichkeit: Untersuchungen zu einer Kategorie der bürgerlichen Gesellschaft* (Neuwied, 1962); and Friedrich A. Kittler, *Aufschreibesysteme 1800/1900* (Munich, 1985).

6 Walter Rüegg, 'Themes', in *A History of the University in Europe: Universities in the Nineteenth and Early Twentieth Centuries*, ed. by Rüegg, pp. 3–13; Christophe Charle, 'Patterns', in *A History of the University in Europe: Universities in the Nineteenth and Early Twentieth Centuries*, ed. by Rüegg, pp. 33–40; Anderson, *European Universities*, pp. 3–4. Some historians have questioned the strict division between a French and a German model. They argue that both systems evolved in parallel and that there were many French educational establishments where research was de facto combined with teaching. According to these historians, the difference is in part a reflection of the contemporary German polemics, and later historiography has been influenced by these allegations. See Anderson, *European Universities*, pp. 63–64 and Gert Schubring, 'Spezialschulmodell versus Universitätsmodell: Die Institutionalisierung von Forschung', in *'Einsamkeit und Freiheit' neu besichtigt: Universitätsreformen und Disziplinenbildung in Preussen als Modell für Wissenschaftspolitik im Europa des 19. Jahrhunderts*, ed. by Gert Schubring (Stuttgart, 1991), pp. 288–96.

here, as at other educational establishments with a distinct profile, that much of French research was conducted. The overall result of these upheavals was that the academic reality in France during the nineteenth century came to be characterised by specialisation and fragmentation.[7]

In Prussia, by contrast, the university as an idea and an institution was headed for a renaissance. Already during the eighteenth century, new elements had been incorporated into the academic activities at several German universities, in particular at Enlightenment Göttingen and Halle. One such element that was particularly important was the requirement that professors should devote themselves to research and not just teach. Another was that lectures had to be complemented by seminars, a forum for scholarly discussion that included both students and teachers who were doing research.[8] In the medieval university the philosophical faculty was the lowest in rank, intended primarily for preparatory studies. By the end of the eighteenth century, increasing numbers of people had begun to question this old but still existing order. Immanuel Kant, Johann Gottlieb Fichte, and Friedrich Schleiermacher all argued that the philosophical faculty should be placed on a par with, and even be given precedence over, the other three. In *Der Streit der Fakultäten* (1798) Kant spoke of a conflict between, on the one hand, the faculty of philosophy and, on the other, the faculties of theology, law, and medicine. In defiance of then-prevalent ideas, Kant argued that the faculty of philosophy was superior because it was independent of demands for utility and free from links to the state. It relied exclusively on reason, and consequently it could 'lay claim to any teaching, in order to test its truth'. Only if the faculty of philosophy was given a higher and more independent position would it be possible for scientific thinking to develop.[9]

---

7 Charle, 'Patterns', pp. 33–47, and, more generally, Schubring, 'Spezialschulmodell'.
8 Charle, 'Patterns', pp. 47–48; Roy Steven Turner, 'University Reforms and Professorial Scholarship in Germany 1760–1806', in *The University in Society: Europe, Scotland, and the United States from the 16th to the 20th Century*, ed. by Lawrence Stone (Princeton, 1974).
9 Immanuel Kant, *The Conflict of the Faculties*, trans. by Mary J. Gregor (Lincoln and London, 1992), p. 45. For a background to Kant's text, see Riccardo Pozzo, 'Kant's *Streit der Fakultäten* and Conditions at Königsberg', *History of Universities*, 16 (2000).

Therefore, the conclusion must be that much of what blossomed during the nineteenth century and became characteristic of the German university had been heralded earlier. Several minor reforms had been realised, and the debate about academic ideals was in full swing during the final years of the eighteenth century. Nevertheless, the emergence and establishment of a distinct Prussian university model must be linked to the major events from the period around the year 1800.

The French Revolutionary Wars and the Napoleonic Wars shaped an entire generation in the German regions. Not all areas were hit equally hard by French warfare and occupation, but in Prussia the humiliating setbacks – the defeats at Jena and Auerstedt, the siege of Berlin – gave rise to a strong and lasting reaction. Out of the resistance to the superior French forces grew an aversion to Enlightenment cosmopolitanism itself. This experience kindled a patriotic awakening, an incipient German nationalism with Prussian overtones. At the same time, the defeats occasioned a self-examination that paved the way for a reform of important social institutions, a reform eagerly anticipated by many people. In contrast to Revolutionary France, the changes were gradual, not seldom defensively directed by men such as Karl vom und zum Stein and Karl August von Hardenberg. In the wake of the Napoleonic Wars significant reforms were undertaken, among them the liberation of the peasants from serfdom, the emancipation of the Jews, freedom of trade, and compulsory military service, which were crucial for transforming Prussia from a feudal into a modern industrial state.[10]

It is impossible to separate the founding of the Berlin university in 1810 from this political and social context.[11] In 1789 there were

---

10 Nipperdey, *Deutsche Geschichte*, pp. 11–101; Hans-Ulrich Wehler, *Deutsche Gesellschaftsgeschichte: Vom Feudalismus des Alten Reiches bis zur defensiven Modernisierung der Reformära 1700–1815* (Munich, 1987), pp. 363–485; David Blackbourn, *History of Germany, 1780–1918: The Long Nineteenth Century* (Malden, 2003), pp. 54–68.

11 A still valuable depiction of the creation and early days of the Berlin university is a work published by Max Lenz in connection with its centenary in 1910, *Geschichte der Königlichen Friedrich-Wilhelms-Universität zu Berlin*, 4 vols (Halle, 1910–1918) (the final volume was delayed because of the First World War and was published eight years after the first volume). In preparation for the bicentenary of Humboldt-Universität zu Berlin in 2010, a new history was written. The six volumes of this history, which were published in 2010–2012 under the joint title *Geschichte der Universität*

thirty-five universities in the German region, almost half of whose students were registered at one of the big four (Halle, Göttingen, Jena, and Leipzig). A quarter of a century later, only sixteen universities remained; the others had been shut down or been forced to close in the aftermath of war and invasion. In addition, in 1807 Prussia lost its erstwhile academic flagship when the university in Halle became a part of the Napoleon-created kingdom of Westphalia. According to the King's oft-quoted words, the state now had to replace the physical losses through spiritual strength – 'der Staat muss durch geistige Kräfte ersetzen, was er an physischen verloren hat'.[12] Even so, one cannot ignore the fact that the transformation of the Prussian educational system was not only an important stage in a general reform effort, but also a concrete attempt to launch an alternative to the Napoleonic special schools. The fact that two other universities, both bearing the epithet Friedrich-Wilhelms-Universität,

---

Unter den Linden, had Heinz-Elmar Tenorth as their main editor. The first three volumes are in the form of a biography of the university and deal mainly with the general transformation of the university in the various German social systems, and they include topics such as financing, statutes, recruitment of professors, student life, relations with the city of Berlin and with the political authorities. See, in order, *Gründung und Blütezeit der Universität zu Berlin 1810–1918*, ed. by Heinz-Elmar Tenorth (Berlin, 2012); *Die Berliner Universität zwischen den Weltkriegen 1918–1945*, ed. by Heinz-Elmar Tenorth & Michael Grüttner (Berlin, 2012); and *Sozialistisches Experiment und Erneuerung in der Demokratie – die Humboldt-Universität zu Berlin 1945–2010*, ed. by Konrad H. Jarausch, Matthias Middell & Annette Vogt (Berlin, 2012). The final three volumes deal with the history of the disciplines and scholarly scientific practices: *Genese der Disziplinen: Die Konstitution der Universität*, ed. by Heinz-Elmar Tenorth (Berlin, 2010), *Transformation der Wissensordnung*, ed. by Heinz-Elmar Tenorth (Berlin, 2010), and *Selbstbehauptung einer Vision*, ed. by Heinz-Elmar Tenorth (Berlin, 2010).

12 Heinz-Elmar Tenorth, 'Eine Universität zu Berlin – Vorgeschichte und Einrichtung', in *Geschichte der Universität Unter den Linden: Gründung und Blütezeit*, pp. 10–16; Rüdiger vom Bruch, 'Die Gründung der Berliner Universität', in *Humboldt international*, ed. by Schwinges, pp. 58–59. According to the most detailed analysis – and in contradistinction to what, for instance, vom Bruch claims – the King's words appear to be authentic; see Hans Ch. Kraus's study of Theodor von Schmalz, the first Vice-Chancellor of the Berlin university (1810–1811), *Theodor Anton Heinrich Schmalz (1760–1831): Jurisprudenz, Universitätspolitik und Publizistik im Spannungsfeld von Revolution und Restauration* (Frankfurt am Main, 1999), pp. 97–104.

were established in Prussia at the same time, in Breslau in 1811 and in Bonn in 1818, does not weaken this impression.[13]

The Berlin university was not, of course, created in an intellectual vacuum. Since the end of the eighteenth century, the idea of the university had been discussed in a good number of publications and debates; the contributions of Kant, Fichte, and Schleiermacher regarding the status of the faculty of philosophy was a part of this discussion, which was far more comprehensive than that. Jena in Thuringia was one important centre of this exchange of opinions. The city's university had been established as far back as the mid-sixteenth century, but towards the end of the eighteenth century it developed into a rare academic free zone. During one period, in particular during the 1790s, the city numbered many of the most prominent thinkers among its professors, among them Schiller, Fichte, Schelling, and August Wilhelm Schlegel. Even more important for the creative atmosphere was the steady stream of authors, artists, and philosophers who came to Jena during these years for shorter or longer stays: Goethe, Hölderlin, Novalis, Schleiermacher, Caroline Schlegel, and Dorothea Veit. This environment inspired ideas about a new kind of educational establishment, an institution which has been called 'the romantic university', with *Bildung*, academic freedom, and the collective research process as its corner-stones.[14]

There are scholars who have claimed that the Berlin university was an 'institutionalisation of the ideal of Jena'.[15] To some extent

---

13 Charles E. McClelland, *State, Society, and University in Germany, 1700–1914* (Cambridge, 1980), pp. 102–08; Schubring, 'Spezialschulmodell', pp. 288–96.
14 *Die Universität Jena: Tradition und Innovation um 1800*, ed. by Gerhard Müller, Klaus Ries, & Paul Ziche (Stuttgart, 2001); Karlsohn, *Originalitetens former*, pp. 82–99. *Bildung* (education, self-cultivation, character formation) is notoriously difficult to translate into English; see below, pp. 36–40 for a discussion on the meaning of this concept.
15 Theodore Ziolkowski, *German Romanticism and Its Institutions* (Princeton, 1990), p. 286. As Thorsten Nybom has framed it, Cardinal John Henry Newman, the other great nineteenth-century ideologue of the university, used an existing institution (Oxford) as a model when writing his *The Idea of a University*, while Humboldt brought together a number of existing ideas and let them coalesce in a new institution, the Berlin university. See Thorsten Nybom, 'A Rule-Governed Community of Scholars: The Humboldt Vision in the History of the European University', in *University Dynamics and European Integration*, ed. by Peter A. M. Maassen & Johan P. Olsen (Dordrecht, 2007), p. 79. For general information on Newman, see Rothblatt, *The Modern University*, and Karlsohn, *Originalitetens former*, pp. 111–26.

it can be seen that way, but the new university that took shape also had its own specific prehistory. As early as 1784, a suggestion had been made to establish a university in Berlin. During the first years of the nineteenth century many of the ideas that had been current in Jena were developed further, and in their writings men like Schelling, Fichte, Schleiermacher, and Steffens laid an intellectual foundation for a new university, guided by ideals of *Bildung* and pure scholarship.[16] In the majority of these outlines for a reformation of higher education, the negatively charged appellation 'university' was shunned in favour of 'institution of higher education' or 'educational institution'.[17] One noteworthy exception was Schleiermacher's *Gelegentliche Gedanken über Universitäten in deutschem Sinn* (1808), which was the most important and widely distributed published work. Inspired by the romantic circles in Jena, he drew up guidelines for a new kind of university. Later interpreters – the best-known being Helmut Schelsky – have questioned Schleiermacher's contribution, because he was not as willing as, for example, Fichte to break with the old order and safeguard the high value of science and scholarship. Today, however, his contribution as an intellectual pioneer for a new concept of the university is emphasised, not least because he contributed to spreading ideas and making them familiar in wider circles.[18]

Moreover, Schleiermacher asked a very concrete question in his *Gelegentliche Gedanken*: 'But why in Berlin of all places?' He believed

---

16 Among the most significant early nineteenth-century texts about the university or higher education are Friedrich von Schelling, *Vorlesungen über die Methode des akademischen Studiums* (Tübingen, 1803), Johann Gottlieb Fichte, *Deduzierter Plan einer zu Berlin zu errichtenden höhern Lehranstalt, die in gehöriger Verbindung mit einer Akademie der Wissenschaften stehe* (1807; published in Tübingen in 1817), Friedrich Schleiermacher, *Gelegentliche Gedanken über Universitäten in deutschem Sinn* (Berlin, 1808), and Heinrich Steffens, *Ueber die Idee von Universitäten* (Berlin, 1809). These writings were later republished in, among other places, *Die Idee*, ed. by Anrich, and *Gelegentliche Gedanken über Universitäten*, ed. by Ernst Müller (Leipzig, 1990). See also Tenorth, 'Genese der Disziplinen', pp. 9–10.
17 Vom Bruch, 'Die Gründung', pp. 57–62; Tenorth, 'Eine Universität zu Berlin', pp. 25–33.
18 Compare Helmut Schelsky, *Einsamkeit und Freiheit*, with Hedwig Kopetz, *Forschung und Lehre: Die Idee der Universität bei Humboldt, Jaspers, Schelsky und Mittelstrass* (Wien, 2002); Rüegg, 'Themes'; and Christoph Markschies, *Was von Humboldt noch zu lernen ist: Aus Anlass des zweihundertjährigen Geburtstags der preussischen Reformuniversität* (Berlin, 2010).

that other Prussian locations would find it easier to attract students and teachers than the expensive and comparatively peripheral capital, but he also saw obvious advantages in Berlin. Berlin already had large libraries, an observatory, zoological and anatomical cabinets, and other facilities that could be of use to the new university. The same was true of the many special schools that had been erected on the banks of and near the river Spree.[19]

The following year, in July 1809, the Prussian king Frederick William III received an official letter with a similar content. In it the author, who had obviously been influenced by Schleiermacher, argued that a general institution of higher education should be established. An important argument for locating it in Berlin was the existence of institutes, collections, and academies in the city, and the fact that full justice would not be done to these if they were not linked to the scholarly teaching at the new university. The idea was that all units would keep their independence but that they would at the same time be deeply interdependent. The official letter bore the signature Wilhelm von Humboldt. He was at this time head of the section for educational and cultural issues in the Prussian ministry of the interior, but he had had time to do many other things before this.[20]

Baron (*Freiherr*) Friedrich Wilhelm Christian Karl Ferdinand von Humboldt was born in Potsdam on 22 June 1767 as the eldest son of chamberlain Alexander Georg von Humboldt and his wife, Marie-Elisabeth Colomb. Together with his brother Alexander, two years younger and destined to become famous as a natural scientist and explorer, Wilhelm von Humboldt had been given a thorough education which was typical for the nobility of his time, provided by prominent governors and private tutors. For one year, 1787, he was registered at the university in Frankfurt an der Oder, but he soon moved to the more dynamic one in Göttingen, where the combination of *Bildung* and Enlightenment made a lasting impression

---

19 Vom Bruch, 'Die Gründung', p. 59; Tenorth, 'Eine Universität zu Berlin', pp. 25–33. During the seventeenth and eighteenth centuries, universities were not usually located in political and commercial centres. Nevertheless, during the nineteenth century a number of new big city universities were established, for instance in London, Manchester, Zürich, Brussels, Athens, Kiev, and Madrid. Consequently, the founding of the Berlin university was part of a general change. See *A History of the University in Europe*, ed. by de Ridder-Symoens, and *A History of the University in Europe*, ed. by Rüegg.
20 Vom Bruch, 'Die Gründung', p. 60.

on him. After studying for four terms he went on a peregrination in Western Europe, experienced revolutionary sentiments in Paris, got engaged to Karoline von Dacheröden, and came into contact with Schiller, Goethe, and Herder, before entering into the service of the Prussian government in 1790. But after only a year or so he left his post, intending to wholeheartedly devote himself to study and writing. For a few fruitful years, 1794–97, he lived in Jena and was able to cultivate his philosophical and philological interests in the company of Schiller, Fichte, and the Schlegel brothers. Next followed a longer sojourn in Romance Europe, mainly with Paris as his base but including several longer journeys to Spain and other countries. Following a brief interlude in Berlin, Humboldt functioned as a Prussian diplomat at the Holy See in 1802–08. This was in many ways the richest period of his life, as he and his wife could enjoy ancient relics and socialise with artists on a daily basis.

Humboldt was, however, recalled to the Prussian capital and employed in Stein's reform cabinet. During sixteen productive months, from February 1809 to June 1810, he would leave a deep impression on the educational system.[21]

---

21 Literature about Wilhelm von Humboldt has been published for more than 150 years. The first comprehensive biographical contributions were Gustav Schlesier, *Erinnerungen an Wilhelm von Humboldt* (Stuttgart, 1843–1845) – divided into three publications, *Von 1767 bis 1794* (1843), *Von 1794 bis 1798* (1843), and *Von 1798 bis 1819* (1845) – and Rudolf Haym, *Wilhelm von Humboldt: Lebensbild und Charakteristik* (Berlin, 1856). Among modern biographies the two volumes by Paul R. Sweet, *Wilhelm von Humboldt: A Biography: 1767–1808* (Columbus, OH, 1978) and *Wilhelm von Humboldt: A Biography: 1808–1835* (Columbus, OH, 1980), are in a class by themselves by virtue of their thoroughness and erudition. Herbert Scurla, *Wilhelm von Humboldt: Werden und Wirken* (Berlin, 1970) is also a sterling biography, which is only slightly marred by the ideological jargon of Eastern European Marxism. In Lothar Gall's *Wilhelm von Humboldt: Ein Preuße in der Welt* (Berlin, 2011), the most recent addition to the major biographies, the phases of the protagonist's life are pursued in their chronological order, with a focus on his achievements as a politician and diplomat. The main features of Humboldt's life also emerge in Eberhard Kessel, *Wilhelm von Humboldt: Idee und Wirklichkeit* (Stuttgart, 1967), Peter Berglar, *Wilhelm von Humboldt* (Reinbek, 1970), Tilman Borsche, *Wilhelm von Humboldt* (Munich, 1990), Manfred Geier, *Die Brüder Humboldt* (Reinbek, 2009), and Franz-Michael Konrad, *Wilhelm von Humboldt* (Göttingen, 2010), as they do in a concentrated form in biographical dictionaries such as Gerhard Masur & Hans Arens, 'Humboldt, Wilhelm von', in *Neue Deutsche Biographie* (Berlin, 1953–), vol. X (1974) and Andreas Flitner,

4 Wilhelm von Humboldt

Humboldt's efforts were initially focused on breathing life into and reforming the Prussian school system. His pedagogic vision encompassed all educational stages, from elementary school through the *Gymnasium* (secondary school) to the university. In the summer of 1809, he therefore sent the previously mentioned official letter to Frederick William III about establishing a new university in Berlin. In August of the same year, the King approved the proposal. It was over a year before teaching and research could commence in October 1810 at the *alma mater berolinensis*. Operations began on a small scale – 262 students and 25 professors during the first term – and not until six years later were there any statutes to speak of. When Georg-August-Universität opened its doors in Göttingen in 1737, it had done so to the accompaniment of an extravagant opening ceremony. In Berlin, which was marked by defeat and years of famine, the opening took place without any pomp and circumstance.[22]

Nevertheless, the new university soon won academic renown, largely owing to the fact that Humboldt managed to persuade so

---

'Humboldt, Wilhelm von', in *Deutsche biographische Enzyklopädie*, ed. by Rudolf Vierhaus, 2nd rev. and enl. edn, 10 vols (Munich, 2005–2008), vol. v (2006). Several older works that are still referred to in studies contribute to the image of Humboldt without being actual biographies: Eduard Spranger, *Wilhelm von Humboldt und die Humanitätsidee* (Berlin, 1909); Siegfried A. Kaehler, *Wilhelm von Humboldt und der Staat: Ein Beitrag zur Geschichte deutscher Lebensgestaltung um 1800* (Munich, 1927); and Clemens Menze, *Die Bildungsreform Wilhelm von Humboldts* (Hanover, 1975). For Humboldt as a linguist, see James Turner, *Philology: The Forgotten Origins of the Modern Humanities* (Princeton, 2014), pp. 134–36. In spite of its size, the literature about Wilhelm von Humboldt can never match that devoted to his younger brother. In a fascinating metabiography of Alexander von Humboldt's many biographies, Nicolaas A. Rupke claims that there are more than 5,000 written works about the great natural scientist, many with a biographical slant. Rupke distinguishes the many faces of Alexander von Humboldt as they have appeared during different periods: the liberal democrat of the decades prior to 1871, the *Kultur*-chauvinist of Wilhelmian Germany and the Weimar Republic, the superhuman Aryan of the Third Reich, the radical abolitionist of East Germany, the cosmopolitan philo-Semite of West Germany, and the globalisation pioneer of today. See Nicolaas A. Rupke, *Alexander von Humboldt: A Metabiography* (Chicago, 2008).

22 Tenorth, 'Eine Universität zu Berlin', pp. 3–75; Heinz-Elmar Tenorth, 'Geschichte der Universität zu Berlin, 1810–2010: Zur Einleitung', in *Geschichte der Universität Unter den Linden: Gründung und Blütezeit*, ed. by Tenorth, pp. xxvi and xxxvii; vom Bruch, 'Die Gründung', pp. 53–54.

many truly prominent scholars to accept important professorial chairs. Fichte became the first holder of the key professorship in philosophy (and, in addition, the Vice-Chancellor – *Rektor* – of the university for a brief period), and was succeeded in 1818 by Hegel. Schleiermacher became the first professor in theology, Carl von Savigny in law, Carl Ritter in geography, August Boeckh in classical philology, and Christoph Wilhelm Hufeland in medicine. A number of significant scholarly environments evolved over the years, for instance around the historian Leopold von Ranke and the physiologist Johannes Müller. By that time, Wilhelm von Humboldt had long ago left his position in the Prussian ministry of the interior. However, beginning in the 1820s his brother Alexander endeavoured to ensure that the natural sciences had a firm foothold in the capital.[23]

The new Berlin university was thus not the work of a moment. On the contrary, it was predicated on the slow reform process during the eighteenth century, the intense intellectual debate in the decades around the year 1800, and the political reaction to the defeat of Prussia.[24] From all of this, a new university system was born. For a long time, it was more of an idea than a reality. It is this idea which will henceforth be at the centre of the present study.

Humboldt's idea

During his entire life Wilhelm von Humboldt was an intellectually active man, but his interests gradually changed over time. His first writings, completed when he was around twenty-five years old, were political texts in a liberal spirit, heavily influenced by the French Revolution. Around the year 1800, Humboldt immersed himself in Greek antiquity and made his first attempts to formulate a theory

---

23 It may be superfluous to point out that the recruitment of professors for the Berlin university was not simply a matter of finding the best minds; sex, religion, and denominational or ideological persuasion disqualified many potential candidates. In addition, the majority of the professors were not particularly famous and were soon forgotten. See Werner Teß, 'Professoren – Der Lehrkörper und seine Praxis zwischen Wissenschaft, Politik und Gesellschaft', in *Geschichte der Universität Unter den Linden: Gründung und Blütezeit*, ed. by Tenorth. For von Ranke's famous *Übungen*, which were not regular seminars, see Kasper Risbjerg Eskildsen, 'Leopold Ranke's Archival Turn: Location and Evidence in Modern Historiography', *Modern Intellectual History*, 5:3 (2008), 427.
24 See also the discussion in Wittrock, 'Modern University', pp. 315–16.

of education. Next came the years 1809–10, when in a number of documents he discussed the Prussian educational system, both concretely and in principle. During the final twenty-five years of his life he initially wrote memoranda and tracts dealing with constitutional policy, but soon concentrated on comparative linguistics. If, in spite of this versatility, a comprehensive idea, his *Lebensthema*, is to be found, it would have to be human beings and their education.[25]

Wilhelm von Humboldt, the ideologue of the university, was not a rebel against the trends of his time. He was a skilled synthesist who became successful by systematically combining thoughts that were in circulation and finding pregnant expressions for his own ideas. During his brief time in Berlin in 1809–1810 he converted his words into action. Perhaps it can be said that Humboldt managed to turn a reform against the university into a reform of the university.

Like no other concept, that of *Bildung* has been linked to Wilhelm von Humboldt – justly so, for it was key to his educational philosophy. At the same time, the word *Bildung* itself has a long history in the German language. It has to do with 'image' (*Bild*), 'depiction' (*Abbildung*), and many other derivations. Its meaning has gradually expanded in the course of the centuries, and in the eighteenth century it was increasingly given the meaning of 'to form' or 'to shape'. It was in the decades surrounding the year 1800 that the word had a real impact on the debate of ideas and in the consciousness of the emerging educated middle classes (*Bildungsbürgertum*). Even if it appeared in various guises, their common sustenance was the specific combination of German New Humanism, Enlightenment thought, and idealism that characterised the intellectual climate in German-speaking Europe at that time. It is significant that *Bildung* lacks a direct equivalent in other major languages. Translations such

---

25 Wilhelm von Humboldt's works were initially published in seven volumes by Carl Brandes, *Wilhelm von Humboldt: Gesammelte Werke* (Berlin, 1841–1852). The Preußische Akademie der Wissenschaften published the more complete *Gesammelte Schriften* (Berlin, 1903–1936) in seventeen volumes, with Albert Leitzmann och Bruno Gebhardt as editors. This edition was republished in 1967–1968. Andreas Flitner and Klaus Giel were the editors of *Werke in fünf Bänden* (Darmstadt, 1960–1981), which contained a detailed critical commentary. The Flitner-Giel edition is the one used for the present study. In 2010 these five volumes were republished in a *Studienausgabe*.

as *éducation*, *formation* or *self-cultivation* do not quite capture the German meaning.[26] As a pedagogical idea, the German *Bildung* is related to concepts that are significantly older. It can be traced back to the Greek *paideia*, an early programme for a comprehensive development of human spiritual, aesthetic, and physical abilities with the aim of moulding a complete and harmonious citizen. The concept of *Bildung* that emerged during the eighteenth century was, in addition, inspired by a late medieval reinterpretation of the old Christian idea that human beings should strive to become an image of God, *imago Dei*.[27] Traces of this way of thinking can, for instance, be found in the works of an influential educational theorist such as Johann Gottfried von Herder. He was one of the first to design a somewhat more coherent pedagogic vision with *Bildung* as its lodestar, where the overarching purpose was to develop the capacities of the individual and break with an ideal that rewarded rote learning of a closed curriculum. Ultimately this had to do with realising what he called *Humanität*. In this way, the educational concept of *Bildung* became a somewhat secularised further development of an older idea. Many of the great figures of the day – Johann Wolfgang von Goethe, Friedrich von

---

26 The pedagogical, philosophical, and historical literature on the concept of *Bildung* is overwhelmingly large. Basic examinations of the history of the concept can be found in Rudolf Vierhaus, 'Bildung', in *Geschichtliche Grundbegriffe: Historisches Lexikon zur politisch-sozialen Sprache in Deutschland*, ed. by Otto Brunner, Werner Conze, & Reinhart Koselleck, 8 vols (Stuttgart, 1972–1997), vol. I (1972), and Ernst Lichtenstein, 'Bildung', in *Historisches Wörterbuch der Philosophie*, ed. by Joachim Ritter, 13 vols (Basel and Stuttgart, 1971–2007), vol. I (1971). A meandering survey of the history of the concept is provided by Reinhart Koselleck in 'Einleitung – Zur anthropologischen und semantischen Struktur der Bildung', in *Bildungsbürgertum im 19. Jahrhundert*, ed. by Werner Conze and Jürgen Kocka (Stuttgart, 1985–), vol. II: *Bildungsgüter und Bildungswissen*, ed. by Reinhart Koselleck (1990), a volume that in addition contains a number of essays on the significance of the concept of *Bildung* to the nineteenth-century middle classes. See also Ulrich Engelhardt, *'Bildungsbürgertum': Begriffs- und Dogmengeschichte eines Etiketts* (Stuttgart, 1986), Aleida Assmann, *Arbeit am nationalen Gedächtnis: Eine kurze Geschichte der deutschen Bildungsidee* (Frankfurt am Main, 1993), and Georg Bollenbeck, *Bildung und Kultur: Glanz und Elend eines deutschen Deutungsmusters* (Frankfurt am Main, 1994).
27 Vierhaus, 'Bildung'; Lichtenstein, 'Bildung'. The classic work on the concept of education in antiquity is Werner Jaeger, *Paideia: Die Formung des griechischen Menschen*, 3 vols (Berlin, 1934–1947).

Schiller, Johann Heinrich Pestalozzi, Immanuel Kant – referred to Herder and contributed to the late eighteenth- and early nineteenth-century dynamic discussion about *Bildung*.[28] Nevertheless, it was not until the actions of Wilhelm von Humboldt that the concept of *Bildung* was truly integrated into an educational programme and given institutional stability. To Humboldt and his contemporaries, *Bildung* had to do with the highest and most harmonious development of natural human abilities. His theoretical expositions on the concept of *Bildung* demonstrated a kind of duality in his thought. On the one hand, he described an educational process in which the unrestricted improvement of each person's personality was at the centre. Humboldt's *Bildung* was based on a subjective acquisition of knowledge that had its origins in and transformed the individual. On the other hand, an individual's development was always considered in relation to history and to the truly human. The realisation of that individual's inner potential took place in a dialectical movement between the self and the surrounding culture. In this dynamics, Humboldt imagined that that which is individual could approach that which is generally human.[29]

One prerequisite for Humboldt's idea of the university was the transformation of the concept of originality that occurred in his time. To Kant, originality was still a capacity that belonged to an exceptional natural talent; but around 1800, creativity more and more often began to be seen as a universal quality that everyone potentially possessed. When originality was not exclusively reserved for artistic geniuses, it could become a lodestar for an entire social institution. Humboldt transferred this way of thinking to the arena of the university. He argued not only for the importance of research, but also for the idea that teaching should be characterised by active dialogic creation that included both students and teachers.

---

28 Koselleck, 'Struktur der Bildung'; Karlsohn, *Originalitetens former*.
29 Wilhelm von Humboldt, 'Theorie der Bildung des Menschen: Bruchstücke', in Wilhelm von Humboldt, *Werke in fünf Bänden*, ed. by Flitner & Giel, vol. I: *Schriften zur Anthropologie und Geschichte* (1960). The literature on Wilhelm von Humboldt's concept of *Bildung* is extensive. See Dietrich Benner, *Wilhelm von Humboldts Bildungstheorie: Eine problemgeschichtliche Studie zum Begründungszusammenhang neuzeitlicher Bildungsreform* (Weinheim and Munich, 2003), pp. 7–10, where the author discusses influential but reciprocally dissimilar understandings of Humboldt's concept of *Bildung*, represented by men like Eduard Spranger, Theodor Litt, and Clemens Menze.

Emulation – not imitation – was to be characteristic of the new pedagogics.[30]

Humboldt was as much a practically disposed as a theoretically orientated man, and his idea about *Bildung* emerges most concretely in the proposals, memoranda, and drafts that he wrote during his years as a Prussian minister. In an official document from 1809, 'Der Königsberger und der Litauische Schulplan', he outlined an educational system that would provide its pupils with what he called *Menschenbildung*. The teaching would not focus on detailed exercises or future professional activities. Instead, pupils would orientate themselves towards the truly human, towards the major intellectual abilities. Humboldt emphasised the importance of wide-ranging studies in languages, history, and mathematics; but the classical subjects, first and foremost Greek, held an obvious special position for him.[31] At the same time, another document from the same year, regarding guidelines for the examination of Prussian administrators, shows that Humboldt's vision of *Bildung* was not narrowly limited to the world of the school. He did not feel that it was essential that future government officials be able to account for statistics or individual facts. Rather, it was the intellectual vitality of the officials and their general ideas about humanity that determined how capable they were. Thus it was qualities and character traits such as these that should be assessed before an individual was allowed to begin to serve the state.[32]

In other words, the idea of *Bildung* held a central position in Humboldt's educational philosophy, both in more general discussions and in concrete plans for the transformation of the school system. The ideal of *Bildung* was also thoroughly foundational to his idea of the university. His academic vision emerges most clearly in 'Über die innere und äussere Organisation der höheren wissenschaftlichen Anstalten in Berlin'. In this short, unfinished manifesto, written

---

30 Karlsohn, *Originalitetens former*, pp. 24–30 and 154–58; Thomas Karlsohn, 'On Humboldtian and Contemporary Notions of the Academic Lecture', in *The Humboldtian Tradition*, ed. by Josephson, Karlsohn, & Östling.
31 Wilhelm von Humboldt, 'Der Königsberger und der Litauische Schulplan', in Wilhelm von Humboldt, *Werke in fünf Bänden*, ed. by Flitner & Giel, vol. IV: *Schriften zur Politik und zum Bildungswesen* (1964).
32 Wilhelm von Humboldt, 'Gutachten über die Organisation der Ober-Examinations-Kommission', in Wilhelm von Humboldt, *Werke in fünf Bänden*, ed. by Flitner & Giel, vol. IV: *Schriften zur Politik und zum Bildungswesen* (1964).

at the end of 1809 or during 1810, many of the basic ideas that later came to be invoked in the Humboldtian tradition can be found.[33]

Next to *Bildung*, the idea of science and scholarship (*Wissenschaft*) was a cornerstone in Humboldt's conception of the university.[34] In his manifesto from 1809/1810, there was an obvious connection between them: Humboldt maintains that the university should be a place where science and scholarship in their most profound, extensive, and pure sense have their abode. He emphasises that 'since these institutions can only fulfil their purpose when each of them bears continuously in mind the idea of pure science and scholarship, their dominant principles must be freedom and seclusion (*Einsamkeit*; in this study, that word is normally translated as "solitude")'. In contrast to schools, which provide fixed and finished knowledge, science/scholarship should be seen as 'an as yet unsolved problem

---

33 Wilhelm von Humboldt, 'Über die innere und äussere Organisation der höheren wissenschaftlichen Anstalten in Berlin', in Wilhelm von Humboldt, *Werke in fünf Bänden*, ed. by Flitner & Giel, vol IV: *Schriften zur Politik und zum Bildungswesen* (1964). I henceforth quote from Wilhelm von Humboldt, 'University Reform in Germany, I: On the Spirit and the Organisational Framework of Intellectual Institutions in Berlin', trans. by Edward Shils, *Minerva*, 8:2 (1970), 242–50. The different suggestions – presented by Adolf von Harnack, Eduard Spranger, Bruno Gebhardt, and others – on how this text is to be dated are discussed in Ulrich Herrmann, Markus Bok, & Günter Erdmann, 'Kommentare und Anmerkungen: Band IV', in Wilhelm von Humboldt, *Werke in fünf Bänden*, ed. by Flitner & Giel, vol. V: *Kleine Schriften, Autobiographisches, Dichtungen, Briefe, Kommentare und Anmerkungen zu Band I–V, Anhang* (1981), pp. 556–57, without there being a final established conclusion. See also Tenorth, 'Eine Universität zu Berlin', pp. 16–26.

34 In German linguistic usage, *Wissenschaft* denotes both the human and the natural sciences. In the present study, the word *Wissenschaft* is usually translated as 'science and scholarship'. See Ringer, *The Decline*, pp. 102–04; Helmut Pulte, 'Wissenschaft', in *Historisches Wörterbuch der Philosophie*, ed. by Joachim Ritter, Karlfried Gründer & Gottfried Gabriel, 13 vols (Basel and Stuttgart, 1971–2007), vol. XII (2004); and Lorraine Daston & Glenn W. Most, 'History of Science and History of Philologies', *Isis*, 106:2 (2015). In *Acolytes of Nature: Defining Natural Science in Germany 1770–1850* (Chicago, 2012), Denise Philipps has, however, established a multi-layered pre-history. Above all, she argues for the idea that the concept of *Naturwissenschaft* (natural science) had a complicated origin and that it was not until the middle of the nineteenth century that the modern sense of the term stabilised.

Wilhelm von Humboldt and his idea

which always calls for further research'. The university stands or falls based on how well it safeguards the principle that science/scholarship should be seen as – to use a key formulation – 'something not yet achieved and as something that cannot ever be completely achieved'. Humboldt is faithful to his idea of *Bildung* when he emphasises that it is only the science/scholarship that originates within people that can shape character, and that it has to be the goal of both the state and humanity to produce character and action, not 'superficial knowledge and empty talk'. In order to achieve this, everything must originate in an ideal, and all types of one-sidedness must be opposed.[35]

Humboldt also develops ideas about academic freedom. The state must not treat its universities as *Gymnasien* or special schools, and it must not use them as store rooms of useful experts. On the contrary, the state must not demand anything from the academy that directly involves the state itself. Instead, writes Humboldt, '[the state] should [...] adhere to a deep conviction that if the universities achieve their purpose, they will realise the purpose of the state as well, and on a far higher plane'. The main duty of the state becomes to ensure that its schools serve the higher scholarly institutions. If these schools are established and managed in an ideal way, their pupils will carry a desire within them to devote themselves to scholarship.[36]

Humboldt's high valuation of academic freedom was thus closely connected to his general ideals of *Bildung* and education. At the same time, academic freedom is a multifaceted concept. In his text Humboldt also discusses the issue of the external organisation of the university, especially how academic posts should be filled. He argues for the idea that it should not be the faculties or the scholarly representatives who should make these decisions. Instead it is the state that should possess this power, for two reasons: the faculties cannot be expected to make a fair assessment of the candidates; and – more importantly – the interests of the state and the university are so intimately connected that the state has to have discretionary power when it comes to appointing professors. This second reason is, according to Humboldt, justified by the fact that the university

---

35 Humboldt, 'On the Spirit', 243–45. Humboldt, 'Über die innere und äussere Organisation', vol. IV, p. 257. Shils translates this passage as 'closed bodies of permanently settled truths' (Humboldt, 'On the Spirit', 244).
36 Ibid., 246–47.

is also an educational institution entrusted with the task of training good officials.[37] Consequently, Humboldt recommended a kind of governmental border control for those who wished to gain access to the university. However, he also felt that the freedom in lecture halls and seminars should be unconditional. This aspect of academic freedom has subsequently come, in some respects, to be expressed in the formula *Lern- und Lehrfreiheit*, a conceptual pair that did not appear in Humboldt's own writings though these concepts have come to form part of the classic German university tradition.[38] It is worth noting that the Prussian official's view of governmental authority differed from the liberal ideas he had previously formulated in *Ideen zu einem Versuch, die Grenzen der Wirksamkeit des Staates zu bestimmen* (1792). In this composition from his youth, he had defended the self-fulfilment of the individual and warned against the unrestricted power of the state.[39]

---

37 Ibid., 249. Humboldt's view on the relationship between the state and the university is discussed in Ursula Krautkrämer, *Staat und Erziehung: Begründung öffentlicher Erziehung bei Humboldt, Kant, Fichte, Hegel und Schleiermacher* (Munich, 1979), pp. 29–77, and Peter Josephson, *Den akademiska frihetens gränser: Max Weber, Humboldtmodellen och den värdefria vetenskapen* (Uppsala, 2005), pp. 51–59. For the earlier history of academic freedom, see Bo Lindberg, 'Akademisk frihet före moderniteten', *Lychnos*, 2014.

38 Josephson, *Den akademiska frihetens gränser*, pp. 57–59. A search of the Deutsches Textarchiv, hosted by Berlin-Brandenburgische Akademie der Wissenschaften, indicates that the first instance of 'Lehrfreiheit' can be found in Friedrich Christoph Dahlmann, *Die Politik, auf den Grund und das Maaß der gegebenen Zustände zurückgeführt* (Göttingen, 1835), p. 290, and of 'Lernfreiheit' in Adolph Diesterweg, *Über das Verderben auf den deutschen Universitäten* (Essen, 1836), p. 12. See http://www.deutschestextarchiv.de (accessed 15 February 2016).

39 Wilhelm von Humboldt, 'Ideen zu einem Versuch, die Grenzen der Wirksamkeit des Staates zu bestimmen', in Wilhelm von Humboldt, *Werke in fünf Bänden*, ed. by Flitner & Giel, vol. I: *Schriften zur Anthropologie und Geschichte* (1960). The text was written in 1792 but was not published until 1851. Three years later it was published in an English translation with the title *The Sphere and Duties of Government*, and it soon came to exert an influence on the political and philosophical debate. John Stuart Mill used a quotation from Humboldt's text as his motto for *On Liberty* (1859). See John Roberts, *Wilhelm von Humboldt and German Liberalism: A Reassessment* (Oakville, 2009).

Towards the end of his text from 1809/1810, Humboldt polemised against the idea that the university should focus on teaching and that research should only be conducted at special academies. The process of science and scholarship is doubtlessly more rapid and lively at the university, he wrote, 'where their problems are discussed back and forth by a large number of forceful, vigorous, and youthful intelligences'. If science and scholarship are not regarded as being changeable, they are not worthy of those designations.[40]

In today's research, many people emphasise Humboldt's unfinished fragment from 1809–1810 as a key document for understanding his idea of the university. Björn Wittrock has called it 'perhaps the most discussed document in the modern history of universities'.[41] From this and a couple of other writings from the same period, the academic principles that have come to be associated with Humboldt can be deduced: academic freedom; the combination of teaching and research; the sense of community between teachers and students; science and scholarship as *Bildung*. At the same time, the Humboldtian tradition is much richer and more nebulous; it cannot be captured in a couple of points. Its transformation during the two centuries that have passed reflects the turbulent history of Germany.

Humboldt's nineteenth century

Wilhelm von Humboldt died on 8 April 1835. During the twenty-five years that had passed since he left his position as the person responsible for education in the Prussian ministry, he had devoted himself to diplomacy and linguistics. Initially he had been an emissary in Vienna and had helped shape the new order of Europe after the defeat of Napoleon. At the end of the 1810s he had retired, settled in Tegel, and dedicated much of the remainder of his life to extensive linguistic studies.[42]

The development of the Berlin university after Humboldt's death has been assessed in various ways. Some narratives about the period from the second quarter of the nineteenth century and forward are characterised by decline and decay. They differ in emphasis; but

---

40 Humboldt, 'On the Spirit', 247–48.
41 Wittrock, 'Modern University', p. 317.
42 Sweet, *Wilhelm von Humboldt*, II: *1808–1835*, pp. 473–91; Scurla, Wilhelm von Humboldt, pp. 608–09.

what they have in common is an interest in how an academic vision, sprung from revolutionary or even utopian dreams, hardened into conservative ideology and Prussian ideas about the national state. These historiographies feature variations on the theme of a slow farewell to the original ideals.[43]

Other scholars construct a more complex balance sheet. In the new history of the university at Unter den Linden, two of the main authors, Heinz-Elmar Tenorth and Charles E. McClelland, offer a comprehensive assessment. Tenorth asserts that Wilhelm von Humboldt played a crucial part in the foundation of the new university, but not in the sense that he formulated a set of philosophical principles that then permeated all official actions and institutional arrangements. Instead, Tenorth emphasises the fact that Humboldt initiated the political-administrative process and reconciled conflicting interests. His idea of the momentous importance of research – what Roy Steven Turner has called 'the research imperative' – had a real impact, but this was because new features of academic practice (which had gradually taken shape during the eighteenth century) were given an institutional basis. Those features were, primarily, that publication of new scholarly/ scientific knowledge was rewarded; that an infrastructure in the form of seminars and laboratories was seen as indispensable; that professors developed a professional identity; and that recruitment to academic posts was based on scholarly/scientific merits. All this contributed to making the research imperative a reality, according to Tenorth.[44]

McClelland for his part maintains that the conditions in which the Berlin university operated were completely different at the beginning in comparison to at the end of the nineteenth century. The university

---

43 Menze, *Bildungsreform*; Fritz Ringer, '*Bildung* and Its Implications in the German Tradition, 1890–1933', in Fritz Ringer, *Toward A Social History of Knowledge: Collected Essays* (New York, 2000); Sven Haase, *Berliner Universität und Nationalgedanke 1800–1848: Genese einer politischen Idee* (Stuttgart, 2012). See also Sven-Eric Liedman, *Karl Marx: En biografi* (Stockholm, 2015), pp. 70–81.

44 Tenorth, 'Eine Universität zu Berlin', pp. 68–70; Heinz-Elmar Tenorth, 'Verfassung und Ordnung der Universität', in *Geschichte der Universität Unter den Linden: Gründung und Blütezeit*, ed. by Tenorth, p. 112. See also Roy Steven Turner, 'The Prussian Universities and the Research Imperative, 1806–1848', unpublished doctoral thesis (Princeton, 1972).

Wilhelm von Humboldt and his idea

was born from a defeat, and for a long time it only had a few students. To the extent that an ideal regarding the combination of research and education became a reality during its first phase, this had more to do with pragmatic necessity than with ideological principles. From the 1870s onward, the university went through rapid expansion, and its reputation grew; at the same time conditions, with respect to both society and science/scholarship, changed during the time leading up to the First World War. McClelland therefore cautions against a simplified historiography, irrespective of whether this takes the form of success stories or narratives of decline.[45]

It is, however, possible to apply a completely different perspective to the legacy from Humboldt. In this perspective, the actual university on Unter den Linden and its development during the nineteenth century are not placed at the centre. Instead it is the symbolism and the formation of myths that surround Humboldt – what in German has come to be called the *Mythos Humboldt* – that is the essential factor. 'The construction of the image of Humboldt and its reception, transmission, and deformation have their own history', Tenorth points out. And it is with the investigation of this history that the present study is associated.[46]

The central proposition of this research about Humboldt is that he was never a point of reference in the German nineteenth-century discussion about the university: his fame did not come until later. The scholar who has most persistently championed the idea of Humboldt's absence is Sylvia Paletschek, but she has been supported by historians such as Mitchell G. Ash, Rüdiger vom Bruch, Dieter Langewiesche, Marc Schalenberg, and Walter Rüegg. According to Paletschek, Humboldt's programmatic texts remained unknown or even unpublished. Presentations of the history of the university contained references to writings by Schleiermacher, Fichte, and Steffens, works written at the time of the foundation of the Berlin university. Other people too, famous in their own time but since forgotten,

---

45 Charles E. McClelland, 'Die Universität am Ende ihres ersten Jahrhunderts – Mythos Humboldt?', in *Geschichte der Universität Unter den Linden: Gründung und Blütezeit*, ed. by Tenorth, pp. 638–53. Among other things, McClelland bases his conclusions on his own research, not least McClelland, *State* and Charles E. McClelland, *The German Experience of Professionalization: Modern Learned Professions and Their Organizations from the Early Nineteenth Century to the Hitler Era* (Cambridge, 1991).
46 Tenorth, 'Geschichte der Universität zu Berlin', p. xliii.

featured in depictions of the early nineteenth-century university. Wilhelm von Humboldt's name was rarely, if ever, mentioned.⁴⁷ According to this line of research, the Berlin university was by no means a beacon in the academic archipelago of the time. Friedrich-Wilhelms-Universität, as it was renamed in 1828, was one university among others. Nothing in its statutes revealed that a new kind of university had seen the light of day. Although many people had eagerly supported another order, the faculty hierarchy remained the same as before: theology, law, medicine, and finally philosophy. Even when it came to its administrative structure, its forms of examination, and the subjects of its professorships, the university in Berlin did not differ significantly from other universities in the German region. Like other innovative or reformed universities it was financed with government funds, though Humboldt himself had argued for a more traditional economic foundation (demesne and prebend) in order to safeguard a certain measure of independence from the state.⁴⁸

Nor did the Berlin university function as an exemplary model in nineteenth-century intellectual discussions. In handbooks, encyclopaedias, and surveys, German New Humanist ideas and Prussian university reform were not presented as turning points in the historical development. Rather, the birth of the modern university was located in the Göttingen and Halle of Enlightenment rationalism. In written histories, the widespread death of universities and the sweeping changes in the administrative structures of the early nineteenth century were accentuated, as was the incipient academic liberalism and the emergence of student associations. In none of these contexts was the creation of the Berlin university given a paradigmatic significance. It was mentioned in passing, often in the same breath as the newly established universities in Bonn (1818) and Munich (1826).⁴⁹

---

47 See Chapter 1 for references to this research. During the nineteenth century attention was paid to Wilhelm von Humboldt not only as a diplomat, a statesman, and a linguist but also, among other things, as a philosopher of history. In his influential *Grundriß der Historik* (Leipzig, 1868), Johann Gustav Droysen paid homage to him as 'a Bacon for the historical sciences' (p. 6). For Humboldt's ideas about history, see Frederick C. Beiser, *The German Historicist Tradition* (Oxford, 2011), pp. 167–213.
48 Paletschek, 'Verbreitete sich', pp. 79–80.
49 Ibid., pp. 97–98. Ludwig-Maximilians-Universität opened its doors in Munich in 1826 but had a long prehistory: in 1472–1800 its predecessor was located in Ingolstadt and in 1800–1826 in Landshut.

Throughout the nineteenth century, a debate continued about the German university. Judging from the number of publications, it was at its most intense during the 1830s and 1840s, although a good deal was also published on this topic around the year 1800 and during the last decades of the century. On the whole, there was agreement regarding the idea that the qualities that above all others distinguished the German university were academic freedom and theoretical-scholarly/scientific teaching. Occasionally the German New Humanist university tracts from the early 1800s were referred to, in particular Schleiermacher's; but the focal points of the debate were often concrete problems concerning examinations, forms of study, and the working conditions of the teachers.[50]

The bringing together of different disciplines was considered to be another distinguishing feature of the German universities; in contrast to the situation in France, all subjects were housed in one and the same university. This was nothing new in itself; indeed, from a historical perspective a strong vein of continuity can be seen to exist between this feature and the basic notions underpinning the medieval university. Kant, Fichte, and Schleiermacher do not seem to have had many followers either. Few argued for the idea that the faculty of philosophy should play a superior or unifying role in the nineteenth-century German university. In all essentials, as was pointed out above, the old hierarchy endured. It was not until towards the end of the nineteenth and the beginning of the twentieth century that the research mission came to the forefront. Before that time, the idea that the systematic production of new knowledge was an academic concern of the highest order was not a majority view.[51]

Consequently, it is impossible to speak of a Berlinesque or a Humboldtian model in the German academic debate during the nineteenth century. It is true that the Berlin university is sometimes mentioned as a young and dynamic university, whose emergence and further expansion were put in relation to Prussia's defeat in the Napoleonic Wars and the ever-increasing importance of the Prussian capital. On the other hand, it did not have any immediate effect on the development of the German university system – neither in ideological nor in institutional terms. The ideals that had been formulated by Wilhelm von Humboldt in his writings around 1810

---

50 Ibid., pp. 98–100.
51 Ibid., pp. 96–98.

did not provide fruitful input in the discussion about the university, and it would be a long time before they materialised into a concrete organisation. Along with the *Gymnasium*, the military system, and classical music, it was claimed that the university was the major successful German export during the era of the German Empire. As the nineteenth turned into the twentieth century, university systems were reformed in line with the German pattern in parts of Europe, North America, and East Asia. The process was lengthy and complex, however, and it evinced many national variations; there was never a question of seamlessly transferring a German model to another culture.[52] In a major study, Marc Schalenberg has disproved all simple theories of diffusion. In France there were many people who were influenced by Germany, but they did not embrace an entire idea; rather, they turned towards their neighbouring country for arguments to use when promoting their own cause. In Britain people were, on the whole, markedly reserved with respect to German notions, and it took a long time before any effect worth mentioning could be observed there, especially at the traditional universities. Besides, neither in the French nor in the British debate was Wilhelm von Humboldt referred to as a key inspirer.[53] Johns Hopkins University, founded in Baltimore in 1876, became the first American university that expressly endeavoured to unite academic education with scholarly/scientific research through, among other means, a special 'graduate school'. During the final decades of the century, a number of researchers who had recently received their doctorates at Johns Hopkins began working at other distinguished American universities, thereby contributing to the dissemination of the new ideas. It should, however, be noted that it was the German

---

52 *Humboldt international*, ed. by Schwinges; Schalenberg, *Humboldt auf Reisen?*; Charle, 'Patterns'; Edward Shils & John Roberts, 'The Diffusion of European Models Outside Europe', in *A History of the University in Europe*, ed. by Rüegg; Jürgen Osterhammel, *Die Verwandlung der Welt: Eine Geschichte des 19. Jahrhunderts* (Munich, 2009), pp. 1132–47; Anja Werner, *The Transatlantic World of Higher Education: Americans at German Universities, 1776–1914* (Oxford, 2013).

53 Schalenberg, *Humboldt auf Reisen?* The British universities were part of global academic networks during this period, but these were often exclusively Anglo-Saxon and included Canada, Australia, New Zealand, and South Africa. See Tamson Pietsch, *Empire of Scholars: Universities, Networks and the British Academic World 1850–1939* (Manchester, 2013).

university that was the model. Wilhelm von Humboldt was not mentioned.[54]

Seen in a broader perspective, the last decades of the nineteenth century were a period of transformation for the major university systems. The scholarly/scientific world became ever more professionalised, specialised, and research-orientated, while at the same time competition among countries intensified.[55] In the turn-of-the-century German Empire, which was in many ways the driving force in this development, the conflicts between different interests and scholarly/scientific ideals intensified. This was where Wilhelm von Humboldt, almost a century after leaving his post in the Prussian ministry of the interior, ended up at the centre of the debate about the idea of the university for the first time.

---

54 Roy Steven Turner, 'Humboldt in North America? Reflections on the Research University and Its Historians' in *Humboldt international*, ed. by Schwinges; Roger L. Geiger, *To Advance Knowledge: The Growth of American Research Universities, 1900–1940* (New York, 1986), pp. 7–9. Abraham Flexner, a prominent American university reformer at the beginning of the twentieth century and originally a student at Johns Hopkins University, praised the spread of the German academic model to the USA in *Universities: American, German, English* (Oxford, 1930). Eventually Clark Kerr would maintain that Flexner had probably been 'too respectful of the German university' and not realised its limitations. See Clark Kerr, 'Remembering Flexner', in Abraham Flexner, *Universities: American, German, English* (London, 1968), p. xvii. Examples of the American reception of the German university model since the nineteenth century are provided by Gry Cathrin Brandser in *Humboldt Revisited: The Institutional Drama of Academic Identity* (Bergen, 2006).

55 Wittrock, 'Modern University', pp. 319–31; Anderson, *European Universities*.

3
The discovery of Humboldt

There were nineteen universities in the German Empire when it was proclaimed in 1871. During the almost fifty years that followed, up until the outbreak of the First World War, the number of students quadrupled. During the same period several institutes of technology and schools of economics were founded, but only three new universities: Strasbourg in 1872, Münster in 1902, and Frankfurt am Main in 1914. Higher education was, strictly speaking, a matter for the individual constituent states; but the university as an institution was seen as a national undertaking and was the subject of a vivid debate in the pan-German public sphere. Within the borders of the Empire the academic norms were similar, and both students and professors moved easily between universities. All this contributed to a sense of the university as a coherent national system.[1]

Prussia, which held half of the students and eleven universities, dominated the united Germany. An exceptionally important figure in this context was Friedrich Althoff. Originally a lawyer, he served between 1882 and 1907 with great power and determination in the Prussian Ministry of Education. During this quarter of a century, the system that would later come to be known as 'System Althoff' prevailed. With forceful, unorthodox methods, Althoff intervened in

---

1 Konrad H. Jarausch, 'Universität und Hochschule', in *Handbuch der deutschen Bildungsgeschichte: 1870–1918: Von der Reichsgründung bis zum Ende des Ersten Weltkriegs*, ed. by Christa Berg (Munich, 1991); Anderson, 'European Universities'. As is often the case when university history is investigated more closely, the establishment of a university is a complicated matter; thus the university in Strasbourg had already been founded in 1631, but after the Franco–Prussian War it was re-established in 1872 as 'Reichs-Universität Straßburg', and five years later it became one of the universities named 'Kaiser-Wilhelms-Universität'. See Stephan Roscher, *Die Kaiser-Wilhelms-Universität Straßburg 1872–1902* (Frankfurt am Main, 2006).

The discovery of Humboldt

recruitment procedures and put forward the candidates he favoured for professorships. By founding new institutes, professorships, and seminars, he was also able to steer developments in the direction he wanted. The main goal was to constantly improve academic quality in Prussia and defend Germany's cultural reputation. Even among his contemporaries, Althoff aroused powerful feelings – he was spoken of as 'the Bismarck of the German university system'– and it was not just Max Weber who felt that he was a domineering schemer who poisoned the scholarly/scientific climate. More recent research has emphasised the idea that he must also be seen as an enlightened bureaucrat in the service of the nation, a man who, without scruples, safeguarded science and scholarship at a time of political polarisation. Irrespective of how Althoff is assessed, it cannot be denied that the Prussian universities, primarily the Friedrich-Wilhelms-Universität of the capital, became the jewel in the German academic crown during the period surrounding the year 1900.[2]

German universities enjoyed a high reputation already at the founding of the Empire in 1871. During the ensuing decades, their importance increased even more; and towards the end of the nineteenth century they were undoubtedly regarded as the foremost in the world. Students from both the rest of Europe and North America flocked to Germany. Here were famous professors in almost all branches of science and scholarship. In the growing rivalry among the European countries, its prominent research milieus became a significant asset for Germany. For many Germans, especially from the educated middle classes, their own academic tradition was an untainted source of national pride. The university was the very quintessence of the pre-eminence attained by German culture.[3]

In spite of their golden-age ambiance, we can see today that German universities at the turn of the century were plagued by inner

---

[2] Althoff and his system in Imperial Germany are discussed in great detail in Bernhard vom Brocke, 'Hochschul- und Wissenschaftspolitik in Preussen im deutschen Kaiserreich 1882–1907: Das "System Althoff"', in *Bildungspolitik in Preussen zur Zeit des Kaiserreichs*, ed. by Peter Baumgart (Stuttgart, 1980) and in *Wissenschaftsgeschichte und Wissenschaftspolitik im Industriezeitalter: Das 'System Althoff' in historischer Perspektive*, ed. by Bernhard vom Brocke (Hildesheim, 1991). On Max Weber's critique of the 'System Althoff', see Josephson, *Den akademiska frihetens gränser*, pp. 169–73.

[3] In great detail in Rüdiger vom Bruch, *Wissenschaft, Politik und öffentliche Meinung: Gelehrtenpolitik im Wilhelminischen Deutschland (1890–1914)* (Husum, 1980); in summary in Anderson, *European Universities*, pp. 151–61.

tensions. The number of students increased rapidly, but permanent jobs became only slightly more numerous. This was especially troublesome for young *Privatdozenten* with *Habilitation* – that is, scholars qualified for a professorship on the basis of a second major work – who were forced to toil, year after year, overshadowed by the powerful professors in their respective subjects. The emergence of a kind of proletariat of docents added fuel to the generational conflict that always lies dormant in the hierarchical academic system. The conflicts, however, ran much deeper than this and were at bottom ideological in nature.[4]

During the 1880s and 1890s, political conflicts increased within the German university. At the time of the February Revolution in 1848, the majority of students and professors had been liberal. Following the unification of the nation, more and more people rallied round national slogans and made Germany's cause their own. A strong state was seen as a guarantor of strong science and scholarship. The intense social development during the final stages of the nineteenth century pushed the academic community to the right; Konrad H. Jarausch has spoken of 'the rise of academic illiberalism'. The German nationalism of which many scholars and scientists were adherents derived its nourishment from Prussian, Protestant, and conservative sources. Catholics, Jews, and political radicals found it more difficult to assert themselves and were sometimes completely excluded from the academic community.[5]

During the same period, competition increased among the academic disciplines. Ultimately, the conflict was about the meaning of the concept of *Wissenschaft*. In a speech from 1892, the Berlin university's rector (this term will be used from now on to refer to the *Rektor*, or vice-chancellor/president, of a German university), Rudolf Virchow, declared that 'the dominance of neohumanism is broken'. Virchow, who was a prominent pathologist and a dedicated amateur archaeologist, had combined his academic work with a career as a liberal politician. To him, it was self-evident that natural science was in alliance with progressive social development. Virchow was

---

4 Alexander Busch, *Die Geschichte der Privatdozenten: Eine soziologische Studie zur grossbetrieblichen Entwicklung der deutschen Universitäten* (Stuttgart, 1959); Anderson, *European Universities*, pp. 153–54.
5 Konrad H. Jarausch, *Students, Society, and Politics in Imperial Germany: The Rise of Academic Illiberalism* (Princeton, 1982); Notker Hammerstein, *Antisemitismus und deutsche Universitäten 1871–1933* (Frankfurt am Main, 1995).

not alone. The late nineteenth century saw a powerful expansion of natural-science subjects in German universities. This was an expansion in quantity, but at bottom it was an advancement for the methodology and knowledge production of the exact sciences. Alongside the rapid industrialisation of Germany during the last decades of the century, a number of institutes of technology were founded, although they were regarded with suspicion by the old universities and long made up a separate sphere of higher education. Around the year 1900, applied research in the natural sciences had nevertheless acquired a real foothold in the large universities. It was not just social-reformist and economic hopes that were tied to this development. During the prelude to the First World War, with growing rivalry among the great powers in Europe, many people put their trust in a marriage between *Macht* ('power') and *Geist* ('mind', 'spirit'). 'Military prowess and science are the two great pillars of Germany's greatness, and the Prussian state has the duty to ensure the preservation of both', maintained the influential church historian and research politician Adolf von Harnack.[6]

But not everyone was carried away by enthusiasm during the years leading up to the 'Great War'. Quite a few observers had a sense of an internal, constantly growing crisis for the university. The representatives of the humanities and theology, *die Geisteswissenschaften*, were particularly troubled. The increasing specialisation not only overthrew the conviction concerning the unity of science/ scholarship; it was a threat to the very idea of *Bildung*, which was in many ways their *raison d'être*. Instead, the natural-scientific worldview was consolidated, and the logic of industrial order risked undermining all spiritual values.[7]

The humanists did not witness this development in silence. In his previously mentioned book about the German mandarins, Fritz K. Ringer has promoted the idea that the general view among the German professors shifted around 1890. The mandarins, primarily prominent scholars within the humanities and social sciences, had long seen themselves as the protectors of the cultural state and the guarantors of civilised society; but now their world was shaken to

---

6 Anderson, *European Universities*, pp. 154–61 (quotations: pp. 154 and 160). See also David Edgerton, 'Science in the United Kingdom: A Case Study in the Nationalisation of Science', in *Science in the Twentieth Century*, ed. by John Krige & Dominique Pestre (Amsterdam, 1997).
7 Jan Eckel, *Geist der Zeit: Deutsche Geisteswissenschaften seit 1870* (Göttingen, 2008), pp. 23–28.

its foundations when the university also adapted to the new deal of the time. The mechanised and commercial Germany was, according to the mandarins, superficial and vulgar, and many felt alienated. They closed ranks within their fraternity, guarded their territory, distanced themselves from current politics and social commitment, and adopted cultural pessimism and anti-modernism. In the Weimar Republic, the mandarins embraced the national-conservative reaction that opposed the democratisation of society in general and of the university in particular.[8]

Ringer's theses have been influential, but he has not escaped criticism. Critics have questioned the representativeness of his characterisation of German scholars; they have criticised his locating the turning point in the 1890s; and they have complained that his interpretations of the turn-of-the-century academic mood were too greatly influenced by posterity's experience of Nazism.[9] In spite of these objections, much of Ringer's general description of the academic climate of the time seems to be correct. The image of the cornered mandarins can be seen to fit into a more comprehensive description of Germany in the transition from the nineteenth to the twentieth century. This was a time of expansion and dynamism in many areas of society; it was a time when faith in the future and ambitious dreams were tied to science and scholarship. But it was also a time of a growing discontent and increasing bewilderment.

Nevertheless, one objection, formulated by Sven-Eric Liedman in a polemical exchange with Ringer, is of great importance for the present study. Liedman argued that Ringer described the mandarins as a far too homogeneous group. It is true that Ringer divided them into an orthodox and a modern faction, but this division was insufficient; the social variety and diversity of opinions among them were greater than that. On the other hand, what the mandarins did have in common, according to Liedman, was a concern with

---

8 Ringer, *The Decline*. On the basis of studies of other countries it is, in addition, possible to question how unique the opinions and attitudes of the German mandarins were. See Sheldon Rothblatt, *The Revolution of the Dons: Cambridge and Society in Victorian England* (London, 1968) and Martin J. Wiener, *English Culture and the Decline of the Industrial Spirit, 1850–1980* (Cambridge, 1981). In later investigations, however, Ringer applied a comparative perspective, for instance in Fritz K. Ringer, *Fields of Knowledge: French Academic Culture in Comparative Perspective, 1890–1920* (Cambridge, 1992).
9 Albisetti, 'The Decline'.

The discovery of Humboldt

the same kind of questions. Among other things, they were able to agree on the exceptional importance of *Bildung*. About everything else they were at loggerheads: the meaning of *Bildung*, its content, and its goals.[10]

The same thing can be said about the idea of the university. All the mandarins attached great value to the German university tradition, but following upon this agreement the questions piled up: What is the place of the university in future? What is the purpose of research and education? With what spiritual values should the nation be imbued? It was while they were searching for answers to these questions that they discovered Wilhelm von Humboldt.

Discovering Humboldt

During the second half of the 1890s, the historian Bruno Gebhardt was working on a book about Wilhelm von Humboldt as a statesman. In an archive he found an unpublished, undated, and unfinished memorandum, 'Über die innere und äussere Organisation der höheren wissenschaftlichen Anstalten in Berlin'. When, in 1896, he published the first volume of *Wilhelm von Humboldt als Staatsmann*, he incorporated excerpts from this ten-page manifesto in the text. Seven years later, Gebhardt would make sure that this text was included when Humboldt's collected works were published.[11]

This short, unfinished text from 1809/1810 suddenly appeared at the turn of the following century in the debate on the university. Not only could it be used to justify basic research in general; it was equally useful for sanctioning the research university, which was only fully developed in Germany around the beginning of the twentieth

---

10 Sven-Eric Liedman, 'Institution and Ideas: Mandarins and Non-Mandarins in the German Academic Intelligentsia', *Comparative Studies in Society and History*, 28:1 (1986), pp. 142–44. See also the debate that followed this contribution: Fritz K. Ringer, 'Differences and Cross-National Similarities among Mandarins', *Comparative Studies in Society and History*, 28:1 (1986) and Sven-Eric Liedman, 'Reply', *Comparative Studies in Society and History*, 28:1 (1986).

11 Bruno Gebhardt, *Wilhelm von Humboldt als Staatsmann*, 2 vols (Stuttgart, 1896–1899); Herbert Grundmann, 'Gebhardt, Bruno', *Neue Deutsche Biographie*, ed. by Historische Kommission bei der Bayerischen Akademie der Wissenschaften (Berlin, 1953–), vol. VI (1964); Paletschek, 'Verbreitete sich', p. 77.

century. Humboldt provided this new type of knowledge institution with an almost hundred-year-long prehistory. Those who wished to do so could claim that developments had proved him right. Sylvia Paletschek has, in several contexts, analysed the place of Wilhelm von Humboldt in the early twentieth-century academic debate. On the basis of her thorough work on the university at Tübingen under the Empire and the Weimar Republic, she has spoken of 'the discovery of Humboldt' around the year 1900. Gebhardt had made an important discovery in the archives, but it was other scholars who emphasised Humboldt as a prominent figure in German university history. Of special importance were Adolf von Harnack and Eduard Spranger.[12]

In 1900, Harnack published a monumental history of the Royal Prussian Academy of Sciences, which celebrated its bicentenary at the time. In his discussion of the early nineteenth century, Harnack foregrounded Humboldt's memorandum and emphasised its epoch-making nature. Not least, he argued that Humboldt had stressed the fact that there should be a close connection between universities and academies.[13] In addition, a few years later, the recently discovered text also provided Harnack with arguments in favour of establishing research institutes outside the university – in other words, a separation of knowledge production and knowledge dissemination. The emergence of large-scale research (*Großforschung*) within the technology and natural-science sphere made completely different demands on the traditional university. In order to uphold Germany's scientific standing in the escalating international competition, the 'Kaiser-Wilhelm-Gesellschaft zur Förderung der Wissenschaften' was founded in 1911. When Harnack, as its first president, was called upon to justify the new independent research institutes, he referred to Humboldt. He pointed out that Germany had the Prussian educational reformer to thank for its scientific brilliance and interpreted Humboldt's hundred-year-old manifesto to mean that scholarly development not only required academies and universities, but also relatively independent institutes. Harnack approvingly quoted Humboldt: 'The academy, the university, and the auxiliary institutes are three equally autonomous and integral units of the

---

12 Paletschek, *Die permanente Erfindung*; Paletschek, 'Verbreitete sich'; Paletschek, 'The Invention of Humboldt'; Paletschek, 'Die Erfindung'.
13 Adolf von Harnack, *Geschichte der Königlich preußischen Akademie der Wissenschaften zu Berlin*, 3 vols (Berlin, 1900), vol. I:II, pp. 594–96.

educational institution as a whole'.[14] To Harnack, the last-named unit was synonymous with the very type of independent research institutes, the *Kaiser-Wilhelm-Institute*, that he was in the process of founding. Rüdiger vom Bruch has pinpointed what is essential in this context: In the period around the year 1900, Humboldt was a name to be invoked by those who wished to create something new in the academic world without breaking with an allegedly strong tradition.[15]

Of exceptional importance for the adoption of Wilhelm von Humboldt as the originator of the modern German university was Eduard Spranger, a leading figure in the pedagogical and educational-political debate for more than half a century. Born in 1882, Spranger had devoted himself to studies in Berlin within a broad spectrum of subjects with an emphasis on philosophy. In 1909, he published his *Habilitation* thesis (as was pointed out above, the second major work of a scholar, qualifying him or her for a professorship) with the title *Wilhelm von Humboldt und die Humanitätsidee*. In this and other contemporary writings, Spranger created an image of Humboldt that proved to be long-lived. The Prussian official had, according to Spranger, transferred his own profound ambition for *Selbstbildung* to a new academic institution. A basic principle that he attributed to Humboldt in this context was the absolute independence of research; another was the organic unity of science. From this followed that the university had to include all subjects, with philosophy as a superposed discipline geared towards creating a unified whole.[16]

---

14 See Humboldt, 'Über die innere und äussere Organisation', vol. IV, p. 266. Shils translates this passage as 'The academy, the university, and the auxiliary institutes constitute three autonomous, integral units of the total system of intellectual institutions' (Humboldt, 'On the Spirit', 250).

15 Bernhard vom Brocke, 'Die Kaiser-Wilhelm-Gesellschaft im Kaiserreich', in *Forschung im Spannungsfeld von Politik und Gesellschaft: Geschichte und Struktur der Kaiser-Wilhelm-/Max-Planck-Gesellschaft*, ed. by Rudolf Vierhaus & Bernhard vom Brocke (Stuttgart, 1990), pp. 17–26; Bernhard vom Brocke, 'Die Entstehung der deutschen Forschungsuniversität, ihre Blüte und Krise um 1900', in *Humboldt international*, ed. by Schwinges; vom Bruch, 'Die Gründung', p. 68.

16 Eduard Spranger, *Wilhelm von Humboldt und die Humanitätsidee*. See also Paletschek, 'Verbreitete sich', pp. 100–02; Benner, *Wilhelm von Humboldts Bildungstheorie*, pp. 22–30; Alban Schraut, *Biographische Studien zu Eduard Spranger* (Bad Heilbrunn, 2007); and Benjamin Ortmeyer, *Eduard Spranger und die NS-Zeit* (Frankfurt am Main, 2008).

Time and again Spranger sang the praises of his own university in enthusiastic speeches and writings, especially at the centenary in 1910. In this year, when he was still a *Privatdozent*, he collected a few of the most important New Humanist documents from the early nineteenth century (by Fichte, Schleiermacher, and Steffens) and expounded on their significance for his contemporaries. These men were influential as innovators; but at the end of the day it was, according to Spranger, Humboldt who had realised the idea of a new university. Spranger did not deny that the flourishing development of the Berlin university had to be explained by way of political liberalism, Prussian reform, and the German nation. Nevertheless, there was no doubt that it was Humboldt who had united free science and scholarship with the state and created a unit imbued with genius. In Spranger, the Humboldt apotheosis reached its zenith so far.[17]

Spranger's ideas were in harmony with the new idealist currents of the time. There was a general tendency in German intellectual life during the first years of the twentieth century to evoke Romantic and New Humanist ideas from the turn of the previous century. Within a number of *Geisteswissenschaften* – Germanic philology, sociology, folklore studies, linguistics, history – a basic idealist stance was coupled to a mission of defining what constituted a common German identity. Under pressure from technological, economic, and scientific advances, many humanists claimed that this was where they had an essential national task.[18] In particular in the historical subjects – and under the aegis of historicism, almost all humanistic research was conducted with historical overtones – a perspective was adopted that made Germany's past synonymous with that of Prussia. According to this historiography, national German development was completed through the Prussian state. And thanks to the agency of the Prussian state, the Berlin university could become a reality and New Humanist ideas could take shape.[19]

---

17 *Fichte, Schleiermacher, Steffens über das Wesen der Universität*, ed. by Eduard Spranger (Leipzig, 1910), pp. vii–xli. At this time Spranger also published *Wilhelm von Humboldt und die Reform des Bildungswesens* (Berlin, 1910) and *Wandlungen im Wesen der Universität seit 100 Jahren* (Leipzig, 1913).
18 Eckel, *Geist der Zeit*, pp. 23–33.
19 It is a well-known fact that the historiography of modern Germany has focused on Prussia. This is also, and to the highest degree, true of university history. A welcome reaction against this bias was James Dennis Cobb, *The Forgotten Reforms: Non-Prussian Universities 1797–1817* (Ann Arbor, 1984).

The discovery of Humboldt

When Spranger drew attention to Wilhelm von Humboldt and the new Prussian founding of universities in 1810, he undeniably departed from the prevalent historiography of his time. During the first years of the twentieth century Friedrich Paulsen, the most prominent pedagogic authority in the German Empire and Spranger's own *Doktorvater* (doctoral supervisor), published two major historical syntheses concerning the German university system. In his description, the universities of Halle and Göttingen emerged as models for what was new. During the second half of the eighteenth century, these universities had been the inspiration for reforms of universities in and outside the German cultural area. Humboldt and the Berlin university did figure in Paulsen's work, but not as the beginning of a new epoch. It is significant that Paulsen spoke of 'the emergence of the modern university' – meaning developments during the eighteenth century.[20]

Spranger's evaluation of Humboldt's importance also differed from Max Lenz's opinion in *Geschichte der Königlichen Friedrich-Wilhelms-Universität zu Berlin*, an extensive work published by Lenz in connection with the centenary in 1910. Lenz, a professor of history and for a time rector in Berlin, was commissioned by his own university to write the four volumes of this work. Although this historiography thus received a kind of official blessing, he saw no reason to emphasise 1810 as a watershed in the development of the German university. In everything he considered important – statutes, administration, organisation, staff structure – the new university in Berlin evinced significant similarities to already existing Prussian universities.[21]

Spranger's depiction of Humboldt has been characterised as classically-idealising by Irmgard Kawohl. She points to this idea of Humboldt as being completely dominant during the first two decades of the twentieth century. Spranger's unconditional appreciation of Humboldt reflected a passion for Classicism and German idealism. This is also true of Harnack and other representatives of this interpretation. In Humboldt they saw a perfect man, a harmonious and thoroughly exemplary figure. He embodied his own idea of *Bildung*.[22]

---

20 Friedrich Paulsen, *Die deutschen Universitäten und das Universitätsstudium* (Berlin, 1902); Friedrich Paulsen, *Das deutsche Bildungswesen in seiner geschichtlichen Entwicklung* (Leipzig, 1906). See also Josephson, Karlsohn, & Östling, 'The Humboldtian Tradition', pp. 3–7.
21 Lenz, *Geschichte*.
22 Irmgard Kawohl, *Wilhelm von Humboldt in der Kritik des 20. Jahrhunderts* (Ratingen, 1969), pp. 11–34.

Over the course of a decade and a half, from Gebhardt's discovery in the archives to Spranger's and Harnack's eulogies around 1910, an image of Wilhelm von Humboldt as the progenitor of the modern German university was created. Sylvia Paletschek sees this as a promotion of the New Humanist idea of the university and finds several underlying explanations. First and foremost, Humboldt's short, unfinished, and hitherto unknown manifesto referred to issues that actively interested academics of various persuasions around the year 1900. His text, like several other New Humanist tracts, offered historical legitimacy to the university as an institution dedicated to research, while simultaneously glossing over the fact that the modern research university was a more recent creation of the 1870s and 1880s. Harnack was the one who most assiduously persisted in claiming that the research imperative was Humboldt's main message. Tellingly enough, he did this in the same breath as he praised the Prussian Academy of Sciences and the new Kaiser-Wilhelm-Gesellschaft. He was less interested in the fact that the rapidly progressing specialisation undermined the idea of the unity of science/scholarship and weakened the link between research and teaching.[23]

In a wider perspective, the image of Wilhelm von Humboldt as a university founder fitted well into the general historiography that dominated in the Empire. It was Prussian, national, idealistic toward the state, and it portrayed great men as the prime movers of history. For the mandarins especially, this historical narrative also provided a degree of comfort when they were threatened by other kinds of academics. Last but not least, the centenary of the Friedrich-Wilhelms-Universität encouraged the glorification of a magnificent academic tradition. Since the first decade of the Empire, the Berlin university had been the subject of special attention from the state, to the detriment of other universities. When, in 1910, it was celebrated as a university surrounded by a special national brilliance, that circumstance was able to reduce the impact of any criticism from the provinces.[24]

The years at the beginning of the twentieth century were in many ways an exceptional phase in the history of the Berlin university. Charles McClelland has characterised this time as a high point for the university, with professors of good repute, many students, and

---

23 Paletschek, 'Die Erfindung', 189–90.
24 Ibid., 190–91.

a significant international reputation. At the same time, this was a period when the signs of crisis began to accumulate. New, external research institutes challenged the primacy of the universities, and competition from other centres of science and scholarship became noticeable. Consequently, the centenary took the form of a defence of an order whose foundations were already rocking.[25]

The traditional ideal of the university and of *Bildung* was also brought to the fore by the many critics who emerged during the decades surrounding the year 1900. One source of inspiration of unrivalled importance for these critics was Friedrich Nietzsche, whose denunciation of the New Humanist concept of *Bildung* reverberated throughout the twentieth century. In several writings, mainly from the 1870s, the German iconoclast condemned the levelling of science and scholarship, the narrowly utilitarian view of knowledge, and ossified, life-denying ideas. Instead he called for an anachronistic *Bildung* for free spirits, a vision of aesthetic and intellectual greatness achieved by a limited elite. The Nietzschean line can be followed throughout Germany's subsequent intellectual history, also within pedagogy and educational philosophy. During the interwar years, reformist educationalists, avant-garde artists, and the youth movement gained strength from Nietzsche in their endeavour to break down the time-honoured concept of *Bildung*. In many cases, however, it was not a matter of expressly criticising Humboldt, but of attempting to breathe life into petrified matter.[26]

The Humboldtian tradition was also the point of departure for more specific university debates during the early twentieth century. This can, for example, be seen from the discussions on the limits and meaning of academic freedom. Important figures such as Harnack and sociologists Robert Michels and Max Weber positioned themselves more or less explicitly in relation to the classic German heritage. The prevailing view of academic freedom at this time, a view which was also close to the one that had been formulated by Humboldt himself, meant that the state was given extensive authority to steer recruitment and exclude undesirable individuals. Once a person had been employed, however, he or she should not have to conform to external or internal authorities. Weber was among those who wished to redefine academic freedom. He wanted to abolish the state's border

---

25 McClelland, 'Die Universität', pp. 639–53.
26 Timo Hoyer, *Nietzsche und die Pädagogik: Werk, Biografie und Rezeption* (Würzburg, 2002); Christian Niemeyer, *Nietzsche, die Jugend und die Pädagogik: Eine Einführung* (Weinheim and Munich, 2002).

control during employment procedures, but suggested that in return a form of discipline should be imposed on teachers while teaching, in the interests of unbiased science and scholarship and political education. Weber's argumentation was shaped by turn-of-the-century political and scientific polemics, but it must simultaneously be seen in the context of the newly awakened interest in the basic values of the classic German university.[27]

Consequently, a number of historical factors underlay the Humboldt renaissance. The Humboldt of Harnack and Spranger was a figure they extracted from the past. He reflected their dreams, their discomfort in the culture of their own time. This line of argument corresponds well with David Armitage's assumption that ideas can be seen both as manifestations of long currents of ideas and as answers to distinct questions specific to a particular era.

It must be emphasised that it was primarily in Berlin that Humboldt was elevated to the position of the German university's ancestor in the period around the year 1900. In analyses of rector's speeches (*Rektoratsreden*), Dieter Langewiesche has shown that for a long time it was only in the capital of the Empire that Humboldt's name appeared in academic laudatory speeches. That was practically the sole place where people maintained that the German university model could be derived from the foundation of the Berlin university in 1810. He calls this historiography 'the Berlin story of origin' (*die Berliner Ursprungserzählung*) and sees it as a building block in a Prussian-German national mythology. After the fall of the monarchy, this story would find it difficult to assert itself.[28]

Beyond the university debate, Wilhelm von Humboldt also figured as a historical personage during the initial decades of the century. After the First World War, Spranger's classically-idealising image of Humboldt was challenged. A radically opposite idea, a romantic-naturalistic one, was tentatively formulated by the historian Siegfried A. Kaehler and eventually blossomed in the work of Germanist Helmut Flenner. Influenced by psychoanalysis, these

---

27 Max Weber developed his view on academic freedom and value-neutral scholarship in a series of texts, of which the most important were a number of university-political writings from 1908–1911 and his essay *Wissenschaft als Beruf* (Munich and Leipzig, 1919), which was based on a lecture he had given in 1917. For a comprehensive analysis, see Josephson, *Den akademiska frihetens gränser*.
28 Langewiesche, 'Die Humboldtsche Universität'; Langewiesche, 'Humboldt als Leitbild?'

The discovery of Humboldt

two men sought to undermine the idealised figure and describe him as an unrealistic romantic.[29] Closely related to this approach was a Faustian-psychologising interpretation, represented during the 1930s by scholar of religion Werner Schultz and later by law scholar Friedrich Schaffstein. Here, too, Humboldt was presented as a dreamer, but also as a figure filled with inner tensions – between classical and romantic, and between ideal and reality.[30]

There were two decidedly Nazi interpretations of Wilhelm von Humboldt. One of them, the *völkisch*-political one, indicated strong abhorrence and emphasised Humboldt's alleged failure to live in the real world. For instance, the historian Wilhelm Grau and the educationalist Hans-Jörg Herkendell depicted him as a prominent figure of liberalism and a friend of the Jews.[31] The other was a favourable picture and can be described as energetically-historical in the sense that Humboldt possessed a strong inner force. He was, claimed philosopher Alfred Baeumler and historian Johann-Albrecht von Rantzau, a Nietzschean strong-willed individual who had conquered rationalism.[32] Finally, the voluntaristically-harmonising image of Humboldt was developed during the 1930s and 1940s by Frenchman Robert Leroux and Swiss Ernst Howald who were, however, inspired by German interpretations from the beginning of the century. In these works Humboldt was portrayed as a classically harmonious figure, whose personality was nevertheless the result of a strong will, an ability to harness the immense powers he harboured within his mind.[33]

---

29 Kawohl, *Wilhelm von Humboldt*, pp. 35–52; Kaehler, *Wilhelm von Humboldt*; Helmut Flenner, *Wilhelm von Humboldt und die Schwermut: Ein Beitrag zur Erkenntnis des Menschen Wilhelm von Humboldt* (Frankfurt am Main, 1953).
30 Kawohl, *Wilhelm von Humboldt*, pp. 53–69; Werner Schultz, 'Wilhelm von Humboldt und der Faustische Mensch', *Jahrbuch der Goethe-Gesellschaft*, 16 (1930); Friedrich Schaffstein, *Wilhelm von Humboldt: Ein Lebensbild* (Frankfurt am Main, 1952).
31 Kawohl, *Wilhelm von Humboldt*, pp. 63–77; Wilhelm Grau, *Wilhelm von Humboldt und das Problem des Juden* (Hamburg, 1935); Hans-Jörg Herkendell, *Die Persönlichkeitsidee Wilhelm von Humboldts und das völkisch-politische Menschenbild* (Würzburg, 1938).
32 Kawohl, *Wilhelm von Humboldt*, pp. 70–77; Alfred Baeumler, *Politik und Erziehung: Reden und Aufsätze* (Berlin, 1937); Johann-Albrecht von Rantzau, *Wilhelm von Humboldt: Der Weg seiner geistigen Entwicklung* (Munich, 1939).
33 Kawohl, *Wilhelm von Humboldt*, pp. 78–85; Robert Leroux, *Guillaume de Humboldt: La formation de sa pensée jusqu'en 1794* (Paris, 1932); Ernst Howald, *Wilhelm von Humboldt* (Zürich, 1944).

Wilhelm von Humboldt was thus a historical figure who was of interest to many German humanists during the first decades of the twentieth century. In his biography were reflected the intellectual and ideological tendencies of the time, from New Humanism and idealism by way of naturalism and psychoanalysis to voluntarism and Nazism. The assessment of him varied in a way that was to a great extent also true of other prominent German figures from the same era – Johann Wolfgang von Goethe, Friedrich Hölderlin, Alexander von Humboldt.[34] However, with the exception of Spranger, none of the Humboldt interpreters made any significant contributions to the literature on the idea of the university. They were philologically, pedagogically, or historically orientated writers who discussed a key figure in German intellectual history from the period around the year 1800. Humboldt's ideal of *Bildung* and outlook on people were at the centre of their depictions, not the Berlin university as a German academic model.[35]

If we turn our attention to those who really took an active interest in the basic issues of the university during the 1920s and 1930s, we find other people than those who wrote about Wilhelm von Humboldt as a person. These were, especially in the Weimar Republic, respected academics who were deeply anchored in a scholarly subject and who had a comprehensive interest in the university as an institution of research and *Bildung*. After 1933 many of the preconditions changed; but in Nazi Germany, too, texts on the principles of the university were written in the context of an extended German tradition.

The Weimar Republic

The First World War is a dividing line in almost all historiography of modern Europe. In some respects, this is also true of the German

---

34 Karl Robert Mandelkow, *Goethe in Deutschland: Rezeptionsgeschichte eines Klassikers: 1773–1918* (Munich, 1980); *Hölderlin in der Moderne: Kolloquium für Dieter Henrich zum 85. Geburtstag*, ed. by Friedrich Vollhardt (Berlin, 2014); Rupke, *Alexander von Humboldt*.

35 In a way, one exception was Alfred Baeumler, from 1933 the holder of a newly established professorship of philosophy and political pedagogics in Berlin. He was a leading educationalist in the Third Reich, and among other things he laid down the guiding principles for a new Nazi education of teachers. However, in his writings Baeumler was more preoccupied with the school than with the university. See Barbara Schneider, *Die Höhere Schule im Nationalsozialismus* (Cologne, 2000).

university. Scholars and scientists from all disciplines had been carried away by enthusiasm for the war and enrolled in the service of the nation. Both students and professors had enlisted and fallen in battle, and ordinary academic work had suffered greatly. The battle lines had been drawn within the learned world, and the conflicts had sown the seeds of dissension in the scholarly community.[36] Nevertheless, the 'Great War' did not bring about an unconditional break with existing academic traditions in Germany. The basic departments remained the same. In the period 1919–45, only two new universities were established; in both cases, Hamburg and Cologne, this happened immediately following the end of the war.[37] In spite of the fall of the Empire, the ideological fragmentation of the interwar period, and

---

36 Notker Hammerstein, 'Epilogue: Universities and War in the Twentieth Century', in *A History of the University in Europe: Universities in the Nineteenth and Early Twentieth Centuries*, ed. by Rüegg; Trude Maurer, *Kollegen – Kommilitonen – Kämpfer: Europäische Universitäten im Ersten Weltkrieg* (Stuttgart, 2006). For a survey of intellectual Europe during the war, see Svante Nordin, *Filosofernas krig: Den europeiska filosofin under första världskriget* (Nora, 1998) and Ernst Piper, *Nacht über Europa: Kulturgeschichte des Ersten Weltkriegs* (Berlin, 2013).

37 The old university in Cologne, founded in 1388, had been closed down in 1798. In 1919 the new university was inaugurated, and it soon became one of the more important ones. See Bernd Heimbüchel & Klaus Pabst, *Kölner Universitätsgeschichte: Das 19. und 20. Jahrhundert* (Cologne, 1988). The case of Hamburg is interesting as a matter of principle. When the idea of establishing a university in the city was discussed with increasing intensity from the end of the nineteenth century, the Prussian universities, especially Friedrich-Wilhelms-Universität in Berlin, emerged as negative models. In the Hanseatic city a new kind of university would be founded, according to promoters such as Werner von Melle and Aby Warburg. The university that was eventually realised in the aftermath of the First World War was, however – as has been emphasised by Emily J. Levine – not that radically different. The motto above the entrance to the main building seemed classic: 'Der Forschung – Der Lehre – Der Bildung' ('To Research – To Instruction – To Bildung'). See Emily Levine, *Dreamland of Humanists: Warburg, Cassirer, Panofsky, and the Hamburg School* (Chicago, 2013), pp. 12, 37, 86 and 92, and, in general terms, Rainer Nicolaysen, 'Frei soll die Lehre sein und frei das Lernen': Zur Geschichte der Universität Hamburg (Hamburg, 2008). In a wider North European perspective, Hamburg had similarities to several universities established in the second cities of several countries during the decades surrounding the year 1900. Like Gothenburg University College (founded in 1891), Åbo Akademi University (1918), and Aarhus University (1928), it was founded on a private initiative and combined the idealism of *Bildung* with mercantile ambitions.

5 Carl Heinrich Becker

the Nazi seizure of power, the university as an institution remained largely intact throughout these turbulent years. On the other hand, the conditions of academic activities changed radically. That had consequences for the interpretation of the Humboldtian tradition.[38]

During the 1920s, it was apparent that the status of German scholars and scientists had declined. They had been compromised by their commitment during the war, and many of them were excluded from the international scholarly community. Individual researchers could still enjoy high esteem and maintain contacts across national borders; but as a collective, German academics were damaged goods. The economic crises of the interwar years impaired the finances of the universities, and from time to time it was difficult to procure funds for literature, journals, and laboratory equipment. In order to remedy this academic poverty, a number of organisations were founded at the beginning of the 1920s, among them the predecessor of the German Research Foundation (Deutsche Forschungsgemeinschaft, DFG). Leading individuals, men such as Adolf von Harnack and Fritz Haber, were convinced that Germany could regain lost ground through large investments in technology and the natural sciences. To some extent they were proved right. German research recovered relatively quickly, but at the price of a permanent shift within the academic system: more of the research would henceforth be carried out outside the universities, and fewer resources would go to the humanities.[39]

This shift in focus intensified the already existing conflict between *Naturwissenschaften* (the natural sciences) and *Geisteswissenschaften* (the humanities). It would, however, be misleading to reduce this opposition to a struggle between 'the two cultures', as this concept was defined by C. P. Snow in the years around 1960. In his book Ringer thus claimed, somewhat schematically, that there were two types of German mandarins. The orthodox

---

38 Developmental tendencies within the university sector during the interwar years – the number of students, the distribution of students among the subjects, the growing share of women in the student population, etc. – can be found in Hartmut Titze, 'Hochschulen', in *Handbuch der deutschen Bildungsgeschichte: 1918–1945: Die Weimarer Republik und die nationalsozialistische Diktatur*, ed. by Dieter Langewiesche & Heinz-Elmar Tenorth (Munich, 1989), pp. 209–12.
39 Vom Bruch, 'A Slow Farewell', pp. 19–20; *The Kaiser Wilhelm Society under National Socialism*, ed. by Susanne Heim, Carola Sachse, & Mark Walker (Cambridge, 2009).

ones made up the majority, a majority who completely rejected the new form of government and harboured a general aversion against industrialised civilisation. The modernists (among others Weber, Tönnies, Troeltsch, Mannheim, and Meinecke) for their part had a more ambivalent attitude to the new democratic state. In the polarisation that characterised the Weimar Republic, the scholarly and scientific ideals became one aspect of a greater ideological battle. Many students now rallied to the cause of National Socialism, and the university never became a bulwark for democracy.[40]

Even if the ideological climate affected conflicts of opinion about the university, this was not a matter of purely political disputes. Just as within the various scholarly and scientific fields, the debate on the basic academic issues followed its own principles. Among other things, it brought up old ideas again, some of them dating back to the time of the Empire. But, as within other intellectual fields, ideas about the university from the Weimar period were not solely shaped by continuity. The strong feeling of crisis that many people experienced elicited fierce reactions – some of them amounting to a defence of an older order, others to a break with tradition.[41]

Sylvia Paletschek characterises the 1920s as a period of consolidation. For some people, the New Humanist idea of the university showed a way out of the crisis and held the promise of a return to a holistic, synthesising kind of science and scholarship. Some people drew parallels between the time following the Napoleonic wars and the time after the First World War. Could Humboldt once again breathe life into the German university? they wondered.[42]

---

40 Ringer, *The Decline*; Titze, 'Hochschulen', pp. 216–20.
41 Peter E. Gordon & John P. McCormick, 'Introduction: Weimar Thought: Continuity and Crisis', in *Weimar Thought: A Contested Legacy*, ed. by Peter E. Gordon & John P. McCormick (Princeton, 2013), pp. 4–6. The idea of a crisis awareness during the Weimar Republic can be problematised, however: see Jürgen John, '"Not deutscher Wissenschaft"? Hochschulwandel, Universitätsidee und akademischer Krisendiskurs in der Weimarer Republik', in *Gebrochene Wissenschaftskulturen: Universität und Politik im 20. Jahrhundert*, ed. by Michael Grüttner et al. (Göttingen, 2010) and, in more general terms, *Die 'Krise' der Weimarer Republik: Zur Kritik eines Deutungsmusters*, ed. by Moritz Föllmer & Rüdiger Graf (Frankfurt am Main, 2005) and Rüdiger Graf, *Die Zukunft der Weimarer Republik: Krisen und Zukunftsaneignungen in Deutschland 1918 bis 1933* (Munich, 2008).
42 Paletschek, 'Die Erfindung', 191.

The debates from the Weimar era on the principles of the university were framed by extensive demands for academic reform that arose in different quarters. As early as the final decades of the Empire, complaints had been made to the effect that studies were insufficiently structured and professors mainly devoted themselves to research. After the war and the defeat, this discussion intensified while the new democratic form of government raised more fundamental issues concerning the character of the university. The large majority of the professors, not least among the mandarins, were monarchists and disliked – as was pointed out above – the ideals of the new era. It was not just democracy they objected to; they were critical of the continually rising student numbers, especially because increasing numbers of students were women.[43]

Paletschek has schematically distinguished two basic positions in the debate of the 1920s. On the one hand, there was a camp that demanded a complete remodelling of the university. On the other hand, there was a camp that wanted to safeguard the structure of the German university and at most make minor adaptations to the demands of the new era.[44] The philosopher Max Scheler must be numbered among the radical critics. In a major work, *Die Wissensformen und die Gesellschaft* (1926), he questioned the university as a coherent institution. According to Scheler, the university had, even after the New Humanist changes, basically kept its mediaeval character. Bringing together character formation, professional education, and research under a common roof no longer worked. Instead he argued for a division of the university into a number of institutions with various tasks, among these scientific colleges for specialised studies.[45]

Eduard Spranger for his part represented a faction in favour of preservation. In order to get out of the crisis, the university should, he argued, hold on to the New Humanist ideals of *Bildung* and scholarship. This, in its turn, required a halt to the increase in student numbers. Together with Werner Jaeger and other more or less orthodox mandarins, Spranger belonged to a group who presented the Humboldtian tradition as a corrective to prevailing tendencies. They had a passion for 'a third humanism' (after

---

43 Ibid., 192.
44 Ibid., 192–95.
45 Max Scheler, *Die Wissensformen und die Gesellschaft* (Leipzig, 1926), pp. 496–502; Schelsky, *Einsamkeit und Freiheit*, pp. 234–43.

Renaissance humanism and New Humanism), a current that – in Humboldt's spirit – wished to unite *Bildung* and harmony with an all-comprehensive view of science and scholarship.[46] However, the notion of a division between radical subverters and conservative defenders entails a danger of over-simplification. One central figure in the academic life of the Weimar Republic was Carl Heinrich Becker. Like Spranger, he supported the classic German model; but at the same time he, more than anyone else, has come to symbolise the academic reform efforts of the 1920s. Becker had his own scholarly roots in Orientalism, and had had a career as an innovative researcher of Islam in Heidelberg, Hamburg, Bonn, and Berlin. He had early on been actively involved in university-political issues, albeit without joining a party. Between 1919 and 1930 he was active in the Prussian Ministry of Culture and Education, first as an undersecretary of state and later as a minister. In writings such as *Gedanken zur Hochschulreform* (1919) and *Vom Wesen der deutschen Universität* (1925), he addressed the German university system.[47]

Under the influence of the First World War and the turmoil that followed in its aftermath, Becker became convinced that the German university had to be transformed. 'The core of our universities is sound', was his contention, and he felt that pure scholarly/scientific research was still alive. But the legacy from Humboldt and Fichte had to be managed and adapted to the new circumstances. The university should have another, more orientating function in the age of parliamentary democracy. In that spirit, Becker recommended, among other things, the creation of new professorships in sociology and political science. At the same time, his notion of *Bildung* was

---

46 Eduard Spranger, 'Das Wesen der deutschen Universität', in *Das akademische Deutschland*, ed. by Michael Doeberl et al., 4 vols (Berlin, 1930–1931), vol. III (1930). The concept 'der dritte Humanismus' ('the third humanism') was coined by Eduard Spranger; see his *Der gegenwärtige Stand der Geisteswissenschaften und die Schule* (Leipzig, 1925).

47 See primarily Guido Müller, *Weltpolitische Bildung und akademische Reform: C. H. Beckers Wissenschafts- und Hochschulpolitik 1908–1930* (Cologne, 1991), but also Erich Wende, *C. H. Becker: Mensch und Politiker: Ein biographischer Beitrag zur Kulturgeschichte der Weimarer Republik* (Stuttgart, 1959). In addition to *Gedanken zur Hochschulreform* (Leipzig, 1919) and *Vom Wesen der deutschen Universität* (Leipzig, 1925), Becker wrote other texts on university politics. Many of these have been collected in Carl Heinrich Becker, *Internationale Wissenschaft und nationale Bildung: Ausgewählte Schriften*, ed. by Guido Müller (Cologne, 1997).

basically idealistic, and he stressed the importance of an all-inclusive formation of character. In this regard, his idea of the university was considerably closer to that of the early nineteenth century than, for instance, Friedrich Althoff's bureaucratically authoritarian system. During the second half of the 1920s, it was clear that Becker would not be successful in changing the German university. His support among the professorial community for carrying out democratic reforms had been very limited even at the outset. When darkness fell in the years surrounding 1930, it became even more difficult to gain a hearing for idealistic and humanistic visions.[48]

Nor can the philosopher Karl Jaspers be assigned to either camp – for or against fundamental change – as a matter of course. In 1923, at the age of forty and recently established as the holder of a professorial chair in Heidelberg, he published the book *Die Idee der Universität*. In the book's preface, he takes the demands for reform that had been raised since 1918 as his point of departure. His conviction was that tradition had to be kept alive by constantly being connected to what was new.[49]

The two main portions of the book consist of a conceptual and philosophical discussion of the prerequisites for scholarly and scientific activity and a significantly more down-to-earth investigation of the legal, bureaucratic, and economic foundations of the university. In a section in the middle of the book, a mere ten pages long, Jaspers nevertheless discusses what he calls the idea of the university. He argues that the university has three objectives, and that they cannot be kept distinct from one another: professional training, *Bildung*, and research. If they were to be separated, for example by the creation of specific educational institutions, the very idea of the university would be abandoned. The fact that a university is distinguished by the connection between research and teaching is one relevant factor in this regard. That connection is a necessity if students are to gain insights into the knowledge process as such. In addition, science and scholarship must strive to come into contact with the totality of existence, according to Jaspers. More concretely, this could mean that every field of knowledge has a philosophical aspect and that it

---

48 The expression 'Der Kern unserer Universitäten ist gesund' can be found in Becker, *Gedanken zur Hochschulreform*, p. 17. It was later picked up by others in a somewhat different form, often a variant of 'die deutsche Universität ist "im Kern gesund"'. See also Müller, *Weltpolitische Bildung* and Schelsky, *Einsamkeit und Freiheit*, pp. 233–34.
49 Karl Jaspers, *Die Idee der Universität* (Berlin, 1923), pp. v–vi.

is an important task for the university to cultivate this dimension. To promote *Bildung* that could form the basis for a worldview is also a foundational task.[50]

Jaspers's contribution was comparatively abstract and contained remarkably few references to the history of the German university. Kant, Weber, and Nietzsche were his general points of reference. Humboldt and the other New Humanist theoreticians of the university were conspicuously absent, however. Jaspers was no iconoclast, unlike Scheler; but nor did he actively seek to restore a tradition that was disintegrating. With his use of language, he evoked academic principles of an unmistakably German kind, with his arguments both for *Bildung* and for 'a unification of research and education'. Immediately after the Second World War, Jaspers published yet another book with the title *Die Idee der Universität*. By then he was an important moral and theoretical authority, and what he wrote resounded in the wider intellectual debate in a completely different way than during the 1920s.[51]

In a broader perspective, Jaspers was typical of the Weimar Republic in that he formulated a holistic ideal for the university. In many academic circles, not just in nationalist and right-wing-radical ones, there was a desire for a coherent outlook. The political and religious visionaries of the interwar period profited from this desire, but broader groups of students and younger academics also found visions of a different kind of university appealing. Very few of the reform proposals that were introduced were implemented, however. Like Becker before him, Jaspers found that there was very little sympathy for reform among the majority of the professors.[52]

The Third Reich

For a long time, there was a prevailing idea to the effect that the majority of academics had gone into a kind of internal exile during the twelve dark years between 1933 and 1945. University departments remained largely intact in the Third Reich. With the exception of National Socialist showpiece subjects – prehistory, folklore studies, scientific racism, *Deutsche Physik* – the regime had not politicised education and research. Most academics had, as far as possible,

---

50 Ibid., pp. 44–53.
51 See Chapter 4.
52 Paletschek, 'Die Erfindung', 195.

fulfilled their scholarly and scientific duties during this difficult time. The conclusion was that the university had been an apolitical reserve in an ideological age.[53] Not until the 1990s did a number of studies manage to revise this established historiography. The new image that emerged was not particularly flattering for the academic community. It is true that few subjects had been remodelled according to Nazi principles; but it is unequivocal that many researchers, simply by continuing to work within the system, contributed to legitimising the ambitions of the regime. Besides, many of the leading scholars and scientists of the post-war period had openly placed themselves in the service of power during the war years.[54]

During the twenty-first century, general scrutiny has continued with a large number of specialist studies and biographies. At the same time, the image has become more complex. It is clear that after 1933 the Nazis attempted to implement regimentation of some academic activities, but this was never a matter of a systematic

---

53 During the 1960s some younger researchers attempted to bring attention to 'the brown university', for example in texts such as *Deutsches Geistesleben und Nationalsozialismus: Eine Vortragsreihe der Universität Tübingen*, ed. by Andreas Flitner (Tübingen, 1965).

54 The reappraisal since the 1990s is discussed in, among other works, *Geschichtsschreibung als Legitimationswissenschaft: 1918–1945*, ed. by Peter Schöttler (Frankfurt am Main, 1997), Notker Hammerstein, *Die Deutsche Forschungsgemeinschaft in der Weimarer Republik und im Dritten Reich: Wissenschaftspolitik in Republik und Diktatur 1920–1945* (Munich, 1999), Notker Hammerstein, 'National Socialism and the German Universities', *History of Universities*, 18:1 (2003), and Mitchell G. Ash, 'Politicizing "Normal Science" in Nazi Germany', *H-Net Book Review*, http://www.h-net.org/ (accessed 15 February 2016). During the last decade, separate studies have been dedicated to many individual universities: see, for instance, Steven P. Remy, *The Heidelberg Myth: The Nazification and Denazification of a German University* (Cambridge, 2002); *Kämpferische Wissenschaft: Studien zur Universität Jena im Nationalsozialismus*, ed. by Uwe Hossfeld et al. (Cologne, 2003); *Universitäten und Hochschulen im Nationalsozialismus und in der frühen Nachkriegszeit*, ed. by Karen Bayer, Frank Sparing, & Wolfgang Woelk (Stuttgart, 2004); Leo Haupts, *Die Universität zu Köln im Übergang vom Nationalsozialismus zur Bundesrepublik* (Cologne, 2007); *Zwischen Diktatur und Neubeginn: Die Universität Bonn im 'Dritten Reich' und in der Nachkriegszeit*, ed. by Thomas Becker (Göttingen, 2008). Likewise, a number of central scholarly disciplines have been discussed with respect to the years 1933–1945. In Johan Östling, 'Tyska historiker i Tredje riket: Historiografi som självprövning', *Historielärarnas förenings årsskrift*, 2010, I discuss aspects of more recent research, using the subject of history as my point of departure.

reconstruction of the university. A new, tough control of the academy (*Führerprinzip*) could coexist with traditional methods of research and teaching. Nor can one claim that the Nazis had a policy of science and research that was wholly logically coherent. Ideologically conditioned research, with *Rasse* ('race') and *völkisch* ('of the people') as key concepts, was assigned to special institutes outside the university, for example the 'Reichsinstitut für Geschichte des neuen Deutschlands' or the 'Forschungsgemeinschaft deutsches Ahnenerbe'. Here, too, could be found Alfred Rosenberg's plans for an elite Nazi university, 'Hohe Schule der NSDAP', plans that were only partially realised. In parallel to this, great investments were made in internationally viable cutting-edge research. In itself, the Nazi leadership was thus not hostile to science and scholarship.[55]

Seen from a wider perspective, it is obvious that many subjects were united via common standards and ways of looking at things without having been subjected to enforced government regimentation. With respect to the humanities, Jan Eckel has highlighted the strong features of continuity that existed from the late nineteenth century to the early 1960s. In all essentials, the basic ideals and theories that took shape during the Empire survived into the early post-Second World War years. Within many humanities disciplines, scholars initially tried to adapt to Nazism by, for example, adopting racist theories; but within the established disciplines racism never became a fundamental element, in contradistinction to the situation within new ones such as *Ostforschung*. But even the well-established humanities subjects contributed in the highest degree toward legitimising the Nazi world of ideas, argues Eckel. His observation is worth considering: the decisive dividing lines of international politics – 1914, 1933, 1945 – are not the same as those of the history of science. Rather, he describes a process in which the issues and concepts of science and scholarship are superimposed on one another and undergo

---

55 In *Gebrochene Wissenschaftskulturen: Universität und Politik im 20. Jahrhundert*, ed. by Michael Grüttner et al. (Göttingen, 2010), much of this important research is summarised. See also Rüdiger Hachtmann, *Wissenschaftsmanagement im Dritten Reich: Die Geschichte der Generalverwaltung der Kaiser-Wilhelm-Gesellschaft*, 2 vols (Göttingen, 2007); Anne C. Nagel, *Hitlers Bildungsreformer: Das Reichsministerium für Wissenschaft, Erziehung und Volksbildung 1934–1945* (Frankfurt am Main, 2012); and Robert P. Ericksen, *Complicity in the Holocaust: Churches and Universities in Nazi Germany* (New York, 2012).

The discovery of Humboldt

6 German students in 1933

a gradual transformation. Revolutions rarely, if ever, take place within the university.[56]

These insights are of vital importance for an assessment of the status of the Humboldtian tradition in the Third Reich. For scholars and scientists who were Jewish, and/or politically opposed to Nazism, the Nazi seizure of power naturally became a horrific watershed. In total between fifteen and twenty per cent of the teaching staff were sent packing, and a number of the most brilliant stars were forced to leave Germany. But for the great majority, the events of the 1930s were not enough to alter their self-image. The mandarins felt that they were still active within the classic German university. With their solid, serious, scholarly-scientific approach, they remained faithful to its leading principles.[57]

---

56 Eckel, *Geist der Zeit*, pp. 131–38. See, in addition, *Nationalsozialismus in den Kulturwissenschaften*, ed. by Hartmut Lehmann & Otto Gerhard Oexle, 2 vols (Göttingen, 2004); *Nazi Germany and the Humanities*, ed. by Wolfgang Bialas & Anson Rabinbach (Oxford, 2007); and Frank-Rutger Hausmann, *Die Geisteswissenschaften im 'Dritten Reich'* (Frankfurt am Main, 2011).
57 Hammerstein, *Antisemitismus*; Notker Hammerstein, 'Humboldt im Dritten Reich', in *Humboldt international*, ed. by Schwinges; Paletschek, 'The Invention of Humboldt'.

If you pan across academic Germany after the Nazi seizure of power, however, no monolithic, completely totalitarian pattern emerges. Particularly during the initial years, it is possible to find different ideas about the university. It is nevertheless striking how much influence the older German model of the university continued to exert; in the Third Reich, too, people were discussing things in relation to the Humboldtian tradition. This is true of the entire spectrum of opinions: those who wholeheartedly supported National Socialism, those who vacillated, those who were critical but kept quiet, and those who openly showed their disgust for the new regime.[58]

In certain circles, it was possible for the classically-idealising image of Humboldt to survive. Above all, it was cherished by older mandarins who had gone into internal exile during the Nazi years. Eduard Spranger is an obvious example. He, who embraced a national-conservative outlook, initially assumed a partially favourable attitude to National Socialism. Soon, however, Spranger reacted strongly against the politicisation of the Berlin university and signalled his critical distance to the new power. Even so, he continued to work as a professor until the end of the war and published a large number of works. A hundred years after the death of Humboldt, in 1935, he dedicated a number of celebratory articles to the Prussian educational reformer; and in the following year, his *Habilitation* thesis from 1909 was republished in a second, unaltered, edition.[59]

Parallel to this state of things, suggestions for a radically different kind of university were drawn up in line with Nazi ideology. Adolf Rein and Ernst Krieck were among the most articulate advocates of such a university. They had both developed the basic characteristics of their philosophy on the university even before the Nazi seizure of power. After 1933, their ideas were adopted by the Nazis and their cause was promoted by Hitler. During the 1930s both men became rectors at distinguished German universities, Rein in Hamburg and Krieck in Frankfurt am Main and subsequently in Heidelberg.[60]

---

58 See, in general, Jost Hermand, *Culture in Dark Times: Nazi Fascism, Inner Emigration, and Exile* (New York, 2013).
59 Ortmeyer, *Eduard Spranger*; Eduard Spranger, *Wilhelm von Humboldt und die Humanitätsidee* (Berlin, 1936).
60 Paletschek, 'The Invention of Humboldt'; Arnt Goede, *Adolf Rein und die 'Idee der politischen Universität'* (Hamburg, 2008); Gerhard Müller, *Ernst Krieck und die nationalsozialistische Wissenschaftsreform: Motive und Tendenzen einer Wissenschaftslehre und Hochschulreform im Dritten Reich* (Weinheim and Basel, 1978).

During the Weimar Republic, Adolf Rein had become known as a national-conservative historian. From his position in Hamburg, he was an eager promoter of 'the political university'. In his manifesto *Die Idee der politischen Universität* (1932), he expressed a nationalist dream of the rebirth of a paralysed institution. This dream met with approval in wide academic circles. Ernst Krieck, an autodidact and influential educationalist during the interwar period, gradually drew nearer to the NSDAP in the years around 1930. In a manner similar to Rein's, but more thoroughly racist, he set himself up as the interpreter of a 'national political education'. Between 1933 and 1944, he was the publisher of the National Socialist journal *Volk im Werden*, publishing a number of articles in this educational periodical.[61]

Although Rein was a traditional academic and Krieck lacked higher education, they had several converging ideas. On the one hand, they both wanted to go beyond the New Humanist concept of the university and enlist science in the service of the Greater German nation. On the other hand, they believed in the union between education and research, opposing a narrowly utilitarian way of thinking about academic matters. Especially Krieck felt at the same time that the German university had to distance itself from the bourgeois nineteenth-century ideology connected to Humboldt's name.

No single vision of a new university has been the subject of so much scholarly discussion as the one presented by Martin Heidegger in his rector's speech in Freiburg im Breisgau on 27 May 1933. For a long time, there was an apologetic tendency in the literature on this philosopher's relationship to Nazism; it was seen as a temporary deviation in his biography, an expression of political naiveté. Since the late 1980s, several critical studies have been published which have analysed the relationship between Heidegger's ideas and National Socialist ideology in great detail. A general conclusion that can be drawn is that he was not an innocent instrument of the men of power, but had genuine motives for becoming rector of the University of Freiburg. During his ten months in office, Heidegger introduced the *Führer* principle and rallied to the support of other Nazi doctrines. With his work in office, he believed he could promote a kind of spiritualised Nazism. When he resigned as rector in the spring of 1934, the reason was not disagreement with the political regime.

---

61 Goede, *Adolf Rein*; Müller, *Ernst Krieck*.

Instead it has been shown that his vision of a new kind of university had encountered resistance within the traditional academic system. Heidegger had been branded as fanciful and unrealistic by others in the professorial community.[62]

There was nothing in Heidegger's fateful speech that could give offence to the new regime. His rector's speech reflected a conscious, ardently desired involvement with the great issues of his time; but it cannot be reduced to a manifesto for a Nazi academy. In spite of its strongly ideological character, it also represented an attempt on Heidegger's part to transfer his ideas to the academic domain.[63]

From the perspective of university history Heidegger's speech was a part of an extended German debate on the basic academic issues. Since the nineteenth century, rectors in German-speaking Europe delivered a *Rektoratsrede* ('rector's address') when they took office

---

62 Martin Heidegger, 'Die Selbstbehauptung der deutschen Universität', in Martin Heidegger, *Gesamtausgabe: Veröffentlichte Schriften 1910–1976: Reden und andere Zeugnisse eines Lebensweges: 1910–1976*, ed. by Hermann Heidegger, Part I, vol. XVI (Frankfurt am Main, 2000). Thought-provoking discussions on Heidegger and Nazism can be found in Hans Ruin, *Frihet, ändlighet, historicitet: Essäer om Heideggers filosofi* (Stockholm, 2013), pp. 151–68, and in Daniel Birnbaum & Sven-Olov Wallenstein, *Heideggers väg* (Stockholm, 1999), pp. 64–76. A translation, by Karsten Harries, of Heidegger's speech is found in *The Review of Metaphysics*, 38.3 (March 1985), 467–502, under the title 'The Self-Assertion of the German University'. International literature on Heidegger and Nazism is extensive and continually proliferating, with Victor Farías, *Heidegger et le nazisme* (Lagrasse, 1987) as a powerful catalyst. Some of the most important works are Hugo Ott, *Martin Heidegger: Unterwegs zu seiner Biographie* (Frankfurt am Main, 1988); Hans Sluga, *Heidegger's Crisis: Philosophy and Politics in Nazi Germany* (Cambridge, MA, 1993); Rüdiger Safranski, *Ein Meister aus Deutschland: Heidegger und seine Zeit* (Munich, 1994); and Emmanuel Faye, *Heidegger, l'introduction du nazisme dans la philosophie: Autour des séminaires inédits de 1933–1935* (Paris, 2005). When Heidegger's so-called Black Notebooks (*Schwarze Hefte*) began to be published in 2014, many scholars thought they had found evidence of his thinking having been more characterised by anti-Semitism than what his defenders after 1945 had claimed. See Peter Trawny, *Heidegger und der Mythos der jüdischen Weltverschwörung* (Frankfurt am Main, 2015).

63 Ruin, *Frihet*, pp. 151–68. For example, Ruin argues that Heidegger's desire for a kind of *Selbstbehauptung* was related to central ideas in his main work *Sein und Zeit* (1927). The argument for science having lost its relationship to the living world was also an emanation of his general philosophy. It is also possible to draw parallels between Fichte, Husserl, and Heidegger in that all three wanted to activate a philosophical and cultural self-control.

and in due course also at the beginning of each academic year.[64] Like many earlier rectors, Heidegger used this opportunity to formulate more general thoughts on the nature of the university. Idealist thinkers from the period around the year 1800 had wanted to unite all forms of knowledge and experience into all-comprehensive knowledge that would be embodied in the university, with philosophy as its cardinal discipline. Heidegger remained sceptical of such pretensions and instead embraced the ancient idea of philosophy as a guide for political power. Consequently, Heidegger was not alien to enlisting the university in the service of the nation's fate. Here, as he put it, there was no room for the 'much celebrated "academic freedom"', because 'this freedom was not genuine, since it was only negative'.[65] Instead, students should be tied to the community of the people, the glory of the nation, and the spiritual mission of the German people.

Heidegger's speech in Freiburg was thus simultaneously a political intervention, a philosophical document, and a contribution to the debate on the idea of the university. His message was strongly marked by the Nazi seizure of power, but his use of concepts and his lines of thought also evinced a dependency on historical predecessors. He worked within a German theoretical tradition concerning the university, but he wanted to go beyond it at the same time. In this respect, there were points of contact between him, Rein, and Krieck. Their examples show that a classic university model remained a significant point of reference in the Third Reich. The academic ideas of Rein and Krieck were an emanation of the radical discussions at the end of the 1920s. At bottom, they held on to the established academic model; but simultaneously they maintained that the university had to be subordinated to the requirements of the nation. Heidegger cherished a dream of a different kind of institution, a vision that entailed a break with all ideas on the university as an autonomous institution.

During the first years after the Nazi seizure of power there was a certain scope for oppositional ideas, including those regarding the fundamental function of the university. Soon thereafter conditions changed. One person who experienced this was René König.[66] In the later period of the Weimar Republic he had moved among different academic settings and humanities subjects; among other things,

---

64 Langewiesche, 'Humboldt als Leitbild?'
65 Martin Heidegger, 'The Self-Assertion of the German University', 477–79.
66 René König, *Leben im Widerspruch: Versuch einer intellektuellen Autobiographie* (Munich, 1980).

he studied under Eduard Spranger. After gaining a doctorate in Romance languages in 1929, he orientated himself towards sociology while working as a publisher's reader at the Berlin publishers 'Die Runde'. It was here, too, that he published *Vom Wesen der deutschen Universität* (approx. 'On the Character of the German University') in 1935. Soon after publication the book was banned, and König was branded by the regime as a hostile intellectual and prevented from continuing his *Habilitation* work. He succeeded in leaving Germany and spent the war years in exile in Switzerland.

Vom Wesen der deutschen Universität was an ambitious survey of the history of the German university, from the beginning of the eighteenth century to the first decades of the nineteenth. König did not openly criticise the Nazi regime, but on the basis of the introduction his message was nevertheless clear. The idea of the university, he emphasised, must be realised once more. Just as the classic German university became a response to those radical forces that wanted to abolish the university as an institution during the age of idealism, it was now necessary to breathe life into the fundamental academic ideals in order to halt the university-hostile currents that dominated the age. In the historical survey Fichte was given the greatest amount of space, but Humboldt was also discussed extensively. In Humboldt, König found an unsolved problem: he did not succeed in uniting a passion for freedom with fidelity to the state. In spite of the imperfections – that the classic German university had contained conflicts and never been completely realised – it was now more than ever necessary to consider the origins and significance of the university. This was the only way in which the idea of the university could be kept alive.[67]

König's words were an act of resistance. The noose had already been tightened, and soon all oppositional voices would be silenced. Those who harboured different ideas left the country or hibernated in internal exile. Not until after the Second World War would a real debate on the idea of the university flare up again.

Humboldt's shifting guises

Wilhelm von Humboldt resurfaced at the turn of the century around 1900 and reappeared now and then during the following decades.

---

67 René König, *Vom Wesen der deutschen Universität* (Berlin, 1935), pp. 11–14, 151–79, and 198–200.

The discovery of Humboldt

But his guises varied. For some people he was a prince of light, full of promise; for others, he was an incarnation of an ossified concept of *Bildung*. It would, however, be reductionist to describe the debate on the idea of the university as a battle between two camps: for or against the Humboldtian model. Even a cursory examination of the different positions, and that is what has been the case here, indicates that the period between the two world wars cannot be described in dichotomous terms.

There were people who stubbornly defended the classic German model of the university. Eduard Spranger is the best example. For many years, his argumentation was characterised by a remarkable continuity. Then there were those who, at bottom, stood up for the academic principles underlying the classic university, but who endeavoured to implement an adaptation to the reality of the Weimar Republic following the First World War. Carl Heinrich Becker was the foremost representative of this position. A person who was considerably more unconditional in his demands for reform was Max Scheler. He decisively rejected the traditional German university as old-fashioned and demanded a transformation of the entire system. Even more categorical were those who attempted to go beyond the entire intellectual tradition and liberate themselves from its alleged trammels.

The significance of one and the same attitude could shift depending on the context. Spranger's defence of the Humboldtian tradition took place during the 1920s, with conservative overtones. He remained dismissive of parliamentary democracy and felt that the only way to safeguard *Bildung* and academic freedom was to put a stop to the influx of students to the universities. A few years later, after 1933, René König returned to the same sources, but for him it was a matter of mobilising a spiritual resistance to National Socialism. There could also be a significant intellectual scope within one and the same position. Heidegger's rector's speech was not exclusively a rousing speech of university ideology; it was also the product of a multifaceted philosophical discussion. This cannot, however, be said of the programmatic contributions made by Rein and Krieck.

Seen from a wider perspective, however, one can see unifying factors operating during the first three or four decades of the twentieth century. All the actors stayed within a common academic conceptual world. Their frames of reference consisted of the national tradition, and no comparative arguments were made. Impulses came from within, the classic German model providing the obvious norm. Even those who rejected that model, or who wished to alter its very foundations, positioned themselves in relation to an intellectual heritage.

'During the twentieth century, references to Wilhelm von Humboldt and New Humanism became an all-purpose weapon [*Allzweckwaffe*]', writes Sylvia Paletschek.[68] This conclusion agrees with my own general points of departure, but it also gives rise to nuances and further questions. First, there is reason to wonder what importance Wilhelm von Humboldt was in fact accorded during the first half of the century. Paletschek and others have argued that Humboldt was discovered or invented around 1900. This renaissance supposedly secured a place for the Prussian educational reformer in the interwar debate on *Bildung*, science, and scholarship. But if we disregard Spranger and Harnack, Humboldt was not an important figure in the most significant interventions in university politics, be they those of Becker, Jaspers, Scheler, Heidegger, or König. One conceivable conclusion is that Humboldt was too much associated with an idealised New Humanist idea of the university whose foremost spokesperson was Spranger. This idea was not embraced by mandarins who were favourably disposed towards modernity, and still less by those who were close to National Socialism. There are thus good reasons for asking just how generally appreciated Wilhelm von Humboldt actually was during the decades prior to the Second World War. If anything, it was the classic German university that was the point of reference.

Second, one may question Paletschek's idea about a kind of *Allzweckwaffe* – the notion that the Humboldtian tradition could be used for all manner of purposes. The observations from the first decades of the twentieth century open the door for other interpretations. It is true that each interpretation of the Humboldtian tradition was embedded in its respective era and was appropriated by different interests. Something partially new could arise that also bore the name of something old, something that could derive its legitimacy from tradition – or from the rejection of tradition – thanks to such an appellation. What was described as a supra-historical idea of the university became a surface for the projection of academic dreams and the scene of intellectual battles. When this has been said, it must nevertheless be emphasised that the classic German ideal of the university was held together by a vocabulary that was more or less constant. It was a vocabulary that made certain attitudes and

---

68 Paletschek, 'Verbreitete sich', p. 103.

The discovery of Humboldt

assertions possible while occluding others. The quantity was not infinite, and the contents were not arbitrary; there were a limited number of main positions. Reflections on the politics of the university had their given framework.

Peter Moraw has introduced an oft-quoted division into epochs for the history of the German universities: a pre-classic phase (up to c. 1800), a classic phase (c. 1800 to the 1960s), and a post-classic phase (from the 1960s onwards).[69] Rüdiger vom Bruch has problematised this division. According to him, it can be argued that the break with classic traditions came at the beginning of the 1930s, provided we do not concentrate exclusively on the stability of departments but also examine the idea of the university as a whole. In Nazi Germany, the ethos of science and scholarship was undermined and academic freedom was curtailed.[70] There is of course a good deal of truth in this picture of developments, but they did not lead to the inexorable decline and fall of the Humboldtian tradition. That tradition remained alive as a contrasting image, as an independent corrective of *realpolitik* and the interests of power. And after 1945, the classic German model was heading for a renaissance.

---

69 Peter Moraw, 'Aspekte und Dimensionen älterer deutscher Universitätsgeschichte', in *Academia Gissensis: Beiträge zur älteren Gießener Universitätsgeschichte*, ed. by Peter Moraw & Volker Press (Marburg, 1982). Moraw modified his chronology somewhat in his later writings; see Peter Moraw, 'Universitäten, Gelehrte und Gelehrsamkeit in Deutschland vor und um 1800', in *Humboldt international*, ed. by Schwinges, pp. 19–21.
70 Vom Bruch, 'A Slow Farewell', pp. 22–24.

4
The rebirth of the university

In the midst of destruction, in some marvellous way, intellectual life sprouted. A small but influential group dedicated themselves to debate, critique, and soul-searching during the early post-war years. Newly written drama was produced in cold basements; newly produced films were shown in mouldy tents. Although this cultural vitality eventually faded, a foundation for post-war Germany was laid here.[1]

The cultural vigour of the first post-war years astonished many thinkers who had been forced to leave Nazi Germany. Theodor W. Adorno had spent the war years in exile in America, but returned to his native country at the end of the 1940s. He had expected to encounter listlessness and cynicism. Instead he saw how young Germans thirsted for art, philosophy, and *Bildung*. In a letter to Thomas Mann, Adorno compared the atmosphere to that which had characterised the period following the Napoleonic wars. Then as now, he noted, the students discussed logical and metaphysical problems with the same gravity that other generations had discussed politics. In a way this was not strange: if the German nation had a future, it was not as a political great power but as an intellectual one. In their present situation, the Germans were – with an echo

---

1 Wolfgang Schivelbusch, *Vor dem Vorhang: Das geistige Berlin 1945–1948* (Munich, 1995); Jörg Echternkamp, *Nach dem Krieg: Alltagsnot, Neuorientierung und die Last der Vergangenheit 1945–1949* (Zürich, 2003). Parts of this chapter build upon earlier texts of mine: Johan Östling, 'The Regeneration of the University: Karl Jaspers and the Humboldtian Tradition in the Wake of the Second World War', in *The Humboldtian Tradition*, ed. by Josephson, Karlsohn, & Östling, and Johan Östling, 'The Swansong of the Mandarins: Humboldt's Idea of the University in Early Post-War Germany', *Modern Intellectual History*, 13:2 (2016), 387–415.

from Hölderlin – 'tatenarm und gedankenvoll' ('poor in deeds, rich in thoughts').[2] It was not only Adorno who experienced the thirst for and the joy of knowledge among the young Germans. Legal historian Helmut Coing spoke of the deep, sincere sense of happiness that unfolded during this time. In spite of the poverty, there was an openness to everything connected with science and scholarship, art, and music, he remembered. Eduard Spranger, the philosopher and educationalist, praised the students he met in the late 1940s. They were the most earnest and dedicated he had ever known.[3]

The university was one of the first societal institutions that were allowed to resume their activities after the surrender of Nazi Germany in May 1945. Much had changed, however. In a very tangible sense, the outcome of the Second World War had transformed the academic terrain. The loss of the eastern territories meant that venerated universities such as Königsberg and Breslau ceased to be German educational institutions. In the Soviet zone a rapid reshaping of the universities, with clear ideological overtones, was immediately begun. Over the next forty years, well-established German educational institutions such as Berlin, Greifswald, Halle, Jena, and Leipzig came under Communist control.[4]

---

2 Wolf Lepenies, *The Seduction of Culture in German History* (Princeton, 2006), pp. 134–38; Theodor W. Adorno & Thomas Mann, *Briefwechsel 1943–1955*, ed. by Christoph Gödde & Thomas Specher (Frankfurt am Main, 2002), pp. 46–47.

3 Christoph Führ, 'Zur deutschen Bildungsgeschichte seit 1945', in *Handbuch der deutschen Bildungsgeschichte: 1945 bis zur Gegenwart: Bundesrepublik Deutschland*, ed. by Christoph Führ & Carl-Ludwig Furck (Munich, 1998), pp. 6–7.

4 Ralph Jessen, 'Zwischen Bildungspathos und Spezialistentum: Werthaltungen und Identitätskonstruktionen der Hochschullehrerschaft in West- und Ostdeutschland nach 1945', in *Eliten im Sozialismus: Beiträge zur Sozialgeschichte der DDR*, ed. by Peter Hübner (Cologne, Weimar and Vienna, 1999); Connelly, *Captive University*; *Hochschuloffiziere und Wiederaufbau des Hochschulwesens in Deutschland 1945–1949: Die sowjetische Besatzungszone*, ed. by Manfred Heinemann (Berlin, 2000); Norman M. Naimark, *The Russians in Germany: A History of the Soviet Zone of Occupation, 1945–1949* (Cambridge, MA, 1995), pp. 440–48; Ilko-Sascha Kowalczuk, *Geist im Dienste der Macht: Hochschulpolitik in der SBZ/DDR 1945 bis 1961* (Berlin, 2003); Gunilla-Friederike Budde, *Frauen der Intelligenz: Akademikerinnen in der DDR 1945 bis 1975* (Göttingen, 2003).

7 The war-damaged Berlin university in 1945

In the west, much of the old system seemed to endure. Nazism, the Second World War, the defeat, and the occupation did not alter the basic order that had been established during the nineteenth century. The organisation, the faculty divisions, the internal hierarchy of subjects – in all essentials, the structure remained the same. Nevertheless, people also faced a number of significant challenges in the western zones of occupation. Several comparatively small university towns, such as Marburg, Göttingen, and Tübingen, were largely spared material destruction; but in many cities, including Hamburg, Cologne, and Frankfurt am Main, lecture halls, libraries, and laboratories had been seriously damaged. Lectures had to be given in temporary facilities, book collections were severely depleted, and access to technical equipment was woefully inadequate.[5]

Getting the academic machinery up and running was not simply a matter of clearing away concrete obstacles and solving practical problems. The university and its future role in German society stood out as a vital issue to many more people than the professors. Dolf

---

5 Wolbring, *Trümmerfeld*, pp. 14–19. The literature on individual universities is quite extensive today. See, for instance, Steven P. Remy, *The Heidelberg Myth*, as well as *Die Universität München im Dritten Reich: Aufsätze*, ed. by Elisabeth Kraus, 2 vols (Munich, 2006–2008). For an overview, see Wolbring, *Trümmerfeld*, pp. 17–19.

Sternberger felt that 'the problem of the university is, crucially, a general problem that in no way concerns academics only'.[6] This was also true of the three powers that controlled occupied Western Germany in 1945–1949. They all identified the university as a key arena for societal transformation. The guiding principles of the Potsdam Agreement – denazification, demilitarisation, and democratisation – would also become those of the German university. Like the educational system at large, the university had to go through a real transformation if it was not to remain an anti-democratic bulwark of reactionary opposition. Ideas as to how this should be done were nevertheless very different among the occupational forces, and the same applied to the degree to which they were prepared for the task. There was no general plan for the future of the university.[7]

The Americans and the British agreed that the best way to bring about re-education was to reform the traditional German university, preferably in close cooperation with democratically minded German academics. The French for their part doubted that it was possible to change the existing university in the desired manner. Democratisation and re-education were matters of too great importance to be entrusted to the Germans themselves. The French solution was to establish new universities (for example in Mainz and Saarbrücken) and to pursue active cultural policies.[8]

At the same time, the will of the allies to change the German educational system was only one side of the matter. These brief but important years also saw ongoing intellectual reflection concerning the idea of the university. One central question which engaged

---

6 Dolf Sternberger, 'Nachbemerkung', in Karl Jaspers & Fritz Ernst, *Vom lebendigen Geist der Universität und vom Studieren: Zwei Vorträge* (Heidelberg, 1946), p. 63.

7 Corine Defrance, *Les Alliés occidentaux et les universités allemandes: 1945–1949* (Paris, 2000); Wolbring, *Trümmerfeld*.

8 Walter Rüegg & Jan Sadlak, 'Relations with Authority', in *A History of the University in Europe: Universities Since 1945*, ed. by Rüegg, pp. 76–84; James F. Tent, *Mission on the Rhine: Reeducation and Denazification in American-Occupied Germany* (Chicago, 1982); David Phillips, *German Universities After the Surrender: British Occupation Policy and the Control of Higher Education* (Oxford, 1983); Stefan Zauner, *Erziehung und Kulturmission: Frankreichs Bildungspolitik in Deutschland 1945–1949* (Munich, 1994); Defrance, *Les Alliés occidentaux*; Paulus, *Vorbild USA?* See also Christian H. Stifter, *Zwischen geistiger Erneuerung und Restauration: US-amerikanische Planungen zur Entnazifizierung und demokratischen Neuorientierung österreichischer Wissenschaft 1941–1955* (Vienna, 2014).

many of Germany's leading thinkers was how to breathe life into the culturally and academically mangled country. What did the dominant ideals for the university look like? What role did the classic German heritage play when it came to vitalising the university? In what way was Wilhelm von Humboldt a point of reference? These questions are at the centre of this chapter.

This limited period of time – the five years following the end of the war – together with the particular conditions that prevailed in occupied Germany provide the prerequisites for realising David Armitage's approach to intellectual history: an investigation of the Humboldtian tradition's significance in a highly specific context. At the same time, the categories drawn from the history of knowledge provide analytic concreteness. The dominant academic mode of presentation during the five years following the end of the war was the lecture, an oral address that was often printed in a journal or published separately subsequent to its delivery. The German mandarins were still the leading agents of knowledge; indeed, these years were the last time they were at the centre of the great debate concerning fundamental academic ideas. Although they had differing views on the history and future of the German university, they were part of the same language sphere and belonged to a shared world of experience. On the precise meaning of the concept of knowledge, however, they could hold conflicting opinions.

Humboldt during the years of occupation

In the three western zones of occupation it soon became obvious that there would be no radical renewal of the German university. The leading professors had no interest in breaking with the older tradition, and the occupation forces lacked the energy and the ideas needed for the implementation of a new order. When, in the autumn of 1945, the Americans were allowed to examine the new statutes of Heidelberg University, they expressed their disappointment that in the main these represented a restoration of old values. Hopes for a new kind of university, however vague and embryonic these ideas might have been, came to nothing.[9]

During subsequent years the western occupation forces instead tried to reform the existing university system, through a gentler and far less comprehensive type of ideological reshaping than that taking

---

9 Wolbring, *Trümmerfeld*.

place in the east. In particular, the Americans and the British took the initiative for several reform conferences and encouraged the various state governments (which gradually took over responsibility for educational issues) to work for change. One common goal was to democratise the structure of universities and place them in the service of the new society.[10] One of the most important initiatives was the 'Marburger Hochschulgespräche', an informal discussion forum that convened several times during the early post-war years. It attracted a good deal of attention in the academic world, especially at first. In a declaration from 1946, the participants stated that the best way to promote democracy was to safeguard scholarly and scientific freedom. After a few years, however, interest in the forum cooled significantly, and in 1949 the discussions in Marburg took place for the last time.[11] Under British guidance, a commission was set up which mainly consisted of reform-minded German academics. They visited most universities in the three western zones, and in 1948 they presented a comprehensive reform proposal, the so-called 'Gutachten zur Hochschulreform' (literally 'experts' report concerning the reform of higher education'). In the 'Blaues Gutachten', thus known because of the colour of its cover, a number of proposals were presented that were aimed at, among other things, opening up German universities and making them accessible to wider social groups. Though many of these proposals were never realised, this document became a point of reference in the more recent West German debate.[12]

In spite of a number of efforts, however, none of the three western allies succeeded in bringing about a profound change of the German university. One important reason for this failure was that both the occupational forces and the leadership of the university were quickly brought face to face with a number of concrete challenges and found themselves unable to muster enough energy to push through changes. One main problem was the question of how the university was to be staffed. Roughly 1,700 Jewish scholars and scientists, 300 of whom were university professors, had been forced to flee, primarily to Great Britain and the United States. Several of them

---

10 Defrance, *Les Alliés occidentaux*; Wolbring, *Trümmerfeld*.
11 *Dokumente zur Hochschulreform 1945–1959*, ed. by Rolf Neuhaus (Wiesbaden, 1961), p. 260.
12 *Dokumente*, ed. by Neuhaus, pp. 289–368; David Phillips, *Pragmatismus und Idealismus: Das 'Blaue Gutachten' und die britische Hochschulpolitik in Deutschland 1948* (Cologne, Weimar, and Vienna, 1995).

were considered to be world leaders in their respective fields. In addition to this, there were those who had left the country during the twelve years of Nazi rule because of ideological or humanistic convictions.[13] A more immediate problem concerned all those professors and lecturers who were politically compromised. Not a few of them had been ideologically dedicated and had worked for the Nazi cause through their academic activities, though the percentage of NSDAP faculty members varied greatly among the universities. Towards the end of the war, almost two thirds of all professors in Heidelberg had joined the Party; in Freiburg the corresponding proportion was roughly half, and in Bonn a quarter.[14]

The academic denazification turned out to be an arduous and delicate task. The process differed from zone to zone, but one basic pattern can be distinguished: Nazi rectors were replaced by new ones everywhere. These individuals had unblemished reputations and had usually held important academic positions before 1933, and many of them were advanced in years. The feeling of returning to normality after a twelve-year-long state of emergency, rather than a break with tradition, was therefore strong. For the occupying authorities, however, replacing the leadership was not enough. As most of the professors had not been party members, but had embraced a national-conservative outlook that had clear points in common with Nazism, much effort was expended in designing a system of categories (*Minderbelastete*, *Mitläufer*, and so on; these two concepts might be translated as 'less tainted' and 'fellow-travellers' respectively) which would differentiate degrees of sympathy and guilt. Though it

---

13 Mitchell G. Ash, 'Scientific Changes in Germany 1933, 1945 and 1990: Towards a Comparison', *Minerva*, 37:4 (1999), pp. 331–34. Friedrich Heer, an Austrian historian of ideas, characterised the intellectual blood-letting that had been caused by this immense academic exodus in a retrospective reflection. 'From the 18th to the 20th century German intellectual life is inconceivable without the explosions of Jewish input', he wrote. 'Everything there has become provincial'. Quoted in Christoph Führ, *The German Educational System since 1945: Outlines and Problems* (Bonn, 1997), p. 5.
14 The literature on the denazification of the universities is extensive. See *Akademische Vergangenheitspolitik: Beiträge zur Wissenschaftskultur der Nachkriegszeit*, ed. by Bernd Weisbrod (Göttingen, 2002); Eckel, *Geist der Zeit*, pp. 88–111; Axel Schildt & Detlef Siegfried, *Deutsche Kulturgeschichte: Die Bundesrepublik – 1945 bis zur Gegenwart* (Munich, 2009); pp. 54–57, and Wolbring, *Trümmerfeld*, pp. 19–23, as well as the literature quoted in Wolbring's book.

turned out to be difficult to apply these schematic categorisations in the real world, an actual denazification process was carried out during the early post-war years, albeit with varying degrees of thoroughness. This process was most zealously implemented in the American zone – the Soviet zone excepted, of course. In Erlangen, only a few lecturers remained after the purges, and in Munich there were not enough competent, unimpeachable people to fill all the academic chairs.[15]

As within other social spheres – the school system, the church, the courts – there was visible opposition to enforced dismissals within the world of the university. This opposition was a combination of esprit de corps, an old aversion to interference in the internal affairs of the academy, and a realisation that it would be difficult to fill the vacancies left by disgraced people. Even so, no more than a few years later many of those who had been ostracised were received back into the fold again. Without much fuss, more and more of the dismissed individuals were reintegrated into the academic community, especially after denazification subsided at the end of the 1940s. In the young Federal Republic people wanted to forget, forgive, and close ranks. This was true not least in the universities.[16]

This is not to say that the universities remained entirely the same. Mitchell G. Ash has distinguished several important processes that characterised the academic *Vergangenheitsbewältigung* (approx. 'coming to terms with the past') that occurred during the years following the Second World War. Though institutional changes took place in the late 1940s – such as the establishment of the Max-Planck-Gesellschaft for basic research (heir to the Kaiser-Wilhelm-Gesellschaft) and the Frauenhofer-Gesellschaft for applied research – universities and research institutes were primarily busy re-establishing the old order that had existed prior to 1933. Alongside this development, the history of each discipline under the Third Reich was reinterpreted so that these years appeared to be an entirely apolitical period, a time when pure science and scholarship prevailed. At the same time, though, the compromised concepts and methods associated with Nazism were quietly eliminated. They were replaced by a scientific vocabulary that was better adapted to the

---

15 Schildt & Siegfried, *Deutsche Kulturgeschichte*, pp. 54–57.
16 *Akademische Vergangenheitspolitik*, ed. by Weisbrod; Koch, *Die Universität*, p. 214.

political culture of the new era. When it comes to cognitive style and scholarly-scientific orientation, there were nonetheless strong veins of continuity running from the late nineteenth century to the early post-war period.[17] Thomas Etzemüller has spoken of 'a strange mixture of continuity with respect to content, methodological innovation, and political adaptation'. That is to say, no intellectual abyss opened up in 1945.[18]

At the end of the 1940s the ideological differences between the eastern zone and the three western zones increased, and in the academic world this phenomenon became very apparent indeed. Immediately following the conclusion of peace, when it was still not entirely clear what the final character of East German society would be, many younger academics had found employment in the Soviet zone. Hans-Georg Gadamer was among those who subsequently became best known; he was rector of Leipzig before actively moving towards the western zones in 1947.[19]

In Berlin, the ideological polarisation became especially obvious. In January 1946 the city's university had reopened, now again bearing the name of Universität Berlin. In his opening address, rector Johannes Stroux stressed that what lay ahead was a renewal of the internal and external character of the university. At the same time, he referred explicitly to Wilhelm von Humboldt and invoked him as a model, among other things through detailed quotations from the manifesto of 1809/1810. Then as now, he said, Germans found themselves in the greatest distress; but owing to idealism and humanism, they

---

17 Mitchell G. Ash, 'Verordnete Umbrüche, Konstruierte Kontinuitäten: Zur Entnazifizierung von Wissenschaftlern und Wissenschaften nach 1945', *Zeitschrift für Geschichtswissenschaft*, 43:10 (1995). Jan Eckel relates a story about Karl Brandi, a historian of the Middle Ages in Göttingen, who presented the lecture series 'The Middle Ages I' during the winter term of 1944–1945 only to continue with 'The Middle Ages II' in the winter term of 1945–1946. Eckel emphasises that this is an anecdote, and that one has to look at the larger patterns, as Ash does. See Eckel, *Geist der Zeit*, p. 89. It can be added that Brandi was an old man and that it was possibly too much to ask of him to come up with a new lecture series at the age of seventy-seven. He died in March 1946.
18 Thomas Etzemüller, 'Auf der Suche nach den "haltenden Mächten": Intellektuelle Wandlungen und Kontinuitäten in der westdeutschen Geschichtswissenschaft nach 1945', in *Die Rückkehr der deutschen Geschichtswissenschaft in die 'Ökumene der Historiker': Ein wissenschaftsgeschichtlicher Ansatz*, ed. by Ulrich Pfeil (Munich, 2008), p. 35.
19 Jean Grondin, *Hans-Georg Gadamer: Eine Biographie* (Tübingen, 2013).

had succeeded in establishing a new kind of university. Here was a source of inspiration and guidance.[20] During the initial post-war years, several suggestions were made to rename the university at Unter den Linden after Wilhelm and/or Alexander von Humboldt. Even so, it was not until February 1949 that the new official name became Humboldt-Universität zu Berlin, after both Humboldt brothers. During the intervening period the university had been transformed in a Communist direction, and the climate had become significantly harsher. In response to that development, oppositional students and teachers established a new university in the American sector in 1948. Through their choice of name, Freie Universität ('the free university'), they wished to safeguard academic freedom.[21]

The years of occupation, 1945–1949, were thus marked by conflicting forces and patterns of movement. On the one hand, it was a particularly eventful period in the history of the German university. It was a time of reckoning, soul-searching, and re-orientation. A number of professors were dismissed, even though many of them returned fairly soon. On the other hand, the early post-war years appear to be the era of unfinished reforms. The form and mission of the university remained intact; the work on renewing it was only a torso.

The discussions about the university were connected with the long German tradition of reflecting on the basic academic issues, but they were also a part of the profound examination of the nation's history that was conducted after Nazism. What may seem to have been a limited exchange of opinions about the university was in point of fact intertwined with greater issues to do with the future of Germany. The university was still what Barbara Wolbring has called a centre for national identification ('Zentralort nationaler

---

20 Reimer Hansen, 'Von der Friedrich-Wilhelms- zur Humboldt-Universität zu Berlin', in *Geschichte der Universität Unter den Linden: Sozialistisches Experiment und Erneuerung*, ed. by Jarausch, Middell, & Vogt (Berlin, 2012), pp. 109–23.
21 Hansen, 'Von der Friedrich-Wilhelms- zur Humboldt-Universität zu Berlin'; Jarausch, Middell, & Vogt, *Geschichte der Universität Unter den Linden: Sozialistisches Experiment und Erneuerung*; Siegward Lönnendonker, *Freie Universität Berlin: Gründung einer politischen Universität* (Berlin, 1988); *Die Freie Universität Berlin 1948–2007: Von der Gründung bis zum Exzellenzwettbewerb*, ed. by Karol Kubicki & Siegward Lönnendonker (Göttingen, 2008).

Identifikation'). This was particularly true of the educated bourgeoisie who still dominated public life. The debate about the university became a point of crystallisation of sorts for the conflicts of the first post-war years.[22] Questions about the foundations of the university were not raised in an intellectual vacuum. In several studies, historian Axel Schildt has stressed how important Christian, conservative thought patterns were for the formation of the landscape of ideas in early post-war West Germany. Instead of affirming temporary trends and impulses, many Germans during the late 1940s and early 1950s put their trust in timeless, supra-individual values which often originated in a classic western tradition. It was as if the Nazi disaster had given rise to a mistrust of the immediate past that was transformed into a mistrust of the immediately contemporaneous.[23]

This reference to the West (*das Abendland*) can be traced in a renaissance both for a humanistic ideal of *Bildung* and for ideas about natural law.[24] The rediscovery was also a way of overcoming the expanding sense of crisis. It was not just a matter of the immediate crisis, the material and humanitarian distress, but of modernity itself as a state of crisis. Technological and natural-scientific developments had rocked society as a whole to its foundations and undermined the stable order. The hope was that a reactivation of permanent values would be able to create a new foundation.[25]

It was not least in this context that great hopes were tied to the university. The academic institutions were assigned a special spiritual task, an ability to administer and refine what was best in the German tradition. But the reconstruction of the university also meant that promises of a new future were kindled in a more general sense.[26]

---

22 Wolbring, *Trümmerfeld*, pp. 5–6.
23 Axel Schildt, *Zwischen Abendland und Amerika: Studien zur westdeutschen Ideenlandschaft der 50er Jahre* (Munich, 1999); Axel Schildt, *Moderne Zeiten: Freizeit, Massenmedien und 'Zeitgeist' in der Bundesrepublik der 50er Jahre* (Hamburg, 1995); Schildt & Siegfried, *Deutsche Kulturgeschichte*.
24 Schildt & Siegfried, *Deutsche Kulturgeschichte*, pp. 54–67.
25 Christina Schwartz, 'Erfindet sich die Hochschule neu? Selbstbilder und Zukunftsvorstellungen in den westdeutschen Rektoratsreden 1945–1950', in *Zwischen Idee und Zweckorientierung: Vorbilder und Motive von Hochschulreformen seit 1945*, ed. by Andreas Franzmann & Barbara Wolbring (Berlin, 2007).
26 Schildt & Siegfried, *Deutsche Kulturgeschichte*, p. 54.

The literature on the university during the years of occupation is not insignificant. A number of works are available that deal with individual universities and aspects of the reform efforts of the allies. But there are few comprehensive studies of this time, and even fewer that deal specifically with the Humboldtian tradition. The most important investigation in this area is without doubt Barbara Wolbring's monumental *Habilitation* thesis about the early post-war debates about the university. She demonstrates how rich and varied the discussion on the role of the university and the meaning of *Bildung* was during these years. By doing so, she emphatically refutes an idea that existed in earlier research: that the years of occupation had been characterised by a vacuum in scholarly-scientific self-understanding. It is true that several of the ideas that had flourished during the previous fifty years had lost their attraction or legitimacy, but opinions as to which direction the future should take were many. One group may be said to have worked for a kind of return of Humboldt's ideas. However, the ideals they associated with him, and the question of how those ideals were connected to the older German tradition, remain unclear; Wolbring's analyses do not focus on these issues.[27]

Nevertheless, a widespread idea features in scholarly literature to the effect that Humboldt and his ideals experienced a renaissance after 1945. It is said that there was a 'noticeable return to Humboldt's ideas' and that leading professors were engaged in an 'evocation of Humboldtian ideals'.[28] Several outstanding experts on modern German university history share the same picture of this period. Sylvia Paletschek writes that in the discussion on the university, 'the

---

27 Wolbring, *Trümmerfeld*. See also my discussion of the book: Johan Östling, 'Rezension zu: Wolbring, Barbara: *Trümmerfeld der bürgerlichen Welt. Universität in den gesellschaftlichen Reformdiskursen der westlichen Besatzungszonen (1945–1949)*', in *H-Soz-Kult*, http://www.hsozkult.de/publicationreview/id/rezbuecher-21761 (11 March 2014) (accessed 15 February 2016).

28 Peter Uwe Hohendahl, 'Humboldt Revisited: Liberal Education, University Reform, and the Opposition to the Neoliberal University', *New German Critique*, 38:2 (2011), 161; Corine Defrance, 'Die Westalliierten als Hochschulreformatoren (1945–1949): Ein Vergleich', in *Zwischen Idee und Zweckorientierung: Vorbilder und Motive von Hochschulreformen seit 1945*, ed. by Andreas Franzmann & Barbara Wolbring (Berlin, 2007), p. 39; Bernd Weisbrod, 'Dem wandelbaren Geist: Akademisches Ideal und wissenschaftliche Transformation in der Nachkriegszeit', in *Akademische Vergangenheitspolitik: Beiträge zur Wissenschaftskultur der Nachkriegszeit*, ed. by Bernd Weisbrod (Göttingen, 2002), p. 26.

return to the "German" or "Humboldtian" idea of the university [became] a central topos', using Freiburg historian Gerd Tellenbach as an example.[29] Konrad H. Jarausch, in a survey of the West German university system, contends something similar but develops his line of argument further. He claims that 'the postwar chaos prompted a return to *Humboldtian rhetoric* as an uncompromised tradition', but that this once inspiring vision 'had rigidified into a ruling discourse'. By re-employing a rhetoric where *Bildung* was a word with favourable connotations, the universities also returned 'to the problems of elitism, arrogance, and apoliticism', continued Jarausch. One consequence of this was that West German universities were plagued by a 'Humboldt syndrome' during the post-war period which made much-needed democratisation and reform more difficult.[30] Ralph Jessen talks about 'the post-war renaissance of the rhetoric of *Bildung*' and demonstrates with several examples how the future was sought via a return to classic New Humanist ideals. In the incipient Cold War, moreover, he sees a looming conflict over who had a right to the German heritage. West German academics and East German academics alike claimed that they alone held the heritage of the Humboldtian tradition in trust.[31]

On the other hand, Dieter Langewiesche is among those who are less inclined to speak of a return to a Humboldtian rhetoric. He has examined 142 German rector's speeches from 1945 to 1950 and found that Humboldt is mentioned on seven occasions only. It was above all in Berlin that the Prussian educational reformer was referred to; in the rest of the German-speaking area, the talk was rather of a German university model.[32] Christina Schwartz has also analysed a large number of rector's speeches from the years of occupation, and she concurs with Langewiesche's conclusion: Humboldt was very rarely mentioned. In contradistinction, many rectors referred back to older academic mottoes (such as '*Bildung*

---

29 Sylvia Paletschek, 'Die deutsche Universität im und nach dem Krieg: Die Wiederentdeckung des Abendlandes', in *Der Zweite Weltkrieg und seine Folgen: Ereignisse – Auswirkungen – Reflexionen*, ed. by Bernd Martin (Freiburg och Berlin, 2006), p. 243.
30 Jarausch, 'The Humboldt Syndrome', pp. 35–38.
31 Jessen, 'Zwischen Bildungspathos und Spezialistentum', pp. 364–67 and 379.
32 Dieter Langewiesche, 'Das deutsche Universitätsmodell und die Berliner Universität', in *Mittendrin: Eine Universität macht Geschichte*, ed. by Ilka Thom & Kirsten Weining (Berlin, 2010), p. 26; Dieter Langewiesche, 'Humboldt als Leitbild?'

durch Forschung', '*Bildung* through research'), and emphasised that the university had a mission of character formation.[33]

The presence of the Humboldtian tradition in the early post-war era debate on the university thus remains insufficiently explained. In order to seek out more profound answers, it is necessary to analyse the most important contributions and investigate how these were related to older German ideals of the university. In this context, it is vital to determine who dominated the debate in the early post-war years. As in West German society at large, an older generation born during the first decades of the German Empire again stepped forward after 1945 and assumed positions of power. Students and younger academics, who had supported Nazism to a considerable extent during the Third Reich, were not allowed to leave their mark on the early post-war period. On the contrary, there were great fears that the younger generation would not allow themselves to be converted to democracy.[34]

However, it was not just the high average age of the participants that gave the debate a special quality. The more elaborate and ambitious contributions came almost exclusively from the mandarins. In Nazi Germany, many of them had – passively or actively – supported the regime; but there were also those who remained at a distance from political power and who were able to step on to the academic stage again after the end of the war. It was this group of mainly older professors from the humanities who played a leading role in the university debate in the wake of the war. Natural scientists and medical researchers were largely absent. The mandarins' claim to be spokespersons for a greater cause lived on in the years after 1945, and that gave their contributions to the debate a distinctive character.[35]

At the same time, it is essential not to adopt posterity's understanding of the mandarins in an uncritical manner. During the 1960s, the mandarins were accused of having wanted to bring back a conservative university.[36] This claim can be problematised. In order

---

33 Schwartz, 'Erfindet sich die Hochschule neu?'.
34 Jaimey Fisher, *Disciplining Germany: Youth, Reeducation, and Reconstruction after the Second World War* (Detroit, 2007); Wolbring, *Trümmerfeld*, pp. 41–123; Sean A. Forner, *German Intellectuals and the Challenge of Democratic Renewal: Culture and Politics after 1945* (Cambridge, 2014).
35 Krohn, 'Intellektuelle und Mandarine', pp. 64–69; Jessen, 'Zwischen Bildungspathos und Spezialistentum', p. 364.
36 Hohendahl, 'Humboldt Revisited', 162.

to understand their ideals, it is necessary to see the debate of the early post-war period against the background of the university's history in the Third Reich. Research from the most recent decades has shown how a large percentage of academics enlisted in the service of the regime and lent ideological support to Nazi policies. In terms of their own self-understanding, however, scholars and scientists had seen themselves as neutral experts who were exclusively knowledge providers. At the same time, it is obvious that Nazism was not anti-modern in the sense of its being opposed to science and scholarship. Pioneering research could be combined with traditional methods of teaching and authoritarian principles of government.[37]

The mandarins who contributed to the debate on the university following the Second World War had thus experienced how the scholarly-scientific institutions had been used, directly or indirectly, by the Nazis during the preceding years. It had never been a matter of an absolute *Gleichschaltung* ('a forcible bringing into line'), but it was certainly a brutal violation of any thought of academic freedom. These experiences were very much alive during the latter half of the 1940s and would come to characterise the discussion.

In what follows I will concentrate on three of the most influential figures in the post-war debate on the university: philosopher Karl Jaspers, historian Gerhard Ritter, and Germanic philologist Werner Richter. All were older mandarins and all had had similar generational experiences: they were born in the 1880s, they had been professors of the humanities during the 1920s, and they had opposed Nazism in different ways. At the same time, their lives between 1933 and 1945 had turned out very differently. While Jaspers and Ritter had stayed in Germany and lived in a kind of internal exile, Richter had fled his native country and spent the war years in the United States.

Karl Jaspers and the rebirth of the university

Jaspers was undeniably a key figure during the years following the end of the war. In speeches, articles, and books he explained in great detail how the university should be vitalised and what the idea of the university should look like after the great catastrophe. In an exchange of views with Romance philologist Ernst Robert Curtius, he was even called 'a Wilhelm von Humboldt of our time'.[38] Jaspers's

---

37 See Chapter 3.
38 Quoted in Mark W. Clark, *Beyond Catastrophe: German Intellectuals and Cultural Renewal after World War II, 1945–1955* (Lanham, MD, 2006), p. 73.

impact on the university debate was enhanced by the fact that during these years, he emerged as a general moral authority in a country that needed moral stature and guidance more than anything else. There is reason to devote special attention to this man.

Karl Jaspers was born in Oldenburg, Lower Saxony, in 1883 and grew up in a well-to-do banking family. After studying law for a couple of terms, he switched to medicine and acquired a doctorate from Heidelberg in 1908 on the basis of a dissertation in psychiatry. Supported by Max Weber and Wilhelm Windelband he orientated himself towards psychology, a subject that was still considered part of philosophy at this time, and in 1913 he published the epoch-making *Allgemeine Psychopathologie*. Jaspers's scientific orientation was decided when, at the beginning of the 1920s, he transferred from a professorship in psychology to one in philosophy. During the interwar period he published several major works that formed the basis of his existential philosophy.[39]

For a long time, Karl Jaspers was the emblem of the apolitical mandarin. The advance of the Nazis did not wake him up; even after the seizure of power he dismissed National Socialism as an operetta. Nevertheless, it was not long before he became aware of how thoroughly the new masters disliked him. In 1933 he was removed from his positions of academic leadership, in 1937 he was forced to take early retirement, and in 1943 he was banned from publishing. Jaspers's sin was not that he had opposed the regime. His crime was that he had refused to divorce his Jewish wife.[40]

During the war years in Heidelberg, the Jaspers family constantly lived under the threat of deportation. On several occasions, they managed to escape at the very last minute. In spite of the persistent worry and intellectual quarantine, Jaspers continued his work in philosophy. To him these difficult years simultaneously meant that he had time for deliberation and that he could devote himself to reflecting on his own and his nation's development. On the basis of his own experiences, he developed ideas about what had caused the German catastrophe and how the Germans could rise again. About a month before the end of the war, he wrote in his diary,

---

39 Suzanne Kirkbright, *Karl Jaspers: A Biography: Navigations in Truth* (New Haven, 2004); Hans Saner, *Karl Jaspers: In Selbstzeugnissen und Bilddokumenten* (Reinbek bei Hamburg, 2005); Kurt Salamun, *Karl Jaspers* (Würzburg, 2006).
40 Kirkbright, *Karl Jaspers*; Saner, *Karl Jaspers*.

8 Karl Jaspers

The rebirth of the university

'Whoever survives this must choose a task to which he will devote himself for the rest of his life.'[41] Karl Jaspers's task came to be the restoration of the intellectual honour of Germany, and during the second half of the 1940s he was involved in several major trials of strength. He felt that the post-war period demanded more than detached observation and abstract thought. As a philosopher, he had to break with the apolitical line of German tradition and formulate a message that reached wider groups and was more influential. In short, he had to take his social responsibility seriously. One important channel became *Die Wandlung*, the monthly journal that Jaspers began publishing in the autumn of 1945 together with, among others, Dolf Sternberger, a journal that was guided by the watchwords humanism, freedom, and spiritual renewal.[42] In the controversial book *Die Schuldfrage* (1946) Jaspers engaged with the moral responsibility for the German crimes, thereby providing one of the most important contributions to German soul-searching directly after the war. A few years later, in 1949, he published a work on the history of philosophy, *Vom Ursprung und Ziel der Geschichte*, in which he introduced the concept of *Achsenzeit* ('axial age') in order to characterise the simultaneous emergence of new ways of thinking in Europe and Asia from the ninth to the third centuries BC.[43]

Jaspers's basic conviction was that a genuine recovery for Germany presupposed a genuine examination of German history. It was not possible to naïvely revert to a pre-Nazi condition. Nor was it possible to imagine such a thing as a clean break with the past. What was required was a historical balance sheet, a summary of the assets and liabilities of the German nation. However, true rebirth was also conditional on utilising what was good and edifying in the German heritage. Universities had a crucial role to play in a spiritual – and, by extension, political – renaissance. If Germany was to rise again, Germans would have to put their trust in the university.[44]

---

41 Quoted in Saner, *Karl Jaspers*, p. 51.
42 Ralf Kadereit, *Karl Jaspers und die Bundesrepublik Deutschland: Politische Gedanken eines Philosophen* (Paderborn, 1999); Clark, *Beyond Catastrophe*.
43 Karl Jaspers, *Die Schuldfrage: Ein Beitrag zur deutschen Frage* (Zürich, 1946); Karl Jaspers, *Vom Ursprung und Ziel der Geschichte* (Munich, 1949).
44 Kadereit, *Karl Jaspers*; Clark, *Beyond Catastrophe*; Jennifer M. Kapczynski, *The German Patient: Crisis and Recovery in Postwar Culture* (Ann Arbor, 2008).

During the initial post-war years, in particular 1945–1946, Jaspers kept returning to the fate of the university. In a large number of talks, essays, and journal articles, he produced variations on the same theme: it is of crucial importance to Germany that the university regains its strong position. At the end of the war, he also finished *Die Idee der Universität* (1946), the most detailed exposition on the nature and purpose of the university published during the early post-war years. Jaspers's book from 1923 had had the same title, but in the preface – dated Heidelberg, May 1945 – he emphasised that the new work 'is not a second edition, nor is it a revision, but a new draft based on the experiences of the last two horrible decades'.[45] Barbara Wolbring points out that Jaspers's text became an important point of reference in a wider discussion during the years following the end of the war, when a common idea was that the rebirth of the university had to begin in the native, New Humanist-idealist tradition. In this way, he made himself the interpreter of a significant current among the professors of the time.[46]

Die Idee der Universität is an important document for understanding Jaspers's comprehensive view of science and scholarship, education, and university. In this 123-page book, he moves from the abstract to the concrete: it begins with theoretical reflections on the nature of science and scholarship, then deals with the function of the university, and finally discusses questions about politics and economics. In the preface to the book Jaspers emphasised, in a concentrated form, ideas about the German university to which he returned and which he developed further in other contexts over the following years. The future of the university depended on a renewal of its original idea, he wrote. For half a century it had been in a period of decline, and finally the deepest downfall had occurred. Re-establishing the university was a critical issue for the whole of German culture, argued Jaspers. It had to be done by reaching back to the older tradition while at the same time transforming it.[47]

For a recreation of Jaspers's vision about how the university could be vitalised and how this rebirth was connected to an interpretation of German history, it is not enough to simply examine his book. Other texts from the same time, primarily a couple of the speeches

---

45 Karl Jaspers, *Die Idee der Universität* (Berlin and Heidelberg, 1946), p. 5.
46 Wolbring, *Trümmerfeld*, p. 425.
47 Jaspers, *Die Idee* (1946), p. 5.

he delivered that were later printed, provide both a broader and a more profound representation of his ideas.[48]

Towards a vitalisation

Two months after the end of the war, in August 1945, Jaspers delivered an address when Karl Heinrich Bauer took over the task of being Heidelberg University's elected rector and teaching there began anew. This speech would later be printed in its entirety in the first issue of *Die Wandlung* under the title 'Die Erneuerung der Universität'. The concept *Erneuerung* should not be understood in the literal sense of 'renewal', but in the sense of vitalising or injecting new life into the university; it is related to rebirth and renaissance.[49]

In this speech, Jaspers presented his vision of the university. He set the tone from the very outset: this was a great day for the university. After twelve years, the university was once more able to elect its own rector; what was now being witnessed was a new beginning. The core of the university had, despite everything that had happened, remained intact. In spite of the Nazis' destruction, in spite of their interference with research and tuition, there were professors and students who had held their own. And because the scholarly-scientific spirit had not been suppressed, the university could now be revived. Those who should be thanked for this, continued Jaspers, were the occupying powers. Their forbearance and perhaps even assistance were a prerequisite for the ability to rebuild the university.[50]

'The new beginning of our university cannot, however, merely consist in connecting on to the conditions that existed before 1933', Jaspers declared in a significant turn of phrase. Too much had happened; the disaster had had too deep an impact. In order to find a new foundation upon which to build, Jaspers felt that Germans had to search their true past: the native region, the native country, the lines that led back to Kant, Goethe, Lessing, and other major figures.[51] It was in this spirit that Jaspers felt the university should

---

48 Several of these speeches and texts have been collected in Karl Jaspers, *Erneuerung der Universität: Reden und Schriften 1945/46*, ed. by Renato de Rosa (Heidelberg, 1986).
49 Jaspers, *Erneuerung der Universität*, p. 293.
50 Karl Jaspers, 'Erneuerung der Universität', *Die Wandlung*, 1 (1945/1946), pp. 95–96.
51 Ibid., pp. 96–97.

be rebuilt. He hoped that the autonomy and the external structures could live on, and also that the students would return and that the conditions for research and tuition would be similar to those that had existed before. But none of this would entail any renewal. Instead, he declared:

> This renewal can really only come about through the work of individuals, through researchers and students, in the community that is made up of their intellectual lives. This community must be guided by the immortal idea of the university, an idea where research and tuition are each other's servants, where academic freedom is a condition for the responsible independence of individual teachers and students, where the purely scholastic is rejected as well as isolating specialisation, and where the unity of the sciences will instead develop in lively communication and intellectual struggle.[52]

The renewal, Jaspers argued, would be apparent through the tone it set in seminars and institutes; it would appear in publications and textbooks. And still there was as yet no common ground upon which to build. The idea of the university had not yet come truly alive again.[53]

Jaspers then applied a historical perspective. In the beginning the university was a unity, he reminded his audience. The three faculties were to serve the basic needs of humanity: the theological the salvation of the soul, the legal the social order, and the medical the well-being of the body. In Jaspers's eyes, it was an abomination when this unity was lost during the second half of the nineteenth century. On the one hand, knowledge was dispersed and mixed with unscientific elements. This development attained its maximum potency during the Nazi era. On the other hand, the loss of unity led to an inability both to deal with the genuine forces of the time, especially technology, and to see how these affected the totality. Renewal had to originate in the past, Jaspers emphasised, partly by extending the university's mission to include all parts of existence, partly by re-conquering the idea of the unity of science. Maybe a new technological faculty should be established, and the faculty of philosophy once again be joined together into a single whole.[54]

There were thus several components in Jaspers's idea about a vitalisation of the university. First, it had to do with safeguarding

---

52 Ibid., pp. 97–98.
53 Ibid., p. 98.
54 Ibid., p. 103.

the scholarly-scientific spirit that had survived the Nazi barbarism. Jaspers claimed that the core of the university was sound, and in doing so he referred to the well-known metaphor that Carl Heinrich Becker had formulated during the 1920s: the German university was 'im Kern gesund' ('healthy at the core').[55] Second, it was important to restore unity; the university could not be an aggregate of vocational training schools and specialist fields.[56] Third, the university had to deal with current problems, not least the role of technology in society, and expand its mission. Last but not least, Jaspers's vision about *Erneuerung der Universität* was closely connected to his understanding of the history of the university. His historiography could be discerned in different speeches and texts during the early post-war period. The most coherent narrative emerged in a speech he delivered in Heidelberg in January 1946. With this address, he initiated a series of lectures by renowned German academics that had the goal of contributing to democratic renewal. The title of the lecture, 'Vom lebendigen Geist der Universität', testified to his belief in a living tradition.[57]

'The university is ancient', Jaspers began his historical exposition. It was an institution whose idea had its conceptual roots in ancient Greece. The university of the Middle Ages had been European, and it had left behind remarkable structures of ideas; but this old university is as distant from us as it is admirable.[58]

Jaspers next trained his gaze on the German area and sketched the development of the university from the Reformation onwards, dividing it into three consecutive stages. *The Protestant university*

---

55 Axel Schildt, 'Im Kern gesund? Die deutschen Hochschulen 1945', in *Vertuschte Vergangenheit: Der Fall Schwerte und die NS-Vergangenheit der deutschen Hochschulen*, ed. by Helmut König, Wolfgang Kuhlmann & Klaus Schwabe (Munich, 1997); Markschies, *Was von Humboldt*, p. 18.
56 He developed these and other aspects of an idea of scholarly-scientific unity further in other writings, not least in Jaspers, *Die Idee* (1946), pp. 37, 43, and 75–76.
57 Jaspers, *Erneuerung der Universität*, pp. 294–95. The title of the lecture referred to a well-known inscription on the Heidelberg university building, 'Dem lebendigen Geist' ('To the living spirit'), formulated by literary historian Friedrich Gundolf during the time of the Weimar Republic. In the Third Reich it was replaced by the motto 'Dem deutschen Geist' ('To the German spirit'), only to be restored to its original wording after 1945.
58 Karl Jaspers, 'Vom lebendigen Geist der Universität', in Karl Jaspers & Fritz Ernst, *Vom lebendigen Geist der Universität und vom Studieren: Zwei Vorträge* (Heidelberg, 1946), pp. 224–25.

had the aim of fulfilling the state's need for clerics and officials. In comparison with the mediaeval university, the universities of the sixteenth and seventeenth centuries represented intellectual limitations.[59] During the eighteenth century, *the classically-humanistic university* came into being. There students liberated themselves and sought out those teachers who had something to offer them. A German-educated bourgeoisie emerged. Scholarship and philosophy became a common concern. Kant, Fichte, and Schleiermacher outlined an idea of the university, and Humboldt found a practical structure that was realised in the establishment of the university in Berlin. The basis was made up of the freedom of research and education – but also their inseparability. Humanism became the foundation of *Bildung*, and the university enjoyed a high prestige in public life.[60]

What Jaspers called *the modern university* originated in the middle of the nineteenth century. Following the March Revolution of 1848, positivistic science and practical realism emerged victorious. At the same time, criticism developed against the fossilised Prussian university, formulated most sharply by Nietzsche. It was clear that the most significant incentives to fresh thought no longer came from inside the university.[61] Its representatives said that they were willing to preserve the old idea, without, however, putting much force behind the words. They developed no principle of their own, and they did not safeguard the unity of the university. Students flocked to the university, the number of professors rose, and a mass university took shape. The level of admission requirements was lowered, teaching became more instrumental, and specialisation increased, Jaspers summarised. The result was that philosophical ideas were crowded out. No one assumed responsibility for the overall view.[62]

According to Jaspers, much of the best in the German cultural tradition derived from the university. This was true of its most original contribution, Protestantism, and only in Germany were the main world-class historical philosophers – Kant, Hegel – simultaneously professors. All this was already apparent by the 1920s.[63] But what followed was of a completely different kind than what Jaspers had expected. A violent political incursion toppled the university.

---

59 Jaspers, 'Vom lebendigen Geist', p. 225.
60 Ibid., pp. 225–26.
61 Ibid., pp. 226–27.
62 Ibid., p. 228.
63 Ibid., pp. 228–30.

The rebirth of the university

Rectors and deans still existed in name, but they were appointed by the National Socialists. Almost completely without resistance, the university and academics capitulated. All the lofty ideals – truth, scholarship, ethics – were left to be defended by individuals, according to Jaspers.[64]

The result, he continued, was that in 1933 the university lost its dignity. For this reason a new university was now required, this time under different conditions and with new tasks. Because one thing had become especially clear during the past twelve years: those who directed the sharpest criticism against the spiritual poverty of the modern university were the Nazis. For this reason, it could be said that the strong sympathy which their criticism encountered in itself demonstrated the extent of the intellectual destitution at the modern university. It is true, Jaspers admitted, that the Nazis seemed initially to wish to change the university in a welcome direction – closing the gaps between the faculties, a synthesis of the sciences, a philosophical seriousness as a basis for all scholarship, a receptiveness to the people and to grand history. All this sounded excellent, and many people allowed themselves to be seduced. But nothing came of it. In point of fact, the Nazis accomplished the very opposite of what they had promised. Instead of insight came empty words, instead of a worldview there followed a hotchpotch of disconnected propositions taken out of context. The intellectual class realised that the bell tolled for them, while the untalented and characterless saw their chances.[65]

Jaspers ended his historical summary with the following statements: 'The Nazi rape has ended. Free research can expand again. Open conflicts of opinion are again allowed and advisable.'[66] After this Jaspers turned to his contemporaries and asked what their common task would be. In an important passage, he stated the following:

> As a consequence of our fidelity to the Humboldtian era we do not strive for a radical transformation of the forms of our institutions; instead we imagine a kind of conservative revolution. But we also know this: we cannot re-establish the, to us, classic German university era. All those social, political, and personal conditions which set the terms for our contemporary existence, our knowledge, and our skills, are different.[67]

---

64 Ibid., p. 230.
65 Ibid., pp. 231–32.
66 Ibid., p. 232.
67 Ibid., p. 232.

That is to say, the university could certainly resume its traditional tasks; but a lot had changed, and the old world of *Bildung* had crumbled. It was not possible to continue on the old track as if nothing had happened. One important task was to construct an image of German history that established connections to the good heritage. This required research; merely re-evaluating earlier views was not a viable approach.[68]

Christoph Markschies has noted that historical opinions about the university can be fitted into either a model of decadence or one of progress. In the former case, one often finds elements of a golden-age myth.[69] This is undeniably the case with Jaspers. His ideal, the classically-humanistic university, gradually took shape during the eighteenth century; but it had begun to be undermined from the middle of the nineteenth century, and with Nazism came the real catastrophe.

At the same time, it is obvious that Jaspers was in two minds about this historical development. On the one hand, he wanted to return to the classic German university and resurrect its ideals. This was a part of the best of the German tradition. On the other hand, he realised that it was impossible to turn back. Far too much had changed.

Karl Jaspers and the Humboldtian tradition

In Jaspers's vision of a vitalisation of the German university, the Humboldtian tradition seemingly played a minor role. In *Die Idee der Universität*, he only mentions Wilhelm von Humboldt a handful of times; and in other texts as well, direct references to the Prussian educational reformer are very infrequent. On one occasion, however, when discussing the relationship between the university and the state, Jaspers quotes Humboldt without an explicit reference: 'The state must always remain aware of the fact that the matter in itself is greatly improved if the state does not interfere.' It is notable that passages with this essential meaning can be found in Humboldt's 'Über die innere und äussere Organisation der höheren wissenschaftlichen Anstalten in Berlin' (1809/1810), although this exact phrasing does not occur there.[70]

---

68 Ibid., pp. 232–35.
69 Markschies, *Was von Humboldt*, p. 20.
70 Jaspers, *Die Idee* (1946), p. 103. Cf. Humboldt, 'Über die innere und äussere Organisation', p. 257.

Humboldt was of course a well-known name for Jaspers, but he did not stand out as one of the main figures in the German university tradition. Kant and Weber were considerably more important sources of inspiration, and Jaspers repeatedly refers to them. Nor was the foundation of the Berlin university in 1810 a milestone in his historical understanding – naturally enough, as Jaspers traced the origins of the classically-humanistic university to the eighteenth century. A unified idea about the university was created around 1800 by philosophers such as Kant and Schleiermacher, and Humboldt is given credit for having put the new university into practice. That is to say, he does not appear as either a thinker or a synthesist.

Against this background, it is hardly surprising that Jaspers found no reason to evoke Humboldt. But in his efforts to vitalise the German university, Jaspers nevertheless looked back to what others have come to associate with Wilhelm von Humboldt. Many of the ideals that Jaspers associated with the classically-humanistic university belong to the Humboldtian tradition. One example of an ideal to which he often returned was the conviction regarding the unity of science. Like many others in the university debate during the years of occupation, Jaspers was concerned about academic specialisation and opposed to the fragmentation of knowledge.[71] Ultimately, this had to do with the educational mission of the university. In *Die Idee der Universität*, he argued for an idea of scholarly-scientific unity in several places. It is true, he wrote, that students come to the university in order to prepare for a profession. But they expect more than that. The university must represent the unity of science, and on the basis of this unity students should be able to form their own worldview.[72]

In addition, Jaspers repeatedly safeguarded 'die Verbindung von Forschung und Lehre' ('the connection between research and tuition'). He opposed the forces that wanted to create a separation and turn the university into a pure research institution. It could not be denied that a good teacher was not necessarily a good scholar or scientist; but unless research and teaching were united, the students could not come into contact with the genuine knowledge process.[73]

Academic freedom, with its many facets, was another major topic where Jaspers worked within a classic German tradition without referring to Humboldt to any noteworthy extent. The very opening

---

71 Wolbring, *Trümmerfeld*, pp. 453–61.
72 Jaspers, *Die Idee* (1946), pp. 37, 43, and 47.
73 Ibid., pp. 41 and 47.

of *Die Idee der Universität* emphasises 'die Freiheit der Lehre' ('the freedom to teach') and 'die Freiheit des Lernens' ('the freedom to learn') as fundamental principles. Jasper returned to this issue several times: researchers shall themselves formulate their tasks and find their way to solutions; students shall have the freedom to choose the direction of their studies themselves.[74] Closely connected to this aspect of academic freedom was the university's relationship to the state. Jaspers acknowledged that the university depended on the state; but in the wake of the Second World War, it seemed self-evident to emphasise a demand for freedom from the state.

The brief mention of these three ideals – the unity of science, the combination of tuition and research, and academic freedom – does not amount to a sufficient characterisation of Jaspers's philosophy of the university. However, these examples from his most central writings illustrate how he worked within the classic German tradition and wished to inject new life into it. With hermeneutic terminology, it can be said that Jaspers attempted to actualise the classically-humanistic heritage, but without actually referring to Wilhelm von Humboldt. He felt that the university to some extent had to be adapted to the modern world, and he emphasised the necessity of strengthening academic freedom after the violent rule of Nazism. He also knew that breathing new life into the German university called for arduous, long-term effort, with little hope of immediate success. But it was the only option.[75]

Karl Jaspers was a prominent figure in the university debate of the early post-war years. But other people also provided important contributions to the discussion. The main issues for them, as for Jaspers, were how the German university could be revived and what direction it should have. And like Jaspers, many people referred to the tradition of the German university, but evaluated it differently and drew dissimilar conclusions. Two examples, Gerhard Ritter and Werner Richter, help to provide a more multifaceted picture of the exchange of ideas during the post-war years.

Gerhard Ritter and the liberal university

Gerhard Ritter, born in 1888, was one of the leading historians of his generation. He mainly devoted himself to the great political,

---

74 Ibid., pp. 111–12 and 277–78. See also Jaspers, *Erneuerung der Universität*, p. 277.
75 Jaspers, 'Erneuerung', p. 105.

The rebirth of the university

military, and religious figures in history. As early as 1925, Ritter had become a professor at Freiburg im Breisgau; he remained faithful to that university, also during the Third Reich. The appreciation that he, with his national-conservative leanings, had initially felt for the new Nazi regime had soon turned into aversion. During the Second World War, he showed his resentment towards Nazism by joining resistance bodies such as the Freiburger Kreis and the Confessing Church. Directly after the end of the war, he wholeheartedly committed himself to rebuilding the demolished German academy. He took part in the local denazification of Freiburg, contributed to the intellectual examination of the origins of Nazism, and played an important role as the first post-war chairman of the German society of historians.[76]

Gerhard Ritter also supplied an elaborate contribution to the discussion on the idea of the university. In October 1945, he delivered the opening address in the first series of public lectures in Freiburg following the war. His contribution was entitled 'Die Idee der Universität und das öffentliche Leben' ('The idea of the university and public life') and would later be printed.[77] It was not the first time that he reflected on the conditions of academic life. In 1936, he had written a volume on the history of Heidelberg University; and he was well acquainted with the Prussian reforms at the beginning of the nineteenth century after having written a biography of Karl vom und zum Stein.[78]

Ritter began where so many other people who spoke out during this time tended to begin: with the Nazi disaster and the search for a new, permanent order. He called for a reliable guide that could indicate a general direction. Society should turn towards science and scholarship in order to get its bearings and understand the deeper causes of the present circumstances. However, the questions were

---

76 Christoph Cornelißen, *Gerhard Ritter: Geschichtswissenschaft und Politik im 20. Jahrhundert* (Düsseldorf, 2001), pp. 371–456; Klaus Schwabe, 'Change and Continuity in German Historiography from 1933 into the Early 1950s: Gerhard Ritter (1888-1967)', in *Paths of Continuity: Central European Historiography from the 1930s to the 1950s*, ed. by Hartmut Lehmann & James van Horn Melton (Cambridge, 1994).
77 Gerhard Ritter, *Die Idee der Universität und das öffentliche Leben* (Freiburg im Breisgau, 1946).
78 Gerhard Ritter, *Die Heidelberger Universität: Ein Stück deutscher Geschichte. Das Mittelalter (1386–1508)* (Heidelberg, 1936); Gerhard Ritter, *Stein: Eine politische Biographie* (Stuttgart, 1931).

many. In his pursuit of answers, Ritter wrote a historical exposition on the idea of the university in Germany.[79]

In quick strokes, Ritter sketched the emergence of the German universities during the Middle Ages. For a long time, at least until the seventeenth century, they were primarily institutions of the intellect, he pointed out. The philosophical-philological missions were more important than professional training programmes. In the absolute monarchies and principalities, however, the practical elements multiplied and pure science and scholarship were pushed back. The dazzling development of the natural sciences during this era primarily occurred outside the university. The same was true of the philosophy of rationalism. There was too little scope for real research at the small, semi-clerical German provincial colleges. In addition, the enlightened rulers of the time showed little understanding for the autonomy of the university or for science and scholarship as an end in themselves.[80]

For Ritter, the centuries of Reformation and confessional division were a period of decay in the history of the university. It was therefore among the major achievements in German intellectual history, he argued, when the university was able to rise from the ruins through internal renewal. He spoke of a 'German movement' which allowed the nation to step forward as the leader of the Occident at the intersection of the eighteenth and nineteenth centuries. Although 'the reform of the German universities during the era of Humboldt, Fichte, and Schleiermacher was merely one aspect of the greater movement', we should today, more than ever, be grateful for this renewal. At the very hour of political defeat, these thinkers achieved a cultural revival of a most unusual kind. One significant result was the reinforcement of scholarly-scientific autonomy, not by means of a reconnection with mediaeval ideals but through the birth of a new kind of university, *the humanistically-liberal state university*.[81]

Ritter next developed a long argument about the features that had characterised the new university. His argumentation was distinctly historical rather than analytic or systematic. It adhered to a chronological line and in many ways took the form of a narrative. From this presentation, it is possible to distinguish the main principles that he believed to be characteristic of the humanistically-liberal university.

---

79 Ritter, *Die Idee*, pp. 3–4.
80 Ibid., pp. 4–6.
81 Ibid., pp. 6–7.

First and foremost, Ritter emphasised the importance of academic freedom. The German university of the nineteenth century was, according to him, characterised by autonomy, in contradistinction to the system of centrally governed state schools that Napoleon had introduced in France. This was a golden age of German science and scholarship, when the free university was allowed to interact with a protective state. Today – yes, especially today – there was hence every reason to reflect once more on the basic principles of the humanistically-liberal university.[82]

Ritter found the first signs of the new university programme in Wilhelm von Humboldt's *Ideen zu einem Versuch, die Grenzen der Wirksamkeit des Staates zu bestimmen* from 1792. For a long time, this little text was considered to be a subversive pamphlet in German-nationalist circles; but after the failures of the totalitarian system, many people realised that the activities of the state had to be surrounded by boundaries. For Humboldt, Ritter pointed out, a limitation of the power of the state could liberate repressed energies, and for this reason his liberal state philosophy was closely linked to his educational vision. Here character formation was at the centre, not professional skills. The goal was free scholarly-scientific research conducted by teachers and students acting together, Ritter stated, referring explicitly to Humboldt.[83]

Even so, the question was whether academic freedom did not risk leading to abstractions and sophistry. 'Of course', replied Ritter, 'freedom for science and scholarship is, like all other freedoms, a very dangerous thing'. But if true scholarship was to be produced, one must dare to take that risk; for as soon as there was interference from the state, the sole results were tendentious writings and propagandistic speeches; this had been proved once and for all by the National Socialist state.[84] On the basis of the Nazi experience, Ritter thus argued that academic freedom had its price, but that one had to be prepared to pay it. The examples to the contrary, taken from the Third Reich, were deterring. The person who provided Ritter with arguments for this cause was Humboldt the liberal.

In his interpretation of the humanistically-liberal university, Ritter connected academic freedom with two other fundamental principles. The first was the pure search for knowledge. Here, too, he referred

---

82 Ibid., p. 7.
83 Ibid., pp. 7–9.
84 Ibid., pp. 9–10.

to Humboldt and claimed that science and scholarship formed 'an eternally ongoing process' whose sole purpose was knowledge. According to Ritter, the state must be aware that such science and scholarship could only be realised by free, creative forces, not on the basis of commissions from the state. It could only flourish 'in Einsamkeit und Freiheit' ('in solitude and freedom').[85]

The second principle had to do with the educational mission of the university. The prominent figures of German idealism had never doubted that free scholarly-scientific work contributed to the formation of character. 'Only science and scholarship which come from the inner depths of the mind and which are cultivated only at those depths can contribute to the transformation of character. [...] [The state and mankind] are both [...] concerned with character and conduct', he quoted approvingly from Wilhelm von Humboldt's memorandum of 1809/1810. Consequently, Ritter concluded, the humanistically-liberal university was not at all cut off from society and its practical needs. On the contrary, the objective, independent search for truth would provide young people with precisely those qualities they needed to work in the service of the public.[86]

Thus far, Ritter had emphasised those ideals that formed the basis of the classic German university. But how well had they been realised? he wondered. The first generations after 1810 were still influenced by impulses from the new educational centres, and he described the following decades as a happy period. 'Never before and never since have German academics played a greater part in social life than between 1815 and 1866', he wrote.[87] Against this golden age, Ritter placed what he himself had experienced during the previous decades: anarchy, individualism, egotism. This decay did not, however, begin under the National Socialists but in the latter part of the Bismarck period.[88]

Two golden ages thus emerged in Ritter's account of modern German history: the first was a time of intellectual innovation in the period around the year 1800, the second came in 1815–1866 when harmonious conditions existed and the humanistically-liberal state university could be realised.[89] During the latter half of the nineteenth century, this unity dissolved. Idealistic philosophy lost its grip on

---

85 Ibid., pp. 7–9.
86 Ibid., pp. 11–12. The quotation comes from Humboldt, 'On the Spirit', 245.
87 Ritter, *Die Idee*, p. 11.
88 Ibid., pp. 11–12.
89 Ibid., pp. 12–13.

The rebirth of the university 115

the human sciences and was replaced by naked materialism and positivism. Academic *Bildung* distanced itself more and more from Humboldt's ideals of comprehensiveness, declared Ritter.[90] After the First World War the situation became more and more critical. Many people experienced a crisis for science and scholarship, and there were resounding calls for total reform of the university. The generation of students that returned from the battlefield was disappointed that the university could not offer any guidance on the major issues of life. Even so, the great reform failed to materialise; and when the universities were filled with women and the unemployed, the university was in danger of becoming an educational facility for the masses. 'And yet the close connection between research and tuition, the very element that forms the distinctive characteristic of our German university as well as its primary advantage, necessarily presupposes close cooperation between teachers and students', declared Ritter, thereby establishing a link to one of the great topics in the Humboldtian tradition: the combination of research and education.[91]

The university had not been in step with the times. It could not offer what young people needed during the 1920s. At the same time, overpopulation was a risk that could result in levelling. This entire threat of superficiality became that much more tangible through the vehement attempts of the Nazis to turn the universities into propaganda centres for a racist worldview. Fortunately, Ritter pointed out, the party's attacks on German scholarship were not carried out with so much determination that the university structure was destroyed. He characterised most representatives of the party as half-educated and claimed that they had failed to make the great majority of professors into spokesmen for a racial ideology. At the same time, he was anxious to avoid whitewashing and pointed out that adaptation to the regime's line varied from subject to subject. Most members of the academy assumed an apolitical stance, however, safeguarding the neutrality of science and scholarship. Ritter's conclusion was that the Nazis, in spite of everything, had had a limited effect on actual research at the universities.[92]

---

90 Ibid., p. 14.
91 Ibid., pp. 14–16.
92 Ibid., pp. 14–17. In another contribution, Ritter had maintained that the German professors who had kept to science and scholarship had not been compromised under the Third Reich. Using himself as an example, he showed that it had been possible to resist the regime even as an academic. See

But what will happen today, when everything is in ruins after the dreadful destruction? Ritter asked. In spite of colossal difficulties, he set his hopes on the German university. He was well aware of the hate and contempt that the Nazis had spread around the world, but the road to rehabilitation for the German people was via science and scholarship. We will not succeed using cheap popular science or the mere transmission of knowledge, Ritter argued. What was required was genuine research for truth and pure scholarship.[93]

Towards the end of the address, Ritter returned to his conviction that science and scholarship must have no other master than pure truth. The university and its lecturers did society the most good when they devoted themselves to their main task, non-utilitarian research. Genuine, pure science and scholarship turned away from the immediately practical needs of life, but that did not mean that they were alienated from life. It was undoubtedly true that academic studies and exams were not guarantees of reason and insight, Ritter rounded off, once more reminding his readers of the previous twelve years. But he wanted to believe, just as Wilhelm von Humboldt once did, that a scholarly-scientific education also had an ethical effect on young people, that it built a free, independent character.[94]

Gerhard Ritter's address had been genuinely historical in nature. He had taken the Middle Ages as his starting-point and moved in a great arc up to the modern era. Like Jaspers, he had searched the past in order to find the sources that could breathe new life into the German university; but to a greater extent than Jaspers, he referred to Wilhelm von Humboldt in the process. It was obvious that Ritter had read Humboldt and saw him as one of several people who contributed to reforming the German university at the beginning of the nineteenth century. He drew special inspiration from Humboldt the young liberal and from his ideas about imposing limitations on the state. A few years after the end of the Second World War, Ritter emphasised academic freedom in the form of university autonomy.

Gerhard Ritter, 'Der deutsche Professor im Dritten Reich', *Die Gegenwart*, 1:1 (1945), pp. 23–26. Readers encountered a diametrically opposed view in Max Weinrich, *Hitler's Professors: The Part of Scholarship in Germany's Crimes against the Jewish People* (New York, 1946). This book, written by a German-speaking writer of Jewish descent, promoted the thesis that German scholarship had supplied the ideas and technologies that had resulted in and justified the Nazi bloodbath.
93 Ritter, *Die Idee*, pp. 17–18.
94 Ibid., pp. 21–27.

Only by safeguarding freedom of research and the pure quest for knowledge could the university regain its importance.

Christoph Cornelißen, Gerhard Ritter's biographer, has emphasised that Ritter's political ideas during the early post-war period were characterised by an increasingly dominant conviction: an absolute and uncontrollable power must at all costs be prevented from ever again gaining dominion over Germany. From this perspective, his ideal of the university can be regarded as an application of a general ideological principle.[95] Samuel Moyn has captured another characteristic of Ritter's from the same period. In 1948, Ritter gave a lecture in Basel about the history of human rights, a lecture which formed the basis of a long article printed the following year in *Historische Zeitschrift*. Moyn demonstrates how Ritter pursued the origins of human rights in specifically Christian sources. He maintains that the Freiburg professor thereby wished to reconstruct and defend a Christian Western identity in a period of crisis and loss.[96]

These examples thus show that Gerhard Ritter attempted to find a new basis to build upon following the Second World War, and that these attempts took place in more than one sphere. As a prominent historian and conservative intellectual, he employed an approach amounting to a revival through the re-establishment of connections. Ritter united a fervent German patriotism with a conviction that Germany must be inspired by the Christian West. His commitment to truth-seeking and unlimited academic freedom, embodied by Wilhelm von Humboldt and the young Berlin university, should be seen in this light.

Ideals under review

Werner Richter (1887–1960) adopted a completely different perspective on the history and future of the German university. He was at bottom a German philologist and had been a professor in this subject at both Greifswald and Berlin. In addition, he had been active in the Prussian Ministry of Culture and Education between 1920 and 1932. As a close colleague of Carl Heinrich Becker, he had participated in drawing up the university reforms of the Weimar Republic. However, because of his Jewish descent he had been forced

---

95 Cornelißen, *Gerhard Ritter*, pp. 416–18.
96 Samuel Moyn, 'The First Historian of Human Rights', *The American Historical Review*, 116:1 (2011).

to leave Germany in 1933 and had eventually ended up in the United States. During the 1940s, he came into contact with several American academic environments and was profoundly influenced by them. Richter returned to his native country a couple of years after the end of the war, initially as a professor and then as rector in Bonn. His interest in the politics of the university and educational policy had by no means faded, and he took an active part in the public debate on research and higher education. During the 1950s, Richter played a decisive role in re-establishing the links between West Germany and the international academic community, not least as the first president of the German Academic Exchange Service (Deutscher Akademischer Austauschdienst, DAAD).[97]

Werner Richter made his first important intervention in the postwar debate on the German university with a lecture that he gave in Marburg and Munich in the summer of 1948. The following year, he had this lecture published under the title *Die Zukunft der deutschen Universität*. In just over forty pages, he developed his ideas about the German tradition and what the future should hold. Like so many others who engaged with these issues after the Nazi disaster, Richter sought means through which to renew the German university. However, his convictions were partially dissimilar, being influenced by his American experiences and by a critical attitude towards elements in the German heritage.[98]

Accordingly, Richter began his lecture by emphasising that his points of departure were different. If the German university wished to lead German culture, the way it had done during the nineteenth century, it had to support a new programme, he declared. But it was inconceivable to talk about its future without considering its magnificent history prior to 1933.[99]

Like Jaspers and Ritter, Richter consequently devoted a significant part of his lecture to a historical exposition on the German university. 'The German university of the nineteenth century [...] has idealistic philosophy and classical-romantic literature to thank for its inception', began Richter. An idealism that reached transcendental heights developed on German soil. 'For Humboldt and his circle, serving scientific truth was a religious experience', wrote Richter,

---

97 Lothar Reinermann, 'Richter, Werner', *Neue Deutsche Biographie* (Berlin, 1953–), vol. XXI (2003), pp. 539–40.
98 Werner Richter, *Die Zukunft der deutschen Universität* (Marburg, 1949).
99 Ibid., pp. 6–7.

meaning that there was a kind of religious motive for Humboldt, Fichte, Schelling, and Schleiermacher in their desire to establish a connection between research and tuition as a fundamental principle of the German university. According to him, Humboldt wanted teachers and students to serve science and scholarship and unite in a joint quest for truth.[100]

At the same time, the scholarly-scientific idea that supported what Richter called *the humanistic university* was characterised by a kind of individualism. Richter pointed out that for Humboldt there was no tension between academic research and life, the way there could be today. In the humanistic university a synthesis of scholarship, *Bildung*, and life would be generated, as it had once been in ancient Greece. Today one could look back at these early nineteenth-century dreams with an elegiac wistfulness, contemplating a time that united bright optimism, faith in human greatness, and a romantic desire for all aspects of life. 'Humboldt himself appeared to have become an archetype for this ideal of life', wrote Richter.[101]

Although Richter cast yearning glances at the humanistic university of the early nineteenth century, he was convinced that it belonged to a bygone age. He reminded his readers that the first phase in the history of the humanistic university had soon reached its end.[102] Leopold von Ranke, professor of history in Berlin between 1825 and 1871, represented the following period. The unifying idea, which had been so central to the founders of the humanistic university, now faded into the background. Gradually – argued Richter – two scholarly-scientific tendencies took shape: a politically-moralising historiography and the expansion of the natural sciences.[103]

In contrast to many of his contemporaries, Richter did not believe that the scholarly ideals of the past provided answers to contemporary questions. What could Humboldt's dreams offer to those who struggled in an age of machines, industry, and overpopulation? he asked.[104] It was obvious that Richter believed that the ideal of the humanistic university which he associated with Humboldt had had its day. Now, with the war a fresh memory, it was difficult to uphold a classically individualistic university ideal. The old idea of

---

100 Ibid., p. 9.
101 Ibid., pp. 9–10.
102 Ibid., pp. 10–11.
103 Ibid., pp. 12–13.
104 Ibid., pp. 13–14.

the full-scale university, *universitas litterarum*, was still cherished by an older generation; but according to Richter, it increasingly came across as a fiction. Richter made comparisons with developments in America, and he predicted that the ideal of professional training would inevitably become predominant in Germany, too. He saw how many young people turned against the old ideas of *Bildung* and affirmed the practical needs of life.[105]

At this point, almost half-way through his text, Werner Richter stopped and asked himself why he had spent so much time on a historical survey. The answer he gave was that Germany at the moment found itself in a political, economic, and intellectual vacuum, and that it must orientate itself guided by those beacons that did exist. Consequently, it was necessary to take a stance with respect to the past, but at the same time Richter was convinced that it was not enough to look back to the nineteenth century. The German university needed to develop a new concept of *Bildung*, a concept that was in harmony both with the political and cultural demands of the time and with the older tradition.[106]

Richter's contention was that one had to listen to criticism of German science and scholarship coming from the Anglo-Saxon countries. This criticism, he said, could be summarised in four points. The first had to do with a tendency on the part of Germans towards pedantry, and the second with their inclination towards the absolute and the abstract. The third critical point had to do with German education being focused so exclusively on preparing students for research and not for the needs of practical life. Finally, the British and the Americans criticised the German university for being incapable of promoting what Richter called 'social life'; it could support individualists and geniuses, but not people who worked in and for collective society.[107] Richter had obviously been permanently influenced by the vitality and innovation that he had encountered during his years of exile on the other side of the Atlantic. Instead of stubbornly holding on to their native ways of thinking, Germans should learn from Anglo-Saxon criticism without automatically imitating American or British models.[108]

Next, Richter turned to the issue of what the educational programmes at the German university should include. His fundamental

---

105 Ibid., pp. 14–17.
106 Ibid., pp. 17–18.
107 Ibid., pp. 19–21.
108 Ibid., pp. 22–24.

The rebirth of the university

opinion was that these programmes had to be based on a respect for Western values.[109] In 1945 he had published a book in English in the United States, *Re-Educating Germany*. Referring to this book, Richter reminded his readers that in it he had promoted an educational ideal aimed at making 'good Europeans' of the Germans. Now, a couple of years later, he was still completely convinced that an orientation toward Western Europe and America was right for Germany. Science and scholarship could contribute to recreating a sense of Western affinity after the discord of the world war. One requirement was that academic scholars, in particular humanists, liberated themselves from their national narrow-mindedness and instead contributed to increasing knowledge of other countries.[110]

Consequently, Richter supported a variant of the *Abendland* ('Occident') rhetoric. However, in contrast to many others who wanted to see a German rapprochement with the West, he had a great deal of respect for the United States and not just for Europe.[111] Like many others, he held up dechristianisation as a major problem. On the one hand, secularisation had led to nihilism and relativism; on the other, it had produced secular utopias. A prerequisite for a real comeback for Europe and Germany was, according to him, a return to religion. Above all, he called for a living Christianity, with Christian humanism as an element of a general cultural and ethical rebirth in the West.[112]

In addition to the necessity of a renewed Western affinity, Richter drew attention to another issue of the greatest importance: Germans must, once and for all, genuinely embrace democracy. In future, democracy – in the sense of personal freedom, human rights, and human dignity – should permeate both politics and everyday life. Richter fully realised that democracy was only weakly rooted in German soil. That was all the more reason to mobilise all available forces for the cause of democracy, including the institutions of higher

---

109 Ibid., pp. 25–26.
110 Ibid., pp. 26–28. In *Re-Educating Germany* (Chicago, 1945), Werner Richter adopts a broad perspective on the German educational system and discusses both school and university, partly via comparisons between American and German circumstances. Towards the end of the book he pleads for 'a new ideal for German education' and states that the only way forward is the 'inclusion in a European, social, and Christian world order' (p. 187).
111 Moyn, 'The First Historian', 67.
112 Richter, *Die Zukunft*, pp. 32–39.

research and education. The university must under no circumstances be content with 'Betrachtungen eines Unpolitischen' ('Reflections of a non-political man', the title of a 1918 treatise by Thomas Mann), he wrote, using a well-known literary reference. It must open its doors to the world; it must promote freedom and social justice. Richter was astonished that it was precisely the German university that was so reluctant to involve itself in work geared to the benefit of society at large. The reason, he believed, was the close relationship between the state and the university. In the United States, academic institutions were happy to stand up for a basic democratic attitude in spite of their generally not being as bound to the state. In contrast to Germany, where the extensive academic freedom had, if anything, isolated the university from the rest of society, Richter believed that American universities had managed to simultaneously promote individual freedom and common responsibility. That was a healthy combination which had strengthened American democracy.[113]

In summary, Richter clearly attached great importance to the Berlin university, on whose initial phase he looked back with a degree of admiration. At the same time, he was utterly convinced that the professors in Germany could not rest on their laurels. When it came to a future programme for the German university, he drew his inspiration from completely different sources than did the other two mandarins. Richter did not emphasise the classic German principles about *Bildung*, academic freedom, or the combination of research and education; instead, he argued for the importance of opening up to the world and supporting democracy. Here, his experiences of having been a German Jew in North American exile shone through.

The mandarins and the Humboldtian tradition

The idea of the university was thus under debate during the years following the Second World War. As we have seen, a number of prominent professors and rectors felt called upon to formulate generally applicable thoughts about the role of research and higher education in post-war Germany. Few, if any, offered a particularly detailed plan for how the university of the future should be organised, however; the more precise outlines usually remained unclear. On certain points they disagreed as to how the German heritage should

---

113 Ibid., pp. 28–30.

The rebirth of the university

be managed and what conclusions should be drawn from the Nazi disaster. But seen from a wider perspective, they were all part of the same academic culture of knowledge. They took up positions on common issues and adapted themselves to the same rhetorical pattern.

There was great unanimity to the effect that the German university must undergo a rebirth. The title of Karl Jaspers's lecture, *Erneuerung der Universität*, could have served as a title for many contributions. After the Nazi period of decay, it was necessary to breathe new life into an old institution. With respect to how the university should be vitalised, it is possible to discern two main paths. One led back to classic German culture, a kind of 'Heimkehr zu Goethe' ('return home to Goethe'). Germans should look inwards and backwards in order to find the rich literary, musical, and philosophical heritage that was part of Germany's history. The other path brought the Germans back into contact with the Christian West. Europe became an *Ersatzvaterland* during the early post-war years, Carlo Schmid pointed out: 'After the collapse of 1945 there were virtually only Europeans in Germany.'[114] The two paths could cross or even be incorporated into a greater whole: by embracing the classic German tradition, Germans understood that they were in the deepest sense a civilised European nation that obviously belonged in a Christian *Abendland*. This was what Jaspers, Ritter, and Richter argued, though the last of these three had a more ambiguous attitude to the German line of thought.[115] It was as if the appropriation of the language and eternal values of idealism were especially attractive after the military and moral bankruptcy of Nazism. The classic German university ideal became a dream of a more dignified and stable order.

Views on how the university could be regenerated were closely linked to a person's opinion on what had historically constituted the modern German university. For Jaspers, the core of the university remained intact in spite of all the destruction that had been caused by Nazism and the world war. In order to remedy the current miserable state of affairs, Jaspers argued for a return to the rich sources of idealism and the German Enlightenment. He imagined that an actualisation of this heritage would be edifying, spreading an atmosphere of creativity while simultaneously contributing to the

---

114 Quoted in Führ, *The German Educational System*, p. 4.
115 In other texts from the same time, 1946–1947, Jaspers displayed an even more unambiguous allegiance to Europe and the Western heritage. See, for instance, 'Europa der Gegenwart' in Jaspers, *Erneuerung*.

re-establishment of the idea of a comprehensive university. Ritter's faith in the capacity of German science and scholarship was also fundamentally undiminished. He did not develop sophisticated ideas about how the university should be reconstructed, but he emphasised that the only way in which it could regain its vigour was by means of concentration on true research and scholarship. To a greater extent than the other two, Werner Richter, for his part, questioned just how sound the German university tradition really was. To him vitalisation meant an opening up, in geographical terms towards Europe and the United States and in political terms towards true democracy. A prerequisite for the university having a bright future was that it became involved in working for the general benefit of society and did not close its doors to the world around it.

One characteristic of the early post-war years is that the ideas about the university that were formulated at that time did not appear most clearly in the form of detailed visions for the future. One explanation for this is that they were expressed in the form of lectures, often as opening or inaugural addresses. Several of them would later be published in the universities' series of publications or in one of the many journals that flourished at the time. The rector's speech was the most frequent format, but many of the more elaborate lectures were given by other professors. On the other hand, few extensive expositions on the university were published during these years. Jaspers's *Die Idee der Universität* was a notable exception.[116]

A more fundamental explanation of the lack of well-developed thoughts about the future was that the discussions were historically orientated. The lines of argument advocating a certain kind of university ideal rested on a backward-looking presentation. This distinctive feature had to do with the fact that the leading actors were academics who were trained historians. However, even more than this, the situation must be viewed in the context of the late 1940s desire to intellectually examine the ways of thinking that had led to Nazism. The historian in the trio, Gerhard Ritter, allowed almost the whole of his lecture to become a recapitulation of the phases of the German university, but Jaspers and Richter also supported their theses with historical analyses.

---

116 That these lectures could attract attention is illustrated by, for instance, Karl Vossler's contribution. The first edition of his *Forschung und Bildung an der Universität* (Munich, 1946) soon sold out, and a second edition had to be printed. See Wolbring, *Trümmerfeld*, p. 326.

At the same time it is striking that none of these scholars dealt with the recent past, for instance by attacking the many Nazis who had populated German universities. Rather, there was a tendency to tone down the effects of Nazism on academic institutions and to gloss over issues that could lead to a conflict in the present. The contributions to the university debate were philosophical or historical in nature, not openly political. Like many other intellectuals during the initial post-war years, these scholars primarily attempted to create an over-arching understanding of the German catastrophe.[117]

And here the depths of history opened up. If the horizons of expectation were limited during the years immediately after the war, the range of experiences was all the greater. Reflections on the idea of the German university were underpinned by centuries-long retrospective reviews. In this respect, Jaspers and Ritter adhered to a historiography that was close at hand. Both turned back to a golden age that was now only a faded memory. They saw how the decay of the German university had begun during the latter part of the nineteenth century. Therefore, neither of them saw 1933 as an absolute turning point, but rather as a culmination. But with the Nazis the university finally lost all its dignity, all of its original spirit. In addition, their experiences of Nazism reinforced their convictions about the value of unlimited academic freedom and the blessings of pure truth-seeking.

However, an interesting difference between them has to do with what they foregrounded as the exemplary era in German university history. Jaspers praised 'the classically-humanistic university' and placed its origin in the eighteenth century. In the middle of the nineteenth century this was replaced by 'the modern university', a pejorative term for Jaspers. In contrast to Jaspers, Ritter ascribed critical significance to the shift from the eighteenth to the nineteenth century. That shift, according to Ritter, was decisive for the creation of a new kind of university, 'the humanistically-liberal state university', with Wilhelm von Humboldt as a prominent figure.

Jaspers and Richter are illustrative of two different attitudes to the Humboldtian tradition. Jaspers's nominal relationship to Humboldt was, as we have seen, weak. He mentioned Humboldt's name on a few occasions, but did not evince any familiarity with

---

117 In other contexts, however, they intervened more obviously in the denazification process. By writing a very critical report, Jaspers, for instance, contributed in a very real sense to Heidegger's inability to retain his appointment after 1945. See Ott, *Martin Heidegger*, pp. 313–23.

his texts and attributed significantly greater importance to other thinkers. Conversely, Ritter referred to several of Humboldt's works and quoted approvingly from them. He repeatedly emphasised the heritage from Humboldt and argued for its continued importance. This was especially true of the university's independence from the state, but also of the importance of a close connection between research and teaching. Generally speaking, Humboldt and the humanistically-liberal state university were incarnations of an ideal of a harmonious unity between practical and theoretical reason, between truth-seeking and *Bildung*.

The historical course of events was at the centre of Werner Richter's line of argument as well, but he put a different emphasis on it and drew dissimilar conclusions. Like Jaspers and Ritter he went back in time, highlighting the 'New Humanist university' of the early nineteenth century. Richter identified a pronounced individualism in its predominant ideal of *Bildung*. This would eventually become disastrous for the German academy, because the inherent individualism distanced the German university from society at large. Richter's relationship to the Humboldtian tradition was hence ambivalent. He was attracted by the New Humanist idea of *Bildung* and scholarly-scientific ideals, but he was convinced that this was a bygone stage. In clear opposition to Ritter, but also to Jaspers, he did not advocate a return to a classic German university ideal. On the contrary, he promoted the idea that tradition had to be renewed through a democratisation of German universities and an overcoming of their national limitations.

In Richter's version of German university history, Wilhelm von Humboldt was a central point of reference. There was thus no self-evident connection between a nominal reference to Humboldt and an intellectual appreciation of (or favourable identification with) the Humboldtian tradition. Ritter referred fairly often to Humboldt, greatly valued the university ideal he associated with him, and advocated a renaissance for the dominant principles of this tradition. Jaspers rarely referred to Humboldt but maintained that the classic humanistic university in a modified form, adapted to contemporary times, could vitalise the German post-war period. Richter referred to Humboldt in appreciative terms and relatively frequently – but held the opinion that the Humboldtian tradition was antiquated and in certain respects even dangerous.

The differences between these three scholars can in many respects be explained by their varying experiences and dissimilar intellectual profiles. For Jaspers, his scholarly and practical activities during the early post-war period had to do with examining the German tradition and creating a new foundation upon which to build. He was anxious for both the German nation and the country's universities to find their places in a changed world. Ritter worked in a related way with a view to re-establishing German academic life, but with conservative overtones. He looked backwards in history and saw an unsullied national line which he now wanted to revive. Richter, with his experiences of exile, adopted a critical fundamental attitude and promoted a radical renewal based on an Anglo-Saxon model. These three thinkers hence fit into the general picture that Axel Schildt and others have drawn of the conceptual landscape of the post-war years; but one must also be aware of variations and nuances. With their different experiences and visions for the future, the three mandarins were thus also representatives of different intellectual and political positions in the late 1940s.[118]

The wider stage

Karl Jaspers, Gerhard Ritter, and Werner Richter all belonged within the *Geisteswissenschaften*; they were all well established, and they had already been professors during the Weimar Republic. While they were behind three of the most substantial contributions to the post-war debate on the university, there were of course other actors too. These actors also adopted a position with respect to the classic tradition, more or less associated with Wilhelm von Humboldt: Was it *im Kern gesund* or *im Kern verrottet* ('healthy or rotten at the core')? This was a question that engaged almost all of the leading academics.[119]

One particular group in the discussion about the university consisted of the rectors. Many of them were elderly humanities scholars, not infrequently shaped by the world of the early twentieth century. In a study of a large number of rector's speeches, Christina Schwartz has distinguished three overarching themes that characterised the initial period after the end of the war: general reflections on human culture, expositions on the current crisis, and ideas about the mission of the university.[120] All the rectors agreed

---

118 Jeffrey K. Olick, *In the House of the Hangman: The Agonies of German Defeat, 1943–1949* (Chicago, 2005); *Rückblickend in die Zukunft*, ed. by Gallus & Schildt. See also Moses, 'Intellectual History'.
119 See Jessen, 'Zwischen Bildungspathos und Spezialistentum', pp. 364–65.
120 Schwartz, 'Erfindet sich die Hochschule neu?', p. 47.

9 Oxford students around 1950

that the university had a crucial role to play. Similarly, they all agreed that the Third Reich had been a disaster and that it would be very difficult to restore the university that had existed prior to 1933. Many representatives of science and scholarship had a share in this guilt, the rectors admitted; but that was not the same thing as questioning the academic institution itself.[121]

Schwartz establishes that the rectors expressed a kind of desire for reform in their speeches. Because the universities had not been able to resist Nazism, it was necessary to transform them. This, however, was not primarily a matter of an internal transformation of hierarchies or organisational structures. What the rectors seized upon was the question of *Bildung*: how would the university be able to contribute to the formation of individuals who simultaneously possessed political judgement and a wide professional range? *Bildung durch Forschung* ('*Bildung* through research') was a leitmotif, supplemented by an ideal regarding the formation of character. *Universitas*, the original mediaeval ideal of the all-comprehensive university, was a kind of model for the rectors. They embraced a holistic idea in which individual academic subjects would engage in dialogue with one another and not remain separate. In this spirit, the students would not specialise but instead strive to obtain a comprehensive education that ultimately benefited society. However, the rectors rarely devoted much space to the question of how these university reforms should be realised.[122]

Karl Vossler is an illustrative example. He was a respected Romance philologist who had survived the Third Reich in spite of his anti-Nazism. In his twilight years, he became rector in Munich. In his inaugural speech in 1946, he said that the university had neglected its more fundamental mission of *Bildung* in favour of a narrower scholarly-scientific education even back in the Wilhelmian period. The ultimate consequences had been experienced during Nazism, when, for instance, physicians had allowed themselves to be enrolled in euthanasia programmes. Science and scholarship must not be isolated from society, was his conclusion.[123]

Another academic leader was law professor Hans Peters. During the period around 1930, he had worked under Werner Richter in the Prussian ministry of education and had devoted time to Carl

---

121 Ibid., p. 48.
122 Ibid., pp. 59–60.
123 Vossler, *Forschung und Bildung*; Wolbring, *Trümmerfeld*, pp. 326–27.

Heinrich Becker's university reform. During the war he had belonged to the conservative opposition against the regime, becoming a dean of the faculty of law in Berlin after 1945 and eventually rector in Cologne.[124] In an unusually critical set of reflections about the university, Peters argued that what was required was not simply a genuine break with Nazism but with the German tradition as such. So far, the re-inauguration of the German universities after the war had been carried out by way of a return to a Humboldtian basic idea, though that idea had arisen in a completely different social and cultural environment.[125] Against this stood the Marxist college with its focus on professional-occupational education. Peters was dismissive of both alternatives.[126] In spite of his attack on the tendency to relapse into old ideas, Peters's own suggestions contained many things that were in line with an older German university tradition. For instance, he repeatedly returned to the need for a vitalised concept of *Bildung* and a renewed combination of research and education.[127]

Vossler, Peters, and many of the rectors belonged to the mandarin class; and they pursued a tradition, established during the nineteenth century, of expounding on the idea of the university. In their evaluations of German university history, they placed their emphases differently and their opinions varied in respect of which conclusions should be drawn. At the same time many things united them, as becomes obvious when their views are compared with other positions held during the years of occupation.

One of the most vocal politicians on university issues was the lawyer Erwin Stein. He belonged to the left-Catholic wing of the Christian Democratic Party and was the minister responsible for culture and education in Hesse from 1947 to 1951. In many contexts, Stein strove for a democratic renewal of the German university system, not least by opening it up to other social classes than the bourgeoisie that had dominated it for so long. Students and politicians took an active interest in this issue, but not so many university professors. However, in other instances Stein had reason to engage with leading academics at close quarters. His view was that academic autonomy

---

124 Hans Peters, *Zwischen Gestern und Morgen: Betrachtungen zur heutigen Kulturlage* (Berlin, 1946); Ulrich Karpen, 'Peters, Hans Carl Maria Alfons', *Neue Deutsche Biographie* (Berlin, 1953–), vol. XX (2001), pp. 240–41.
125 Peters, *Zwischen Gestern und Morgen*, p. 65.
126 Ibid., p. 66.
127 Ibid., pp. 52 and 58.

The rebirth of the university

had to be limited, because the university had proved itself incapable of working for the good of society. In Nazi Germany the professors had betrayed their ideals, and after the war they had simply safeguarded their own privileges. But his criticism was more fundamental than that, and it was directed against the ideals that formed the very basis of academic freedom. In Stein's eyes, Wilhelm von Humboldt's ideas on the classically-liberal university were harmful. They had contributed to the neglect of social responsibility and to academic life having been cut off from society at large.[128]

Erwin Stein is an example of a politician who intervened in the academic debate about the idea of the university, combining analyses of the Humboldtian tradition with concrete suggestions. His historical examination could not match those of the leading mandarins, but his assessment of the classic German tradition was in line with those of, for example, Ritter and Peters.

Similar strains could be heard from the other side of the Atlantic. A sizeable number of German refugees had been employed at American universities, and they followed the reconstruction of the old country from their exile. Frederic Lilge had begun his studies in Germany, but from the mid-1930s he had been active in the United States. In 1948, he published the book *The Abuse of Learning: The Failure of the German University*. Lilge was an educationalist by profession, and against the backdrop of the great catastrophe he subjected the university to a thorough scrutiny. In his historiography, the eighteenth century was presented as a miserable period for the German university; but towards the turn of the century in 1800 came what he called 'the brief flowering of German humanism'. Humboldt stood out as one of the major facilitators. With idealism, however, embodied in Fichte, began what Lilge called a political misuse of the educational tradition. During the course of the nineteenth century, there emerged an alloy of idealistic abstraction and worship of science and scholarship that eventually turned into irrationalism and fascist mythology. The universities did not manage to resist the assault of unreason.[129]

Lilge's book had a patent affinity to Richter's contribution. Both men regarded German history from a shared American viewpoint. They had high opinions of Humboldt and the university that he had

---

128 Wolbring, *Trümmerfeld*, pp. 137–42, 275–78, and 379–85.
129 Frederic Lilge, *The Abuse of Learning: The Failure of the German University* (New York, 1948).

helped create. But unlike Richter, Lilge concentrated on a historical analysis, and he had few suggestions as to what the future should hold. In a wider perspective, it is possible to see how Lilge's study fitted into a critical line of thought in the historiography on modern Germany that developed among German researchers in American exile during the early post-war period. In the focus of their analyses were the trends and structures that had led Germany on to its fatal historical path. Lilge's book was never published in his mother tongue, and it probably influenced the Anglo-Saxon image of the German university more than it did the native German debate.[130]

Ambivalence toward the German university tradition could also find expression in other ways. The 'Blaues Gutachten', the above-mentioned reform proposal from 1948, contained a number of concrete suggestions regarding organisation, financing, exams, and so on. In addition, the document contained basic reflections on the nature and the fundamental ideals of the academic system. The commission agreed that a reform of the university was necessary. The university had not been able to keep pace with the transformations in society and had educated specialists rather than persons. Without reform, a new political disaster would be inevitable. This being said, the commission wanted to emphasise that the German university was the bearer of an old and 'im Kern gesunde[r] Tradition' ('tradition [that was] healthy at the core'). Every institution of such a kind had to be continually reformed; those who merely wanted to create something

---

130 Many of the leading American researchers on Germany had fled from the Third Reich. They might differ when it came to their ideological and scholarly orientation, but they were united in a critical attitude to the traditions in the German state and intellectual life that had supported Nazism. The basis for their interpretations of Germany's past was not infrequently a kind of unspoken idea of a unique path of German development. This was true of figures who were as different from one another as Franz Neumann, Hajo Holborn, Ernst Fraenkel, Leonard Krieger, Hans Rosenberg, George L. Mosse, and Fritz Stern. During the decades after 1945, several of these German-born researchers in exile published studies that anticipated the West German *Sonderweg* ('special path') debate of the 1970s and 1980s. Younger German researchers working at American universities were inspired by these interpretations. See Johan Östling, 'Tysklands väg mot moderniteten: Hans-Ulrich Wehler och *Sonderweg*-tesen', in *I historiens skruvstäd: Berättelser om Europas 1900-tal*, ed. by Lennart Berntson & Svante Nordin (Stockholm, 2008) and Udi Greenberg, *The Weimar Century: German Émigrés and the Ideological Foundations of the Cold War* (Princeton, 2015).

completely new risked killing the very essence of the institution. The commission pointed to the fact that the European university had trained the leading social classes ever since the Middle Ages, and that it still bore a living heritage of Christian humanism. 'The German university can be particularly proud of its characteristic tradition, derived from Humboldt, which embodies the unity and freedom of research and tuition in an exemplary manner', they wrote, maintaining that the upcoming reform had to safeguard this healthy core and promote further development in accordance with the requirements of the time.[131]

In spite of this professed allegiance to the German university tradition, the 'Blaues Gutachten' also contained critical reservations. It warned against blind faith in pure scientific thought. Academic studies risked leading to specialist knowledge only. In order to remedy this shortcoming a *studium generale* was recommended, a kind of general educational programme according to an American model whose ultimate purpose was to strengthen political democracy. Instead of a New Humanist concept of *Bildung* where individual studies of art, literature, and philosophy predominated, an ideal was emphasised where political science, economics, and sociology would strengthen democratic involvement. This socially orientated attitude had its proponents among German rectors and professors; but not a few of them, Jaspers being one, disliked seeing character formation give way to an education of citizens. Student associations also reacted unfavourably to the enlisting of the concept of *Bildung* in the service of political democracy. They welcomed the *studium generale*, but felt that it should promote independent scholarly-scientific thinking and a classically based idea of *Bildung*.[132]

The 'Blaues Gutachen' and the ideas about a *studium generale* illustrate the fact that there were several competing opinions regarding the concept of *Bildung* during the years of occupation. In a wider perspective one also has to ask how unique the German debate was, and whether there were contemporaneous parallels in other countries.

Many European universities had suffered badly during the Second World War. The rapid recovery after 1945 has been characterised by Walter Rüegg as 'one of the most astonishing post-war achievements'. At the same time, he notes that 'this phenomenon has only been partially studied'. The number of students at the universities

---

131 *Dokumente*, ed. by Neuhaus, pp. 290–91.
132 Wolbring, *Trümmerfeld*; Phillips, *Pragmatismus und Idealismus*.

increased significantly during the initial post-war years, and all across Western Europe higher education was considered to be a major issue in relation to the future – technologically, economically, and intellectually. Even so, radical changes of the academic system failed to materialise. In Italy and France, reconnections were made with the ideals of the interwar period. The same applied to many countries that had been under German occupation. In cases where the university became the subject of wider public scrutiny, for instance in the work of the 1945 Swedish parliamentary drafting committee on universities, this did not lead to a substantial transformation of the system. It would be at least another decade before a real discussion of reforms got off the ground.[133]

This, however, does not amount to saying that there was an absence of exchanges of opinion about the nature and fundamental mission of the university. On the contrary, the Germans seem to have been far from alone in discussing these issues in the wake of the war. It is true that Robert D. Anderson in his work on the history of British universities pointed out that neither of the world wars was a real watershed: between the turn of the century and the early 1960s, academic culture retained its social and intellectual character in all essentials. However, there had long been a conflict between advocates of utilitarian and free knowledge respectively. During the years prior to and during the Second World War, the idea of disinterested science and scholarship gained more adherents.[134] For example, in *Red Brick University*, the most influential publication about the university from the 1940s, Bruce Truscot argued for the importance of free research. He felt that this was being neglected, not least at the newer universities in the large English industrial cities. Truscot also eagerly promoted a vitalisation of the academic sense of community, partly with religious overtones.[135] Indeed, a pervasive spiritual undertone could be detected in the British university debate during the years following the Second World War. That undertone was especially apparent in philosopher Walter Moberly's *The Crisis*

---

133 Rüegg & Sadlak, 'Relations with Authority', pp. 74–76.
134 Robert D. Anderson, *British Universities: Past and Present* (London, 2006), pp. 113–24.
135 Bruce Truscot, *Red Brick University* (Harmondsworth, 1951). Bruce Truscot was a pseudonym for Liverpudlian Hispanic philologist Edgar Allison Peers, who published his book in two parts, in 1943 and in 1945, respectively, and in 1951 in an omnibus volume. See Anderson, *British Universities*, pp. 124–25.

of the University (1949). According to him the world was in a crisis, and the university had an obligation to deal with it. He defined the university as 'a community in pursuit of truth', but at the same time claimed that the cult of research and objectivity had led to a neglect of societal engagement.[136]

The comparison with Britain shows up both similarities and differences between the United Kingdom and Germany. On both sides of the English Channel, there was a strong idealistic undercurrent in the academic debate during the initial post-war years. At a time of spiritual crisis, it was felt that the university had a vital obligation. In both countries the debaters, who were mainly active in the humanities, felt that it was an essential task of the university to furnish moral and cultural education, not to provide practical skills. In contrast to the situation in the West German zones of occupation, a critical examination of the national tradition was not a key theme in the British discussion. Nor was the strong emphasis on academic freedom, in the form of a line of demarcation between state and university, anywhere near as marked in Britain. The British case underlines how interwoven the German discussions were with the greater national processing of the impact of Nazism following its demise.

Similarly, it is difficult to find an equivalent of the German examination of the university tradition in Britain. Systematic historical reflection on the origins of academic ideals and their importance for the future was a German speciality. However, during the early postwar period in Norway there were debaters who rejected the German university model (without mentioning Wilhelm von Humboldt by name). It was branded old-fashioned and conservative. In a country that had been under Nazi occupation from 1940 to 1945, Germanness in itself was a counter-argument. Prominent scholars from Oslo and Bergen promoted an Americanisation of the Norwegian university instead – in line with what Richter had advocated, but expressed in more categorical terms.[137]

The university reborn

This brief geographic survey indicates that the German debate had a distinctive character. It was exceedingly historical in nature, and it

---

136 Walter Moberly, *The Crisis of the University* (London, 1949), pp. 106–47.
137 Fredrik W. Thue & Kim G. Helsvig, *Universitetet i Oslo 1945–1975: Den store transformasjonen* (Oslo, 2011).

was so in two respects: partly because the coveted academic principles were drawn from the past and the arguments were supported by historical narratives, partly because many contributions referred – directly or indirectly – to older commentaries, primarily from the early nineteenth century or the interwar period. In addition, the German case was characterised by its intensity and extent. The debate was wide-ranging and passionate; the vitalisation of the university was seen as a decisive issue for the future of the nation. Finally, the divergence of opinion about the fundamental academic values was integrated into a greater national processing of the German catastrophe. Ultimately, the discussion had to do with how post-war Germany would overcome the calamities of history.

In all this, the Humboldtian tradition was of great significance. Regardless of whether Humboldt's name was mentioned, one can see how variants of a classic German university were used as an exemplary or dissuasive model. The historical argumentation hence provided the debaters with a rhetorical arsenal, but also with a point of orientation in a tumultuous period.

However, to evoke – as was done in several earlier studies – an image of a Humboldtian renaissance in the wake of the Second World War is simplistic. There was never anything akin to the Goethe cult which the Bard of Weimar inspired in connection with the bicentenary of his birth in 1949.[138] On the other hand, an idealistic pathos and an invocation of an older tradition did characterise the discussion about the university. None of the influential mandarins recommended that nineteenth-century ideals should be re-established without modification; they all said, in different ways and with differing emphases, that the university had to go through a process of rebirth. In this process Wilhelm von Humboldt and the young Berlin university was a source of inspiration, although certainly not for everyone.

Konrad H. Jarausch, one of the few scholars who have presented a comprehensive interpretation of the importance of the Humboldtian tradition after 1945, has claimed that the rhetoric of *Bildung* brought the university back to 'the problems of elitism, arrogance, and apoliticism'. A consequence of this was that West Germany has been haunted by what Jarausch called a Humboldt syndrome which prevented a democratisation of the university.[139]

---

138 Karl Robert Mandelkow, *Goethe in Deutschland: Rezeptionsgeschichte eines Klassikers: 1919–1982* (Munich, 1989).
139 Jarausch, 'The Humboldt Syndrome', pp. 35–38.

Jarausch's critical assessment is reminiscent of the 1960s accusations against those leading professors who after the war had remained silent about the academics' ideological support of Nazism, thereby placing obstacles in the way of democratic reform.[140] Peter Uwe Hohendahl, however, has warned about the dangers of too facilely appropriating the way in which the 1960s understood the early post-war period. Hohendahl asks whether Jaspers and his contemporaries adopted a conservative attitude and argues that we have to distinguish between different types of conservatism. According to his classification, the mandarins can be considered conservatives in the sense that they wanted to establish connections to a classic tradition; but they were not necessarily conservatives in the political sense, or in the sense of being opponents of change.[141] Above all, it is mandatory to get away from simple dichotomies of the 'conservative versus modern' type. The majority of the mandarins had experienced the research and educational policy of the Third Reich at first hand, where innovative investments in cutting-edge research were combined with traditional educational models and authoritarian academic governance. When they formulated their ideas on the university after 1945, they did not simply evoke a classic model. They also drew conclusions from their experiences of Nazism.

In a wider perspective the university debate of the early post-war period was linked to other major topics in the intellectual history of modern Germany. The theme of crisis was such a topic. Already during the Weimar Republic, a discourse of crisis had developed that to a very great extent included the university. After the heyday of the German Empire, German science had fallen into disrepute; but the academic crisis was also seen as a symptom of the serious crisis for all of classic modernity that many people experienced during the interwar years.[142] After the Second World War the crisis discourse appeared in different guises, and the question might be asked whether twentieth-century German university history could be written as a history of continuous crises.[143]

---

140 Moses, *German Intellectuals*, pp. 131–59.
141 Hohendahl, 'Humboldt Revisited', p. 162.
142 John, '"Not deutscher Wissenschaft"?'
143 Stefan Gerber et al., 'Einleitung', in *Traditionen – Brüche – Wandlungen: Die Universität Jena 1850–1995*, ed. by Stefan Gerber et al. (Cologne, 2009), p. 5; Paletschek, 'The Writing of University History', p. 154.

Another major theme was the masses. The fear that the university would become overcrowded existed as early as the nineteenth century. When this metaphor showed up during the early post-war period, for instance in Ritter, it was not, however, simply a matter of rising student numbers and a lowering of the level of knowledge. Rather, the criticism was connected to a conservative distantiation from mass society as such. In Friedrich Meinecke's oft-quoted book *Die deutsche Katastrophe* (1946) the origin of Nazism had, in a similar manner, been sought in the rise of the masses and their infatuation with power. The discussion on the mass university would continue throughout the post-war period.[144]

In her extensive study of the university debate during the years of occupation, Barbara Wolbring advances the thesis that restorative tendencies have been exaggerated in earlier research. The early post-war period cannot merely be described as a series of failed attempts at reform or as a return to older academic ideals. In the debates about the university that took place directly after the Second World War, new arguments and oppositional positions took shape that would in due course characterise the Federal Republic. She uses the debate on the meaning of the concept of *Bildung* as an example, but also the discussions that were held about the university as a socially closed unit, a stronghold of the bourgeoisie. The latter view was a criticism that would return with renewed vigour fifteen years later.[145]

However, my own findings do not support Wolbring's conclusion that the basic patterns of the West German university policy emerged already during these early years. At least when it comes to the contributions of the leading debaters, I find it difficult to be persuaded that she is right. Rather, both Wolbring's book and my investigation show how the discourse was shaped during a very specific phase in the history of modern Germany. The proposals that Jaspers, Ritter, Richter, and several others formulated during the early post-war period were anything but timeless; they were expressions of the experiences and ideals of a particular generation. These debaters sought a rebirth of the university, but what they witnessed was the swan song of the mandarins.

When discussions about the university flared up again in the early 1960s, a new generation had assumed power, and the focal

---

144 Friedrich Meinecke, *Die deutsche Katastrophe: Betrachtungen und Erinnerungen* (Zürich, 1946).
145 Wolbring, *Trümmerfeld*, pp. 12–13.

point had shifted. The main actors took a stand with respect to the place of the developing mass university in a modern, democratic, industrial society. They, too, posed questions about the freedom of research, the meaning of *Bildung*, and the orientation of studies against the backdrop of the German university tradition; but their answers were based on dreams of the future and notions of reality which belonged to another era.

5
Tradition under debate

During the final years of the 1950s, the period of actual reconstruction came to an end. Material standards had risen considerably, and the sombre, anxious atmosphere that was typical of the first half of the decade had given way to confidence in a brighter future. An artistic avant-garde broke with prevalent aesthetic principles; a public reckoning with Nazism gradually got under way; and a younger generation began to make itself heard in social debate. Many said farewell to the Adenauer era even before the ageing Federal Chancellor left his post in 1963. These years, c. 1957–1965, stand out as a comparatively distinct phase in West German post-war history, a phase that can be separated from the preceding and ensuing ones. 'Dynamic times' is a label given by historians to this period of just under ten years.[1]

In spite of the growth and spread of prosperity, there was a simmering discontent in many circles. One underlying cause was the incomplete democratisation. True, the parliamentary system had taken hold and been consolidated; but West German society was not seen as entirely democratic. More and more people made more and more insistent demands for *reform* – a keyword for the 1960s. Especially the younger generation did not feel at home in an order where older men held all the important positions of power. As an

---

1 *Dynamische Zeiten: Die 60er Jahre in den beiden deutschen Gesellschaften*, ed. by Axel Schildt, Detlef Siegfried & Karl Christian Lammers (Hamburg, 2000); Schildt & Siegfried, *Deutsche Kulturgeschichte*, pp. 179–244. Other important interpreters of the history of the Federal Republic use a similar vocabulary: In *Die geglückte Demokratie: Geschichte der Bundesrepublik Deutschland von ihren Anfängen bis zur Gegenwart* (Stuttgart, 2006), Edgar Wolfrum speaks of the 1960s in terms of 'dynamism and liberalisation' while 'transformation' and 'the euphoria of modernity' are keywords in Ulrich Herbert, *Geschichte Deutschlands im 20. Jahrhundert* (Munich, 2014).

ever-increasing number of people obtained first-hand experience of other Western countries, domestic standards and social structures were challenged. The demands for democratic reform came to be directed not least at the educational system.[2]

In her thorough study of reforms and revolts in the university world during the long 1960s, Anne Rohstock has presented a complex picture of this situation. She maintains that a strong sense of crisis spread during the period around 1960. There was a widespread belief that there was an alarming educational deficit, a *Bildungsnot*. According to this belief, West German science and scholarship were dysfunctional and incapable of living up to their ideals; this was considered to be particularly true of the university. That was something many people could agree on. In contrast, there were differing opinions about how the problem should be described, what the reason for this state of affairs was, and what solution would be the best one.[3]

When the Soviet Union launched the rocket containing the Sputnik 1 satellite in the autumn of 1957, this was not simply the beginning of the space race. In several Western countries, the launch triggered a self-critical discussion on technological and scientific capacities. People have spoken of a Sputnik effect that directly or indirectly incited educational debates and led to new investments. As far as West Germany is concerned, a new direction in research and educational policy could in any case be discerned during the final years of the 1950s. Higher education and advanced research were emphasised as crucial for Germany's ability to hold its own in international competition. The Cold War would not be won by soldiers but by the 'people who safeguarded their educational system most carefully', it was said in the debate. Influential politicians from different camps rallied in support of similar slogans. The Christian Democratic president Heinrich Lübke spoke of the 'vital importance' of science and scholarship, and leading Social Democrat Carlo Schmid described advanced education as a fateful issue for the nation. In his government policy statement from 1963, Federal Chancellor Ludwig Erhard suggested that educational and research issues now had the same dignity as the social question had had during the nineteenth century.[4]

---

2 Schildt & Siegfried, *Deutsche Kulturgeschichte*, p. 204.
3 Rohstock, *Von der 'Ordinarienuniversität'*, pp. 3–12 and 17–18.
4 Ibid., pp. 17–18. On the Sputnik Crisis, see Paul Dickson, *Sputnik: The Shock of the Century* (New York, 2001) and Nicholas Barnett, ' "RUSSIA WINS SPACE

10 Protesting students in Munich in 1968

This general support for science and scholarship was gained under duress. It was not merely the triumphs of the Eastern bloc that worried people and called for action. Even in comparison to other countries, primarily the United States, Great Britain, and France, the West German research and educational system appeared neglected and underfunded. The domestic universities and scientific institutes had unquestionably fallen behind, claimed Helmut Coing, first chairman of the *Wissenschaftsrat* (the Science Council), in a lecture in 1959; and he would be supported by several reports published during subsequent years. Engineering and the natural sciences were singled out as special problem areas.[5]

One obvious sign of the Federal Republic's having lost its academic attraction was the stream of younger researchers who left the country and sought their fortunes elsewhere, primarily at American universities. Both pull and push factors were behind this exodus. The conditions for work and research appeared decidedly more favourable on the other side of the Atlantic. At the same time, the German system with its rigid, hierarchical character appeared intimidating to younger scholars. Rudolf Mößbauer, Nobel Prize winner in physics in 1961 and for several years a researcher in California, condemned the scholarly-scientific form of organisation in West Germany as antiquated and backward. He was not alone.[6]

The threat of an academic drain was paired with the threat of overcrowded universities. During a single decade, from 1955 to 1965, the number of students more than doubled, from 150,000 to 308,000. The result was not only a lack of premises, an increased workload, and other practical problems. In addition, some professors were extremely sceptical with regard to the increase in the number of students. One important reason for this, according to Anne Rohstock,

---

RACE": The British Press and the Sputnik Moment, 1957', *Media History*, 19:2 (2013). An additional sign of the urgency of issues of education and *Bildung* during the period around 1960 is that several prominent German-speaking thinkers, who had not otherwise concerned themselves with these topics to any particular extent, now took them up for discussion. See, for instance, Hannah Arendt, 'Die Krise in der Erziehung: Gedanken zur "Progressive Education" ', *Der Monat*, 124:11 (1958–1959) and Theodor W. Adorno, 'Theorie der Halbbildung', *Der Monat*, 132:11 (1959).

5 Rohstock, *Von der 'Ordinarienuniversität'*, pp. 18–23; Paulus, *Vorbild USA?*, pp. 163–68 and 337–71.
6 Rohstock, *Von der 'Ordinarienuniversität'*, pp. 23–25; Paulus, *Vorbild USA?*, pp. 275–335.

was that the growing number of students was thought to undermine the old Humboldtian ideal, which saw *Bildung* as an end in itself. Consequently, it was not only a matter of the professors feeling that they themselves had more to lose than gain from the expansion.[7]

At the same time, a significant – and seemingly growing – percentage of students displayed an interest in pronouncedly vocational educational programmes. This tendency was seen by professors, primarily in the faculty of philosophy, as proof of the functionalisation of higher education; indeed, it even came close to 'treason against the Humboldtian idea of the university'. In this debate Friedrich Schiller's inaugural lecture from 1789 was quoted, along with his distinction between bread-and-butter scholars and philosophers. Leading representatives of the academy warned that the former were taking over, something that resulted in an intellectual impoverishment of the student population. In a series of articles that attracted a lot of attention, published in 1963 in *Die Zeit*, literary scholar Walther Killy criticised students for no longer wanting to give themselves up to an 'adventure of the intellect', but simply aiming to earn their bread. According to Killy, the students aspired to social prestige and security, not truth and *Bildung*.[8]

Underlying the discontent with this development, several factors can be discerned: a genuine concern for the tradition of *Bildung* and academic freedom; a defence of personal privileges; a bourgeois repugnance toward working-class children gaining entrance to the universities; and so on.[9] In a wider context, criticism of the new students must be seen as a result of a deeper dissatisfaction with the state of the West German educational system. No one embodied this better than theologian and educationalist Georg Picht. In February 1964, he published a series of articles in the weekly *Christ und Welt* under the headline 'Die deutsche Bildungskatastrophe' (approx. 'the German educational disaster'). This article attracted an enormous amount of attention, and later in the same year Picht collected his texts and the reactions to them in the book *Die deutsche Bildungskatastrophe*. Picht demonstrated how bad the situation was

---

7 Rohstock, *Von der 'Ordinarienuniversität'*, pp. 25–33 (quotation on p. 33); Führ, 'Zur deutschen Bildungsgeschichte', pp. 14–16.
8 Rohstock, *Von der 'Ordinarienuniversität'*, pp. 33–35. For Schiller's terms, see Friedrich Schiller, 'The Nature and Value of Universal History: An Inaugural Lecture [1789]', *History and Theory*, 11:3 (1972), 322; Schiller distinguished between 'ein Brotgelehrter' and 'ein philosophischer Kopf'.
9 Rohstock, *Von der 'Ordinarienuniversität'*, pp. 35–37.

in West German schools: pupils were less proficient than in other countries; far too few graduated from upper secondary school; and the difference between city and countryside was startling. Although Picht concentrated on primary and secondary schools, his writings triggered an animated debate that included the entire educational system.[10] The sense of crisis was thus widespread during the early 1960s, although it did not dominate completely. It was coupled with feelings of the end of an era and premonitions of the dawning of a new one. Leading people in power had, with an increased emphasis, underscored the importance of research and education for the wellbeing of society. In 1957, the *Wissenschaftsrat* had been established and given the task of functioning as advisers and stimulating the development of scholarly-scientific institutions in West Germany. The council soon began recommending an expansion of higher education and the establishment of new universities.[11] At the same time, the production of knowledge about research and education went through a process of renewal. An older pedagogy rooted in the humanities and philosophy gave way to empirical and civic-minded educational research. The Max Planck Society's 'Institut für Bildungsforschung', founded in West Berlin in 1963 at the initiative of Hellmut Becker, symbolised what was new.[12]

---

10 Georg Picht, *Die deutsche Bildungskatastrophe: Analyse und Dokumentation* (Olten and Freiburg im Breisgau, 1964); Wolfgang Lambrecht, 'Deutschdeutsche Reformdebatten vor "Bologna": Die "Bildungskatastrophe" der 1960er-Jahre', *Zeithistorische Forschungen/Studies in Contemporary History*, 3 (2007). For general information about the university in West German public life, see Sebastian Brandt, 'Universität und Öffentlichkeit in der Expansions- und Reformphase des deutschen Hochschulwesens (1955–1967)', in *Universität, Wissenschaft und Öffentlichkeit in Westdeutschland*, ed. by Brandt et al.
11 Bartz, *Der Wissenschaftsrat*; Moritz Mälzer, '"Die große Chance, wie einstens die Berliner Universität so heute eine Modell-Universität zu schaffen": Die frühen 1960er Jahre als Universitätsgründerzeiten', *Jahrbuch für Universitätsgeschichte*, 13 (2010); Mälzer, *Auf der Suche*.
12 *Bildungsforschung und Bildungspolitik: Reden zum 80. Geburtstag von Hellmut Becker* (Berlin, 1993). For the burgeoning research on the university, see Wilfried Rudloff, 'Der politische Gebrauchswert der Hochschulforschung: Zum Verhältnis von Hochschulforschung und Hochschulpolitik in den Jahren von Bildungsboom und Hochschulexpansion (1960 bis 1975)', in *Universität, Wissenschaft und Öffentlichkeit in Westdeutschland: (1945 bis ca. 1970)*, ed. by Sebastian Brandt et al. (Stuttgart, 2014).

At this stage, when despair vied with hope, debates were held about the mission and orientation of the university. Many of the contributions focused on concrete measures, but in parallel to these there was intellectual reflection on the basic academic issues. In her above-mentioned study, Anne Rohstock has convincingly argued for the importance of the reform discussions of the early 1960s. She maintains that the influence of the student movement and the sixty-eight movement during the latter half of the decade has been overrated in explanations of changes in the university. It was the thoughts and suggestions formulated in the period around 1960 that were of decisive importance for the future.[13]

The West German history of the university of the 1960s is not completely uncharted. Rohstock's work appears quite central and is the closest thing to a comprehensive analysis, although strictly speaking she concentrates on Bavaria and Hesse. But newer investigations also flesh out the picture in important ways: Olaf Bartz on the *Wissenschaftsrat*, Stefan Paulus on Americanisation, and Nikolai Wehrs on professors' reactions to left-wing radicalism. In addition to this, there are a number of contributions in anthologies and journals, as well as accounts of individual universities.[14]

In none of these studies, however, was the primary focus the importance of the Humboldtian tradition or even the fundamental reflections on the ideal university in this particular period. That is not to say that there are no attempts at interpretation. One opinion is that there was a prevalent Humboldtian ideal which

---

13 Rohstock, *Von der 'Ordinarienuniversität'*, p. 415. See, however, Uwe Rohwedder, 'SDS-Hochschuldenkschrift und VDS-Neugründungsgutachten', in *Hochschulreformen früher und heute: Zwischen Autonomie und gesellschaftlichem Gestaltungsanspruch*, ed. by Rainer Pöppinghege & Dietmar Klenke (Cologne, 2011).

14 Rohstock, *Von der 'Ordinarienuniversität'*; Bartz, *Der Wissenschaftsrat*; Paulus, *Vorbild USA?*; Wehrs, *Protest der Professoren*. Among the anthologies can be found *Zwischen Idee und Zweckorientierung: Vorbilder und Motive von Hochschulreformen seit 1945*, ed. by Andreas Franzmann & Barbara Wolbring (Berlin, 2007); *Gebrochene Wissenschaftskulturen*, ed. by Grüttner et al.; and *Universität*, ed. by Brandt et al. The 1960s are discussed more or less extensively in numerous works on individual post-war universities, but there are also separate studies, such as Stefan Bichow, *Die Universität Kiel in den 1960er Jahren: Ordnungen einer akademischen Institution in der Krise* (Frankfurt am Main, 2013). The main theme of *Jahrbuch für Universitätsgeschichte*, 8 (2005), is the university in divided Germany during the 1960s.

functioned as a kind of constraint on the changes of the 1960s. Olaf Bartz, for example, argues that the principle of professorial chairs was so strong up to the middle of the decade that it placed obstacles in the path of those who argued for other ways in which to organise the university. After this, however, one cannot speak of wide-ranging support for Humboldt, according to Bartz.[15] Sylvia Paletschek represents another line of argument. In a brief sketch, she has foregrounded the period from the beginning of the 1960s as a phase in which the Humboldtian tradition gained renewed currency. During this and the following decade, the Humboldtian ideals legitimised the research orientation of the university. At the same time, she claims, a culturally pessimistic conviction spread to the effect that Humboldt was defunct in the age of the mass university.[16]

What these ideas have in common is that they are rather poorly supported. Therefore, this chapter will subject some of the most significant contributions to the early 1960s discussion on the idea of the university to a fairly thorough analysis. On the basis of knowledge of the interwar years and the first post-war years, there is reason to ask in what way these contributions mirrored the academic situation of the time. The general conditions – the growth of student numbers, the birth of the mass university, the large-scale social planning – had their analogies in other countries; but, as is so often the case in the history of the German university, sweeping changes brought about an investigation of the classic academic tradition. The concrete, time-bound manifestations of the long Humboldtian line will hence be a main concern in this chapter as well.

As in the previous chapter, the main part of the intellectual-historical analysis will be conducted within a framework set by the history of knowledge. The media forms of knowledge at the centre of the discussion are publications of university ideology that were published during the early 1960s. In contrast to the publications

---

15 Olaf Bartz, 'Bundesrepublikanische Universitätsleitbilder: Blüte und Zerfall des Humboldtianismus', *die hochschule*, 2 (2005), 105–07. See also Wilfried Rudloff, 'Ansatzpunkte und Hindernisse der Hochschulreform in der Bundesrepublik der sechziger Jahre: Studienreform und Gesamthochschule', *Jahrbuch für Universitätsgeschichte*, 8 (2005), and Anne Rohstock, 'Hemmschuh Humboldt oder Warum scheitert die Hochschulreform: Universitäre Neuordnungsversuche zwischen Sputnik-Schock und Bologna-Prozess, 1957–2009', *Zeitschrift für pädagogische Historiographie*, 2 (2009).
16 Paletschek, 'Die Erfindung', 203.

from the years of hardship in the late 1940s, these were voluminous books. They could be distributed and discussed in wide circles, not least because of paperback publishing and because the West German press already had an interest in these issues. The knowledge actors, those behind these publications, were active in the academy; but they were not as homogeneous with respect to age and opinions as their predecessors during the years of occupation. A generational shift had taken place, both at the university and in public life, without a new, uniform class having taken over. Just as in earlier periods, all actors used a more or less consistent vocabulary. The meaning of these concepts of knowledge was, however, the subject of sharp polemics.

The person who is given most attention below is Helmut Schelsky. In many ways the most important figure in the decade's reflection on the history and relevance of the Humboldtian tradition, Schelsky was a man who presented his own agenda, an agenda in relation to which other people were forced to react, willingly or not. Like no other person, Schelsky brought Humboldt into the centre of the debate on the development of the modern university.

A Humboldt for the post-war world

Helmut Schelsky was born in Chemnitz in 1912 and began his academic career in Königsberg, studying philosophy, German philology, and history. He soon moved to Leipzig, where he came under the influence of Hans Freyer and Arnold Gehlen. Like many others in the so-called Leipzig school, Schelsky had been attracted by an idealistic *Jugendbewegung* ('youth movement') inspired by nature romanticism, and during the 1930s he displayed clear sympathies for National Socialism. Even prior to the Nazi seizure of power he joined the Nazi student association, and in 1937 he became a member of NSDAP. In 1935 he published his doctoral thesis about the natural law of Fichte, whereupon he completed a *Habilitation* thesis on Thomas Hobbes. During the war years he initially moved among different academic settings, but his career was cut short when he was conscripted into the army.[17]

---

17 There is no detailed scholarly biography of Helmut Schelsky. Basic biographic and historical information can, however, be found in *Helmut Schelsky als Soziologe und politischer Denker: Grazer Gedächtnisschrift zum Andenken an den am 24. Februar 1984 verstorbenen Gelehrten*, ed. by Ota Weinberger & Werner Krawietz (Stuttgart, 1985); *Helmut Schelsky – ein Soziologe in*

Like many others of his generation, Schelsky went through an act of ideological transformation following the Second World War. In 1949, after a short period in academic quarantine, he was offered a professorship in sociology in Hamburg. During the 1950s his reputation grew, and in 1960 he was offered a post at the University of Münster, where he at the same time became director of one of the German Federal Republic's most important centres of empirical social science, the 'Sozialforschungsstelle an der Universität Münster' in Dortmund. During these first post-war decades Schelsky embraced a technocratic ideal of modernisation, and in political terms he was close to Social Democracy. In a rapid succession of works, he explored the social conditions of modern industrial society. He wrote about institutions and the school system, automatisation and youth unemployment, sexuality and family formation; but he also produced intellectual-historical writings on the basic features of German sociological thinking. Schelsky must undoubtedly be numbered among the founding fathers of West German sociology. His talent lay not least in the way he captured contemporary tendencies and formulated them in cogent social-science terms. 'No one read the signs of the times earlier than Helmut Schelsky and nobody described them in the same accessible way', Ralf Dahrendorf would note much later.[18]

---

der Bundesrepublik: Eine Gedächtnisschrift von Freunden, Kollegen und Schülern, ed. by Horst Baier (Stuttgart, 1986); Volker Kempf, Wider die Wirklichkeitsverweigerung: Helmut Schelsky – Leben, Werk, Aktualität (Munich, 2012); and in the autobiographical texts in Helmut Schelsky, Rückblicke eines 'Anti-Soziologen' (Opladen, 1981). The most detailed and scholarly treatment of Schelsky's life and work is provided in the articles in Helmut Schelsky – der politische Anti-Soziologe: Eine Neurezeption, ed. by Alexander Gallus (Göttingen, 2013) and in Patrick Wöhrle, Zur Aktualität von Helmut Schelsky: Einleitung in sein Werk (Wiesbaden, 2015).

18 Karl-Siegbert Rehberg, 'Vom soziologischen Neugründungs-Pragmatismus zur "Anti-Soziologie": Helmut Schelskys Position in der Nachkriegsgeschichte des Faches', in Helmut Schelsky, ed. by Gallus; Klaus Dammann & Dominik Ghonghadze, 'Helmut Schelskys sozialdemokratische Konversion und seine Einbindung in Leipziger/Königsberger Netzwerke', in Helmut Schelsky, ed. by Gallus; Carl-Göran Heidegren, Antropologi, samhällsteori och politik: Radikalkonservatism och kritisk teori: Gehlen – Schelsky – Habermas – Honneth – Joas (Göteborg, 2002); Ralf Dahrendorf, Über Grenzen: Lebenserinnerungen (Munich, 2002), p. 179; Gerhard Schäfer, 'Der Nationalsozialismus und die soziologischen Akteure der Nachkriegszeit: Am Beispiel Helmut Schelskys und Ralf Dahrendorfs', in Soziologie und Nationalsozialismus: Positionen, Debatten, Perspektiven, ed. by Michaela Christ & Maja Suderland (Berlin, 2014).

During the 1960s Schelsky became increasingly involved with questions regarding the university.[19] When Schelsky took up his duties as a new professor in Münster in 1960, he gave an inaugural lecture entitled 'Einsamkeit und Freiheit: Zur sozialen Idee der deutschen Universität' ('Solitude and freedom: On the social idea of the German university'). As a representative of sociology, a critical science engaged in contemporaneous affairs, he took the opportunity to analyse his own academic world. Above all, he wanted to shed light on a comparatively unknown side of the German idea of the university. 'In all our discussions on the university, the idea of the university formulated by Wilhelm von Humboldt plays an important role', he pointed out, 'but in spite of its being generally known, it seems to me as if one half of it has been forgotten, namely the *social* component.'[20]

Three years later, in 1963, Schelsky had developed the thirty-page address into a 350-page book, *Einsamkeit und Freiheit: Idee und Gestalt der deutschen Universität und ihrer Reformen*. A strikingly large number of the basic ideas and key formulations in the book can be found in a concentrated form in the lecture; but he had expanded the historical survey and deepened the contemporary analysis considerably.[21]

Considered as a book, this was a hybrid between a learned historical account of the birth of the modern German university, a sociological analysis of the scholarly-scientific world of the post-war era, and an indirect call for a reform of the contemporary German

---

19 Schelsky's involvement with university issues during the 1960s is analysed in Kopetz, *Forschung und Lehre*; Clemens Albrecht, 'Gefundene Wirklichkeit: Helmut Schelsky und die geistige Physiognomie politischer Konversion', in *Was war Bielefeld?*, ed. by Asal & Schlak; Herman Lübbe, 'Die Idee einer Elite-Universität: Der Fall der Universität Bielefeld', in *Was war Bielefeld?*, ed. by Asal & Schlak; Alfons Söllner, 'Mehr Universität wagen! Helmut Schelsky und die Hochschulpolitik der 1960er Jahre', in *Helmut Schelsky*, ed. by Gallus; and Mälzer, *Auf der Suche*. In addition, an exhibition catalogue produced by the university archive in Bielefeld contains a great deal of valuable matter from the period: '*Wie gründet man Universitäten?': Helmut Schelskys Konzept und der gelungene Start der Universität Bielefeld*, ed. by Martin Löning et al. (Bielefeld, 2011).
20 Helmut Schelsky, *Einsamkeit und Freiheit: Zur sozialen Idee der deutschen Universität* (Münster, 1960), pp. 6–7.
21 Schelsky, *Einsamkeit und Freiheit* (1963). For the relationship between the lecture and the book, see Albrecht, 'Gefundene Wirklichkeit', pp. 67–71.

university. It was published in Rowohlt's well-received series for non-fiction, *rowohlts deutsche enzyklopädie* (rde). Under the motto 'Das Wissen des 20. Jahrhunderts' (approx. 'The knowledge of the 20th century'), the publisher had brought out a large number of titles in a great many areas of knowledge since 1955, usually written by leading German and foreign thinkers. Together with, among others, Hans-Georg Gadamer, Mircea Eliade, Karl Löwith, Alexander Mitscherlich, and J. Robert Oppenheimer, Schelsky was a member of the scholarly advisory board of the series. Some works had the nature of an introduction to a subject; others were closer to forming independent contributions to intellectual debate. Schelsky's book accomplished both at the same time.[22]

In his preface, Schelsky explained the kind of book he had written. He accused the generations most directly preceding his own of having had a single-mindedly historical bent to their reflections on the university. However, in its attempt at finding new ways for scholarship and *Bildung*, this volume also took the German tradition of ideas as its point of departure. 'This book proceeds from the conviction, and the belief that it can prove, that Wilhelm von Humboldt's ideas on the nature of the university, *Bildung*, and university policy are still valid today and may well leave their mark on our future university. And yet it will upset those who see themselves as legitimate protectors of the Humboldtian ideas.'[23]

With this declaration, the principal argument of the book was stated. What might appear a contradiction – that Schelsky found inspiration in Humboldt's ideas while distancing himself from those who said they wanted to preserve these ideas – he explained by claiming to have adopted a sociological way of looking at the university. He considered it his duty to analyse the social reality of the university in the past as well as in his own time, and to place the university's goals in relation to this social reality. In order to achieve this aim, he divided his book into two parts. The former was historical and was taken up by the birth of the Berlin university and its main principles; the latter was sociological and took the form of an investigation of the predicament and the potential of the German post-war university.[24]

---

22 *100 Jahre Rowohlt: Eine illustrierte Chronik*, ed. by Hermann Gieselbusch et al. (Reinbek bei Hamburg, 2008).
23 Schelsky, *Einsamkeit und Freiheit* (1963), p. 8.
24 Ibid., pp. 9–10.

The idea of the Berlin university

The discussion of German university history was knowledgeable and rested on an extensive reading of the pertinent literature. Schelsky sought the mediaeval roots of the university and described the changes after the Reformation and the incipient Enlightenment. But this was not a neutral presentation. The emphasis was on the university reforms and what could be learned from them. Schelsky saw these periodically recurring and sometimes successful efforts to renew the university as a way for the university to confront itself.[25]

An ambition to bring the academic reform tradition to life guided Schelsky as he wrote the history of the university. This became obvious when he approached the eighteenth century. He conjured up a sombre picture of a university system in decay, dominated by tired professors who had inherited both their curricula and their positions. It was a provincial world, circumscribed by a guild spirit, wretchedly poor for keen minds. During the last decades of the eighteenth century, criticism had increased against this 'university, ossified in a guild system' ('im Zunftwesen erstarrte Universität'); and Schelsky distinguished four 'front lines of university policy' in existence at the turn of the century in 1800.[26]

The first front line was made up of traditional, conservative forces that safeguarded the status quo. These were challenged by the second front line: radical Enlightenment men who called for useful knowledge and vocational training in a utilitarian spirit. The desire to abolish the university as an institution was not infrequently heard among them. The third front line was also inspired by the Enlightenment, but it was not quite as revolutionary in its demands. Instead, representatives of this group recommended pragmatic organisational changes of the university, with Halle and Göttingen as models. The fourth grouping envisioned a new kind of university. Although they formed a unified front against the other three, they were able to share certain points of departure with them: like the traditionalists, they criticised the cult of utility; like the radical supporters of the Enlightenment, they demanded a new ideal of science and *Bildung*; and like the moderate supporters of reform, they wanted to keep the university as an institution. In the shift between the eighteenth and nineteenth centuries these four currents existed in parallel, Schelsky emphasised; but in hindsight we can see how the fourth

---

25 Ibid., p. 13.
26 Ibid., pp. 13–44.

front line broke through and became a political force that aimed to transform the university in accordance with a particular idea while simultaneously counteracting other ideas. Thanks to the influence of Wilhelm von Humboldt, this group could, according to Schelsky, emerge as the winner of the battle for the university.[27]

Schelsky's sympathies were no doubt with Humboldt and the fourth front line. Having used three chapters to bring German university history up to the decades surrounding the year 1800, he devoted half a dozen chapters to the Berlin university and its foundational ideas. As was self-evident with such an approach, Schelsky put Humboldt, his ideas, and his practical achievements at the centre. Schiller, Fichte, and Schelling were also given plenty of space as intellectual trail-blazers for the new university. However, Schelsky was indifferent to Schleiermacher; unlike the others, Schleiermacher was considered merely to have wanted to reform the old order, not create a new university.[28]

Before dealing with the Berlin university, Schelsky returned to methodical considerations. As a sociologist, he saw his most important scholarly task in the uncovering of the forces that shaped a certain period, a proceeding that enabled him to open up opportunities for future action. In this way, sociologists could contribute to shaping the future without being either politicians or social planners. Consequently, Schelsky argued, his project did not amount to writing the history of the university for its own sake; rather, it was a matter of highlighting a past that was still relevant. René König's opinion from 1935 was still valid: 'The idea of the university found in German idealism is the normative frame within which all German university reforms are drawn up.' Schelsky wanted to approach the classic German university in order to find out what was still valid. That was the overarching goal of his investigation; but in order to achieve it, it was necessary to understand the context in which the Berlin university had been created.[29]

One important point of departure for Schelsky was that what happened in the Prussian capital in 1810 was not a *Reform* but a *Gründung* (a 'foundation' or 'establishment').[30] In other words, a new type of institution had seen the light of day. Under the influence

---

27 Ibid., pp. 44–47.
28 Ibid., pp. 48–130. He repeatedly returned to criticising Schleiermacher on, among other places, pp. 60–64, 151, and 156.
29 Ibid., p. 48.
30 Ibid., pp. 48–57.

of Gehlen, Schelsky had, in various writings, developed a theory of institutions on which he now proceeded to base his understanding of the uniqueness of the Berlin university. In contrast to organisations, institutions possessed a greater measure of stability and were of fundamental importance to society. According to this theory, a new institution takes shape when the existing ones are no longer capable of fulfilling a pressing social need. In addition, this need has to be concentrated into a conception of norms that an established social group can embrace and that can become the foundational idea of the new institution. In the case of the Berlin university, this conception of norms consisted of two components: an intellectual one (*Sachidee*) that was expressed in the slogan *Bildung durch Wissenschaft* ('*Bildung* through science and scholarship'), and a social one (*Sozialidee*) that was captured in the formula *Einsamkeit und Freiheit* ('solitude and freedom').[31]

The first ideal, *Bildung* through science and scholarship, was completely contrary to the idea that the university should offer knowledge that was practically useful. Schelsky agreed with Humboldt that the primacy of research had to prevail and that the task of the university was never to convey a series of dogmas, but to give students a normative basic attitude in life (*Sittlichkeit*, approx. 'morality') and teach them to become intellectually independent.[32] Both students and professors had to be part of the same organisation, without therefore replacing the free search for knowledge with the teaching and learning of fixed material. It was *Lernfreiheit* (the 'freedom to learn') – not *Lehrfreiheit* (the 'freedom to teach') – that was fundamental to Humboldt.[33]

The other principle, *Einsamkeit und Freiheit*, embodied the basic social idea of the university. Schelsky had taken this conceptual pair from Humboldt's famous manifesto about the higher scholarly-scientific institutions in Berlin (1809/1810). On the one hand, 'solitude' meant that an ideal academic life required a certain measure of social seclusion. This was necessary in order to keep elements of distraction outside the walls of the university. On the other hand, there was in Humboldt an idea that truth led to solitude. Whoever was looking for truth had to be content with being at a distance from the surrounding society. Schelsky reminded his readers

---

31 Ibid., pp. 57–69. On Schelsky's institutional theory, see Heidegren, *Antropologi*, pp. 77–92.
32 Schelsky, *Einsamkeit und Freiheit* (1963), pp. 79–87.
33 Ibid., p. 92.

of the fact that distancing solitude was not simply a pre-industrial, pre-urban ideal for the scholar, but that the idea of unconditional independence could also be found in Karl Mannheim and Alfred Weber.[34]

The meaning of 'freedom' was also a dual one in Schelsky. He sided with science and scholarship in favour of non-utilitarian research (*Zweckfreiheit der Wissenschaft*, approx. 'the freedom of science from the pursuit of a purpose') in polemics against the idea of the university as a scholarly-scientific vocational college, aiming towards designated professions and practical skills. But he also claimed that the freedom to learn and teach was a condition for the creation of a combination of *Forschung* and *Lehre* ('research' and 'tuition') that included both students and teachers. Only by such means would they be able to shape knowledge together.[35]

Solitude and freedom were reciprocal concepts in the German university tradition, Schelsky emphasised. He saw them as two sides of the same coin: solitude stood for the social duties of the university, freedom for its social rights. In contemporary literature on the university Schelsky found much about academic freedom, but the word *solitude* no longer seemed to play a role. To him this was proof of impoverishment, a result of individualised people in the bosom of the welfare state being used to freedom but thinking they had no obligations. In addition, the experience of Nazism had made freedom appear superior to everything else.[36]

In spite of these positively charged words, *solitude* and *freedom*, Schelsky never recommended that the university should separate itself from the state. Once again he found support in the founding fathers of the Berlin university. These New Humanist theoreticians of the university had criticised a concept in which the state and its university policy promoted the interests of bourgeois society. In contrast, they had not been sceptical of the idea that the state would, as such, wield power. Thus it was again the Enlightenment philosophers and their university ideals that came under fire. Humboldt, argued Schelsky, had not required that the university should be free from the state in the sense that it should be self-administering. He

---

34 Ibid., pp. 67–69 and 115–18. In 'Der Königsberger und der Litauische Schulplan', Humboldt had also foregrounded 'Einsamkeit' and 'Freiheit' as desirable principles for the university. See Humboldt, 'Der Königsberger und der Litauische Schulplan', p. 191.
35 Schelsky, *Einsamkeit und Freiheit* (1963), pp. 68–69 and 92–97.
36 Ibid., pp. 115–120.

had turned against the state's insistence on vocational education. Humboldt and those who agreed with his ideas did not simply find the state as an instance of power unproblematic; on the contrary, they supported it as an alternative to the old university doctrine of self-administration. Ultimately, the state was a prerequisite for realising the idea of *Bildung* in the university.[37]

Supported by Humboldt's theories, Schelsky made an important differentiation in this respect, distinguishing between a policy that favoured the university as a cultural and educational institution and one that interfered in the content of that education.[38] Germany's scholarly and scientific successes during the nineteenth and early twentieth centuries had only been possible thanks to this boundary between a state university policy with cultural aims and one with character-forming and instructional aims, claimed Schelsky. But with Nazism, the character-forming and instructional aspects had taken over completely.[39]

In his youthful publication from 1792, Humboldt had been convinced that science, scholarship and *Bildung* were best promoted when the state remained at a distance. Less than twenty years later, he used the state as a tool in order to realise his new university. Schelsky did not interpret this as a volte-face. What Humboldt had defended in his youth was the freedom of the individual vis-à-vis the dirigistic state of the Enlightenment, that is to say against the educational pretensions of the state, not against the state as such. Schelsky argued that Humboldt's ideas from 1809/1810 were simply a new attempt at formulating ideas about the limitations of the state. He was still against the state's representing special interests, but had no objection to the state's cherishing a general idea of *Bildung*.[40]

For Schelsky, the establishing of the Berlin university also raised the question of whether it was possible to see any general patterns in the academic reforms. He noted the fact that the German university reforms had always been connected to great social upheavals. One type of reform was the radical transformation which Germany had experienced through the Nazis in 1933 and the Communists in 1945. On both occasions, an extreme educational policy had triumphed and autonomy had been completely abolished. Another type of university reform was the one that came from within the

---

37 Ibid., pp. 131–33.
38 Ibid., pp. 134–45.
39 Ibid., p. 145.
40 Ibid., pp. 145–47.

administration or the professorial community. In the German case this had happened in 1848 and in 1945 (in the western parts of the country). These reform attempts from within rarely entailed a genuine renewal of the university. The third type of reform, the state-instigated cultural university reform, meant that the cultural state endeavoured to create a new institution which would be in harmony with the concept of *Bildung* as combined with science and scholarship that was supported by leading academics. The classic example of this, to Schelsky's mind, was Wilhelm von Humboldt and the Prussian Berlin university; but Carl Heinrich Becker and his reforms during the Weimar Republic fulfilled the criteria as well. This third type of reform had the best prospects of success.[41]

Before leaving the historical investigations on academic reforms and the relationship between state and university, Schelsky compiled a few lessons for his contemporaries. The first he called the principle of foundation: in order to create something truly new while reforming something old, founding a new institution with connections to an already existing one constituted a successful recipe. According to another of his conclusions, there was a need for an idea that was not merely able to capture the contemporary ideals of science, scholarship and *Bildung*, but that could also serve as a supporting structure for the new institution. Only when this idea was manifested in a particular social way of life (for example *Einsamkeit und Freiheit*) could it become a guiding principle of the new university. The third and final lesson that Schelsky presented was that a new idea of the university could not become truly effective unless the entire social order was shaken to its foundations at the same time. One could not expect government reform measures alone to be very long-lasting.[42]

'The "validity" of these insights appears to be based on the fact that we are now to a great extent facing a situation that is similar to the one that Humboldt and his contemporaries encountered *before* the establishment of the new educational institution in Berlin', wrote Schelsky. Now as then, he continued, it would be natural either to obey the demands of conservatives for the restoration of an old ideal of *Bildung*, or to pragmatically adapt to the seemingly inevitable passage of time. But Schelsky rejected both alternatives. 'The importance of Humboldt's university to us today', he explained instead, 'is thus not found in the contents of the idea of the university

---

41 Ibid., pp. 159–62.
42 Ibid., pp. 171–72.

or of *Bildung* [...], but in the *structures* of intellectual and social action which are associated with the establishment of a university.'[43]

This conviction formed the basis for Schelsky's own ideas about the university. Before he could be in a position to answer the question of whether the old ideals from Humboldt's days might still serve as models for the post-war university, however, a sociological analysis of his own time was required.

The theoretical university

When considering the development of the university in the Federal Republic, Schelsky became despondent. During the first post-war years there had, naturally enough, been many debates about the idea of the university. In general terms, the suggestions for reform had been linked to the Humboldtian tradition; but soon the debate had led on to practical deliberations, organisational plans, and so on. Most people seemed to believe that the core of the German university was sound and that there was no reason for scrutinising its foundations.[44]

At the same time, there were many tendencies that were contrary to the basic principles of the Humboldtian university. Although science assumed a more and more central place in modern industrial society, academic life increasingly consisted of activities like those of primary and secondary school, with tests and grades, fixed curricula and vocational elements, increasing bureaucratisation and transformation into a *Gymnasium*-like institution. In addition, the social idea of the older university tradition was no longer a guiding principle. Neither students nor professors were able to withdraw into productive solitude any longer. The Socratic dialogue was an illusion in times of anonymity and lack of contact.[45]

Against all this, Schelsky set the genuine reform work that had been undertaken during the early years of the Weimar Republic under the aegis of Carl Heinrich Becker. Becker had been aware that his reforms would have to be accompanied by an intellectual renewal of the university if they were to have any real effect. Becker's diagnosis, too, was still valid: the specialisation, the bureaucratisation, the isolation of the faculties, the mass influx of students. Schelsky was

---

43 Ibid., pp. 172–73.
44 Ibid., pp. 178–79.
45 Ibid., pp. 180–204 and 207–10.

less sure about Becker's solution. He did sympathise with the idea of promoting subjects with a potential for synthesis (philosophy, sociology, pedagogy) in order to encourage a unity of science/scholarship. But when Becker advocated limiting the *Lernfreiheit* of the students in favour of a more regulated curriculum, Schelsky objected that this was indubitably a violation of the ideals of the Humboldtian university.[46]

On the whole, Schelsky nevertheless found Becker a worthy exponent of the classic programme. Schelsky felt that the greatness of the erstwhile German Minister of Education as a reformer was based on the fact that he had possessed both a politician's practical experience and a university teacher's knowledge of academic reality.[47] Schelsky was inspired by yet another person from the intellectual world of the interwar period, the philosopher Max Scheler. During the 1920s, Scheler was the only person who presented a proposal on the issue of the university and *Bildung* that was based on the theory of science. Scheler opposed Becker's institutional proposals, even though the two men embraced the same diagnosis and concept of *Bildung*. In spite of this, Schelsky argued, we could regard Scheler as the first representative of 'the realistic direction' among university reformers, that is to say, a modern university ideal that turned against the classic one.[48]

Scheler subjected the university to a type of analysis from which Schelsky drew inspiration. From his position in 1920s Germany, Scheler distinguished five main tasks for the university: the tradition-related task, the educational task, the research task, the *Bildung* task, and the task of educating the wider public. From this Scheler had drawn the conclusion that the organisation of the university was dysfunctional; far too many tasks were in conflict with one another. He had questioned the idea that a single institution should perform so many tasks. In order to solve the inherent conflicts, Scheler had suggested a differentiation of the university. Unlike Becker, he wanted to divide the institution into four or five new ones that would be responsible for the various tasks.[49]

Schelsky showed great respect for Scheler's ideas and argued that the tensions were even greater in the 1960s than they had been forty years earlier. In contrast to all the reform proposals of

---

46 Ibid., pp. 229–32.
47 Ibid., pp. 233–34.
48 Ibid., p. 234.
49 Ibid., pp. 234–42.

the post-war years, Scheler had attempted to deal with the totality and had not simply proceeded on the basis of the premise that the German university was sound.[50] That made an impression on Schelsky, who subjected the post-war university to a sociological functional analysis. In line with the pace of increasing scientific specialisation, he saw a need for a division of the university's functions; but as an institution it had instead amassed even more functions. There was now considerable discrepancy between the idea of the university and the tasks that it actually performed. The various sectors developed their own goals, which were never merged into a common, coherent ideal for the university.[51]

When Schelsky himself endeavoured to formulate a vision for the contemporary university, he found inspiration in the classic ideals. But he reinterpreted them throughout and placed them in relation to his sociological analysis of the post-war university. The old slogans had to be formulated in a new way, was his motto. One example was scholarly-scientific specialisation. Schelsky did not regard this as problematic in itself, but as a necessary consequence of the modern division of labour. The problem was that one-sidedness was rewarded. A reform of the university must consequently strive towards an integration of the branches of science and scholarship, preferably with the classic ideal *Einheit der Wissenschaft* (the 'unity of science/scholarship') as a guiding principle – not as a philosophical system but as an institutional arrangement.

Similarly, the ideal of *Einheit von Forschung und Lehre* (the 'unity of research and tuition') continued to be relevant, though it was not simply a matter of bringing research and education together but of combining a large number of different functions. An additional task that had to be given a new form was the relationship of the university to the practical needs of society, for instance the vocational education of the students and the professors' role as experts. In this area, too, it was impossible to hold on to an obsolete order. New ways had to be found to realise an old ideal about *Einsamkeit und Freiheit*.[52]

The concept of *Bildung* also remained of key importance. According to Schelsky, creating a true world citizenship ought to be a goal at the present time. The university should promote civilisations growing together, not looking inwards. Another goal would be for

---

50 Ibid., pp. 240–45.
51 Ibid., pp. 266–74.
52 Ibid., pp. 275–78.

the students to develop intellectual freedom vis-à-vis the coming scientised world. Just as the New Humanist concept of *Bildung* had aimed to elevate human beings over the merely practical in life, a modern concept of *Bildung* had to aim at making human beings transcend science and scholarship. Only those who understood science and scholarship well could master them, he said.[53]

Contemporary *Bildung* must also include an ideal of openness towards society and towards existence in general terms. The individual fields of knowledge can create and classify the world, but scholarly-scientific education expands people's opportunities and responsibilities.[54] Just like the classic idea of *Bildung*, the modern conception of it should ultimately include a pursuit of *Humanität* ('humanity' in the sense of 'humaneness'), an endeavour to develop a person's inherent qualities. To Schelsky, who was a modern social scientist rather than a New Humanist philosopher, there was never a question of classical languages having a privileged position.

Consequently, Schelsky's concept of *Bildung* consisted of elements from several traditions. Here was a civic ideal of a person opening up to the world and taking part in social life. Here was also an element of a more traditional, character-forming ideal which meant that each person should realise his or her full potential. And then there was a notion of *Bildung* as being able to draw on science and scholarship to lift the individual out of a thoroughly rationalised existence, a notion akin to the ideas of the humanities as compensatory branches of scholarship which were advocated by Joachim Ritter at the same time.[55]

This brought Helmut Schelsky to his conclusions. In the twenty-first and last chapter of the book, he posed the question of the extent to which prevailing conditions would allow the implementation of a true reform of the university today.[56] His thesis was that it would not be possible to realise a fundamental reform of the German university. The university of today was far too multifaceted for a common formula to be found, and the danger was that an attempt would go no further than a glorification of past greatness.[57] Instead,

---

53 Ibid., pp. 296–99.
54 Ibid., pp. 299–301.
55 Carsten Dutt, 'Zweierlei Kompensation: Joachim Ritters Philosophie der Geisteswissenschaften gegen ihre Popularisatoren und Kritiker verteidigt', *Scientia Poetica*, 12 (2008).
56 Schelsky, *Einsamkeit und Freiheit* (1963), p. 305.
57 Ibid., pp. 306–07.

Schelsky's answer was a more differentiated university – but the goal should still be that its various elements would together preserve and renew an ideal of *Bildung* based on science and scholarship.[58]

Against this background he suggested the establishment of a new kind of university, *the theoretical university*. Such a university would not have vocational education or scholarly specialisation as its goal, but be a combined research and educational institution. He outlined a university with unrestricted *Lernfreiheit* that had no limiting regulations for those who wished to study. Activities should be focused on the theories of the various branches of science and scholarship, and collaboration between subjects would be encouraged. It was thus not a matter of a series of loosely connected research institutes with advanced specialisations. In addition, a crucial element for promoting a true formation of character was that students and professors came into direct contact with one another.[59]

Schelsky harboured certain hopes that such a university could breathe new life into the academic system as a whole and make old universities try new forms of teaching and research. But he did not believe that the theoretical university could become a new common basic model.[60]

Schelsky and the Humboldtian tradition

Wilhelm von Humboldt was undoubtedly a bright star in Schelsky's intellectual firmament. Schelsky's views on people and society were influenced by his association with Fichte, Hobbes, Gehlen, and Freyer; but when it came to the ideal university, the Prussian official was in a class by himself. Already in Schelsky's inaugural lecture from 1960, it was self-evident that Humboldt would form a point of departure for his argument. He even maintained that Humboldt had become a kind of Church Father of the German university.[61]

Schelsky had a very vital relationship to Humboldt the man; it was never simply a matter of access to a rhetorical resource or formula. In *Einsamkeit und Freiheit* he displayed a thorough familiarity with Humboldt's writings, and not only with them but also with the philosophical and social world in which the Berlin university was conceived. Schelsky's knowledge of the Humboldtian tradition, both

---

58 Ibid., p. 308.
59 Ibid., pp. 312–13.
60 Ibid., p. 317.
61 Schelsky, *Einsamkeit und Freiheit* (1960), p. 7.

11 Helmut Schelsky

at the turn of the century around 1800 and subsequently, is without parallel among German university theoreticians from the twentieth century. At the same time, his relationship with Humboldt was dynamic and not paralysed by awe; he did not regard Humboldt as an unimpeachable national icon, but as an inspirational teacher who could take on several roles.[62]

First – and in a way foremost – Humboldt served as an example as the ideal *founder* of a new institution. In Schelsky's institutional theory, the need for a new institution was not in itself enough for such an institution to take shape. This need had to be underpinned by a general idea which an influential social group could embrace. Here, Humboldt emerged as both an interpreter of the idea of the new institution and as a practically active person who could turn thoughts into action. This was the social act to which Schelsky attached so much importance; it was this – rather than a specific programme of *Bildung* – that he admired. Without Humboldt, the Berlin university would have remained at best a reform of an old educational institution. Instead, he had brought about the founding of a new institution.

At the same time, there was a set of distinct ideals which Schelsky cherished and for which Humboldt had been one of the most eloquent exponents. Schelsky was fully aware that many of these principles could not be connected exclusively with Humboldt, but were generally disseminated among philosophers of the university around the turn of the century in 1800. Already in Schiller's famous inaugural lecture from Jena in 1789, a lecture which Schelsky honoured by calling it the first 'university publication', he saw several of the basic ideas that would guide Fichte, Humboldt, and others: the repudiation of vocational education and fixed curricula, the insight that knowledge is continuously modified by research, and the conviction that a wholeness of knowledge creates harmony.[63]

Generally speaking, Schelsky was not afraid to relativise Humboldt's role as a fundamental innovator. For instance, he repeatedly cited *Einheit von Forschung und Lehre* as a key principle. But in the historical parts of his book he emphasised that it was in Schelling,

---

62 Naturally there have been prominent experts on the German university tradition whose knowledge and broad outlook could well measure up to Schelsky's, from Max Lenz and Eduard Spranger to Heinz-Elmar Tenorth and Sylvia Paletschek. Like no one else, however, Schelsky combined historical knowledge with his own theoretical contributions.
63 Schelsky, *Einsamkeit und Freiheit* (1963), pp. 76–77.

more precisely in his lecture from 1802, that this principle was formulated with some clarity for the first time. Additional examples of the same kind of conceptual self-reflection are not hard to find.[64]

According to Schelsky, two principles permeated the Berlin university and made it a new and independent institution. One was *Bildung durch Wissenschaft*, an intellectual ideal that was unequivocally associated with New Humanist theoreticians from the turn of the century around 1800. He therefore named one of his historical chapters 'Bildung durch Wissenschaft', and on many occasions he returned to this expression. In the latter half of the book, when he focused on his own era, he discussed both the conditions of science and scholarship and the content of *Bildung*; but he did not put the connection between them at the centre of the discussion. Rather, he maintained that a contemporary concept of *Bildung* had to be based on science and scholarship and designed in relation to a world characterised by them. The process itself – *Bildung* through science and scholarship – did not, however, occupy Schelsky's thoughts.

The second principle, *Einsamkeit und Freiheit*, had given Schelsky the title of the book, and it formed his most original contribution to the history of Humboldt interpretations. Like no one else, he stressed this social idea as a central and dynamic motif. The concept itself could be directly derived from Humboldt. The conceptual pair struck a special chord in Schelsky the sociologist. It did not just capture a cognitive principle but the social conditions of the ideal university. In addition, each concept, solitude and freedom, had two sides, one with respect to the individual and one with respect to the institution. For the individual, solitude meant a condition that was necessary for devoting oneself to true science and scholarship; for the university, it was desirable that a certain distance was maintained from the society around it. In a similar fashion, freedom had related meanings for both individual and institution. It was a vital prerequisite for research and for the knowledge process at large; but it was manifested in different ways depending on whether it was seen from the perspective of the students, the professors, or the university as an academic unit.

Schelsky was more ambivalent about another concept connected with the Humboldtian tradition, *Einheit der Wissenschaften*. Extremely critical of one-sidedness, he upheld a broad concept of *Bildung*. At the same time, he saw scholarly-scientific specialisation

---

64 Ibid., p. 74.

as an inexorable consequence of the division of labour in the modern world. One of his principal conclusions was that the university today had so many functions that it was not held together by a common vision. For this reason, it was pointless to try to promote a unity of science/scholarship in the classic sense, for instance as a coherent and non-contradictory philosophical system.

With his extensive knowledge of the philosophical debate concerning the university during the late eighteenth and early nineteenth centuries, Schelsky was able to articulate his own interpretation of the Humboldtian tradition. He proceeded from many of the central concepts and foregrounded them as ideals; but he was programmatically convinced that the old nineteenth-century principles had to be placed in relation to the social and scholarly-scientific reality of the post-war era if they were to have continued relevance. On many occasions, it was necessary to fill them with new content.

The necessity of finding new expressions was evident not least from Schelsky's line of reasoning about the meaning of *Bildung*. Schelsky emphasised its continued importance; but he did not unreflectingly evoke a New Humanist conception, for instance. Instead, he first presented his own analysis of the conditions of science, scholarship and education in the industrial society. On the basis of that analysis, he went on to formulate his own theory of *Bildung*. The ideals of openness and world citizenship could be found in an early twentieth-century tradition of realistic education for citizens, but they could also be seen as expressing general positive values in an international and democratic post-war world. However, the idea that students should learn to transcend science and scholarship came from a more specific understanding of how rationalism circumscribed the life world of individuals. The ideal of humanity was the most classic element in Schelsky's theory of *Bildung*; here he expressly invoked New Humanist ideals.

But it was not merely as a founder and exponent of a series of academic ideals that Humboldt served as an example for Schelsky. Schelsky also wholly shared Humboldt's view on the nature of the state's influence on the university. Humboldt had conducted what Schelsky called a state-instigated cultural university policy that was a model for how the state should exercise its power over the world of learning. The state should promote comprehensive educational work and make sure the conditions for that work were generally good; but it should not otherwise interfere and above all should not use the university to instruct students in how to be useful subjects.

A profound respect for Humboldt the statesman also surfaces in Schelsky's work on a couple of occasions. In Humboldt, Schelsky appears to have seen a person who combined a philosophical mind with political knowledge of the world. He thus argued that Humboldt did not really represent a different idea of the relationship between state and university in 1809–1810 than he had done in his youthful text from 1792, but that he had simply formulated it on the basis of his position as an acting statesman.[65] Humboldt hence served as an example to Schelsky in a number of guises. In some cases, this was directly tied to the individual and thinker Wilhelm von Humboldt; in other cases it had to do with ideals encompassed within the broader Humboldtian tradition.

As the 1960s progressed, Schelsky transformed himself from a theoretician into a politician. In 1965 he was given an assignment by Paul Mikat, Minister of Education in North Rhine-Westphalia, to develop a proposal for a new university. In the spring of 1966, the two men jointly presented an ambitious programme, *Grundzüge einer neuen Universität* (approx. 'Essential features of a new university'), which contained both fundamental considerations and concrete proposals. Many of the underlying thoughts are recognisable from *Einsamkeit und Freiheit*, not least the emphasis on research, academic freedom, and the combination research–education. The research imperative was most vigorously promoted in the outline for 'Zentrum für interdisziplinäre Forschung' (ZiF), an institute for advanced interdisciplinary studies that resembled the theoretical university in several essential respects.[66]

It was not until 1969 that the new university opened in Bielefeld. Schelsky had not only exerted influence as an ideologue, but also as an influential chairman of the committee that developed the plans for the new university. However, during the final years of the 1960s the spirit of the times changed character. Increasingly radical forces among the students and younger academics demanded the right of co-determination and called for a democratisation of the proposed

---

65 Ibid., p. 147.
66 Paul Mikat & Helmut Schelsky, *Grundzüge einer neuen Universität: Zur Planung einer Hochschulgründung in Ostwestfalen* (Gütersloh, 1966). For Schelsky and Bielefeld University, see Albrecht, 'Gefundene Wirklichkeit'; Lübbe; 'Wie gründet man Universitäten?', ed. by Löning et al.; Gerhard Sprenger & Peter Weingart, 'Zentrum für interdisziplinäre Forschung', in *Reformuniversität Bielefeld 1969–1994: Zwischen Defensive und Innovation*, ed. by Peter Lundgreen (Bielefeld, 1994); and Mälzer, *Auf der Suche*.

elite university. Schelsky was forced to resign as chairman of the committee after his youthful Nazi sympathies were revealed. In spite of his increasing bitterness over the radicalisation of academic life, he initially served as director of ZiF; but at the beginning of the 1970s, he chose to leave Bielefeld and returned to a professorship in Münster.[67]

As early as 1969, Schelsky had aired his resentment in the acerbic pamphlet *Abschied von der Hochschulpolitik* ('A farewell to university politics'). He did not mince words when polemising against the inability of politicians and the radical left to think clearly on academic matters. In this book he also collected a number of texts he had written on university issues, among them a lecture delivered in 1967 at the West German rectors' conference on the occasion of the bicentenary of Wilhelm von Humboldt's birth. Here he recapitulated the main points of Humboldt's programme. In the last paragraph, Schelsky admitted that he had been critical of Humboldt's concept of the state in his youth, but that practical experience of university life in the last few years had turned him into an admirer of Humboldt's ideas and achievements.[68]

A couple of years later, in 1971, Schelsky published a second edition of *Einsamkeit und Freiheit*. In a newly written preface and postscript, he expressed his pessimism concerning the course of history. He described how his original intention with the book had been to find a new form for the German university by returning to the Humboldtian model and drawing attention to its significance, but how he had instead witnessed the decline of an institution. 'The last few years have demonstrated that a 150-year-old era in the history of the German university is drawing to a close', he observed.[69]

During the 1970s Schelsky moved steadily to the right and joined the 'Bund Freiheit der Wissenschaft', an association of liberal, conservative, but also social-democratic professors who shared a conviction that the traditional basic academic values had to be defended in a time of politicisation. He excoriated the sixty-eight

---

67 Söllner, pp. 109–14; '*Wie gründet man Universitäten?*', ed. by Löning et al.
68 Helmut Schelsky, *Abschied von der Hochschulpolitik oder die Universität im Fadenkreuz des Versagens* (Bielefeld, 1969), pp. 151–67. Schelsky's lecture was unfavourably reviewed by Manfred Nast in the East German journal *Das Hochschulwesen*, and this text was also printed in Schelsky's book. See, in particular, pp. 176–77.
69 Helmut Schelsky, *Einsamkeit und Freiheit: Idee und Gestalt der deutschen Universität und ihrer Reformen* (Düsseldorf, 1971), pp. 9 and 241–68.

movement in a large number of writings. When Schelsky died in 1984, he was lauded as one of the great post-war sociologists; but his capricious nature and political diatribes had made him many enemies and few real disciples.[70]

Schelsky's *Einsamkeit und Freiheit* was of immense importance for the West German 1960s debate on the idea of the university. This book was without doubt the single most important text published during these years. There were several reasons for that. First, Schelsky had written the most thorough presentation of the Humboldtian tradition to be published during the post-war years; indeed, in many ways it is the most substantial work on this topic in existence. It was historically and philosophically sophisticated but also contained a comprehensive sociological analysis of the contemporary era. When the work was published, Schelsky had a reputation as a productive and respected social scientist. All this paved the way for the book's impact in academic and intellectual circles, especially as it was distributed in a popular paperback series.

The sudden changes in Schelsky's biographical career attracted attention. When he first stepped on to the West German university-ideological stage at the beginning of the 1960s, it was as a representative of an establishment that embraced modernity. When his brown past was revealed a few years later, he was branded as part of the reaction, and not only by the increasingly radical student movement. It can be claimed that Schelsky's gradual transition from theory to politics during this decade led him away from the centre and out towards the periphery, but it is not quite as simple as that. With his well-founded defence of the basic academic principles, he forced his antagonists to take a stand with respect to the Humboldtian tradition.

Schelsky's method of argumentation was of great importance in this respect. His book was never intended simply as a contribution to an understanding of the past. Based on German university history, Schelsky instead engaged in a kind of conceptual intervention. He focused on central terms, but promoted his own interpretations and introduced them forcefully. The most obvious example is contained in the very title of the book, *Einsamkeit und Freiheit*.

---

70 Nikolai Wehrs, 'Auf der Suche nach einem "Pronunciamento": Helmut Schelsky im Hegemonialkampf der "Reflexionseliten" in den 1970er Jahren', in *Helmut Schelsky*, ed. by Gallus, and more generally in Wehrs, *Protest der Professoren*.

This conceptual pair can be derived from the writings of Wilhelm von Humboldt; but no particular importance had been attached to it in the discussions that took place during the first half of the twentieth century. By contrast, Schelsky brought it to the centre of the debate and gave it a prominent place in his theory about the ideal university.

Two examples, a liberal one and a socialist one, demonstrate how the conceptual intervention functioned during the 1960s.

Ralf Dahrendorf and the liberal university

Ralf Dahrendorf (1929–2009) was awarded his PhD in the city of his birth, Hamburg, at the early age of twenty-three, having written a thesis on Karl Marx. His second dissertation, this time at the London School of Economics, had a more sociological orientation, and from that time onwards the Anglo-Saxon social sciences formed his lodestar. In the years around 1960, he established himself in the Federal Republic as a young, inventive, and energetically productive sociologist. In addition to publishing a number of pioneering scholarly works, he intervened in many of the important debates of the time. His main topic, both as a social scientist and as a liberal intellectual, was the theory and practice of freedom, its potentials and inhibitions.[71]

The mid-1960s was a particularly intensive phase for Dahrendorf. He held a professorship at Tübingen, published several authoritative works and was actively involved in the newly established university in Konstanz. In addition, he was increasingly drawn to practical politics. In 1965, he published two books that revealed his views on the German university tradition and the need for reforms, *Gesellschaft und Demokratie in Deutschland* ('Society and democracy

---

71 Jürgen Kocka, 'Dahrendorf in Perspektive', *Soziologische Revue*, 27:2 (2004); Jürgen Kocka, 'Ralf Dahrendorf in historischer Perspektive: Aus Anlass seines Todes am 17. Juni 2009', *Geschichte und Gesellschaft*, 35:2 (2009); Jens Alber, 'In memoriam Ralf Dahrendorf (1. Mai 1929–17. Juni 2009)', *Soziologie*, 38:4 (2009). See also Dahrendorf, *Über Grenzen*, and Franziska Meifort, 'Der Wunsch nach Wirkung: Ralf Dahrendorf als intellektueller Grenzgänger zwischen Bundesrepublik und Großbritannien 1964–1984', *Geschichte in Wissenschaft und Unterricht*, 65:3/4 (2014).

in Germany') and *Bildung ist Bürgerrecht* (approx. '*Bildung* is a civil right').[72] In *Gesellschaft und Demokratie in Deutschland*, a book of over 500 pages, Dahrendorf combined historical explanation, sociological analysis, and a commitment to democracy. The central issue was why the political values of liberalism had found it so difficult to gain a true foothold in Germany. Dahrendorf described the country's long and difficult progress towards modernity and made connections to older interpreters of a German *Sonderweg*-thesis (Helmuth Plessner, Thomas Mann, Friedrich Meinecke), but even more to contemporary liberals such as Friedrich August von Hayek, Raymond Aron, and Karl Popper. Dahrendorf painted a picture of an authoritarian, antidemocratic, hierarchical society with an abundance of metaphysics and militarism and a shortage of rationalism and enlightenment. His passionate plea for the principle of liberal democracy had a great effect during the 1960s and gave him a reputation as the foremost liberal intellectual in West Germany. Much later, Jürgen Habermas would call the book 'probably the treatise that had the greatest impact on shaping the political mentality of the population on West Germany's long path to find itself'.[73]

---

[72] Ralf Dahrendorf, *Gesellschaft und Demokratie in Deutschland* (Munich, 1965); Ralf Dahrendorf, *Bildung ist Bürgerrecht: Plädoyer für eine aktive Bildungspolitik* (Hamburg, 1965). Franziska Meifort analyses both these texts in an essay. In a praiseworthy manner, she places them and Dahrendorf's achievements with respect to educational politics in the context of the 1960s; but she is not interested in his relationship to the Humboldtian tradition. See Franziska Meifort, 'Liberalisierung der Gesellschaft durch Bildungsreform: Ralf Dahrendorf zwischen Wissenschaft und Öffentlichkeit in den 1960er Jahren', in *Universität, Wissenschaft und Öffentlichkeit in Westdeutschland: (1945 bis ca. 1970)*, ed. by Sebastian Brandt et al. (Stuttgart, 2014).

[73] Michael Prinz, 'Ralf Dahrendorfs "Gesellschaft und Demokratie" als epochenübergreifende Interpretation des Nationalsozialismus', in *Politische Zäsuren und gesellschaftlicher Wandel im 20. Jahrhundert: Regionale und vergleichende Perspektiven*, ed. by Michael Prinz & Matthias Frese (Paderborn, 1996); Jens Hacke, 'Pathologie der Gesellschaft und liberale Vision: Ralf Dahrendorfs Erkundung der deutschen Demokratie', *Zeithistorische Forschungen/Studies in Contemporary History*, 2 (2004); Östling, 'Tysklands väg mot moderniteten'; Jürgen Habermas, 'Die Liebe zur Freiheit', *Frankfurter Allgemeine Zeitung*, 18/6 2009, translated into English as 'Rationality out of Passion', in *On Liberty: The Dahrendorf Questions*, ed. by Timothy Garton Ash (Oxford, 2009), p. 13; Meifort, 'Der Wunsch nach Wirkung'; Schäfer, 'Der Nationalsozialismus'.

Out of the twenty-eight chapters in the book it was only one, the eleventh, that dealt with science and the university, 'Die deutsche Idee der Wahrheit' ('The German idea of truth'). Dahrendorf began this chapter by reminding his readers that Wilhelm von Humboldt had, in his proposal from 1810, distinguished between two institutions: the university, which was closer to the state and the practical needs of life; and the academy, a bastion of free research. Between these two, productive competition would arise to the benefit of science and scholarship.[74]

Dahrendorf sympathised strongly with this idea of a fruitful rivalry; it was completely in accordance with his liberal view of society. He felt that the university traditionally had two different tasks. On the one hand, its mission was to provide knowledge for professions and prepare the individual for life as a citizen. In this respect it was tied to prevailing norms, forming an expression of the interests of the state, and in that sense it was conservative. On the other hand, the university had another mission: research. For this, freedom and openness were necessary. Here, just as in politics, there was always an element of uncertainty; in neither case was the outcome given.[75]

In the real-world Berlin university, however, the division between an institution of learning and an academy had never taken place. The two had remained united. In his short and unambiguous historiography, Dahrendorf describes how Humboldt instead realised the principle of 'Einheit von Forschung und Lehre'. That principle set a pattern and spread to other universities. In theory, the Berlin university, according to Dahrendorf, managed to combine the governmental conservative dimension with the liberal progressive one, although this was not always a successful combination in practice. The reason for this failure formed the point of departure for Dahrendorf's continued discussion.[76]

There were several reasons why a university reform was necessary at the beginning of the nineteenth century. The 'university, ossified in a guild system' – without naming names Dahrendorf used Schelsky's characterisation – was not adapted to the needs of the time. In addition, the university had become nothing more than a teaching institution. We are experiencing something similar today, 150 years later, Dahrendorf interjected. This prompted him to ask whether

---

74 Dahrendorf, *Gesellschaft und Demokratie*, pp. 175–76.
75 Ibid., p. 176.
76 Ibid., p. 177.

teaching always had a tendency to crowd out research. Could it be, he wondered, that the conservative forces have a fundamental advantage, and that there is a kind of gravitational force that pushes the centre of gravity from demanding research towards the less strenuous activity, teaching?[77]

Dahrendorf posed the question but did not provide an answer in this text. Instead, he presented another reason why the university always threatened to transform itself into a higher school in Germany. During the nineteenth century there existed – in Humboldt, Hegel, and Dilthey, among others – a critique of empirically based science and scholarship, which were seen as far too limited in their perception of reality. Instead of experimental research, philosophical speculation or historical understanding was recommended.[78]

Dahrendorf was critical of the concept of science and scholarship that had characterised the German university during the nineteenth century. Above all, he perceived institutional consequences of the fact that a dogmatic resistance to an experimental approach had become predominant. This anti-empirical attitude had its domicile in the philosophical faculty, which by virtue of its exceptionally strong position had relegated other scholarly-scientific ideals to the margins. As a consequence, neither technology nor the natural or social sciences were able to compete with the humanities.[79]

But the anti-experimental dominance had other consequences which Dahrendorf found even more troubling. 'All science and scholarship requires freedom; however, the combination of freedom and solitude is surely more important to historical speculation than to experiments and empirical research', he began, but he did not stop there. The traditional humanists may have made do with this inner freedom to be left alone to seek out the truth. For the experimental sciences, however, the outer, political freedom, the one manifested in public life and in controversies, was a fundamental prerequisite. In polemics against the ideal of *Einsamkeit und Freiheit*, Dahrendorf wanted to name this objective, critical spirit *Disput und Freiheit* or *Kritik und Freiheit* ('Argument/Dispute and freedom' or 'Critique/Criticism and freedom'). The Humboldtian leitmotif fenced in the individual researcher and divided the scholarly world into small garden patches where each scholar was allowed to grow his or her

---

77 Ibid., p. 177.
78 Ibid., pp. 178 and 181–82. Dahrendorf used *empirical science, experimental science,* and *experiential science* as largely interchangeable terms.
79 Ibid., pp. 182–83.

own truth. In the experimental sciences there were no fences. On the contrary, cooperation, exchange, and conflict were encouraged.[80] Even so, the political parallels were what interested Dahrendorf most. The solitary, introspective humanist could flourish in authoritarian and totalitarian states as well, he claimed. By contrast, empirical science could only exist in a liberal society; in other political contexts, its own rules of the game became invalid. He regarded the approach of empirical science as analogous to that of political freedom. Knowledge was only possible if many people participated, through collaboration, competition, and conflict. Disproving theories that did not stand up to scrutiny was a prerequisite for the progress of knowledge. Understanding and speculation did not presuppose resistance and conflicts of opinion in anything like the same manner.[81]

Here Dahrendorf saw a crucial difference between the empirical ideal of science and scholarship and the one that had dominated German universities since the beginning of the nineteenth century. In Germany, profundity and thoroughness had characterised scholarly life, not experimental imagination or theoretical brilliance. Consequently, the vitality and dynamism that characterised the empirically orientated natural and social sciences were lacking. Here Dahrendorf identified an important reason why the German university drifted into conservatism. Besides, German academic culture encompassed a hankering for the syntheses and great connections that only researchers of genius could capture. According to that conception, scholarly truths sprang from the visions of the solitary thinker rather than originating in schisms and critical exchanges of ideas.[82]

Speculation and understanding had pushed out the empirical acquisition of knowledge, with the consequence that instances of critical empiricism had failed to gain a foothold. Instead, an authoritarian relationship between teachers and students had been permitted at German institutions of learning, a relationship which reflected a hierarchical society. Dahrendorf's thesis was that the weak position held by the liberal mind-set at the academic institutions had had a structurally inhibiting effect on liberal democracy in Germany.[83]

The second book published by Dahrendorf in 1965 set a different tone. *Bildung ist Bürgerrecht* was crisply written and openly polemical.

---

80 Ibid., p. 184.
81 Ibid., pp. 184–85.
82 Ibid., pp. 185–87.
83 Ibid., pp. 190–91.

With the subtitle 'Plädoyer für eine aktive Bildungspolitik' (approx. 'A plea for an active policy of *Bildung*'), its aim was to intervene in the extremely lively educational debate of the mid-1960s. Picht's previously mentioned debate book *Die deutsche Bildungskatastrophe* was an obvious point of departure; but Dahrendorf also referred to topical contributions on school policy by Hellmut Becker, Friedrich Edding, and Hildegard Hamm-Brücher.

Dahrendorf wished to affect the direction in which the discussion was moving. He was convinced that West Germany had to open up its schools and universities in order to remain prosperous; he argued that the *Wirtschaftswunder* (the 'economic miracle') of the post-war era should be followed by a *Bildungswunder* (an 'educational miracle'). Such a development called for an active educational policy and radical reforms, but Dahrendorf looked in vain for a unifying idea.[84]

Dahrendorf's own bid could be summarised in the motto *Bildung ist Bürgerrecht*. First, he saw education as a basic social right and a prerequisite for a well-functioning civil society. Second, he emphasised the equality principle: no group should be favoured or disadvantaged because of their origins or their economic situation. Third, the aim of education was to enlighten citizens about their rights and broaden their horizons with respect to knowledge and wishes. This last aspect was the strongest and most revolutionary, and had the greatest potential to change people's lives.[85] 'An active educational policy with the purpose of realising the rights of citizens is the major task in German domestic politics', argued Dahrendorf. He regarded the process of modernisation, of liberating people from unwanted ties and opening up new opportunities, as unfinished in Germany, thereby establishing a connection to the main thesis in his *Gesellschaft und Demokratie in Deutschland*. Working for education as a citizen's right was consequently an even more urgent task in the Federal Republic than in Great Britain or the United States. The principal goal of the active educational policy was therefore to lay the foundations for a free and modern society.[86]

After this declaration of principles, Dahrendorf proceeded to devote several chapters to an examination of the obstacles and opportunities that existed for educational reform. A baseline in his argument was the need for a general expansion of the educational

---

84 Dahrendorf, *Bildung ist Bürgerrecht*, pp. 7–11.
85 Ibid., pp. 11–24.
86 Ibid., pp. 24–28.

system in order to encourage more people to graduate from upper secondary school and from university; another was that educational policy had to strive to modernise society and increase the educational levels of disadvantaged groups, above all working-class children, girls, children from the countryside, and children from Catholic families.[87]

Dahrendorf devoted one of his chapters to university reforms. Here, too, he argued for a general expansion, but called attention to the fact that the university often defended itself against reforms and regarded them as encroachments on academic autonomy. In addition, he emphasised the fact that there were inherent problems that would not be solved simply by increasing the number of professorships or universities. This gave rise to a reflection on the distinctive character of the German university.[88]

Traditionally, argued Dahrendorf, academic reform had been a matter of adapting the idea of '*Bildung* through science and scholarship' to changes in the meaning of *Bildung* and of science/scholarship. The most striking adaptation of this kind had happened when the Berlin university was founded. The basic principle was that scholarly-scientific research should be a medium for education. Dahrendorf felt that this idea still prevailed, but that the steadily increasing student numbers made it difficult to maintain the ideal of *Einheit von Forschung und Lehre* in practice. But he also had more principle-based objections.[89]

In order to realise *Bildung als Bürgerrecht* one could not, according to Dahrendorf, take the idea of *Bildung durch Wissenschaft* as one's point of departure, as had previously been the case. The strong orientation towards research that had existed for a long time prevented the growing number of students from getting an adequate education. In this respect, the contemporary German university was out of sync with the times.[90] Unfortunately, Dahrendorf could not see that anybody was endeavouring to find a real solution to the problems, neither the *Wissenschaftsrat* nor the new universities. One fundamental mistake was that a reform of the scholarly-scientific system became mixed up with a reform of the educational system.

---

87 Ibid., pp. 28–100. In another text from the same year, *Arbeiterkinder an deutschen Universitäten* (Tübingen, 1965), Dahrendorf specifically performed a class analysis of recruitment to higher education.
88 Dahrendorf, *Bildung ist Bürgerrecht*, pp. 101–06.
89 Ibid., pp. 107–08.
90 Ibid., pp. 107–09.

If the aim was to promote education as a civil right, as Dahrendorf felt it was, a reform of research was not necessary. Conversely, a research policy that was not coordinated with educational policy might fail.[91]

Dahrendorf's recipe for getting more students to graduate and for vitalising science and scholarship at the university was called division and differentiation. Inspired by Clark Kerr, president of the University of California, he wanted to transform the university into a *multiversity*, a knowledge centre that included a multiplicity of institutes, campus areas, and research centres. But that would require radical reforms. The combination of research and teaching had to be replaced by a more flexible idea, claimed Dahrendorf. All universities should be educational institutions, but not all should engage in research.[92]

He had no difficulty predicting that his proposal would meet with opposition in the academic world. Making tuition and not research the primary task of the university would trigger litanies about lost *Bildung*, the end of a great tradition, levelling, and transforming the university into a *Gymnasium*-like institution. But German universities – in contrast to English ones, which had retained a part of their pre-modern character – did not offer any real place for students who did not want to do research. German universities should create special supplementary educational programmes for future researchers, argued Dahrendorf. In other respects, teaching should be prioritised.[93]

One prerequisite for this entire reform was that the professors changed their attitude to their profession. To many of them, teaching the broader strata of society was an occupation below their dignity. 'Solitude and freedom are very problematic as points of orientation for a general education', wrote Dahrendorf, reminding his readers that the concept of *Wissenschaft* could be used as an alibi for a multitude of sins. It was necessary to adopt a clear-sighted approach and admit that the universities, no matter how prominent, were to a large extent institutions of teaching. Research was by no means conducted everywhere.[94]

In order to meet the demand for expansion and realise the motto *Bildung ist Bürgerrecht*, the German university had to abandon, or

---

91 Ibid., p. 110.
92 Ibid., pp. 111–13.
93 Ibid., pp. 114–16.
94 Ibid., p. 116.

at least thoroughly modify, the Humboldtian tradition. That was Dahrendorf's firm conclusion. He realised that there were strong legal obstacles against encroaching on academic autonomy, and that tradition-minded academics would protest. But to most students, a concept like *Lernfreiheit* was an empty phrase in any case.[95]

In 1965, Dahrendorf thus presented two publications that proceeded from distinct aspects of the German university tradition. In *Gesellschaft und Demokratie in Deutschland*, he traced a pernicious line in the German past and connected it with a general understanding of the country's modern history. His political message formed a framework for his analysis of the German university, and at the same time his observations from the scholarly-scientific sphere supported his thesis on social development in Germany. The anti-empirical speculation that had governed the academic world had its counterpart in the anti-liberal and authoritarian sentiments that had characterised social life at large. *Bildung ist Bürgerrecht* had a more concrete aim. In this work, Dahrendorf energetically promoted an expansion of the entire educational system, and in this process a basic reform of the university was necessary. The German academic ideals were outmoded and put obstacles in the way of desirable developments. In both texts, he hence argued for the necessity of liberating oneself from tradition. Only then could Germany become a genuinely liberal and democratic society.

Dahrendorf had adopted historical perspectives in several of his works. This was true not least in *Gesellschaft und Demokratie in Deutschland*, which may to a considerable extent be characterised as a scrutiny of social and intellectual patterns in the modern history of Germany. At the same time, his discussion of the German university did not come close to exhibiting the same interest in the historical dimension as, for instance, Schelsky's had done. Dahrendorf's presentation was linear, and there was no attempt to find complications. With him, indeed, the past served an almost instrumental purpose: that of showing how dysfunctional the classic model was in the age of mass education and democracy.

Although Dahrendorf displayed nothing like the familiarity with university history that Schelsky possessed, he was nevertheless dependent on the vocabulary of the Humboldtian tradition. In order to characterise one leitmotif in German academic life, he used the concept *Einheit von Forschung und Lehre*; and without going into

---

95 Ibid., p. 129.

its meaning to any significant extent, he repeatedly returned to this principle. The same was true of *Bildung durch Wissenschaft*. In both cases, there was something formulaic about Dahrendorf's usage; the concepts were manifestations of the old university that the reforms aimed to overcome. He found *Einsamkeit und Freiheit* even more problematic. This was an ideal that functioned as a symbol for an introverted, anti-social kind of scholarship. As a social phenomenon it was ominous.

It is notable that Dahrendorf did not polemise openly against Helmut Schelsky and his idea of the university. There were no explicit references to the book *Einsamkeit und Freiheit*, or to any other of Schelsky's contributions to the debate on the university. On the other hand, Schelsky was present as an important but never expressly identified point of reference. When Dahrendorf referred to the ideal of solitude and freedom without citing any source, it was Schelsky's interpretation that he responded to.

Dahrendorf's ambition to intervene in the educational debate was also reflected in his use of certain concepts. He exhibited his lack of satisfaction with the idea of solitude and freedom by launching the concepts *Disput und Freiheit* and *Kritik und Freiheit*. To debate and to criticise were much more desirable activities than cutting oneself off from society and searching for one's own truth. Being a liberal, he had, not surprisingly, fewer problems with *Freiheit*. In contrast to Schelsky, however, he did not elaborate on the meanings of academic freedom in these texts. He merely provided brief hints to the effect that some of the traditional freedoms (such as *Lernfreiheit*) were mostly illusions, and that his proposed reforms would involve an encroachment on the autonomy of the university. But all this was to the benefit of a greater freedom, a freedom for students and citizens.

'Hochschule in der Demokratie'

'Der Sozialistische Deutsche Studentenbund' (SDS) was founded in Hamburg in 1946 and initially attracted many left-leaning former soldiers. It was formally independent of the Social Democratic party, but in reality there were close connections. That became apparent during Helmut Schmidt's time as chairman, when several Communist sympathisers were expelled. During the 1950s, the SDS was actively engaged against what were regarded as reactionary and militaristic tendencies in West German society. But as the SPD gradually renounced the radicalism of Marxism, a renunciation manifested in the new Godesberg programme of 1959, antagonism between the student organisation and the Social Democratic movement grew. In 1961, the party leadership forced a break with the SDS and instead tied a new student association to the party. During the years that followed, the SDS would function as an umbrella organisation for a number of left-wing groups, and during the latter half of the 1960s it formed the nucleus of the extra-parliamentary opposition before it was disbanded in 1970 as a consequence of factional infighting and internal ruptures.[96]

At an SDS conference in Frankfurt in October 1961, a working group from West Berlin presented a 180-page typewritten memorandum, *Hochschule in der Demokratie*. Behind the text were four students born between 1938 and 1940 who studied history, philosophy, sociology, and jurisprudence, respectively, at the Freie Universität: Wolfgang Nitsch, Uta Gerhardt, Claus Offe, and Ulrich K. Preuß. They all belonged to a younger generation who had been children during the Second World War, and who would be at the forefront of the confrontation with the older generation's unfinished reckoning with Nazism during the 1960s. *Hochschule in der Demokratie* was not just any text; in student circles, it would become almost synonymous with a radical left-wing university programme.[97]

The four students had obviously been influenced by Marxist theory and empirical social science. More specifically, they invoked the critical investigations of the university and society that had taken shape at the 'Institut für Sozialforschung' in Frankfurt during the

---

96 Willy Albrecht, *Der Sozialistische Deutsche Studentenbund (SDS): Vom parteikonformen Studentenverband zum Repräsentanten der Neuen Linken* (Bonn, 1994); Siegward Lönnendonker, Bernd Rabehl, & Jochen Staadt, *Die antiautoritäre Revolte: Der Sozialistische Deutsche Studentenbund nach der Trennung von der SPD: 1960–1967* (Opladen, 2002); Tilman P. Fichter & Siegward Lönnendonker, *Kleine Geschichte des SDS: Der Sozialistische Deutsche Studentenbund von Helmut Schmidt bis Rudi Dutschke* (Essen, 2007).

97 *Hochschule in der Demokratie: Denkschrift des Sozialistischen Deutschen Studentenbundes zur Hochschulreform* (Frankfurt am Main, 1961). The memorandum lacked information about the authors, and on p. 1 its collective origins were emphasised. From other material, however, it is clear that it was Wolfgang Nitsch, Uta Gerhardt, Claus Offe and Ulrich K. Preuß who were the primary authors. See Lönnendonker, Rabehl, & Staadt, *Die antiautoritäre Revolte*, pp. 34–36; Fichter & Lönnendonker, *Kleine Geschichte*, p. 108; and Rohwedder, 'SDS-Hochschuldenkschrift', p. 160.

1950s. In 1957 Jürgen Habermas had published an article in this context with the title 'Das chronische Leiden der Hochschulreform' (approx. 'The chronic disease of university reform'). He argued that it was wrong to try – as had Karl Jaspers and others during the early post-war era – to re-establish the old university. Instead, he insisted that critical reflection on the roles of science and scholarship and the university in society must form the point of departure for all reforms. This was a fundamental idea that was discussed in *Hochschule in der Demokratie*.[98]

The purpose of this text was to intervene in the current university-political debate from a Socialist point of view. One of the authors' aims was to address the situation of students, reaching out to anybody who was thinking in a 'genuinely democratic' way.[99] The democratisation of higher education was consequently a recurring theme. The authors argued firmly for the democratic representation of students, an improved situation with respect to student welfare, greater social relevance on the part of subjects, and other similar demands; but they also analysed the place of the university in modern society at a theoretical level. The target for them was the conservative professorial establishment. They especially criticised those who wanted to find a solution to the university crisis by way of backward-looking utopias and unrealistic concepts of *Bildung*.[100]

Already in the introduction to *Hochschule in der Demokratie* the four socialist students presented their main theses. The crucial point was that the university was nowadays a part of the industrial mode of production. The intellectual and organisational model for the German university since the beginning of the nineteenth century was

---

98 Lönnendonker, Rabehl, & Staadt, *Die antiautoritäre Revolte*, pp. 34–35; Jürgen Habermas, 'Das chronische Leiden der Hochschulreform', *Merkur*, 3 (1957). Habermas's article was based on the introduction to an empirical investigation that he had written in close cooperation with Theodor W. Adorno. See Jürgen Habermas, *Protestbewegung und Hochschulreform* (Frankfurt am Main, 1969), p. 51.
99 The category 'genuinely democratic' came directly from the vocabulary of the Frankfurt School. It was, for instance, used in the investigations that Jürgen Habermas, Ludwig von Friedeburg, Christoph Oehler, and Friedrich Weltz conducted and that were published in collected form as *Student und Politik: Eine soziologische Untersuchung zum politischen Bewußtsein Frankfurter Studenten* (Neuwied am Rhein, 1961). Horkheimer spoke of 'genuine democracy', *genuine Demokratie*.
100 *Hochschule in der Demokratie* (1961); Lönnendonker, Rabehl & Staadt, *Die antiautoritäre Revolte*, pp. 35–36.

therefore outmoded and needed to be reconsidered. According to the authors, the classic German university had its roots in Humboldt's reforms and had been guided by three principles: 'Einsamkeit und Freiheit', 'Autonomie der Universität', and 'Einheit von Forschung und Lehre'. The last-mentioned ideal had proved to be particularly productive, while the first two were an attempt on the part of the reformers to create a space for liberty in relation to the late absolutist state.[101]

As industrialisation progressed, however, these old principles lost their relevance. With the emergence of technological, natural-scientific, and economic educational programmes during the nineteenth century, the university increasingly became a producer of scholarly and scientifically trained specialists in the service of society. The goal was no longer to educate learned officials. The idea that the university should represent non-utilitarian scholarly-scientific research that benefited *Bildung* thus became obsolete. Even so, the idea itself lived on and could be used by those who wished to use science and scholarship for political purposes. The Third Reich was the most apparent, but far from the only example of this, argued Nitsch, Gerhardt, Offe, and Preuß.[102]

During the post-war era, it became perfectly clear that the classic principles had been emptied of all meaning. When they were used it was, at best, as an expression for a romantic escapism; but more often they concealed special interests within and outside the university. The idea that the German university tradition was 'im Kern gesund' ('healthy at the core') was repeated as fervently as though it were a creed. Nor did the ideal of *Bildung* find any favour with these authors. That ideal justified the exaggerated social prestige of German academics and thereby contributed to strengthening the anti-democratic potential of society. Besides, it supported the authoritarian idea that there was an intellectual elite who had the right to govern the uneducated masses. Consequently, the concept of *Bildung* was a means of ideological indoctrination rather than an expression of the principle of rationality. It cemented the prevailing order.[103]

The authors' opinion was clear: if the university was not to become a tool of the Counter-Enlightenment, it had to formulate a

---

101 *Hochschule in der Demokratie* (1961), pp. 3–4.
102 Ibid., pp. 4–5.
103 Ibid., pp. 5–6.

new understanding of itself. During the last 150 years the German university had always been an apologist for the reaction, despite the belief of academics that they remained neutral in the conflicts of society. The four authors therefore proposed that the autonomy of the university should be reformulated and instead be given the meaning of freedom from manipulation by society. The goal had to be an emancipation of the individual. Only by such means could the university maintain a critical distance to society and prevent science and scholarship from supporting the position of those in power.[104] It was also important, emphasised the authors, to remind people that an advanced division of labour was an absolute necessity in science and scholarship, as it was in modern society as a whole. This was a fact that could not be concealed beneath romantic references to 'Einheit der Wissenschaften'. On the contrary, the realisation that specialisation was necessary should form a point of departure for attempts to overcome narrow-minded scholarly-scientific thinking.[105]

The four writers derived their general conclusion from this line of argument. The activities of the university, they argued, needed to be directed toward permanent criticism both of the various branches of science and scholarship and of conditions in society. They emphasised that this goal was not at odds with science and scholarship, but was very much compatible with their true purpose: standing up for critical rationality in the service of humanity.[106]

In the introduction to its text, the 'Sozialistische Deutsche Studentenbund' thus presented fundamental criticism of the German university. In the course of the ensuing years the four authors developed their arguments, and in 1965 they published a voluminous book of almost 500 pages with a similar-sounding title, *Hochschule in der Demokratie*. The subtitle, 'Kritische Beiträge zur Erbschaft und Reform der deutschen Universität' ('Critical contributions to the heritage and reform of the German university'), specified its orientation. According to the authors, the 1961 version had been characterised by a programmatic approach. Now they wanted to find a firmer basis for their arguments and discuss alternatives. In particular, they expanded the intellectual-historical sections of the

---

104 Ibid., pp. 6–7.
105 Ibid., pp. 7–8.
106 Ibid., pp. 8–9.

book and placed the post-war university in relation to a longer German tradition.[107]

In a preface Jürgen Habermas expressed his appreciation for the young authors. 'The reading [of this book] may be provocative for those who want to see a continuation of a grand, unbroken tradition', he wrote, but emphasised that the students' criticism seemed so merciless because they made such severe demands. The writers identified with ideals that were as lofty as those once championed by the German university, argued Habermas.[108]

Hochschule in der Demokratie discussed the university's organisation and place in society, along with democracy and scholarly-scientific freedom, the university's ideology, and the situation of the students. A concluding excursus was devoted to 'Women and the university', as though this were a marginal topic. The authors' relationship to the German university tradition became particularly obvious in an introductory historical chapter and in the third part of the book. Like the text from 1961, the new book was characterised by a fundamentally critical approach. However, the questioning tone was more restrained, and the presentation had become more nuanced. It included references to Jürgen Habermas, Herbert Marcuse, Alexander Kluge, Hans Rosenberg, and other writers who had contributed to the intellectual examination of German society during the 1950s and early 1960s.

Nitsch, Gerhardt, Offe, and Preuß wanted to transform the university of their own time. Today's academic system, they wrote, had been given its modern form before Germany was a democracy. Therefore it was necessary to uncover the historical context in which the German university had taken shape.[109] In the historiography that the writers developed in the introductory chapter, the German university system was compared to those of France and Great Britain. In the German states, economic life had been weak during the seventeenth and eighteenth centuries, with the result that no alternative foundation for scholarly-scientific institutions had been

---

107 Wolfgang Nitsch et al., *Hochschule in der Demokratie: Kritische Beiträge zur Erbschaft und Reform der deutschen Universität* (Berlin and Neuwied, 1965), p. xiii. In addition, a lightly edited version of the text from 1961 was published in book form: *Hochschule in der Demokratie: Denkschrift des Sozialistischen Deutschen Studentenbundes* (Frankfurt am Main, 1965).
108 Jürgen Habermas, 'Vorwort', in Wolfgang Nitsch et al., *Hochschule in der Demokratie*, pp. v–vi.
109 Nitsch et al., *Hochschule in der Demokratie*, p. 5.

created outside the traditional universities. Patronage was poorly developed; few people sponsored the Muses. In contrast to the situation in France and Britain, German scholars remained public servants. A kind of civil-service ethos settled across the university, limiting the intellectual field of vision.[110]

On the basis of this socio-economic analysis, the writers hence identified a historical circumstance that was particularly characteristic of German academic culture. Next they turned to the upheavals during the years around 1800 and the foundation of the Berlin university. In spite of a flourishing debate, the university remained a concern of the state. At the same time, the state's tasks and character changed. After the defeat suffered by Prussia against Napoleon, the Prussian focus of power shifted to the intellectual arena. In the idea of a cultural state that then took shape, the goal was no longer to educate civil servants for a specific professional area, but for the civil servants to safeguard the political order.[111]

In light of this general change, the writers discussed the classic university treatises from the early nineteenth century. Even though Schleiermacher, Fichte, and Schelling received some attention, it was Humboldt who was at the centre. His idea was that the new scholarly-scientific establishment in Berlin should distance itself from the – using Schelsky's expression – 'university, ossified in a guild system'. Here a new relationship would arise between professors and students; together, they would create an intellectual community. The overarching goal was to promote the process of *Bildung* of both the individual and the collective. A crucial prerequisite for this was 'Einsamkeit und Freiheit'.[112]

From this line of reasoning, the authors concluded that Humboldt's university was neither a corporate body of teachers nor a research-focused institute. It could be best characterised as a scholarly educational establishment for students. True research, if it existed at all, was conducted outside the universities, at academies or similar institutions.[113] Consequently, it was wrong – as constantly happened – to refer to Humboldt's ideas about 'the combination of research and tuition as the constituent principle of the *university*'. Here, the authors expressly referred to Schelsky's formulation in *Einsamkeit und Freiheit*, polemising against his perspective. Likewise,

---

110 Ibid., pp. 5–11.
111 Ibid., pp. 9–13.
112 Ibid., pp. 14–19.
113 Ibid., pp. 19–21.

they questioned his contention that this had been an 'institutional fundamental idea' in Humboldt.[114]

The critique of Schelsky, indirect or undisguised, did not stop at this. The four students valued Schleiermacher considerably higher than Schelsky had done. According to them, Schleiermacher had seen the combination of research and education as a structuring principle in a completely different way than had Humboldt. At the same time, when they considered the new university that took shape in the Prussian capital, they could not escape the impression that it lived up neither to Humboldt's nor to Schleiermacher's ideals. It had been characterised by a large number of students who only saw the university as a higher-level special school. In practice, there had been an institutional division between research and education. The professorial community had been a non-political guild-like association which had held all the power within the university, but had itself been subordinate to the ministry.[115]

The authors described how this university changed during the course of the nineteenth century but how its basic features endured. The post-war era academic institutions consequently traced their origins back to a pre-democratic stage. The Berlin university in all essentials served the interests of the state, not the free search for knowledge or society as a whole. What was described as its characteristic feature, the combination of education and research, was a chimera. It was the process of *Bildung* that had been at the centre.

Further on in the book, historical discussions recurred. The point of departure was the idea that the university as the quintessence of science/scholarship and *Bildung* was still defined by New Humanism and a philosophical idealism with roots in the early nineteenth century. The authors were critical of this; but they also identified an opposition between the actual tasks of the university (supplying highly specialised professional education) and its claim that it formed personalities through scholarly *Bildung*. The very idea of the university, in the form of a philosophically formulated notion of the unity of science/scholarship, seemed problematic to them. It was an ideal that did not consider the transformation of society, an ideal whose character chiefly amounted to an ideological declaration of the status quo.[116]

---

114 Ibid., p. 21.
115 Ibid., pp. 22–27.
116 Ibid., pp. 240–42.

Tradition under debate

The authors' presentation revolved around the theoretical discussions at the turn of the century in 1800 and the transformation of the scholarly-scientific system since then. From this historiography, five critical points could be extracted which also became decisive when the authors gave their verdict on the contemporary university. The first point had to do with the ahistorical attitude. The authors underscored that the process of *Bildung* was the central aspect of the New Humanist university. By doing science and scholarship for their own sake, a kind of internal ethical standard was created in those who pursued such activities, a standard which underpinned a moral course of action, according to the way of thinking that prevailed at the time. When humanity educated itself, it liberated itself from bourgeois society at the same time. *Bildung* led to individuality; and in consequence of that, all research acquired an individual stamp. During the course of the nineteenth century, however, it became increasingly difficult to maintain this idea. Today, argued the authors, it was deeply problematic to simply take over an older conception of the university. An ideal of *Bildung* could not be cut loose from its social and intellectual-historical origins.[117]

The second critical point revolved around the anti-social ideals of the Berlin university. A central idea in Humboldt was that the individual should realise his or her inner perfection, and that the outer harmony of society would be guaranteed as a result. In this model, the interests of the individual and of the state coincided. With the aid of idealist philosophy, an older, static worldview was overcome. It was therefore completely logical, argued the authors, that Humboldt made *Lernfreiheit* and productive solitude his principles. The individual development of students presupposed freedom from society; only the inner ties to science and scholarship were necessary for moral instruction.[118]

Their thesis was thus that the new university had isolated students and professors. This was not only a matter of distance to the surrounding world or a quiet place for intellectual labours. Underlying this sequestration was an endeavour to ensure that human beings were not compelled to be incorporated into the chain of production and subjected to alienation.[119] Besides, the authors said that Humboldt's university had been reserved for an intellectual aristocracy. His idea

---

117 Ibid., pp. 251–55.
118 Ibid., pp. 256–58.
119 Ibid., pp. 258–59.

of *Bildung* inevitably belonged to an older world, which had been brought to an end by the social differentiation and industrialisation of the nineteenth century.[120]

In this line of reasoning, two additional objections could be discerned that were later developed further. One of these, which was thus the third point, can be described as the illusion of ideas. That expression implied that the ideas behind the Berlin university were never realised. Instead, the authors of *Hochschule in der Demokratie* emphasised the fact that the older function of the university in many ways remained intact after 1810. The new university took over a good deal of that which was old, and it never managed to create its own social form. By contrast, the *idea* of the university was incorporated into the academic self-understanding without modification. In spite of the university having merged with other segments of society over the most recent 150 years, the academic regarded him- or herself as different from other citizens. When scholarly-scientific *Bildung* became more important as a status symbol, academics acquired positions of power.[121]

A fourth critical point was based on a more comprehensive analysis of society. On several occasions, the authors brought the changes in science and scholarship during the nineteenth and early twentieth centuries and the transformations in the economic order together. They argued that specialisation and differentiation gave science and scholarship a somewhat business-like character. At the classic university, an academic education had not been a matter of learning a profession or special methods, but of cultivating thinking and reason. However, the industrialisation of society made this idea increasingly obsolete. The university became part of the reproduction of society. A consequence of this was that a discrepancy arose between the *Bildung* that was provided by the university and the education required by modern society. Once more, the authors' conclusion was that the New Humanist idea was completely anachronistic.[122]

Finally, the German academic tradition was labelled as antidemocratic. This criticism contained several dimensions. One was historical: the Berlin university had been formed in pre-democratic conditions, and its ideals mirrored the society of that time. Another dimension was structural: the university was the bearer of an authoritarian heritage, and even at the present time professorial

---

120 Ibid., p. 259.
121 Ibid., pp. 260–62 and 301–02.
122 Ibid., pp. 260–62 and 299–302.

domination constituted an obstacle to the influence of students and democratic participation in decision-making. Yet another dimension was intellectual: during the interwar era, educational theorists such as Carl Heinrich Becker and Max Scheler had aired conservatively coloured disapproval of the mass university and the academic freedom of students. Such attitudes still lived on.[123]

All five forms of criticism were variations on a common theme: the obsolescence of the Berlin university. With Humboldt at the forefront, that university had been conceived during the pre-modern age of idealism and aristocracy. As early as the interwar years, it was obvious that it had not adapted to the new scholarly-scientific and social conditions, conditions characterised by industrialism, positivism, and large-scale research. To a great extent this was also true of the post-war era, the authors emphasised. In spite of many reform proposals presented during the last fifteen years, no adaptation had taken place. Above all, criticism had not been directed against the idea but against the concrete form of the university.[124]

At a time when the unity of science/scholarship had been dissolved, philosophy had lost its status as the central discipline, and the social role of science and scholarship had changed radically. Leading representatives of the university were still under the delusion that an idea from the early nineteenth century could serve as a guide. This was the basis for the criticism expressed by the SDS members. True, several reform proposals had been presented during the period following the Second World War, proposals aimed at changing the form of the university and adapting it to society while safeguarding its basic ideals. And it was precisely this last-mentioned circumstance that was the crux of the matter: the idea of the university – of this the authors were convinced – could not simply be transferred to contemporary times, but had to be placed in relation to a specific social order. If not, it just turned into a petrified ideology.[125]

Nevertheless, it was not enough to establish that changes in society, and in science and scholarship, called for a new course for the university. To the authors, it was important to formulate an idea of *Bildung* that was in harmony with the reality of the industrial world. In doing so, they at the same time openly attacked Helmut Schelsky, who had claimed that *Bildung* had to do with creating an intellectual independence vis-à-vis the world's insistence on action.

---

123 Ibid., pp. 327–29.
124 Ibid., p. 290.
125 Ibid., pp. 292–97.

His isolationism, which seemed to presuppose a somewhat ascetic way of life, was essentially different from the society-orientated ideals of Nitsch, Gerhardt, Offe, and Preuß.[126]

With his concept of *Bildung*, Schelsky had established connections to a classic line of thought concerning character formation. Conversely, *Hochschule in der Demokratie* recommended that each student should learn the virtues of a profession while at the same time scrutinising the praxis and social function of that profession. The Socialist students regarded this combination of vocational training and critical rationality as a model. It was an idea of university education that took its point of departure in the realities of industrial society, but that also turned higher education into a critical school.[127] However, there were institutional conditions to consider. First, one had to introduce a form of professional knowledge that was based on the critical social sciences. Further, it was important that future teachers, theologians, physicians, and engineers were given a theoretical understanding that could subvert their naive attitude to their respective profession. Last but not least, this part of an education must not be limited to specific knowledge about various professional traditions. Instead, students should learn to scrutinise the ideologies, stereotypes, and socio-economic circumstances that surrounded professional life.[128]

In two texts, a memorandum from 1961 and a book from 1965, the Socialist students in the Federal Republic had thus stated their views on the German university. While the earlier text was written in the form of theses and intended as a contribution to an internal discussion, the latter was more complex and aimed at a wider readership.[129] In its substance, however, the criticism was the same. The basic notion was that the Humboldtian tradition was obsolete and constituted an obstacle to the university's falling into step with the times.

The historical sections referred explicitly to Wilhelm von Humboldt and his ideas. Fichte, Schleiermacher, and other theoreticians who were Humboldt's contemporaries were also discussed, but it was

---

126 Ibid., p. 304.
127 Ibid., pp. 332–44.
128 Ibid., pp. 344–46.
129 Later, Wolfgang Nitsch said that he and his co-authors crossed out the most radical phrases in order to have a better chance of reaching out to 'progressive, bourgeois, idealistic people'. See Lönnendonker, Rabehl, & Staadt, *Die antiautoritäre Revolte*, pp. 39–40.

Humboldt who was the central figure. The origin of the authors' historiography was the same as, for instance, that of Ritter and Schelsky: the upheavals around the turn of the century in 1800, the New Humanist treatises, and the foundation of the Berlin university. Their evaluation, on the other hand, had a different character. These writers did not look back at a golden age that had later changed into a long period of steady decline. However, they were not as unambiguously critical, especially not in the book, of the utopia that Humboldt and those who thought like him had drawn up. They were certainly critical of the undemocratic spirit, and they emphatically turned against the ideal according to which academics should be kept apart from their surroundings; but they did not reject the idea of *Bildung* in itself. Instead, their basic objection was that the idea of the university had not been adapted to the world of the industrial society. There was clear irritation towards the attitude of *im Kern gesund*, an attitude which they regarded as a complacent refusal to see the problematic aspects of the German tradition, and which they felt was lamentably widespread among leading academic representatives. It is natural to regard this as an aspect of young people's general resentment at conservative self-satisfaction during the late Adenauer era. During the second half of the 1960s, this smouldering discontent would flame up into protests and revolts.

It is worth noting that these young students with a radical self-perception afforded so much space to historical discussions about the German university. Whether they liked it or not, they used the classic tradition as their point of departure. The strong links to the principles of the Humboldtian model also became obvious when the SDS members drew up their own visions. Starting out from strong concepts taken from tradition – *Einsamkeit und Freiheit*, *Einheit von Forschung und Lehre*, *Autonomie der Universität* – they claimed that these had lost their original meanings. In this context, it is symptomatic that they either frankly declared that a concept had lost its meaning (such as *Einsamkeit und Freiheit*) or that a concept needed to be reformulated (such as *Autonomie der Universität*). Their own contributions to the academic vocabulary were limited. In many ways, they depended on reinterpretations of an established terminology.

Hochschule in der Demokratie was not characterised by Marxist jargon or by the rhetoric of class struggle. More important as sources of inspiration were Jürgen Habermas, Herbert Marcuse, and – more generally – the Frankfurt School analyses of science and society. The concept of praxis, which was not defined in any detail, was central, as were critical, relatively concrete lines of reasoning about the social conditions of students and of working life. On a more overarching level, the authors made connections to an ongoing discussion about industrial modernity which engaged people of varying ideological colours.[130]

On this point, there was a clear connection between the young Socialists and Helmut Schelsky, who had repeatedly discussed the predicament of modern society in his writings. His interpretation of the Humboldtian tradition and his idea of the university of the 1960s were fixed points of reference for the Socialist students, and they constructed parts of their historiography on the basis of his *Einsamkeit und Freiheit*. In all essentials, however, they remained critical of Schelsky's statements and evaluations. This was true with respect to aspects of German university history, where they, for instance, valued Schleiermacher more highly than did Schelsky, but in return did not care much for Becker and Scheler. More important, though, was their repudiation of Schelsky's conception of the university. They condemned his social ideal ('Einsamkeit und Freiheit') as isolationist, his comprehensive vision ('Einheit von Forschung und Lehre') as illusory, and his ideal of *Bildung* as outmoded. Nor did his new creation, 'the theoretical university', find favour with them. In their opinion, it was a mistake to separate the theoretical elements into a special institute; on the contrary, theoretical-critical elements should permeate all academic educational programmes.[131]

The West German students consequently intervened in a discussion on the ideal university that had been going on for a long time. During the earlier half of the 1960s this discussion was conducted with special overtones, characterised, as this period was, by the expansion of the university and increasingly loud demands for reform. Schelsky's intervention breathed life into the debate. Anyone who wanted to offer a substantial intellectual contribution had to adopt a stance with respect to his ideas, whether the contributor sympathised with him or not.

Debating tradition

In 1960, the Humboldt-Universität zu Berlin celebrated its 150-year anniversary. In the years leading up to it, several university jubilees

---

130 Hacke, *Philosophie der Bürgerlichkeit*.
131 Nitsch et al., *Hochschule in der Demokratie*, p. 292.

Tradition under debate

had been celebrated in the GDR – in Greifswald in 1956, in Jena in 1958, and in Leipzig in 1959. They had, in various ways, taken the form of celebrations of the new Socialist university; but they had also triggered conflicts between a younger, ideologically persuaded group of academics and an older faction of more conservatively aligned professors. The festivities in East Berlin in 1960 also aimed to demonstrate the role of the university in a Socialist society. In the East German capital, the Cold War was a grimly insistent reality at the same time. In the following year, 1961, the Berlin wall would be built and would stand as a manifestation of ideological division. Leading academic and political figures in the GDR therefore attempted to use the anniversary in order to emphasise that the Humboldt-Universität was the obvious centre of scholarly life in the city. The rivalry with the Freie Universität was plain for all to see. Invitations to the festivities were sent out during the spring of 1960 to universities in the Federal Republic and in other Western countries, but not to the West Berlin university. In protest, the Freie Universität turned to the West German rectors' conference, exhorting the latter as well as the rest of the West

12 Humboldt University anniversary celebrations in 1960, in the GDR period

German universities to boycott the official celebration. Its demand was accepted.[132]

The struggle between East and West could also be studied in the publications that were produced for the occasion of the 150-year anniversary. The official East German Festschrift was given the title *Forschen und Wirken* (approx. 'Doing research and working [towards a purpose]') and was published in three volumes of more than 2,500 pages in total. The first of these contained contributions on important personalities and events in the history of the university; the last two contained current research articles from various disciplines.[133] In the historical presentation at the beginning of the first volume, a picture was painted of the development of the university during the early nineteenth century. The writer of this text was Kurt Schröder, mathematician and rector between 1959 and 1965. He emphasised the crucial importance of Wilhelm von Humboldt for the foundation of a new kind of university inspired by the Enlightenment and the French Revolution. Schröder adopted the mandated historiography in the continuation of his account, in particular in his treatment of Fascism and the Socialist transformation after 1945. In a contribution following that of Schröder, educationalist Heinrich Deiters supplied a rosy picture of the person and innovator Wilhelm von Humboldt.[134]

The same year saw the appearance of a sort of counter-publication, *Idee und Wirklichkeit einer Universität* ('The idea and the reality of a university'). The editor was the philosopher Wilhelm Weischedel, supported by other professors in West Berlin. In the preface, however,

---

132 Tobias Schulz, *'Sozialistische Wissenschaft': Die Berliner Humboldt-Universität (1960–1975)* (Cologne, Weimar, and Vienna, 2010), pp. 76–81; Matthias Middell, 'Die Humboldt-Universität und die Hochschulpolitik der DDR, 1960–1985', in *Geschichte der Universität Unter den Linden*, ed. by Konrad H. Jarausch, Matthias Middell & Annette Vogt, pp. 263–73.

133 *Forschen und Wirken: Festschrift zur 150-Jahr-Feier der Humboldt-Universität zu Berlin 1810–1960*, ed. by Friedrich Herneck, 3 vols (Berlin, 1960). The fact that the 150-year anniversary of the Humboldt university coincided with the 250-year anniversary of the Charité hospital formed the point of departure for another celebratory publication: *Die Humboldt-Universität gestern – heute – morgen: Zum einhundertfünfzigjährigen Bestehen der Humboldt-Universität zu Berlin und zum zweihundertfünfzigjährigen Bestehen der Charité*, ed. by Gerhard Krüger (Berlin, 1960).

134 Kurt Schröder, '150 Jahre Humboldt-Universität zu Berlin', in *Forschen und Wirken*, ed. by Herneck, vol. I; Heinrich Deiters, 'Wilhelm von Humboldt als Gründer der Universität Berlin', in *Forschen und Wirken*, ed. by Herneck, vol. I.

Eduard Neumann, rector of the Freie Universität, emphasised that the West German rectors' conference was behind the book. It thus had a kind of official blessing. The text was essentially a publication of sources and contained a large number of key documents from the first decade of the nineteenth century (including Humboldt's memorandum), as well as a selection of texts from the turn of the century in 1900. The idea behind the work, explained Weischedel, was that the contemporary university should be able to consider its origins and examine whether its heritage was still felt to constitute an obligation. He himself felt that that was the case, and at the end of his introduction he stressed the importance of academic freedom, albeit without expressly mentioning conditions at the Communist universities. To Weischedel, Humboldt was obviously a vitally important intellectual and organisational figure in the history of the Berlin university. At the same time, the publication of documents in itself made it clear that Humboldt had been a far from solitary force.[135]

The Festschriften were components in the German–German interpretational battles about places of national commemoration that were fought over and over again during the time that the country was divided.[136] On repeated occasions during the anniversary year, the East Berlin academic establishment underlined that they saw themselves as bearers of the true Humboldtian spirit. There was a diametrically opposed evaluation in the Federal Republic. *Frankfurter Allgemeine Zeitung*, for example, maintained, in an article in November 1960, that the old Berlin university no longer existed, even if lectures were still given in the buildings at Unter den Linden. 'For twelve years, there have been two universities in Berlin: Freie Universität in the West and Humboldt-Universität in the East. One of them has taken over Humboldt's original idea and the other the building', claimed the conservative newspaper.[137]

In a broader context, beyond the acute situation that prevailed in Cold War Berlin, the Western reactions point to an interesting state of affairs. In his text, Wilhelm Weischedel made no independent

---

135 *Idee und Wirklichkeit einer Universität: Dokumente zur Geschichte der Friedrich-Wilhelms-Universität zu Berlin*, ed. by Wilhelm Weischedel (Berlin, 1960), pp. vii, xvi–xvii and xxxiv.
136 Many examples can be found in *Deutsche Erinnerungsorte*, ed. by Etienne François & Hagen Schulze, 3 vols (Munich, 2001) and in *Erinnerungsorte der DDR*, ed. by Martin Sabrow (Munich, 2009).
137 Quoted in Schulz, 'Sozialistische Wissenschaft', p. 81.

attempt to explain the relevance of the national university tradition to his contemporaries in any great depth. Celebrating the 150-year anniversary with a voluminous publication of sources demonstrated, if anything, the general deep respect that many professors in the West still felt for the classic German model at the beginning of the 1960s. In a contribution from a few years earlier, the chairman of the West German rectors' conference, mediaeval historian Hermann Heimpel, had repeated Becker's credo from the interwar era: the German university was 'im Kern gesund'.[138] And he was not alone. Another person who openly invoked an older idea of the university was the historian Ernst Anrich. At this time, Anrich published several books expressing this spirit.[139]

Even the grand old man of German university reflections, Karl Jaspers, made an effort to intervene in the debate. In 1961, he published a book entitled *Die Idee der Universität* – identical to the title he had used in 1923 and in 1946. This time, however, he had a co-writer, philosopher Kurt Rossmann. The publication took the form of an extensive inventory of the origins, ideals, and structure

---

138 Hermann Heimpel, *Probleme und Problematik der Hochschulreform* (Göttingen, 1956), p. 7. Heimpel expressed a similar attitude on later occasions. See, for instance, the address which he gave a little less than a decade later under a characteristic title: *Liebeserklärung an die deutsche Universität: Festvortrag* (Regensburg, 1965; an approximate translation would be 'A declaration of love for the German university: A celebratory lecture'). Several other contemporary texts of a similar nature – addresses, pamphlets, articles – are listed in Marion Junge, *Wilhelm von Humboldts akademischer Bildungsanspruch: Ein Beitrag zur Entideologisierung der klassischen deutschen Universitätsidee* (Hamburg, 1970), pp. iv–xiv.

139 Ernst Anrich (1906–2001) had joined the NSDAP in 1930 and had, as a historian, been involved in Nazi *Westforschung* during the Second World War. After the conclusion of the peace he worked as a publisher; among other things he published nationalist and right-wing extremist literature. He published his thoughts on the university in *Die Idee der deutschen Universität und die Reform der deutschen Universitäten* (Darmstadt, 1960). A few years before this he had published five of the classic New Humanist university texts in *Die Idee der deutschen Universität*, ed. by Anrich. See Peter Schöttler, 'Die historische "Westforschung" zwischen "Abwehrkampf" und territorialer Offensive', in *Geschichtsschreibung als Legitimationswissenschaft 1918–1945*, ed. by Peter Schöttler (Frankfurt am Main, 1999), and Lothar Kettenacker, 'Ernst Anrich und die Reichsuniversität Strassburg', in *Les 'Reichsuniversitäten' de Strasbourg et de Poznań et les résistances universitaires 1941–44*, ed. by Christian Baechler, François Igersheim, & Pierre Racine (Strasbourg, 2005).

of the university. The two authors stated that professing older values was no longer enough; the German university had to be given a new form. They presented a number of proposals for how this aim could be realised, among other things a recommendation that pronounced vocational training should be assigned to specialised colleges. But even though they eagerly promoted reforms, their efforts belonged within the framework of the great, established German tradition.[140]

In spite of the book's scope and level of ambition, it did not attain anywhere near the same importance for reflections on the university in the 1960s as Jaspers's earlier publication had done in the early post-war era. Back then, he had been an impressive figure. Now he was seventy-eight years old, and despite attempts at renewal it was obvious that he was no longer at the centre of things. Those who came to dominate the scene during this decade were decidedly younger than he, and they were the bearers of different experiences. Even so, it was not simply a matter of a new generation replacing an old one.[141]

Helmut Schelsky stands out as the single most important figure in the debate on the idea of the university during the 1960s. He indubitably belonged to another generation than the mandarins of the years of occupation, but at the same time he was a well-established professor; when *Einsamkeit und Freiheit* was published in 1963, he was fifty-one years old. Schelsky's formative experiences belonged to the time before 1945, but his entire professional life had taken place after the war, all of which he was old enough to have experienced. When it was over, he, like so many of his generation, tended to keep silent and look forward rather than confront and criticise. But even for this generation, feelings of guilt and a loss of previously cherished values were a reality.[142]

Here Schelsky differed from his antagonists of the early 1960s. In a study of German intellectuals and the Nazi past, A. Dirk Moses used the concept 'the forty-fivers'. This is a designation for

---

140 Karl Jaspers & Kurt Rossmann, *Die Idee der Universität: Für die gegenwärtige Situation entworfen* (Berlin, 1961).
141 See Kirkbright, *Karl Jaspers*.
142 Basic background about the concept of generations: Karl Mannheim, 'Das Problem der Generationen', *Kölner Vierteljahreshefte für Soziologie*, 7:2 (1928); Ulrike Jureit, *Generationsforschung* (Göttingen, 2006), pp. 20–25. Specifically about various German generations and their relationship to the issue of guilt: Barbro Eberan, *Vi är inte färdiga med Hitler på länge än* (Eslöv, 2002), pp. 245–61.

a generation of intellectual people born between c. 1922 and 1932 who shared similar experiences. Their youth had been marked by Nazism and the Second World War, and their transition to adulthood had coincided with the end of the war and the first post-war years. Taken altogether, these experiences produced a will and a propensity to confront the German heritage at a profound level and to reflect over the origins of the great catastrophe.[143]

Ralf Dahrendorf was a typical representative of the forty-fivers. He devoted a significant part of his work to examining the authoritarian foundations of German society and trying to promote a liberalisation, not least within the educational system. The most influential forty-fiver – Jürgen Habermas – was born in the same year, in 1929. On the basis of a critical, Marxist-inspired analysis, he involved himself in a number of fundamental discussions in the Federal Republic from the end of the 1950s, concerning, among other things, questions of pedagogy and educational policy. Habermas did not recommend a return to the nineteenth-century ideals but promoted a concept of *Bildung* that would give students the skills they needed to deal with rational and technological modernity. In contrast to Schelsky – with whom he had a critical, if not completely antagonistic, relationship – Habermas gave the emerging student movement his support in several texts written during the late 1960s. He collected these in the book *Protestbewegung und Hochschulreform* (1969; the title might be translated as 'Protest movement and university reform'). The volume may be read as a plea for radical reformism, but it did not contain any coherent conception of the ideal university.[144]

The students behind the SDS publication *Hochschule in der Demokratie* were born around the outbreak of the war. Their childhood and youth belonged to the 1940s and early 1950s. Together with somewhat younger people of their own generation, they would make up the nucleus of the sixty-eight movement. One

---

143 Moses differentiates between two kinds of forty-fivers: on the one hand 'the non-German Germans', who were represented by liberal or left-leaning intellectuals such as Jürgen Habermas, Peter von Oertzen, Ludwig von Friedeburg, and Werner Hoffmann; on the other hand 'the German Germans', who were represented by conservative or bourgeois figures such as Wilhelm Hennis, Hermann Lübbe, Odo Marquard, and Andreas Hillgruber. See Moses, *German Intellectuals*, pp. 55–68.

144 Habermas, *Protestbewegung und Hochschulreform*; Stefan Müller-Doohm, *Jürgen Habermas: Eine Biographie* (Berlin, 2014), pp. 163–67.

of their most powerful driving forces was a revolt against fathers, literally or figuratively speaking. Schelsky was one of these father figures.

In the university-ideological terrain of the early 1960s, there were thus several different types of knowledge actors. The oldest were represented by the last few of the mandarins. In the wake of the war, these men had shaped the discussions; but now their contributions mostly appeared as lingering echoes. They no longer had the ability to steer the debate. An important reason for this was that the intellectual and cultural life of West Germany changed during the dynamic times in the shift between the 1950s and the 1960s. The prominent figures of public life became younger and in some sense more diversified. The clashes of opinion about the university reflected this state of affairs. Contrary to what had been the case fifteen years earlier, there were now different groups who stood against one another. That created a different kind of friction and confrontation.

In spite of crucial differences in age, experience, and outlook, one also has to point to the common denominators that united the university debaters of the 1960s. They all moved entirely in the post-war world, and they were all busy reflecting over the place of the university in a modern, democratic industrial society. Their assertions were based on historical and often critical examinations of the German academic tradition. The debate was formed by these circumstances – a common realisation that there was a need to reform the university system, but with different suggestions as to how that reform should be carried out.

Just as in earlier periods, the discussions about the university can be incorporated into the greater intellectual patterns of the time. From the end of the 1950s, German history began to be subjected to a more openly critical scrutiny. There was far too much from the recent past that remained unexamined, and there were many former Brownshirts in the administration, the courts, and the schools who went on with their lives as though nothing had happened. But now, in the years around 1960, a change in the atmosphere could be discerned, and new winds blew across the country. Heinrich Böll's *Billard um halb zehn* (*Billiards at Half Past Nine*) and Günter Grass's *Blechtrommel* (*The Tin Drum*) were both published in 1959, heralding the new decade's wealth of artistic reckonings with the Third Reich. During the following years, Nazism was brought to the fore through a number of legal cases and political events that attracted much attention: the Eichmann trial in 1961–1962, the

Spiegel affair in the autumn of 1962, and the Auschwitz trials in Frankfurt am Main in 1963–1965.[145] As part of this processing of the recent past, West German historians and social scientists began to investigate the origins of the Nazi catastrophe more systematically. They shone a light on the dark heritage of history in order to uncover lingering authoritarian structures. Many of them later subscribed to some variant of the *Sonderweg* thesis. In this interpretation, Germany became a special case in the modern history of the West – an undemocratic, militaristic, authoritarian state that had set out on the fateful path that ended in Auschwitz back in the nineteenth century. In the university debate Dahrendorf was a clear exponent of this view, but it is possible to trace the same mental image in the SDS students, too. Schelsky did not concur with this historiography; but he also evinced a strong desire to investigate central pathways in German intellectual and social life.[146]

If the *Sonderweg* proponents tended to have Socialist or left-liberal sympathies, Schelsky supplied points of contact with a more conservative debate on ideas. In his book, Schelsky repeatedly disclosed his lack of understanding of radical Enlightenment thinkers. His fundamental criticism in that direction was that they had an ambition to enlist the university in the service of the state. He objected to the idea that universities, in a utilitarian spirit, should provide practically useful knowledge as well as to the state's pursuing a policy of character formation and instruction. Schelsky thereby invoked a broader current in early post-war Germany, a current that was critical of the Enlightenment. This anti-Enlightenment mind-set might have Marxist overtones, as in Max Horkheimer and Theodor W. Adorno; but during the 1950s there were also several bourgeois intellectuals and academics who developed a critique of the Enlightenment project, especially against its alleged dirigisme, hubris in respect of reason, and exaggerated faith in large-scale planning.[147]

---

145 *Lexikon der 'Vergangenheitsbewältigung' in Deutschland: Debatten- und Diskursgeschichte des Nationalsozialismus nach 1945*, ed. by Torben Fischer & Matthias N. Lorenz (Bielefeld, 2007).
146 Östling, 'Tysklands väg mot moderniteten'.
147 Hacke, *Philosophie der Bürgerlichkeit*; Moses, *German Intellectuals*. For an interesting example, Reinhart Koselleck, see Olsen, and also Hans Erich Bödeker, 'Aufklärung über Aufklärung? Reinhart Kosellecks Interpretation der Aufklärung', in *Zwischen Sprache und Geschichte: Zum Werk Reinhart Kosellecks*, ed. by Carsten Dutt & Reinhard Laube (Göttingen, 2013).

Generally speaking, the exchange of opinions about the idea and origin of the university was an aspect of the contemporaneous commitment to democracy. Since the late 1950s, more and more people had begun to question the conservative political culture in the Federal Republic. To be sure, parliamentarism had a firm foothold in the new Germany; but that was not the same thing as society being democratised. Inspired by tendencies in other Western countries – the new American president John F. Kennedy serving as the primary symbol – there was a call for a liberalisation of German social norms and institutions. Demands for an increased emancipation of women and freer sexual morals went hand in hand with a growing criticism of traditional authorities. Pluralism became a common leitmotif.[148]

These examples show that the West German debate on the university formed an integral part of greater national issues. In another respect as well, it was expressly national: its focus on processing the Humboldtian tradition and finding its strong or weak points. The recurring evaluation of the national academic heritage lent a distinctive quality to the West German discussion; it was historically profound and culturally narrow at the same time. In comparison with the mandarins who had dominated the years after 1945, however, the main figures were not quite as enclosed within their own German world. To several of the major topics that were discussed – the expansion of the university, the direction of studies, the conditions of research – clear contemporary parallels could be found in other countries. Besides, in some cases it was obvious that international impulses had permeated West German reality.

During the Cold War era, there was a competitive relationship between West and East Germany within all spheres of society. For the West German universities, the conflicts were accentuated not least in connection with the academic anniversaries; but the rivalry was latent the whole time, and it had a constitutive effect. Soviet science had proved capable of great deeds, and in the years around 1960 several Nobel Prizes went to that country's researchers. At this time, science/scholarship and higher education became a prioritised social concern within the Eastern bloc as well. Johannes Hörnig, who was

---

148 Anselm Doering-Manteuffel, *Wie westlich sind die Deutschen? Amerikanisierung und Westernisierung im 20. Jahrhundert* (Göttingen, 1999); Gabriele Metzler, 'Am Ende aller Krisen? Politisches Denken und Handeln in der Bundesrepublik der sechziger Jahre', *Historische Zeitschrift*, 275:1 (2002); *Streit um den Staat*, ed. by Geppert & Hacke.

responsible for science and research issues in the GDR for several decades, pushed for a change to the East German system during the 1960s.[149] A decision indicating the direction of the reconfiguration of the university system was made by the Communist Party in 1963. In order to master technological developments and hasten the Socialist transformation, the so-called third university reform was completed in 1967–1968. Its aim was to make university activities more efficient and strengthen the bonds between the university and the business sector; but also, once and for all, to break the ascendancy of the old professors and introduce a sectional structure. Research would be concentrated in special institutes and the universities would primarily be given the task of teaching. As a result, the idea of a combination of research and education would finally be abandoned. In practice, though, this division of property was not quite so clear-cut.[150]

University and science were thus elements in the general systemic competition that existed between the two German states. During the 1960s, both states moved further away from the original shared model in consequence of their respective reform processes. During this course of events, each German state functioned as a negative point of orientation for the other, at least when it came to its official self-representation. In practice, West and East were united not only in a general enthusiasm for planning, but also with respect to several concrete issues. This was, for instance, true of discussions about the university's commitment to society at large and about the professorial chair as a central component of the organisational structure.[151]

In spite of the status achieved by the United States as a leading country in the 1950s and 1960s, it is impossible to speak of an

---

149 Hannes Hörnig, *Zu einigen Problemen im Hochschulwesen beim umfassenden Aufbau des Sozialismus in der DDR* (Berlin, 1965); Lambrecht, 'Deutsch-deutsche Reformdebatten'.

150 Jessen, *Akademische Elite*; *Wissenschaft und Wiedervereinigung: Disziplinen im Umbruch*, ed. by Jürgen Kocka & Renate Mayntz (Berlin, 1998); Peer Pasternack, *Wissenschaft und Politik in der DDR: Rekonstruktion und Literaturbericht* (Wittenberg, 2010).

151 Tobias Kaiser, 'Planungseuphorie und Hochschulreform in der deutschdeutschen Systemkonkurrenz', in *Gebrochene Wissenschaftskulturen: Universität und Politik im 20. Jahrhundert*, ed. by Michael Grüttner et al. (Göttingen, 2010). See, in addition, Emmanuel Droit & Wilfried Rudloff, 'Vom deutsch-deutschen "Bildungswettlauf" zum internationalen "Bildungswettbewerb"', in *Geteilte Geschichte: Ost- und Westdeutschland 1970–2000*, ed. by Frank Bösch (Göttingen, 2015).

unequivocal Americanisation of the West German university. As previous chapters showed, the American occupational forces had not implemented a comprehensive change of the academic system during the early post-war years but had, to a great extent, left it to the Germans themselves to put their own stamp on it. As more students and teachers were given an opportunity to stay for longer periods of time in North America, there were a growing number of people who were greatly influenced by the different nature of the studies, the good conditions for research, and the vibrant academic environment in general. From the early 1960s onwards, the American model emerged as a laudable example in reform publications and university-political contributions. In a thorough study of this topic, however, Stefan Paulus demonstrates that very little of this had any concrete institutional repercussions in West Germany. Attempts to introduce more efficient leadership, bring in assistant professors, or replace professorial chairs (*Lehrstühle*) with departments failed. There was a vigorous resistance to changing the German academic order.[152]

For the issues that have been at the centre of this chapter – the intellectual debate about the basic character of the university – there were considerable synchronous parallels in other countries. At the same time, 1963, that Schelsky published *Einsamkeit und Freiheit*, Clark Kerr's *The Uses of the University* appeared. Three years earlier, as president of the University of California, Kerr had launched the California Master Plan for Higher Education. Its aim was to draw up a coherent system that would simultaneously include the most prominent research environments and broad educational institutions for a growing number of students. In *The Uses of the University*, which was based on a lecture he had given at Harvard, Kerr promoted the above-mentioned idea of a multiversity. The modern university, the one that had developed in the United States under German influence from the late nineteenth century, had been a coherent unit. But today, argued Kerr, an academic community no longer existed. The new multiversity was made up of a multitude of overlapping social and scholarly communities.[153]

In spite of Kerr's using his Californian experiences as a point of departure, there was a clear conceptual kinship between him

---

152 See Paulus, *Vorbild USA?*
153 Clark Kerr, *The Uses of the University* (Cambridge, MA, 1963); Roger L. Geiger, *Research and Relevant Knowledge: American Research Universities since World War II* (New Brunswick, NJ, 2004), pp. 73–82 and 234–37.

and Schelsky. Both men emphasised the idea that the university had to find a form that was adapted to post-war society, and both recommended increased differentiation. At the beginning of the 1960s, they were able to attract attention for their prescient visions; but only a few years later they were branded as reactionary by the radical student movement.

In Great Britain, too, one of the most important post-war documents of university policy was published in 1963 – the Robbins Report. For two years, the economist Lionel Robbins had chaired a committee appointed by Prime Minister Harold Macmillan. The committee would become a symbol for the expansion of the university during the post-war era. In his report, Robbins formulated the principle that everyone who had the qualifications and the desire should have access to higher education. From this followed a recommendation that the government should make large investments in the university system, which also happened during the following two decades. In Britain, as in other comparable countries, the sector expanded very considerably. Robbins also contemplated the basic tasks of the university in his report. In contrast to Schelsky and Kerr, though, the changes in society did not make him reconsider the basic recipe for research and higher education: in all essentials he adhered to the Oxbridge model.[154]

In a wider perspective, it is possible to trace a general change in the view of the university in Western Europe during the years around 1960. The individual universities went from having been regarded as solitary units to becoming components in a country's university system. At this time, too, a coherent national research and university policy evolved. Entirely in accordance with the period's ideal of large-scale planning, bureaucrats and politicians seriously began to see research and higher education as key societal resources. In parallel with this nationalisation of the university, an internationalisation was under way. The Fulbright Program, Alexander von Humboldt fellowships, and supranational rectors' associations brought academics into contact with one another, evoking a sense that a republic of the learned still existed.[155]

---

154 *Higher Education: Report of the Committee Appointed by the Prime Minister under the Chairmanship of Lord Robbins 1961–63* (London, 1963); Anderson, *British Universities*, pp. 131–62.
155 Rüegg & Sadlak, 'Relations with Authority', pp. 95–101. Using Finland as an example, Marja Jalava has convincingly illustrated how the reforms of the university system in the 1960s and 1970s were a national affair

These changes were fully discernible in the Federal Republic. Anne Rohstock has spoken of the first half of the 1960s as 'the true moment of birth for university policy'. For a time, Social Democrats, Liberals, and Christian Democrats could unite in a kind of modernisation euphoria.[156] The university-theoretical publications of Schelsky, Dahrendorf, and the Socialist students came into being at this moment of preparation for change. Their will to reform the university was paired with an examination of its history. This attraction to the past appears to be a distinctive feature, specifically characteristic of the German debate.

With Helmut Schelsky's book *Einsamkeit und Freiheit*, 'Wilhelm von Humboldt' or 'the Humboldtian tradition' finally gained a foothold in the West German academic consciousness. Certainly, Humboldt had appeared as a point of reference since the turn of the century in 1900; but even during the late 1940s, leading figures such as Jaspers preferred to refer to the classic German university. Schelsky's intellectual intervention brought Humboldt to the centre of attention.

One conceivable explanation for the increasing interest in Humboldt has been presented by Anne Rohstock. During the 1960s and 1970s, she points out, new demands began to be made on the university. On the basis of theories of human capital, the OECD and other similar organisations encouraged institutions of research and higher education to cooperate with the business sector, stimulating economic growth. Rohstock argues that some academics based in the humanities reacted to the new proposals by vitalising or reformulating an older ideal of *Bildung*. This reaction might manifest itself differently in different countries, but the Humboldtian tradition became a kind of unifying watchword.[157]

Rohstock's thesis is well worth considering, but it requires a degree of nuance. In the West German case, it appears more appropriate

---

that was closely linked with social and commercial policy endeavours. See Marja Jalava, *The University in the Making of the Welfare State: The 1970s Degree Reform in Finland* (Frankfurt am Main, 2012).
156 Rohstock, *Von der 'Ordinarienuniversität'*, p. 121.
157 Rohstock, '"Some Things Never Change"'. The Swedish case is analysed in Fredrik Bragesjö, *Bilda eller samverka? En studie av bakgrunden till universitetets tredje uppgift* (Göteborg, 2009) and Thomas Kaiserfeld, 'Massuniversitetets forskningspolitik: Samverkan och innovation i slutet av 1960-talet', in *Universitetets gränser*, ed. by Peter Josephson & Thomas Karlsohn (Göteborg, forthcoming).

for a later stage than for the early 1960s. Ideas associated with different forms of academic adaptation to the market had little or no impact during the period that has been at the centre of this chapter, at least not in the intellectual debate. To Schelsky and his adversaries, adapting the university to industrial, democratic modernity was the key issue. Arguing for or against cooperation with the business sector was not something that mattered to them. When they entered the discussion about the meaning of *Bildung* and the basic mission of the university, their aim was to provide a contribution to the evaluation of their own national tradition.

However, next time the debate about the basic academic issues recurred with full force, during the Bologna process of the early twenty-first century, the competitiveness of the German university was a central topic.

6
From Berlin to Bologna

The universities of the Federal Republic had undoubtedly fallen behind. This conclusion was drawn by the West German rectors' conference at the beginning of the 1980s. The modest number of Nobel Prize winners and the limited number of patents were obvious to everyone, as were the overcrowded lecture rooms and the countless students who never seemed to reach graduation.[1] In spite of these complications and problems – caused by, among other things, ever larger student cohorts and ever more shrinking funds – the big discussions about principles never took place. The intense intellectual interest that German academics had devoted to the question of the university in the 1960s had no equivalent in the final stage of the old Federal Republic. The fundamental academic ideals and the relationship to the German tradition did not seem capable of inspiring the same enthusiasm as before.[2]

---

1 George Turner, *Universitäten in der Konkurrenz: Möglichkeiten und Grenzen von Wettbewerb im Hochschulbereich* (Stuttgart, 1986), pp. 17–28; Christine Burtscheidt, *Humboldts falsche Erben: Eine Bilanz der deutschen Hochschulreform* (Frankfurt am Main, 2010), pp. 11–12; Mitchell G. Ash, 'Humboldt the Undead: Multiple Uses of "Humboldt" and His "Death" in the "Bologna" Era', in *The Humboldtian Tradition*, ed. by Josephson, Thomas Karlsohn, & Östling, p. 85. Parts of this chapter are based on Östling, 'Humboldts idé'; Johan Östling, 'Universitetets historia: Humboldttraditionen som akademiskt historiemedvetande', in *Historiens hemvist: Etik, politik och historikerns ansvar*, ed. by Patricia Lorenzoni & Ulla Manns (Göteborg, 2016); and Johan Östling, 'Universitetets moderna tid', in *Tiden: Symposier på Krapperups borg nr 10*, ed. by Kim Salomon (Göteborg, 2017).
2 Burtscheidt, *Humboldts falsche Erben*, pp. 12–14; Ash, 'Humboldt the Undead', pp. 84–85. Scholarly literature on Wilhelm von Humboldt and the German university tradition was published during these years as well. The following may be mentioned: Menze, *Bildungsreform*; Sweet, *Wilhelm von Humboldt*; Ulrich Hübner, *Wilhelm von Humboldt und die Bildungspolitik: Eine*

In the debate on ideas that did take place, it was not difficult to sense a mood of crisis. When the university in Heidelberg celebrated its 600-year anniversary in 1986, a few of post-war Germany's most prominent academics were asked to deliver an address under the heading 'Die Idee der Universität', a tribute to Heidelberg Professor Karl Jaspers. Several of the contributors – Hans-Georg Gadamer, Jürgen Habermas, Wolf Lepenies, Manfred Eigen – started out from the German university tradition.[3]

It was Gadamer who adopted Humboldt's model most unconditionally. He described how the Prussian state had existed in darkness at the beginning of the nineteenth century. The new Berlin university had, with its emphasis on *Bildung* and research, brought with it a new ideal, the aim of which was to make the entire horizon of reality visible. Today, argued the leading proponent of hermeneutics, the university was again in a crisis, and this was a consequence of industrial society rewarding vocational training and practical skills to the detriment of *Bildung* and basic research. A new balance was sorely needed. However, Gadamer argued, a difficult problem had appeared in that the students had been alienated from Humboldt's original idea. One reason for their alienation was that rising student numbers created obstacles for those who wanted all academic activities to be research-orientated. Another problem had to do with specialisation leading to increased distances between subjects. Still, the most serious factor was that young people no longer saw their studies as a mission in life, but as an assignment to be got through. At the same time, Gadamer saw promising opportunities, even though these were incredibly difficult to realise. One task would be to utilise the freedom that existed in a life of ideas, beyond '[society's] institutionalized structures of being'. Research, or at least insights into the unforeseeable knowledge process, could be one possible route. Another objective would be to encourage the development of students' judgement and their openness to new directions. Finally, Gadamer cherished hopes that the university would be able to engender a kind of solidarity, a sense of belonging

---

Untersuchung zum Humboldt-Bild als Prolegomena zu einer Theorie der historischen Pädagogik (Munich, 1983); *Wilhelm von Humboldt: Sein Leben und Wirken, dargestellt in Briefen, Tagebüchern und Dokumenten seiner Zeit*, ed. by Rudolf Freese (Darmstadt, 1986); *Wilhelm von Humboldt: Vortragszyklus zum 150. Todestag*, ed. by Bernfried Schlerath (Berlin, 1986); and Christina M. Sauter, *Wilhelm von Humboldt und die deutsche Aufklärung* (Berlin, 1989).

3 These contributions were collected in Manfred Eigen et al., *Die Idee der Universität: Versuch einer Standortbestimmung* (Berlin, 1988).

to a tradition that did not exclude criticism but instead encouraged new questions, new 'possible ways of shaping our own lives'.[4]

In his reflections Gadamer combined personal observations, a profound familiarity with the German intellectual heritage, and an aspiration to identify suppressed potentialities. He received a kind of rejoinder, formulated on the basis of another theoretical position, in the contribution written by Jürgen Habermas. In his contribution, Habermas polemised against two positions. On the one hand, he turned against the idea that an organisation like the university embodied an idea; that notion was a relic of the bourgeois *Bildung*-elitist mandarin ideology. The opinion of Habermas, quoting K. Reumann, was that 'the assertion of unbroken fidelity to Humboldt is the existential self-deception of our universities'. This verdict, however, did not stop Habermas from devoting a large portion of his statement to scrutinising idealism and the ideas of the early 1960s.[5] On the other hand, Habermas criticised theories of the kind employed by Niklas Luhmann, theories in which research and higher education merely became elements in a system and not part of the life-world. His own proposal for how the university should be adapted to contemporary times was to a great extent concerned with a differentiation of its main tasks. Instead of idealistically holding on to an ideal of unity, he felt that the combination of research and education needed to be modified in order to be in harmony with modern working life. Similarly, he recommended a redefinition of the link between science/scholarship and *Bildung*. Toward the end of his text, he nevertheless argued for some sort of coherent idea of the university and emphasised the importance of communicative processes.[6]

It is worth noting that Habermas, in spite of his sometimes harsh criticism of older idealist ways of thinking, ultimately argued for an

---

4 Hans-Georg Gadamer, 'Die Idee der Universität – gestern, heute, morgen', in Manfred Eigen et al., *Die Idee der Universität*, translated into English as 'The Idea of the University – Yesterday, Today, Tomorrow' in *Hans-Georg Gadamer on Education, Poetry, and History: Applied Hermeneutics*, ed. by Dieter Misgeld and Graeme Nicholson, transl. by Lawrence Schmidt and Monica Reuss (Albany, 1992). The two quotations can be found on pp. 57 and 59.

5 K. Reumann, 'Verdunkelte Wahrheit', quoted in Jürgen Habermas, 'Die Idee der Universität: Lernprozesse', in Manfred Eigen et al., *Die Idee der Universität*, p. 141. English translation in Jürgen Habermas, 'The Idea of the University: Learning Processes', transl. by John R. Blazek, *New German Critique*, 41 (2014) (quotation on p. 4).

6 Habermas, 'Die Idee der Universität', pp. 164–70.

adjustment of the existing German system, not for its overthrow. In other words, it was a matter of academic emancipation within a clearly defined framework. A desire to bring the classic ideals into the modern age was also present in another vocal university debater from the same time period, Konstanz philosopher Jürgen Mittelstraß. In a dialogue with prominent German figures from the previous two centuries, Mittelstraß – for instance in *Die unzeitgemäße Universität* (1994; approx. 'The old-fashioned university') – opened the door to a more heterogeneous academic system. As was the case with Gadamer and Habermas, Wilhelm von Humboldt and the model he embodied was an explicit reference here.[7]

These philosophical reflections on the idea of the university were not disconnected from the general reform discussions that slowly got under way during the second half of the 1980s. However, historical circumstances meant that much of the work of renewal had to be put on hold. Instead, considerable energy had to be spent on remodelling the East German universities in the 1990s. At the same time, difficult times led to economic cutbacks, and the whole sector suffered from underfunding. The consequence was that the attempted vitalisation ground to a halt and that the West German model was preserved. By the end of the decade, there was a severely pent-up need for reform.[8]

At this time, more precisely in April 1997, President Roman Herzog delivered a speech that aroused a good deal of attention. He criticised the German university system for no longer providing the education that was required in an increasingly interconnected and globalised world. Above all, there had to be greater freedom. Herzog exhorted those in power to free the university from bureaucratic governance and to promote the development of a more differentiated selection of educational programmes. If the principles of competition were not realised, the German academic system would go under in the struggle for students, scholars and scientists, and research funding. At the same time, Herzog called for an adaptation of education to a changeable labour market. It was no longer the case that all students could be expected to end up in a traditional academic profession.[9]

---

7 Jürgen Mittelstraß, *Die unzeitgemäße Universität* (Frankfurt am Main, 1994). See also Kopetz, *Forschung und Lehre*.
8 Burtscheidt, *Humboldts falsche Erben*, p. 12; *Wissenschaft und Wiedervereinigung: Bilanz und offene Fragen*, ed. by Jürgen Kocka (Berlin, 2010).
9 Roman Herzog, 'Aufbruch in der Bildungspolitik', in *Aufbruch in der Bildungspolitik: Roman Herzogs Rede und 25 Antworten*, ed. by Michael Rutz (Munich, 1997). See also Burtscheidt, *Humboldts falsche Erben*, p. 7.

From Berlin to Bologna 211

In the year before this, in 1996, the Social Democratic educational politician Peter Glotz had published a book entitled *Im Kern verrottet?*, a reference to Carl Heinrich Becker's phrase from the time of the Weimar Republic. Glotz was pessimistic about the situation but optimistic about possibilities of renewal, and he prescribed an increased dose of autonomy.[10] Only two years later, the prayers of both Herzog and Glotz were heard. In 1998, changes were made to the law that laid down the framework for the national university system (*Hochschulrahmengesetz*): the provisions that stipulated a certain inner and outer organisation were deleted. Deregulation and self-government were the watchwords of the day.[11] At the turn of the millennium, the *Wissenschaftsrat* rallied to the support of the same slogans. In a number of theses concerning the development of the German scholarly-scientific system, the major questions for the future were identified: internationalisation, a reinforced connection to praxis, and quality assurance through competition. Increased autonomy was a condition for all this.[12]

These shifts were taking place against an international background. In the middle of the 1990s, the OECD had determined that research and the expansion of the university sector were key factors in creating employment and growth in the so-called knowledge society. The European Union adopted these ideas in the Lisbon Strategy, which defined as a target that the EU would become the most competitive knowledge-based economy in the world. At the same time, new ideas were introduced for how the authorities and the public sector should be governed more efficiently. Inspired by the market solutions of private industry, New Public Management (NPM) became an umbrella term for management by objectives (MBO), decentralisation, putting out to tender, and follow-ups through quantitative evaluation. Eventually, the new management philosophy became a reality in German universities as well.[13]

---

10 Peter Glotz, *Im Kern verrottet? Fünf vor zwölf an Deutschlands Universitäten* (Stuttgart, 1996).
11 Burtscheidt, *Humboldts falsche Erben*, pp. 12–15.
12 Ibid., p. 7.
13 The scholarly literature on New Public Management is nowadays difficult to survey. The university and research sectors are discussed in, among other works, *Education and the Knowledge Based Economy in Europe*, ed. by Bob Jessop, Norman Fairclough, & Ruth Wodak (Rotterdam, 2008); Mats Benner, *Kunskapsnation i kris? Politik, pengar och makt i svensk forskning* (Stockholm, 2009); Chris Lorenz, 'If You're So Smart, Why Are You under Surveillance? Universities, Neoliberalism, and New Public Management',

At the turn of the millennium, there were thus important forces who wished to transform research and higher education in Germany. Influential groups advocated increased autonomy, increased competition, and increased adaptation to the labour market. But they would encounter vigorous resistance – from both students and professors. During the first decades of the twenty-first century, a series of battles were fought about the university and its mission. All in all, this phase comes across as one of the most debate-intensive periods in modern German history – fully comparable to the 1920s, the late 1940s, and the 1960s.

Several specific circumstances imparted particular fervour to the debate. The years following 2000 witnessed the publication of several works which revealed the serious condition in which the German educational system found itself. The first report that PISA (Programme for International Student Assessment) presented in 2001 undoubtedly came in for the most attention. It gave rise to a 'PISA shock' which had an impact on public discussion of the school system for a long time. Parallel to this, a torrent of international ranking lists and evaluations were published, all of which made it clear how difficult it was for German universities to compete with the most prominent Anglo-Saxon ones. The Europeanisation of policies concerning higher education and research that took place during the noughties, manifested in the creation of the European Research Council (ERC) in 2007, also intensified the competition. As a result, the German mood of crisis, which had taken shape during the final stages of the previous century, was further reinforced.[14]

At the centre of twenty-first-century German university debates, however, was the Bologna process. At a meeting in 1999 in the historic north Italian university town, ministers of education from twenty-nine countries agreed to create a uniform university landscape for Europe. The overarching goals were to promote mobility, employability, and the general competitiveness of the continent. During

---

Critical Inquiry, 38:3 (2012); and *Transformations in Research, Higher Education and the Academic Market: The Breakdown of Scientific Thought*, ed. by Sharon Rider, Ylva Hasselberg & Alexandra Waluszewski (Dordrecht, 2013).

14 *PISA & Co: Kritik eines Programms*, ed. by Thomas Jahnke & Wolfram Meyerhöfer (Hildesheim, 2007); Johanna Ringarp & Martin Rothland, 'Is the Grass Always Greener? The Effect of the PISA Results on Education Debates in Sweden and Germany', *European Educational Research Journal*, 9:3 (2010); *European Integration and the Governance of Higher Education and Research*, ed. by Alberto Amaral et al. (Dordrecht, 2009).

the ensuing decade, a new, joint education and examination system was gradually introduced. In most European countries the reform was realised without any notable opposition, but in Germany the Bologna process gave rise to heated discussions in the public sphere. A large number of texts were published, and the resistance even produced physical manifestations. In Mainz, the exegete Marius Reiser stepped down in protest against what he saw as the levelling of academic studies. On repeated occasions students took to the streets to demonstrate, and the culmination was reached with the great *Bildungsstreik* ('*Bildung* strike') of 2009.[15]

Another important tendency during the early twenty-first century was the investment in scholarly-scientific excellence that was made in a number of countries. In Germany, the extensive research-excellence programme came to be called the *Exzellenzinitiative* (actually 'Exzellenzinitiative des Bundes und der Länder zur Förderung von Wissenschaft und Forschung an deutschen Hochschulen', approx. 'Initiative of excellence by the federal and state governments for the promotion of science, scholarship, and research at German universities'). By adding extra funds, the *Deutsche Forschungsgemeinschaft* and the *Wissenschaftsrat* wished to stimulate a genuine scholarly-scientific advance, not least in order to increase German visibility in the international world of research. After long negotiations between the federal and state governments, the first selection round was implemented in 2005–2006. Three universities were considered to have particularly good future prospects and were dubbed 'elite universities'. In addition, around twenty prominent research environments (*Exzellenzcluster*) were identified, and roughly as many postgraduate research schools were created. This process was repeated in another two rounds, the last one beginning in 2012. In a report presented in January 2016 by an international commission led by Swiss physicist Dieter Imboden, the substantial German investment in research excellence was highly commended. The commission recommended that the programme should continue, but also offered suggestions for further developments.[16]

---

15 Philipp Eckardt, *Der Bologna-Prozess: Entstehung, Strukturen und Ziele der europäischen Hochschulreformpolitik* (Norderstedt, 2005); Burtscheidt, *Humboldts falsche Erben*.

16 *Die Exzellenzinitiative: Zwischenbilanz und Perspektiven*, ed. by Stephan Leibfried (Frankfurt am Main, 2010); and Hristina Markova, *Exzellenz durch Wettbewerb und Autonomie? Deutungsmuster hochschulpolitischer Eliten am Beispiel der Exzellenzinitiative* (Konstanz, 2013). See the final report

13 Student protests in Magdeburg in 2010

The *Exzellenzinitiative* encountered some criticism; but it did not trigger any waves of protest of the same magnitude as the Bologna process. Nor did the excellence initiative shake the foundations of the academic system. The large number of contributions to the debate published in the years after 2000 – from sober analyses to splenetic pamphlets – were essentially aimed at the Bologna process. And as never before, Wilhelm von Humboldt and the tradition that he represented were at the centre of things.

The morphology of the Bologna process

Closer inspection shows that it was primarily during the second half of the noughties, in particular between 2006 and 2009, that the waves of debate were at their highest. This was a time when the Bologna process became a reality at the universities, and its possible implications dawned on students and professors alike. It

---

of the so-called Imboden Commission, 'Internationale Expertenkommission zur Evaluation der Exzellenzinitiative: Endbericht', https://www.bmbf.de/files/Endbericht_Internationale_Expertenkommission_Exzellenzinitiative.pdf (accessed 15 February 2016). For historical observations, see Margit Szöllösi-Janze, '"Der Geist des Wettbewerbs ist aus der Flasche": Der Exzellenzwettbewerb zwischen den deutschen Universitäten in historischer Perspektive', *Jahrbuch für Universitätsgeschichte*, 14 (2011).

was also a time when the first rounds of the *Exzellenzinitiative* were implemented. The situation at that particular juncture was described in an endless number of newspaper articles and a large number of books, not infrequently with an extremely sharp point directed against the prevailing tendencies of the time.[17] The longer, more substantial writings were of dissimilar kinds. One group was made up of scholarly works, characterised by a matter-of-fact tone and aimed at description and investigation.[18] Other publications were clearly of greater importance in influencing public opinion. Some of these were general and could, for instance, deal with the concept of *Bildung*, while some concerned more specific phenomena. Another influential group was made up of theoretical or classic university texts.[19]

---

17 During the final years of the noughties, the leading newspapers and magazines of the German-speaking world – *Frankfurter Allgemeine Zeitung, Neue Zürcher Zeitung, Der Spiegel, Süddeutsche Zeitung, Die Welt, Die Zeit* – contained article upon article about the Bologna process and the criticism of the great educational reform. In trade journals, too, in particular *Deutsche Universitätszeitung (duz)*, these issues were discussed in great detail. An unusually explicit defence of the concept of the elite was presented by Heike Schmoll in *Lob der Elite: Warum wir sie brauchen* (Munich, 2008), a book that at the same time censured the pseudo-elitist initiatives involved in the *Exzellenzinitiative*.

18 Eckardt, *Der Bologna-Prozess*; Burtscheidt, *Humboldts falsche Erben*; Markova, *Exzellenz*. Naturally, it can be difficult to draw a sharp line between the scientific and the polemic. An example of this difficulty is seen in the case of Richard Münch. In three works – *Die akademische Elite: Zur sozialen Konstruktion wissenschaftlicher Exzellenz* (Frankfurt am Main, 2007), *Globale Eliten, lokale Autoritäten: Bildung und Wissenschaft unter dem Regime von PISA, McKinsey & Co.* (Frankfurt am Main, 2009), and *Akademischer Kapitalismus: Über die politische Ökonomie der Hochschulreform* (Frankfurt am Main, 2011) – Münch made a considerable contribution to the sociological understanding of the university debate, wishing at the same time to intervene in the discussion through his writings. See my interview with Münch: Johan Östling, 'Richard Münch: Marknadsekonomin har koloniserat universitetet', *Respons*, 2012, no. 1. See, in addition, George Turner, *Von der Universität zur university: Sackgassen und Umwege der Hochschulpolitik seit 1945* (Berlin, 2013).

19 Among the more general works – often critical, sometimes ironic, sometimes essayistic – the following may be mentioned: Julian Nida-Rümelin, *Humanismus als Leitkultur: Ein Perspektivenwechsel* (Munich, 2006); Uwe Kamenz & Martin Wehrle, *Professor Untat: Was faul ist hinter den Hochschulkulissen* (Berlin, 2007); Jochen Krautz, *Ware Bildung: Schule und Universität unter dem Diktat der Ökonomie* (Kreuzlingen, 2007); and *Bildung? Bildung!*

A distinct category was the just over half-dozen anthologies that explicitly discussed the Bologna process. Behind them were usually academics who, to a varying extent, combined scholarly-scientific claims with critical analysis. *Was ist eine Universität?*, published in 2008 by theatre scholars Ulrike Haß and Nikolaus Müller-Schöll, was typical in many respects. In this case around ten contributions had been collected from, above all, social scientists and humanists. One common denominator in their texts was a critical illumination of an increasing adaptation to the market, an accelerating separation of research and teaching, and a profound shift in meaning when it came to academic key concepts. The denunciation of the Bologna process was harsh; but like other books of the same kind, this one lacked edifying future visions and innovative programmes. Behind the criticism of contemporaneous demands for economic efficiency and dreams of scholarly-scientific excellence, it was possible to discern an idealisation of a recent past.[20]

In this anthology, as in companion volumes such as *Der Bologna-Prozess und die Veränderung der Hochschullandschaft* (2007), *Humboldts Albtraum* (2008), *Bachelor bolognese* (2009), and *Bologna-Schwarzbuch* (2009), a historical dialogue with the German university tradition was not the main issue. Nevertheless, 'Humboldt' was frequently invoked as a rhetorical concept, an ally for those who fought against utilitarianism and market adaptation.[21]

---

26 *Thesen zur Bildung als Herausforderung im 21. Jahrhundert*, ed. by Andreas Schlüter & Peter Strohschneider (Berlin, 2009). The publication or republication of theoretical or classic university writings included Jacques Derrida, *Die unbedingte Universität* (Frankfurt am Main, 2001); Theodor W. Adorno, *Theorie der Halbbildung* (Frankfurt am Main, 2006); *Was ist Universität? Texte und Positionen zu einer Idee*, ed. by Johanna-Charlotte Horst (Zürich, 2010); *Was passiert? Stellungnahmen zur Lage der Universität*, ed. by Johanna-Charlotte Horst (Zürich, 2010); Jan Masschelein & Maarten Simons, *Jenseits der Exzellenz: Eine kleine Morphologie der Welt-Universität* (Zürich, 2010); and Plínio Prado, *Das Prinzip Universität (als unbedingtes Recht auf Kritik)* (Zürich, 2010).

20 *Was ist eine Universität? Schlaglichter auf eine ruinierte Institution*, ed. by Ulrike Haß & Nikolaus Müller-Schöll (Bielefeld, 2008).

21 *Der Bologna-Prozess und die Veränderung der Hochschullandschaft*, ed. by Georg Bollenbeck & Waltraud 'Wara' Wende (Heidelberg, 2007); *Humboldts Albtraum: Der Bologna-Prozess und seine Folgen*, ed. by Franz Schultheis et al. (Konstanz, 2008); *Bachelor bolognese: Erfahrungen mit der neuen Studienstruktur*, ed. by Andrea Liesner & Ingrid Lohmann (Opladen, 2009); and *Bologna-Schwarzbuch*, ed. by Christian Scholz & Volker Stein

Other writings had a more specialised aim, for instance against the humanities or the elite-orientated research initiatives.[22] The books testified to the wide range and the emotional intensity of the engagement which had been triggered by the Bologna reform. Although there were original thoughts and observations in the anthologies, the limited space allotted to each writer rarely permitted any extensive discussions. Many contributions were quite similar; indeed, there was something formulaic about them. However, there were other writings that were more distinctive in their style and argumentation. These were monographic works by more or less prominent German-speaking academics, mostly with a background in the humanities and the social sciences. The larger format permitted a combination of historical and contemporary reflections. Directly or indirectly, they invoked the long German tradition of discussing the idea of the university.

Jochen Hörisch's *Die ungeliebte Universität* – with the subtitle *Rettet die Alma mater!* (approx. 'The unloved university – save the alma mater!) – attracted attention when it was published in 2006. The writer was a well-known scholar of literature and media with an extensive output; besides, he was present in public life and on the theatre stage. As in many other contemporary writings, the Bologna process came under fire; but Hörisch's approach was a more comprehensive one, and it assumed the form of a general scrutiny of academic culture at large. The growing workload, the application hysteria, the altered social position of professors, the dictates and primacy of money – all were taken up for discussion.[23]

Unlike other, more pamphlet-like works, Hörisch's book did not summon Wilhelm von Humboldt as a saviour. As a Germanic philologist, Hörisch was well acquainted with the period that had

---

(Bonn, 2009). A few years later, *Bologna-Bestiarium*, ed. by Johanna-Charlotte Horst et al. (Zürich, 2013), appeared – a collection of short, alphabetically arranged articles about the keywords and phrases of the Bologna process and the academic newspeak of the contemporary era: *Excellence, Employability, Evaluation, Peer Review*, etc.

22 *Universität ohne Zukunft?* ed. by Dorothee Kimmich & Alexander Thumfart (Frankfurt am Main, 2004); *Die Illusion der Exzellenz: Lebenslügen der Wissenschaftspolitik*, ed. by Jürgen Kaube (Berlin, 2009).

23 Jochen Hörisch, *Die ungeliebte Universität: Rettet die Alma mater!* (Munich & Vienna, 2006). See my comment, Johan Östling, 'Bolognaprocessen ett ramverk att fylla', *Svenska Dagbladet*, 16 May 2007 and Ash, 'Humboldt the Undead', p. 89.

shaped Humboldt. This was precisely the reason why he could keep an ironic distance to the many genuflections and bows before the Prussian educational reformer. This did not prevent him from personally dealing with the Humboldtian tradition in his analysis of what was wrong with the contemporary university. Hörisch argued that something wholly fundamental in the classic German research university had been lost: students and professors no longer loved their alma maters. The powerful emotional relationship to the university, the almost erotic desire, that had distinguished academics in earlier periods was lacking today. In order to breathe life into this slumbering romantic relationship, a new academic community needed to be created, both between and within the student and professorial collectives. Only in this way could a free academy and a true concept of *Bildung* be restored, argued Hörisch.

In the same year, 2006, the Austrian philosopher Konrad Paul Liessmann intervened in the discussion with his essay *Theorie der Unbildung*. In contrast to 1959 – when Theodor W. Adorno wrote his critical article 'Theorie der Halbbildung' – worrying about the spread of semi-education was not worth the trouble, according to Liessmann. The fragmentation and commercialisation of knowledge had made all talk of *Bildung* irrelevant. With this as a premise, he subjected the entire knowledge society to a furious scrutiny. Beautiful words about lifelong learning and research excellence were contrasted with infotainment and the educational factories of the real world.[24]

The philosopher from Vienna used the philosopher from Frankfurt as his point of departure and devoted a special chapter to the Bologna process. Liessmann was extremely critical. In his eyes, all that the new order brought was a single-minded orientation towards the skills of working life. The free, inquiring spirit had given way to proto-scientific vocational education for the willing lackeys of the market, where efficiency and adaptability were rewarded to the detriment of profound learning and original analysis. Bologna was a farewell to the European idea of the university, he concluded.

Liessmann relied on Humboldt's writings in his statement of the facts, but his book was a polemic intervention rather than a discussion about the topicality of the classic university tradition.

---

24 Konrad Paul Liessmann, *Theorie der Unbildung*. He later returned to the same issues in, among other places, *Bildung ist ein Lebensprojekt: Im Gespräch mit Konrad Paul Liessmann*, ed. by Martin Kolozs (Innsbruck, 2011) and *Geisterstunde: Die Praxis der Unbildung: Eine Streitschrift* (Vienna, 2014).

More complex and energetic in its exegesis was the collection of texts and speeches that Christoph Markschies published on the eve of the bicentenary of the Berlin University in 2010, *Was von Humboldt noch zu lernen ist*. Markschies, who had at that point been rector of Humboldt-Universität for four years, was at bottom a theologian, a patristics scholar, and a professor of church history with an international reputation. His references ranged from Christendom in classical antiquity via Friedrich Schleiermacher to completely contemporaneous events.

In his book, Markschies made use of the insights of university history in order to distinguish two main types of debater in the discussions on educational policy: the constant development pessimist and the irrepressible progress optimist. The former, he said, experiments with a kind of decadence model, where we have step-by-step distanced ourselves from a golden age (regardless of whether this age was located in 1810, 1900, or 1965). The progress optimist, in return, claims that the university is 'im Kern gesund' and has boundless faith in that institution's power to grow.

To begin with, the Protestant theologian Markschies answered the basic question in his book – what we can still learn from Humboldt – by posting a number of theses. He rejected the insubstantial reverence for Humboldt the monument that was expressed in empty festive speeches, maintaining that we have to read the original documents in order to see what Humboldt and his contemporaries really have to tell us. The early nineteenth-century idea of the university was permeated with Romantic dreams of unity and wholeness. While perceiving obvious limitations in those dreams, he had a strong faith in the ability of today's university to overcome dualistic ways of thinking and create an understanding that went far beyond specialist studies, or the boundaries between subjects. To Markschies, Humboldt became something of a conversational partner, an intellectual innovator to whom one could return in order to discuss things and test one's ideas.

Even after the culmination of the Bologna debate in 2009, voluminous books were written with reference to Humboldt. In *Wozu noch Universitäten?* (2011), philosopher Reinhard Brandt described the rise and fall of the German university of *Bildung*.[25] Julian Nida-Rümelin, a philosopher close to the Social Democratic Party, argued in favour of a renewal of the humanistic heritage

---

25 Reinhard Brandt, *Wozu noch Universitäten? Ein Essay* (Hamburg, 2011).

of *Bildung* and for a closer relationship between philosophy and pedagogy. Yehuda Elkana and Hannes Klöpper assumed a different position in *Die Universität im 21. Jahrhundert* (2012). They painted a picture of a number of major challenges for the future, but argued that the German university was far too deeply rooted in the structures and ways of thinking of the nineteenth century to take up these challenges. Even so, the subtitle of their book sounded unmistakably Humboldtian: 'Für eine neue Einheit von Lehre, Forschung und Gesellschaft' (approx. 'For a new unity of tuition, research, and society'). And in the book *Die digitale Bildungsrevolution* (2015), the authors Jörg Dräger and Ralph Müller-Eiselt referred to Wilhelm von Humboldt in their argumentation for the opportunities of digital transformation. Humboldt would have been in favour of digitalisation, they argued, because his motto had been '*Bildung* für alle' ('*Bildung* for everyone'). So many more people can access education because of the new technical and media-related opportunities.[26]

Consequently, the Bologna debate, with its preludes and epilogues, gave rise to a large number of publications. These publications might be of different kinds; but the strong presence of Humboldt was conspicuous in them all.

The ubiquity of Humboldt

Some characteristics of early twenty-first century disagreements about the Bologna process distinguished these disputes from earlier debates about the idea of the university. References to the classic ideals were seemingly more numerous than ever before. Above all, it was Wilhelm von Humboldt's name that kept appearing again and again. Journalist Martin Spiewak, who covered university and research issues in depth for *Die Zeit*, put it in the following terms in an article from 2009:

> There is a lot of death about in German universities. The deceased is always the same person: Wilhelm von Humboldt and 'his' university. Physically, this learned man has been dead for a long time, more

---

26 Julian Nida-Rümelin, *Philosophie einer humanen Bildung* (Hamburg, 2013); Yehuda Elkana & Hannes Klöpper, *Die Universität im 21. Jahrhundert: Für eine neue Einheit von Lehre, Forschung und Gesellschaft* (Hamburg, 2012); Jörg Dräger & Ralph Müller-Eiselt, *Die digitale Bildungsrevolution: Der radikale Wandel des Lernens und wie wir ihn gestalten können* (Munich, 2015); Jörg Dräger & Ralph Müller-Eiselt, 'Humboldt gegen Orwell', *Die Zeit*, 2015, no. 39.

precisely since 8 April 1835. Usually, a commemorative community dwindles as the distance in time grows. This is different only with respect to founders of religions – and to Humboldt. The longer the real Humboldt has been buried, the greater and more numerous is the multitude of mourners.[27]

The significance of Humboldt was seldom exactly defined. It is, however, obvious that to many people, the Prussian educational reformer became a corrective of the contemporaneous market ideology and neo-utilitarianism. He could also serve as a clear antithesis to an instrumental view on education and research. This was especially true of humanists, who were able to mobilise Humboldt whenever they experienced an ever more apparent marginalisation.

At the same time, there was something paradoxical in all this backing for Humboldt. During the noughties, he was extracted from his historical context in a manner utterly different from the approaches applied during the post-war era. Humboldt, and the tradition that he embodied, was reduced to a set of timeless values. This tendency is not contradicted by the fact that a couple of historically orientated reflections on the university were published as well, for instance by Jochen Hörisch and Christoph Markschies. But for the majority of the contributions to the debate, the older German history lacked significance – regardless of all those references to Humboldt. During the 1940s and 1960s, the university debate had been incorporated into a broader processing of the recent past. This processing had, in part, been a matter of coming to terms with German history and its destructive potential. That was not the case during the twenty-first century. In spite of all the historical references, the Bologna debate was, in all essentials, concerned with the present day.

The writings published in previous years, with Schelsky's *Einsamkeit und Freiheit* as a catalyst, had brought Humboldt's name into the German public sphere. In the era of the mass university, he could be used by academics who wanted to safeguard their privileges, but also by all those – from radical students to conservative representatives of professorial chairs – who objected to the university being reformed in line with an Anglo-Saxon model and placed in the service of the business sector.

Even so, it is not until the last twenty-five years that Humboldt has truly ended up at the centre of the debate. After the reunification

---

27 Martin Spiewak, 'Falsches Vorbild', *Die Zeit*, 2009, no. 26.

of Germany in 1990, he became a symbol for a recently acquired academic freedom in the new federal states in the East. Soon, however, the Humboldtian tradition also came to be associated with the process that reconfigured the East German universities and adapted them to the West German model, not least among the thousands of academics who lost their positions. But when a new deal was presented a few years later, embodied by the Bologna process, Humboldt's model seemed preferable after all.[28]

The increased twenty-first-century interest in Humboldt has given rise to some comparatively coherent interpretations. Susan Wright chose to regard this interest as a stage in the market adaptation of higher education. Supported by the OECD, governments in various countries have conducted policies intended to expose the university to competition ever since the 1990s. Wright believes that governments have indulged in a kind of double shuffle in order to gain backing for these measures: a two-way move partly towards more academic capitalism, partly towards an increased academic autonomy. 'Humboldt' has become a signal concept which conceals the first movement while the rhetoric of freedom surrounding the other tendency suppresses all criticism. In reality, the promised freedom never materialises. Power is transferred to the university management and to the executors of 'the audit society'.[29]

Wright's observations are plausible and thought-provoking, but they are placed at a general level and say nothing about national variations. Mitchell G. Ash suggests another, more context-bound understanding, based in a German-speaking context. His thesis is that the frequent use of Humboldt in the university debate of the last twenty years represents the presence of an absence. There is simply no new cultural code that would have been able to replace the old one embodied by Humboldt. Ash sees this as a considerable flaw in the Bologna process. Ultimately, it has to do with the inability of the architects behind the new European educational system to

---

28 Guy Neave, 'On Scholars, Hippopotami and von Humboldt: Higher Education in Europe in Transition', *Higher Education Policy*, 16:2 (2003), 135–40; Ash, 'Humboldt the Undead', p. 86.
29 Susan Wright, 'Humboldt, Humbug! Contemporary Mobilisations of "Humboldt" as a Discourse to Support the Corporatisation and Marketisation of Universities and Disparage Alternatives', in *The Humboldtian Tradition*, ed. by Josephson, Karlsohn, & Östling, pp. 161–63. Wright has borrowed the term 'double shuffle' from Stuart Hall. On the concept 'the audit society', see Michael Power, *The Audit Society: Rituals of Verification* (Oxford, 1997).

formulate a vision for the university that transcends an economic or administrative logic, or even to muster sufficient interest to attempt such a vision in the first place.[30]

Ash, too, captures something essential about the contemporary situation. The question is, however, whether it is possible to attain greater depths in our understanding of the rebirth of Humboldt in the decades surrounding the year 2000. For instance, how is this phenomenon connected to over-arching modifications in our relationship to the past, and to the general view of research, *Bildung*, and knowledge? Is it possible to relate the transformation of contemporary academic culture to greater dislocations? And how are we to understand the place of the Humboldtian tradition in modern German history as a whole? It is time to return to the basic issues, assemble the insights of the investigation, and expand the field of vision.

The Humboldtian tradition's intellectual history and history of knowledge

Throughout the entire modern era, the battles over the university formed part of larger cultural and social issues. Sometimes the conflicts were an aspect of something broader; at other times they themselves were at the centre of attention. They could always be inserted into wider historical patterns. In the introduction to this book, I set out to investigate the Humboldtian tradition's changing meanings in German history. An intellectual reflection over fundamental academic ideals has been at the centre of this investigation, a reflection viewed from a perspective of intellectual history as well as of the history of knowledge. It has become an analysis of university history, both as related to distinct periods and with regard to changes over the long timeline.

One important insight is that the Humboldtian tradition has appeared in three basic guises. The most concrete form may be called *Humboldt's name* and pertains to explicit references to, or rhetorical invocations of, Wilhelm von Humboldt as a person. This nominal

---

30 Ash, 'Humboldt the Undead', pp. 94–96. Peter Weingart has presented a similar interpretation; see 'Humboldt im Ranking', in *Bildung? Bildung!*, ed. by Schlüter & Strohschneider (Berlin, 2009). See, in addition, Konrad H. Jarausch, 'Demokratische Exzellenz? Ein transatlantisches Plädoyer für ein neues Leitbild deutscher Hochschulen', *Denkströme: Journal der Sächsischen Akademie der Wissenschaften*, 1 (2008).

relationship could be paired with well-founded knowledge of his university ideals; but it could also exist in spite of a lack of any real knowledge about his thought. Not least the most recent decades have illustrated the latter phenomenon. Moreover, on a higher level of abstraction one can talk about *Humboldt's concepts* in order to refer to the basic academic vocabulary that has played such a decisive role in the debate about the modern German university. Concepts such as academic freedom, *Bildung*, the combination of research and education, and a few additional ones belong to this group. To varying extents, these concepts have been associated with Wilhelm von Humboldt the man; but for a long time they were primarily seen as part of the classic German university tradition. In a third, mostly abstract, meaning, the Humboldtian tradition is equivalent to *Humboldt's model*, that is to say a coherent idea about the ideal university. Here, too, Humboldt the person may be of more or less central importance. The fact that the model embraces a comprehensive idea about the university matters more: its fundamental academic norms, its place in history, its task. The conditions, framework, and limitations of the German debate have been provided by this classic model for more than two hundred years.

A tripartition of the fundamental forms of the Humboldtian tradition – the name, the concepts, the model – should not, however, mislead anyone into believing that there was a strict separation between them. In certain contexts they could appear simultaneously, imparting a particular power to the tradition. But an analytical distinction of this kind invites a more coherent interpretation of the main guises and functions of the tradition during various periods. In addition, it enables me to reconsider some basic assumptions that have evolved during the last two decades in research about the history of the university.

This research, most emphatically so as represented by Sylvia Paletschek, has promoted the idea that Wilhelm von Humboldt the university ideologue was discovered at the turn of the century in 1900 and became the object of an increasing mythologisation. Langewiesche has added nuance to this claim, underscoring that Humboldt was hardly ever referred to in rectors' speeches before the 1970s and pointing out that the early mania for him was limited to, at most, certain Prussian circles, above all in Berlin. Nevertheless, the thesis of a 'Humboldt myth' has taken a firm hold in research during the twenty-first century.

The present study, however, provides good reasons for a re-examination of this interpretation. One conclusion that can be drawn from the preceding chapters is that it was not until after the mandarins had left the public sphere and their academic positions during the 1960s that Humboldt began to become a widespread reference. It is true that some people – such as Spranger and Ritter – had made early attempts to bring him to life, but for a long time the classic German model was not synonymous with Wilhelm von Humboldt. The person who played a crucial role in the transformation of Humboldt into an uncontested central figure in the German university tradition was Helmut Schelsky. He had a good command of German intellectual history while his academic profile was primarily that of an innovative social scientist. Schelsky could thus not be accused of being a backward-looking mandarin. With his combination of solid learning and polemical talent, he was able to transform his university-historical insights into interventions in university policies. When Schelsky's brown biography was revealed and his aversion to the sixty-eight movement grew in strength, he was dealt hard blows in the debate. But the controversial aspects of his character may have contributed to establishing Humboldt as symbolic figure, because not even Schelsky's antagonists could refrain from referring to Humboldt's ideas. When Gadamer, Habermas, and Mittelstraß discussed the university in the 1980s, Humboldt was a given reference.

Investigations of countries other than Germany indicate that Wilhelm von Humboldt did not become a generally cherished watchword until late in the twentieth century. The earliest explicit references in Norwegian debates showed up in the latter half of the 1960s, and in Switzerland it was not until 1970 that his name was frequently included in rector's speeches. In Belgium, too, it was not until the end of the century that Humboldt's name was on everybody's lips. Once this happened, he could, as Pieter Dhondt has proved, be invoked for widely divergent purposes and without historical discernment.[31]

The case of Humboldt's impact in Sweden is an interesting example of his influence outside Germany. Here, too, he was something of a

---

31 Sivert Langholm, 'Das "Humboldt-Modell" in Norwegen: Symbol, Begriff und Wirklichkeit', in *Humboldt international*, ed. by Schwinges, pp. 226–28; Langewiesche, 'Das deutsche Universitätsmodell', p. 26; Pieter Dhondt, '"Humboldt" in Belgium: Rhetoric on the German University Model', in *The Humboldtian Tradition*, ed. by Josephson, Karlsohn, & Östling, pp. 106–10. See also Marja Jalava, 'When Humboldt Met Marx: The 1970s Leftist Student Movement and the Idea of the University in Finland', in *The Humboldtian Tradition*, ed. by Josephson, Karlsohn, & Östling.

late arrival. True, the great early and mid-twentieth-century Swedish encyclopaedias contained rather detailed articles on Wilhelm von Humboldt; but it was his efforts as a statesman, diplomat, and humanist that were emphasised, especially his philological achievements. A single sentence mentions that he was employed in the Prussian ministry of the interior in 1809, and that he founded the university of Berlin in this position; but no great importance was attached to that fact. Nor did Wilhelm von Humboldt or the Berlin university play leading parts in accounts of the history of the university.[32] By way of illustration, the *Svensk uppslagsbok* article 'Universitet', which contains a relatively detailed discussion of developments from the Middle Ages onwards, states the following:

> In many ways the eighteenth century signified a renewal of the university system; this was the case in France after the abolition of the Jesuit order (1764) and in Germany, where the universities in Halle (1693) and Göttingen (1737) were at the forefront. The last-mentioned university also acquired a great international reputation. Especially worth noting is the increasing importance of the faculties of philosophy, with innovative activities within linguistics, historical research, mathematics, and the natural sciences; the dominant position of the faculty of theology was undermined during this century. [...] A new period with respect to the establishment of new universities began at the dawn of the nineteenth century. After a time of dissolution during the Revolution, the French universities were reorganised during the first decade of the nineteenth century. In the area of the university, nationalist tendencies were expressed through a number of new establishments: in Germany, where many universities had vanished or been moved during the Napoleonic wars, the universities in Berlin (1809), Bonn (1818), and Munich (1826) were added; in Belgium among others in Brussels (1834), in Norway in Christiania [Oslo] (1811), and in Greece in Athens (1837).[33]

---

32 'Humboldt, Friedrich Wilhelm Christian Karl Ferdinand', *Nordisk familjebok*, 38 vols (Stockholm, 1904–26), vol. XI (1909); 'von Humboldt, Wilhelm', *Svensk uppslagsbok*, 2nd edn, 32 vols (Malmö, 1947–1955), vol. XIII (1955). It is worth noting that the articles on Alexander von Humboldt were more extensive and contained more multifaceted character descriptions than the ones about his elder brother. See 'Humboldt, Friedrich Wilhelm Heinrich Alexander', *Nordisk familjebok*, 38 vols (Stockholm, 1904–1926), vol. XI (1909) and 'von Humboldt, Alexander', *Svensk uppslagsbok*, 2nd edn, 32 vols (Malmö, 1947–1955), vol. XIII (1955).

33 Ingvar Andersson, 'Universitet', *Svensk uppslagsbok*, 2nd edn, 32 vols (Malmö, 1947–1955), vol. XXX (1958), column 511. *Svensk uppslagsbok* was the leading encyclopaedia in Sweden in the mid-twentieth century. The corresponding

The Berlin university hence did not represent anything different in principle, and it did not in any way mark a paradigm shift. Rather, it was connected with a general national awakening in Europe at the beginning of the nineteenth century. The new and noteworthy could instead be found in Halle and Göttingen. The Swedish historiography on the university was thus to a significant degree the same as the one that had prevailed in Germany since the nineteenth century. Not until the very last decades of the twentieth century would Swedish commentators come to view the Humboldtian tradition as a constituent element for the modern university. In *Nationalencyklopedin* from the 1990s, the Berlin university was mentioned as one of the leading universities, 'created on the basis of Wilhelm von Humboldt's programme of *Bildung*'. At this juncture, Humboldt himself was described as the ideologue behind the new university.[34]

Similarly, Humboldt did not become a reference in Swedish contributions to the history and theory of the university until late in the twentieth century. In writings published during the 1960s and 1970s, readers look in vain for his name; this also applies to publications written by eminent academics, such as Torgny T. Segerstedt.[35]

---

article in *Nordisk familjebok*, another widely disseminated encyclopaedia in the early twentieth century, gave a similar account of history. Halle was described as 'the first truly modern university', which came to share the leadership with Göttingen during the latter half of the eighteenth century. Berlin was mentioned simply as one of the new universities founded at the beginning of the nineteenth century, a university that had 'managed to attach renowned professors to itself and now stands among the foremost in Europe'. See Frans Eugène Fahlstedt, 'Universitet', *Nordisk familjebok*, 38 vols (Stockholm, 1904–1926), vol. XXX (1920), p. 1110.

34 Tore Frängsmyr, 'Humboldt, Wilhelm von', *Nationalencyklopedin*, 20 vols (Höganäs, 1989–1996), vol. IX (1992). *Nationalencyklopedin* was the successor of *Svensk uppslagsbok* and *Nordisk familjebok* in the later part of the twentieth century. See also Kjell Jonsson, 'Bildning, utveckling och frihet: Om Wilhelm von Humboldt och *Om gränserna för statens verksamhet*', in Wilhelm von Humboldt, *Om gränserna för statens verksamhet*, transl. by Erik Carlquist (Umeå, 2012), pp. 7–8.

35 See Torgny T. Segerstedt's trilogy on academic freedom – *Den akademiska friheten under frihetstiden: En sammanställning* (Uppsala, 1971), *Den akademiska friheten under gustaviansk tid* (Uppsala, 1974), and *Den akademiska friheten 1809–1832* (Uppsala, 1976) – but also his more polemical writings with a greater degree of analysis of his own times, *Studentrevolt: Vetenskap och framtid* (Stockholm, 1968) and *Hotet mot den högre utbildningen* (Stockholm, 1974). See, in addition, Sverker Gustavsson, *Debatten om*

It was not until the following two decades that Humboldt began to appear, although few people evinced any deep familiarity with his ideas. It was, for instance, obvious that a researcher on education as internationally prominent as Torsten Husén had a completely different knowledge about the American classics (Flexner, Kerr, and others) than about the German ones.[36] Only in the years around, or even after, the turn of the millennium was Humboldt widely and seriously discussed. He, or the model he embodied, then became part of the intellectual common knowledge of academic debate.[37]

---

forskningen och samhället: En studie i några teoretiska inlägg under 1900-talet (Stockholm, 1971). Wilhelm von Humboldt is not mentioned in the most voluminous Swedish work on university history published during these decades, the history of Lund University in four volumes; see Krister Gierow, *Lunds universitets historia: Utgiven av universitetet till dess 300-årsjubileum: 3. 1790–1867* (Lund, 1971) and Jörgen Weibull, *Lunds universitets historia: Utgiven av universitetet till dess 300-årsjubileum: 4. 1868–1968* (Lund, 1968).

36 For instance *Universitet och samhälle: Om forskningspolitik och vetenskapens samhälleliga roll*, ed. by Thorsten Nybom (Stockholm, 1989); Birgitta Odén, *Forskarutbildningens förändringar 1890–1975: Historia, statskunskap, kulturgeografi, ekonomisk historia* (Lund, 1991); Göran Blomqvist, *Elfenbenstorn eller statsskepp? Stat, universitet och akademisk frihet i vardag och vision från Agardh till Schück* (Lund, 1992); and Torsten Husén, *Bokslut: Essäer om utbildning* (Stockholm, 2002). In his textbook on intellectual history and the history of science in the modern age, published in several editions during the 1980s and 1990s, Gunnar Eriksson characterised the Berlin university as 'a new establishment of exceptional importance', claiming that Wilhelm von Humboldt had outlined 'a new ideal for the university' where research assumed a key position. See Gunnar Eriksson, *Västerlandets idéhistoria 1800–1950* (Stockholm, 1983), p. 132.

37 Bo Sundqvist, *Svenska universitet – lärdomsborgar eller politiska instrument?* (Hedemora, 2011); Göran Bexell, *Akademiska värden visar vägen* (Stockholm, 2011); Carl-Gustaf Andrén, *Visioner, vägval och verkligheter: Svenska universitet och högskolor i utveckling efter 1940* (Lund, 2013); Stig Strömholm, *Resonerande katalog: Minnen 1958–2003* (Stockholm, 2014). It was also during the twenty-first century that Swedish research on the Humboldtian tradition began in earnest – for instance *The Humboldtian Tradition*, ed. by Josephson, Karlsohn, & Östling – and that translations of Wilhelm von Humboldt's writings began to be published, such as Wilhelm von Humboldt, 'Om den inre och yttre organisationen av de högre vetenskapliga läroanstalterna i Berlin', transl. by Thomas Karlsohn, *Psykoanalytisk Tid/ Skrift*, 26–27 (2009); Wilhelm von Humboldt, *Om språket*, transl. by Johan Redin (Stockholm, 2011); and Wilhelm von Humboldt, *Om gränserna för statens verksamhet*.

A question that has yet to be answered is to what extent the international Humboldtian Renaissance towards the end of the century had anything to do with internal German developments. A study by Gry Cathrin Brandser maintains that it is an American understanding of the German university tradition that has been brought forward in the contemporary European debate. In American sociology and history of the 1950s and 1960s, 'the German university' had been branded a hotbed of reactionism – anti-democratic and illiberal, dedicated to metaphysics, and a forum for social preservation. Brandser argues that a reinterpretation occurred during the following decades: Humboldt was combined with a tradition of Anglo-Saxon liberal education at a time of an accelerating market adaptation of the university; and it was in this form that Humboldt's ideas returned to Europe. As in all such processes of circulation, the transfer from one culture to another has meant that the intellectual contents have been transformed.[38]

Brandser's thesis is a very interesting one, but it could have done with more in the way of corroboration. What speaks in its favour is that many Western European countries, and maybe especially those of Scandinavia, received decisive international impulses from British and American university life during the post-war era. Germany did not function as a model, and there were few outsiders who followed the German-language debate at close quarters. For instance, few of the Swedes who began to invoke Humboldt at the end of the twentieth century had actually been influenced by the debate on ideas in Germany.[39]

---

38 Brandser, *Humboldt Revisited*, pp. 342–50.
39 Obviously it is possible to find exceptions. For instance Thorsten Nybom, an important figure in the Swedish debate on the university during the 1990s and the early twenty-first century, was very knowledgeable about German circumstances. He actively contributed to introducing newer insights on the Humboldtian tradition, for instance in Thorsten Nybom, 'A Rule-Governed Community of Scholars'; Thorsten Nybom, 'Humboldts Vermächtnis: Betrachtungen zu Vergangenheit, Gegenwart und Zukunft des europäischen Hochschulwesens', in *Humboldts Zukunft: Das Projekt Reformuniversität*, ed. by Bernd Henningsen (Berlin, 2008); and Thorsten Nybom, 'The Persistent Use and Abuse of Wilhelm von Humboldt in History and Politics', in *Aurora Torealis: Studies in the History of Science and Ideas*, ed. by Marco Beretta, Karl Grandin, & Svante Lindqvist (New York, 2008). Other Swedes who combined an active interest in university and research policy with considerable knowledge of the German university tradition at this time include Sverker Gustavsson, Sven-Eric Liedman, Stig Strömholm, and Björn Wittrock.

The Humboldtian Renaissance of the last few decades must be explained by a variety of factors. One basic prerequisite was the transformation of the old university during the post-war era and the emergence of a mass university. As people left an older order behind, a need developed for a recipe that would capture this earlier state of things – whether this was a surface for the projection of dreams, an expression of phantom pains, or a dark past against which the progress attained could be outlined. To many people, Humboldt became this recipe. When the universities of the world were drawn into global competition in the last decades of the twentieth century, and ever more innovation and collaboration with the business sector were decreed, the Prussian educational reformer was mobilised. Some people saw him primarily as a mercenary who could be used in order to fight the prevailing tendencies. Others were inspired by his philosophy and argued that he stood for a coherent alternative. As Ash has pointed out, Humboldt's popularity has to be explained by the fact that there was no attractive and all-comprehensive recipe that could give meaning to the new academic deal.

All this was also true with respect to Germany; but here other circumstances played a role as well. The Humboldtian tradition was a part of the national culture and self-perception in a completely different way from its manifestations in other countries. Its ups and downs must be placed in relation to the social and intellectual transformations of modern Germany.

There is a German intellectual attitude that may be described as a preference for culture over politics. Wolfgang Lepenies has examined this leitmotif throughout intellectual history and found that it shows up in a number of different constellations after the eighteenth century. He follows in the footsteps of others (Norbert Elias, Fritz K. Ringer, Georg L. Mosse, Fritz Stern) when he postulates that a high valuation of cultural achievements and what George Peabody Gooch called 'a strange indifference to politics' have been characteristic of the German context. Lepenies rejects the *Sonderweg*-thesis, the idea that there is a special German path to modernity; but his ideas can nevertheless be incorporated into such a debate. The aversion to both parliamentarianism and capitalism among many German thinkers derives from this basic attitude. This is also true of their propensity to prescribe culture as a cure for the ills of society.[40]

---

40 Lepenies, *The Seduction*, pp. 4–13 and 132–38.

The Humboldtian tradition, which Lepenies does not discuss in detail, may reasonably be regarded as a variant of this greater German theme. First, it is indisputable that the classic ideals have been cited as a defence against political intervention in the academic sphere. A variety of arguments lent themselves to this purpose: anti-democratic ones during the Weimar Republic; culturally vitalising ones during the years of occupation; technocracy-rejecting ones in the 1960s; and anti-economistic ones in the Bologna era. Second, Humboldt's ideas have been seen as a means of healing a diseased university body. This was the case as early as the turn of the century in 1900; and culture, in the form of a specific academic heritage, continued to be credited with healing properties in various subsequent periods. That was primarily the situation in the devastated landscape of the years immediately after 1945; but the notion showed up in the twenty-first century as well.

A closely related interpretative perspective can be applied in order to illustrate the connection between the Humboldtian tradition and the social and cultural history of *Bildung*. In one of the most important books on intellectual history in this area, *Bildung und Kultur* (1994), Georg Bollenbeck advocated the thesis that a special relationship between 'culture' and '*Bildung*' developed in Germany during the nineteenth century: originating in a New Humanist reaction against the rational Enlightenment, this relationship meant that culture became a medium for *Bildung*. At first liberal and progressive, the concept of *Bildung* became ever more tied to the national cause during the Empire, a shield for those who wanted to defend themselves against the destructive forces of modernisation. Bollenbeck spoke of the connection culture – *Bildung* as a '*Bildung*-bourgeois pattern of interpretation', because it was primarily supported by *das Bildungsbürgertum* ('the educated bourgeoisie') as a social group and it reflected their view of the world. As a paradigm it was at its strongest in the years around 1900, but thereafter it gradually lost its power over people's minds. The orientation towards the West and the economic miracle of the post-war era finally sealed its fate.

It is not hard to see parallels between the transformation of the Humboldtian tradition on the one hand and that of the greater *Bildungsbürgertum*-shaped pattern of interpretation on the other. Both had their origins in the idealism and New Humanism of the early nineteenth century; but in both cases a reformulation with national overtones also occurred towards the turn of the century in 1900, a reformulation which was in many respects a reaction to the emergence of industrial society and the crisis of modernity.

In both instances, too, a gradual weakening occurred during the ensuing decades; and even though there were periods of newly awakened interest – in the aftermath of the Second World War, for example – that was mostly a matter of lingering echoes.

Here Bollenbeck makes an important observation. Reactivating a cultural critique is not the same thing as restoring a pattern of interpretation and re-establishing its influence, he writes. Besides, there was no hegemonic class of the kind once made up of the *Bildungsbürgertum* during the post-war era.[41] The same may well apply to the Humboldtian tradition. It could be reactivated as a culture-critical or nostalgic interpretation, but it could not represent a vital and realistic idea about the university unless it was supported by a socially and intellectually influential class. To Bollenbeck, this class consisted of the German *Bildungsbürgertum*.

In the history of the Humboldtian tradition, it was a particular segment of this group that acted as mainstays: the mandarins. They were a kind of high priests of the *Bildungsbürgertum*, schooled in theory and with a self-imposed mission to interpret shared beliefs. In the first years following 1945, the mandarins made their final major appearance. Those who came after this period, not least in the 1960s, were keen either to distance themselves from the older generation or to fundamentally reformulate that generation's ideals. When the discussions about the Bologna process took place, the last mandarins had disappeared completely, and one could no longer speak of a bourgeois dominance. To be sure, there were outspoken professors who came to the defence of an older ideal of *Bildung*; but there were also younger and more radical people who saw Humboldt as an ally in the battle against the capitalist university.[42]

Consequently, the transformation of the Humboldtian tradition was closely connected with the fate of the mandarins, and of the whole German bourgeoisie, during the modern era. In more general terms, this is a history of how one of the knowledge actors lost influence during the twentieth century. The mandarins had had considerable power to shape the meaning of *Bildung* and the university during the first half of the century, but in the post-war era they were gradually replaced by new intellectual types. Not only did these new types have dissimilar ideals; they also presented a different appearance to the

---

41 Ibid., pp. 301–04.
42 On the transformation of the German bourgeoisie after 1945, see *Bürgertum nach dem bürgerlichen Zeitalter: Leitbilder und Praxis seit 1945*, ed. by Gunilla Budde, Eckart Conze & Cornelia Rauh (Göttingen, 2010).

world and held different social positions. The order of knowledge depended on the social order and vice versa.

A unifying factor for the Humboldtian tradition was its own vocabulary. These concepts of knowledge contributed to forming a linguistic community which was, in its turn, a prerequisite for an academic community. The concepts facilitated a conversation about the basic issues of the university that transcended epochs and social systems, but they also imposed limits on what could be formulated. In some cases, the continuity over time was illusory in that a term could certainly recur, but its more precise meaning varied from one context to another. On the basis of the earlier chapters and searches in digital corpuses, a few main conceptual types can be distinguished.[43]

One type of concept was derived from Humboldt's ideas but displayed an anything but even frequency. 'Einsamkeit und Freiheit' ('solitude and freedom') is an illustrative example. It could be found in Humboldt's writings, but it was not until the 1960s that it was brought into the debate. It then acquired a specific meaning. A similar case was 'Einheit von Forschung und Lehre' ('unity of research and tuition') and its variants. Although the exact wording cannot be found in Humboldt, the essence was there. Even so, it was not until the end of the 1950s that its frequency increased significantly, only to then diminish and stabilise two decades later. It is not far-fetched to imagine that the increased use of these concepts reflected the problem of maintaining an ideal involving the combination of research and education at a time when mass universities emerged.[44]

---

43 Using Google Books Ngram Viewer, it is possible to search for concepts or short sentences in digitally available corpuses based on a large number of printed sources from the sixteenth century until today in, for instance, the German language. See https://books.google.com/ngrams. The opportunities for historical research with Google Ngram – but also the methodological and source-critical considerations that are brought to the fore in this context – are discussed in Jean-Baptiste Michel et al., 'Quantitative Analysis of Culture Using Millions of Digitized Books', *Science*, 331 (2011); Lev Manovich, 'Trending: The Promises and the Challenges of Big Social Data', in *Debates in the Digital Humanities*, ed. by Matthew K. Gold (Minneapolis, 2012); and Steffen Roth, 'Fashionable Functions: A Google Ngram View of Trends in Functional Differentiation (1800–2000)', *International Journal of Technology and Human Interaction*, 10:2 (2014).

44 https://books.google.com/ngrams (accessed 15 February 2016). Search terms: 'Einsamkeit und Freiheit' and 'Einheit von Forschung und Lehre'. Corpus: 'German'.

An example of another type of concept is 'academic freedom'. This concept has a long history; but during the nineteenth and twentieth centuries, it was gradually incorporated into the understanding of what constituted the modern university. 'Akademische Freiheit' displayed a higher frequency during certain periods, most markedly in the years around 1810, 1850, 1910, and 1960. A similar pattern applies to close variants of this concept, such as 'Lernfreiheit' ('freedom to learn') and 'Lehrfreiheit' ('freedom to teach').[45] But it is precisely because it is possible to draw such a long line through history that the need for contextualisation increases. The form of academic freedom that Humboldt promoted in his capacity as a high-ranking Prussian official meant that the state should have significant power to exclude unwanted individuals from the universities, but that extensive liberties would be extended to those who did manage to get in. Barely a hundred years later, Weber argued for the opposite order. Academic freedom could, in addition, be used in order to determine the relationship between the university and the surrounding society. During the years following the Second World War, the ideal of freedom espoused by the classic German model was invoked in order to demarcate the university from the dangerous state. In the conflicts of opinion regarding the Bologna process, people referred to the same kinds of principles; but now the state was more of an ally, and the damaging influence came from the business sector.

There are other crucial concepts which have a more general usage and cannot be said to belong exclusively to the Humboldtian tradition. '*Bildung*' is one of these. The distribution and meaning of this concept are so much wider that it cannot be seen to reflect the ups and downs of the university debate in a similar way. In a more limited sense, though, valuable observations may be made. '*Bildung durch Wissenschaft*' ('*Bildung* through science and scholarship') did have a certain upswing in the 1820s, but the real increase in frequency came during the years around 1960. Again, it is reasonable to view the expansion of the university and the discussions that accompanied that expansion as an important background. Still more general concepts such as 'Krise' are even more difficult to connect with the varying expressions of the Humboldtian tradition. Nevertheless, there is good reason to claim that a kind of crisis consciousness

---

45 https://books.google.com/ngrams (accessed 15 February 2016). Search terms: 'akademische Freiheit', 'Lernfreiheit', and 'Lehrfreiheit'. Corpus: 'German'.

has marked German debates about the fundamental academic issues during large parts of the twentieth century, at least when it comes to the manner in which those debates were conducted by leading intellectuals.[46]

The name 'Wilhelm von Humboldt' yields interesting results in the digitalised text collections. An initial peak was attained in the years around 1870, which was not a period that has generally been emphasised as a turning-point in university history; but this could be explained by his being mentioned in connection with his brother Alexander, who appeared in many German-language publications during these years. It is worth observing that the so-called discovery of Wilhelm von Humboldt as a university ideologue at the turn of the century in 1900 has not left any unequivocal traces. By contrast, the frequency rises directly after the Second World War, during the 1960s, and in the years that precede 1990, receding between these points in time.[47]

A premise of the history of knowledge is that all knowledge presupposes a medium. This medium is never an innocently empty container; it contributes to shaping and reshaping the content and character of the knowledge. These media forms of knowledge have been important to the conversational order in the history of the Humboldtian tradition as well. During the early post-war era, ideas about the university were usually presented in the form of addresses. This form restricted the scope of the texts and gave them a particular rhetorical structure. Their range was initially limited; but if the addresses were subsequently printed in one of the many journals and newspapers published at the time, they could reach a considerable audience. Fifteen years later, conditions were very different. Book-publishing in the Federal Republic was extensive, and the most influential contributions had the form of regular books. This created a completely different opportunity to develop lines of reasoning and provide extensive and detailed argumentation. In addition, distribution was facilitated by the fact that the books were marketed by professional publishers and published in paperback editions. The West German public sphere was well developed, and university-theoretical writings were not seldom reviewed and debated

---

46 https://books.google.com/ngrams (accessed 15 February 2016). Search terms: 'Bildung', 'Bildung durch Wissenschaft', and 'Krise'. Corpus: 'German'.
47 https://books.google.com/ngrams (accessed 15 February 2016). Search terms: 'Wilhelm von Humboldt', 'Alexander von Humboldt', and 'Humboldt'. Corpus: 'German'.

in the press, on the radio, and on TV. Consequently, these writings were included in the existing media system of the 1960s. The same thing happened during the early twenty-first century. At that point, book production was even more extensive, although a good deal of what was published appeared in anthologies. The new digital media were an additional factor.[48]

The history of the Humboldtian tradition also illustrates how the spaces of knowledge have changed during the modern period. The changes in Germany's borders since 1871 – geographically, politically, legally – have had an impact on the university debate. During some periods, the spaces of knowledge have coincided with the German nation state; at other times, they have been greater or smaller than the German cultural sphere. Similarly, the degree of openness to the world has varied. In spite of – or because of – Germany being occupied after the end of the war in 1945, foreign influences on the domestic debate were extremely limited; instead, the debate in all essentials assumed the form of national introspection. In the 1960s, a growing awareness of the international scene is discernible; but the frames of reference were still mainly German. At the beginning of the twenty-first century, however, Germany was part of a European or even a global reality in a completely different way. The economic and administrative processes that could be identified in Germany were similar to those found in other countries.

Nevertheless, strong national characteristics remained in the German reflections on the university. It was as if Germany's fate as a nation of research, science, and scholarship – dominance at the beginning of the twentieth century, followed by the First World War and Nazi pillaging followed by reconstruction and processing – had laid the foundations for a distinctively introverted way of approaching the university. Rather than applying a broad perspective and seeking international inspiration, Germans looked backwards and inwards.

The Humboldtian tradition and the modern university

To anyone who adopts a wide-ranging perspective, it is clear that the German university tradition has been a source of academic renewal, offering solutions to real problems, during certain periods. At other

---

48 See, generally, *Mediengeschichte der Bundesrepublik Deutschland*, ed. by Jürgen Wilke (Cologne, 1999); Schildt & Siegfried (2009); and Daniela Völker, *Das Buch für die Massen: Taschenbücher und ihre Verlage* (Marburg, 2014).

times, by contrast, it has been depicted as the problem that posed obstacles in the way of desirable changes. Following the Second World War, the German heritage was, according to the leading mandarins, most of all a sound, unsullied well from which to draw. For most of the debaters of the 1960s, however, that tradition was primarily an encumbrance, something to liberate oneself from, although a central figure such as Schelsky evinced a more ambivalent attitude. During the twenty-first century, many people felt that the German university was in the process of renouncing its heritage altogether. To them, Humboldt could be put forward as an alternative to the prevailing tendencies of the time. Obviously, then, the historical tradition may be adduced both for and against an existing order.

The new, historicising research on the Humboldtian tradition that has taken shape during the last twenty years has adopted a kind of critical constructivism. Paletschek has spoken of 'the invention of the Humboldtian university'; an important scholarly anthology was given the name *Mythos Humboldt*; and the designation 'the Humboldt myth' has been used on a number of occasions. The chief intention behind the use of these concepts has been deconstruction: demonstrating that the Humboldtian tradition is not a 'given', immutably stable thing.[49]

These unmasking activities can be justified, and they have had an unmistakable value. But they may restrict the scope for understanding. Mitchell G. Ash has emphasised that the concept of myth as employed in research on Humboldt has been aimed at separating a lie from the truth. The problem is that a false idea can also shape a debate. Ash therefore recommends adopting an anthropological way of looking at things. Instead of disproving the Humboldt myth, studies should be orientated towards the historiography that surrounds it. That historiography emerges as a significance-bearing academic *Gründungserzählung* (approx. 'foundational narrative') – beyond true and false.[50]

---

49 See Chapters 1–3. *Mythos Humboldt: Vergangenheit und Zukunft der deutschen Universität*, ed. by Mitchell G. Ash (Vienna, 1999), was a German translation of Ash, *German Universities Past and Future*.

50 Ash, 'Humboldt the Undead', pp. 82–83. A similar way of looking at things is assumed in Herfried Münkler, *Die Deutschen und ihre Mythen* (Berlin, 2009), although this is a book that focuses on political myths and does not discuss the Humboldtian tradition. A brief discussion of the Humboldt brothers as a German national monument can be found in Rudolf Vierhaus, 'Die Brüder Humboldt', in *Deutsche Erinnerungsorte*, ed. by Etienne François & Hagen Schulze (Munich, 2001), vol. III (2001).

Ash thus did not want to puncture an inflated balloon, but narrow down what he calls a cultural code. In a broader context, his ambition is hardly radically new – on the contrary, he agrees with the main lines in the cultural history of recent decades – but he contributes to an important shift in perspective in research on the German university tradition.

Even so, an anthropological concept of myth cannot completely capture that which makes the German debate on the university so distinctive, namely its historical character. Other ways of understanding are more appropriate for that purpose. In the theoretical discussion, a historical consciousness clarifies the connections between an interpretation of the past, an understanding of contemporary times, and expectations for the future. These connections may also be described as the context in which people exist when they orientate themselves in time, shaped as they are by their images of the past and their ideas about the future. The historical consciousness links the three tenses – past, present, future – and emphasises the interaction among them. A culture of history is made up of concrete manifestations of a historical consciousness: the artefacts, institutions, and arenas where a particular encounter between past, present, and future is expressed.[51]

The German university community seems to have included an *academic historical consciousness* that has contributed to shaping a particular self-perception. In their ambition to bring clarity to their own time and draw up guidelines for the future, the members of that community orientated themselves on the basis of a classic German university ideal. Consequently, there was always a distinct historical element – sometimes in the form of an elaborate historiography, sometimes in the form of isolated images of the past. In brief, there was a basic retrospective reflex in the German university debate.

A historical consciousness never includes an entire nation, an entire class, or an entire profession; social, cultural, and generational factors divide and separate. Those who by tradition supported the academic historical consciousness and articulated its meaning were the mandarins; but their successors in the scholarly scene were also strikingly historical in their orientation. This is not to say that the historical consciousness has been one and the same during the entire modern era. For the professors of the years of occupation, brought

---

51 A classic definition of 'historical consciousness' was formulated in Karl-Ernst Jeismann, 'Geschichtsbewußtsein', in *Handbuch der Geschichtsdidaktik*, ed. by Klaus Bergmann, 2 vols (Düsseldorf, 1979), vol. I.

up on the ideals of the early twentieth century, the history of the university offered security and edification after the great disaster of Nazism. The road ahead was lined with the watchwords of New Humanism. The protagonists of the 1960s were preoccupied with opening up the academic sector to the modern, democratic industrial society. Monitoring the intrinsic transformation of an awareness of history hence presupposes sensitivity both to the longer timeline and to a clearly demarcated historical context. This is a credo in line with David Armitage's programme for transtemporal history. An academic historical consciousness can consequently have dissimilar meanings and produce diverging conclusions during different periods in time – even though they form a common whole when taken altogether.

In a wider context, however, the German case is distinguished by the fact that the fundamental academic principles have continually been formulated within the framework of a major historical tradition. Visions of the ideal university have taken shape in an explicit or implicit dialogue with the past. This tendency to look backwards – whether it is a matter of finding strength or of emphasising deterrent examples – has given the discussion its points of reference, its inner logic, and its outer conditions.

The modern university was shaped in the shift between the eighteenth and nineteenth centuries. As a historical period, epoch-making qualities have been accorded to these years by many leading interpreters. Reinhart Koselleck called it *Sattelzeit* ('saddle time') and viewed it as a transition from the old world to the modern one, and Jürgen Habermas analysed it as the emergence of a new bourgeois public sphere. Michel Foucault placed the break between the *épistème* of classical and modern times in the same period, while Eric J. Hobsbawm traced the origins of the long nineteenth century by emphasising the importance of the double revolutions, political (the French) and socio-economic (the industrial), respectively.[52]

The modern university, with its gradual formation in Prussia during the same era, has rarely been incorporated into a grand system of modernity. One exception is Björn Wittrock, who wishes to view the changes in the university since the Enlightenment in the light of three major transformations, which he regards from a

---

52 Koselleck, 'Einleitung'; Habermas, *Strukturwandel der Öffentlichkeit*; Michel Foucault, *Les mots et les choses: Une archéologie des sciences humaines* (Paris, 1966); Eric J. Hobsbawm, *The Age of Revolution: Europe 1789–1848* (London, 1962).

wider social perspective. The first of these began during the late eighteenth century and is associated with the Berlin university; the second gathered momentum a hundred years later and involved the rise of research-intensive, specialised institutions; and the third was equivalent to the emergence of the post-war mass university. In the first comprehensive transformation, Wittrock has identified crucial changes within three different but connected areas. On the cognitive level, a mechanistic outlook was challenged by a holistic one. In parallel to this, science and scholarship were given a new social organisation when the professional scholar/scientist replaced the learned amateur. Finally, new institutional forms for higher education and research evolved. Taken together, these circumstances created the prerequisites for a new kind of university in the decades around the year 1800.[53]

In an earlier chapter, I referred to new research and demonstrated how there were a number of specific factors that interacted in order to pave the way for a new kind of university in Prussia – everything from the transformation of the book market to military defeat at the hands of Napoleon. Wittrock's argument lifts the problem to a more general level when he claims that the modern university was a part of a greater social and epistemic transformation. That claim raises the question of how the Humboldtian tradition has been a part of modernity in a more fundamental manner.

One way of approaching this issue is to proceed from what François Hartog has called the modern regime of historicity. In his major work *Régimes d'historicité* (2003), he claims that a particular perception of history has permeated the West since the end of the eighteenth century. This modern regime of historicity was characterised by openness towards the future, a lack of interest in the past, and an underlying idea of progress.[54] The new Prussian university model was an exponent of the new regime of historicity. In the mediaeval and early modern university, the passing on of older knowledge had been a principal task; that university had hence had a fundamentally historical orientation. With the new research imperative, the orientation of knowledge was shifted towards the contemporary period or towards the future. The major historical

---

53 Wittrock, 'Modern University', pp. 315–16. William Clark also places the emergence of the research university in relation to the modern state, but from different points of departure.
54 François Hartog, *Régimes d'historicité: Présentisme et expériences du temps* (Paris, 2003).

scholarly projects during the nineteenth century were also orientated towards the future in the sense that they developed new knowledge for the benefit of society or culture.[55] The Humboldtian tradition was an aspect of the modern in other respects as well. The major discussions about the university that were conducted during the twentieth century were, as has been shown, connected to other and even bigger discussions – about the elite and the masses, democracy and dictatorship, crisis and tradition, science/ scholarship and progress. This affinity between fundamental academic issues and reflections on the nature of modernity surfaced again and again. When Jaspers, Ritter, and others in the aftermath of the Second World War contemplated the history of the German university, there were patent parallels with the ways in which contemporary thinkers such as Friedrich Meinecke, Karl Löwith, Theodor W. Adorno, and Max Horkheimer analysed the self-destructiveness of Western society. Similarly, the university debate of the 1960s had an affinity with the philosophical and sociological diagnoses of industrial society that were articulated during the same period.[56]

During the last two centuries, the shifts in the relationship to the university tradition have consequently had to do with greater shifts in the relationship to history, time, and the modern project in general. For a few decades now, however, more and more people have been asking whether the modern regime of historicity has been broken up. Hartog is one of these people. According to him, after 1989 we have witnessed how the dominance of the present has grown in strength, and the ubiquity of presentism is threatening to replace all other orders of time. In Aleida Assmann's *Ist die Zeit aus den Fugen?* (2013; 'Is the time out of joint?'), a similar thesis about the destruction of the basic temporal logic of modernity is advanced. The future no longer carries the same promises, the present is impossible to survey, and the past keeps reappearing in different guises, argues Assmann. In contrast to Hartog, she welcomes the

---

55 Hartog, *Régimes d'historicité*. See, in addition, Hartmut Rosa, *Beschleunigung: Die Veränderung der Zeitstrukturen in der Moderne* (Frankfurt am Main, 2005) and *Obsession der Gegenwart: Zeit im 20. Jahrhundert*, ed. by Alexander C. T. Geppert & Till Kössler (Göttingen, 2015).
56 Meinecke, *Die deutsche Katastrophe*; Karl Löwith, *Meaning in History: The Theological Implications of the Philosophy of History* (Chicago, 1949); Max Horkheimer & Theodor W. Adorno, *Dialektik der Aufklärung: Philosophische Fragmente* (Amsterdam, 1947). On the 1960s, see Hacke, *Philosophie der Bürgerlichkeit*.

dissolution of the coherent, clearly tripartite orientation of time. She regards this dissolution as a liberation that opens up for new relationships to the past – memory, oblivion, passing on, configuring.[57] Helge Jordheim in his turn has used the ideas of Hartog and Assmann as a starting-point, but has questioned why the fall of the dominant regime of historicity would necessarily be replaced by a new unambiguous order. He emphasises that modernity's perception of time – homogeneous, linear, teleological – was continually challenged by other orders of time, with different rhythms, different narratives, and different chains of events. Jordheim instead wants to argue for the possibility of the existence of multiple temporalities. In other words, the fall of the modern regime may pave the way for a simultaneously new and old multiplicity of orders of time.[58]

If we assume that Hartog, Assmann, and Jordheim are right in their observations, this could mean that a new relationship to the past can be initiated. Ever since antiquity, history had been envisaged as a teacher of life, *historia magistra vitae*, that allowed people to repeat the successes of the past instead of falling into its mistakes. Reinhart Koselleck has, in an elegant line of argument, shown that the perception of history as a collection of didactic narratives gradually began to dissolve during the eighteenth century. With historicism, this notion finally collapsed. Many of the historians of the twentieth century felt that the only lesson one could learn from history was that one could not learn any lessons; anyone who claimed anything different could be dismissed as a speculative metaphysician. Post-modernism finally drained history of meaning, but in its paradoxical way also invited the historian back in as a solitary interpreter and imaginative co-creator of histories.[59]

The question here is what a basic shift in the perception of time and history can mean to the academic orientation and ultimately to the notion of the ideal university. In one of the foundational documents of post-modernism, *La condition postmoderne* (1979),

---

57 Hartog, *Régimes d'historicité*; Aleida Assmann, *Ist die Zeit aus den Fugen? Aufstieg und Fall des Zeitregimes der Moderne* (Munich, 2013). See, in addition, Erling Sandmo, *Tid for historie: En bok om historiske spørsmål* (Oslo, 2015), pp. 215–28.
58 Helge Jordheim, 'Introduction: Multiple Times and the Work of Synchronization', *History and Theory*, 53:4 (2014).
59 Reinhart Koselleck, 'Historia Magistra Vitae: Über die Auflösung des Topos im Horizont neuzeitlich bewegter Geschichte', in Reinhart Koselleck, *Vergangene Zukunft: Zur Semantik geschichtlicher Zeiten* (Frankfurt am Main, 1989).

Jean-François Lyotard developed his ideas about how the metanarratives that had supported modernity had lost their strength. Among these were the 'narratives of the legitimation of knowledge' that Lyotard associated with the Berlin university and Wilhelm von Humboldt.[60] The following year an even more renowned French philosopher, Jacques Derrida, predicted that Humboldt's idea of the university was becoming outmoded:

> The Western university is a very recent *constructum* or artifact, and we already sense that it is *finished*: marked by finitude, just as, as its current model was established, between *The Conflict of the Faculties* (1798) and the founding of the University of Berlin (October 10, 1810, at the close of the mission entrusted to Humboldt), it was thought to be ruled by an idea of reason, by a certain relation, in other words, with infinity.[61]

In the more concrete and delimited German culture of history, there are signs indicating that the German university also entered a new phase at the end of the old century and the beginning of the new. In the wake of the radicalism of 1968, academic festivities had fallen into disrepute, and during the 1970s and 1980s remarkably few celebratory volumes were published. In the most recent years, however, we seem to have entered a new era of history and memory. Once more it has become obvious that universities should celebrate their significant anniversaries, and this has also happened across the German-language area: ETH in Zürich celebrated 150 years in 2005, Greifswald 550 years in 2006, Jena 450 years in 2008, Leipzig 600 years in 2009, Berlin 200 years in 2010, and Vienna 650 years in 2015.[62] As historical-cultural events, these celebrations have made a divided impression. On the one hand, ambitious, research-based multi-volume works were written about the history of the universities, usually with detailed and critical chapters about academic life during the eras of dictatorship and the world wars. On the other hand, many of the official celebrations came to be about marketing the

---

60 Jean-François Lyotard, *La condition postmoderne: Rapport sur le savoir* (Paris, 1979), translated into English as *The Postmodern Condition*, transl. by Geoff Bennington and Brian Massumi (Manchester, 1984); the quotation can be found in the translation on p. 31.
61 Jacques Derrida, 'Mochlos, or The Conflict of the Faculties', in Jacques Derrida, *Eyes of the University: Right to Philosophy 2*, transl. by Jan Plug et al. (Stanford, 2004), p. 90.
62 Paletschek, 'The Writing of University History', p. 146. See also *University Jubilees*, ed. by Dhondt.

universities and strengthening their trademarks. There was rarely an ambition to stimulate a more profound or reflective interest in history.⁶³

One interesting circumstance is that Humboldt as a symbol for the ideal university gained a foothold in the academic consciousness at a time when the basic truths of modernity began to be questioned in earnest, and not only by French philosophers. The theoretical death-blows were combined with a vague but rising mistrust of rationality, progress, and enlightenment in Western societies during the last twenty-five years of the twentieth century. It is possible to see the belated exaltation of the old Prussian educational reformer as an expression of an insight that something essential had been lost.

The contemporaneous German debate, which – in the era of the Bologna process – has points in common with the debate in other European countries as well, moves between two poles. On the one hand, it is marked by presentism, a preoccupation with the present. The discussion not only lacks a deeper historical dimension, it also lacks a comprehensive and long-term goal that has to do with something other than what is immediately at hand. In brief, there is a lack of a well-developed idea about the task and character of the university. On the other hand, enormous funds are invested in research and higher education in many parts of the world. There is an immense faith in the ability of science and scholarship to take on the 'great societal challenges' and contribute to solving the problems of humanity. One depressing interpretation is that the large investments and the rhetoric of excellence merely conceal the prevailing presentism, where history – not least in the form of references to the Humboldtian tradition – becomes nothing more than a source of empty rhetoric.

However, it does not have to stop there. Humboldt's ideals can have a deeper and broader relevance in the future, too.

---

63 This discrepancy has its equivalent in other parts of the contemporary culture of history. During the past two decades, research about the Holocaust has provided knowledge that is increasingly empirically and theoretically well founded. During the same period, genocide has, to a growing extent, become a symbol for all the things the EU project does not represent. In this respect, debates in the European Parliament during the twenty-first century illustrate a dehistoricisation of a basic historical experience. The respective attitudes of politics and the humanities to the past seem essentially different. See Daniel Levy & Natan Sznaider, *Erinnerung im globalen Zeitalter: Der Holocaust* (Frankfurt am Main, 2007) and Anne Wæhrens, *Erindringspolitik til forhandling: EU og erindringen om Holocaust, 1989–2009* (Copenhagen, 2013).

Humboldt's topicality

In his book *What Are Universities For?* (2012), the British intellectual historian Stefan Collini emphasises that anybody who studies the debates on the value and goals of the university throughout history must develop a high degree of tolerance for repetition. Those who succeed will notice that the understanding of the university is often locked into pairs of binary opposites: utilitarian versus non-utilitarian, *Bildung* versus vocational training, pure research versus applied research.[64]

While Collini chose to express himself in a pointed manner, his observation invites reflection. If it were to be placed in the context of a debate on historical methodology, it could be assigned to the David Armitage camp. Collini seems to mean that a limited number of themes and ideals recur in the history of the university. In Armitage's terminology, these would be investigated through a series of synchronous contextualisations brought together into a transtemporal history in the form of a comprehensive analytical chain. Peter E. Gordon employs a similar line of thought but carries the argument further. He underlines the importance of the historical context, but maintains that far too many studies of intellectual history (not least in imitation of Skinner) have overemphasised the importance of the local and delimited context. Gordon argues that ideals and notions can survive from one era to another, and that the connection between them should also be seen as a relevant context. Historians should, he says, remain sceptical of semantic continuity and of the belief that the ideas of the past are still immediately accessible to posterity. But at the same time a researcher must be receptive to the idea that there are contexts with a very long range. Otherwise, there is a danger that each period becomes an isolated island. The understanding of the contemporary period will then become distorted, and our own era will appear to be completely separate from historical courses of events and currents that have their origins in older processes. 'No epoch exists in sublime isolation from its temporal antecedents, and no era should imagine itself as so detached from the past as to flatter itself with the fantasy of intellectual independence', Gordon concludes.[65]

This attitude is well in keeping with the perspective I have applied to the history of the Humboldtian tradition: there is a set of basic

---

64 Stefan Collini, *What Are Universities For?* (London, 2012), p. 39.
65 Peter E. Gordon, 'Contextualism and Criticism in the History of Ideas', in *Rethinking Modern European Intellectual History*, ed. by Darrin M. McMahon & Samuel Moyn (Oxford, 2014), pp. 32–46 (quotation on p. 46).

14 A photo from present-day Berlin, showing the 'Humboldt-Box' – a futuristic exhibition venue – on the left. The rebuilt city palace on the right will house the 'Humboldt forum', a new centre for world culture

ideals which can, to a greater or lesser extent, be traced back to early nineteenth-century Prussia; but in order to understand what these ideals have meant, and how they have been articulated over the subsequent two centuries, they must be incorporated into specific eras and contexts. By extension, this approach to the principles of the German university opens up for reflections with a bearing on the present situation. If the point of departure is not that Humboldt's ideals are monolithic or eternal, it is instead possible to ask what insights of importance for our own time can be gained from them, without for that reason foregoing a scholarly understanding of history. The new culture of history that was outlined above is particularly capable of providing such opportunities. When the modern regime of historicity has fallen, it might become easier to combine ambitions to historicise while remaining alive to current circumstances.

In this respect, Hans Joas can offer qualified guidance. In his book about the history of human rights, *Die Sakralität der Person* (2011), he strives to avoid both an ahistorical legitimisation of timeless, universal norms and an unconditional deconstruction of the historical origin of these rights. 'Neither Kant nor Nietzsche' is his motto, and with that motto as a premise he introduces the idea of an affirmative genealogy.[66]

Joas, who is inspired by Ernst Troeltsch's idea of a kind of existential historicism, argues for a genealogy that is aware of the contingency of historical constructions. At the same time, it should be affirmative in the sense that an investigator, who is never free from his or her own value system, opens up to the normative appeal that may exist in historical contexts of meaning. 'Affirmative' does not imply support for actual historical conditions but for ideals in the past and the values associated with them.[67] Joas emphasises that affirmative genealogy presupposes two manoeuvres. On the one hand, it is necessary to interpret the historical meaning that the norms possessed during the period in question. On the other hand, the interpreter must have a realistic picture of the situation in his or her own time in order to realise the historically shaped ideals and the potential that still remains to be found in them. The values cannot remain pure abstractions. They only retain their relevance if they are defended in argumentation, supported by institutions, and embodied in practices.[68]

Inspired by these thoughts about affirmative genealogy, I would like to argue that it is possible to reconcile a critical understanding of the Humboldtian tradition with support for several of its fundamental ideas. There is no contradiction. But this requires, just as Joas emphasises, a historical sensibility that is combined with a genuine sense of reality.

Identifying highly time-bound interpretations of the German academic heritage is not difficult. Nor is it hard to see that some features were more prominent during certain periods than in others. The German – or Prussian – dimension was, for instance, strong at the turn of the century in 1900 and directly after the Second World War, while it is possible to speak of a kind of de-Germanisation of Humboldt in the early twenty-first century. It is also possible to see how the meaning of liberty, the content of *Bildung*, and the university's relationship to the state have varied. More generally, it is obvious that the university which Humboldt helped realise was an elitist, aristocratic institution – far from the egalitarian, democratic mass university that has developed during the post-war era.

---

66 Hans Joas, *Die Sakralität der Person: Eine neue Genealogie der Menschenrechte* (Berlin, 2011).
67 Ibid., pp. 187–95.
68 Ibid., p. 203.

This being said, the vigorous strands of consistency must be emphasised. There are a limited number of fundamental ideals in the Humboldtian tradition that have turned out to have a particular ability to survive and speak to various university cultures. These ideals have served as a model and a landmark in extremely dissimilar periods. I would like to believe that this is where the topicality of Humboldt can be found even today. Taken together, the Humboldtian ideals may form the basis for a kind of normative academic appeal, an idea about the university for our own time.[69]

First, the Humboldtian tradition has been used throughout the modern era in order to defend an acquisition of knowledge that goes beyond vocational programmes and instrumental usefulness. This happened at the turn of the century in 1800, 1900, and 2000, respectively. In our own time, which is at least as beset by utilitarianism as any other, it contains an understanding of how studies can promote civic and human development. The Anglo-Saxon liberal-arts tradition encompasses a related pedagogic vision, but that vision usually lacks any elaborate idea about the importance of research for the dynamics of knowledge.[70]

Second, the Humboldtian model has often been used as a synonym for the modern research university. There is a very good reason for this: the free search for new knowledge has been a cornerstone from the very beginning. Science and scholarship should, in Humboldt's

---

69 For attempts at topicalising the importance of the Humboldtian tradition for today's academy, see several of the contributions in *The Humboldtian Tradition*, ed. by Josephson, Karlsohn, & Östling, especially Wright; Hans Ruin, 'Philosophy, Freedom, and the Task of the University: Reflections on Humboldt's Legacy'; Ylva Hasselberg, 'Reclaiming Norms: The Value of Normative Structures for the University as Workplace and Enterprise'; and Sharon Rider, 'The Very Idea of Higher Education: Vocation of Man or Vocational Training?'

70 The Anglo-Saxon liberal-arts tradition, with its roots in John Henry Newman, has repeatedly, and on the basis of different points of departure, been invoked in the American debate. For important contributions from the most recent decades, see Allan Bloom, *The Closing of the American Mind: How Higher Education has Failed Democracy and Impoverished the Souls of Today's Students* (New York, 1987); Martha C. Nussbaum, *Cultivating Humanity: A Classical Defense of Reform in Liberal Education* (Cambridge, MA, 1997); Martha C. Nussbaum, *Not for Profit: Why Democracy Needs the Humanities* (Princeton, NJ, 2010); Hanna Holborn Gray, *Searching for Utopia: Universities and Their Histories* (Berkeley, 2012); and Fareed Zakaria, *In Defense of A Liberal Education* (New York, 2015).

words, be regarded as dealing with 'as yet unsolved problem[s] which always [call] for further research'. When research is reduced to a set of great societal challenges, usually defined by policy-makers and bureaucrats, people need to be reminded of the importance of having the ability to formulate original questions and test bold hypotheses against reality. Otherwise, there is a danger that research in the true sense of the word will wither away.

Third, the idea of the combination of research and education is closely linked to this notion of the significance of research. Underlying that principle is the conviction that there should be a dynamic connection between these two academic activities. Their coalescence stimulates movement in both directions and contributes to a continuous renewal of the education and a firmer anchoring in reality for research. Today, this ideal may serve as a memento for those who, in various ways, promote a division between the dissemination of knowledge and its incrementation.

Finally, at a higher level, the Humboldtian model may be viewed as an unusually coherent and well-thought-out idea of what distinguishes an ideal university. This idea is underpinned by a set of clear academic principles that permit variation at the same time – principles which have, thanks to their adaptability, had relevance in various historical contexts. Without being tied to a certain societal system or committed to a particular political movement, the Humboldt model has, more than any other comparable vision, represented an idea about the university as an autonomous world with its own logic and its own system of norms that are not the same as those of ideology, the market, or usefulness for the state.[71]

Seen in this light, there is an unquestionable value in bringing the Humboldtian tradition into the contemporary debate and recalling what it has represented in various ages. As a historically evolved phenomenon, it harbours a wealth of reflections and experiences, of sobering correctives and intoxicating dreams.

---

71 There are, of course, other similar systems of norms, such as Robert K. Merton's CUDOS principles (an acronym that has come to stand for 'Communalism, Universalism, Disinterestedness, Originality, and Scepticism'), although this has to do with science and scholarship rather than with the university as such. See Robert K. Merton, 'The Normative Structure of Science', in *The Sociology of Science: Theoretical and Empirical Investigations* (Chicago, 1973), and the discussion in Hasselberg, 'Reclaiming Norms'.

Bibliography

Adorno, Theodor W., 'Theorie der Halbbildung', *Der Monat*, 132:11 (1959)
——, *Theorie der Halbbildung* (Frankfurt am Main, 2006)
Adorno, Theodor W. & Thomas Mann, *Briefwechsel 1943–1955*, ed. by Christoph Gödde & Thomas Specher (Frankfurt am Main, 2002)
Ahlbäck, Anders, & Laura Hollsten, 'Changing the Narratives of University History', *Kasvatus & Aika*, 9:3 (2015)
'Akademische Freiheit', corpus 'German', https://books.google.com/ngrams (accessed 15 February 2016)
Alber, Jens, 'In memoriam Ralf Dahrendorf (1. Mai 1929–17. Juni 2009)', *Soziologie*, 38:4 (2009)
Albisetti, James C., 'The Decline of the German Mandarins After Twenty-Five Years', *History of Education Quarterly*, 34:4 (1994)
Albrecht, Clemens, 'Gefundene Wirklichkeit: Helmut Schelsky und die geistige Physiognomie politischer Konversion', in *Was war Bielefeld? Eine ideengeschichtliche Nachfrage*, ed. by Sonja Asal & Stephan Schlak (Göttingen, 2009)
Albrecht, Willy, *Der Sozialistische Deutsche Studentenbund (SDS): Vom parteikonformen Studentenverband zum Repräsentanten der Neuen Linken* (Bonn, 1994)
'Alexander von Humboldt', corpus 'German', https://books.google.com/ngrams (accessed 15 February 2016)
Amaral, Alberto et al., eds, *European Integration and the Governance of Higher Education and Research* (Dordrecht, 2009)
Anderson, Robert D., *British Universities: Past and Present* (London, 2006)
——, *European Universities from the Enlightenment to 1914* (Oxford, 2004)
Andersson, Ingvar, 'Universitet', *Svensk uppslagsbok*, 2nd edn, 32 vols (Malmö, 1947–1955), vol. XXX (1958)
Andrén, Carl-Gustaf, *Visioner, vägval och verkligheter: Svenska universitet och högskolor i utveckling efter 1940* (Lund, 2013)
Anrich, Ernst, *Die Idee der deutschen Universität und die Reform der deutschen Universitäten* (Darmstadt, 1960)

Bibliography

——, ed., *Die Idee der deutschen Universität: Die fünf Grundschriften aus der Zeit ihrer Neubegründung durch klassischen Idealismus und romantischen Realismus* (Darmstadt, 1956)

Arendt, Hannah, 'Die Krise in der Erziehung: Gedanken zur "Progressive Education"', *Der Monat*, 124:11 (1958–1959)

Armitage, David, 'What's the Big Idea? Intellectual History and the *Longue Durée*', *History of European Ideas*, 38:4 (2012:4)

Armitage, David & Jo Guldi, *The History Manifesto* (Cambridge, 2014)

Asal, Sonja & Stephan Schlak, eds, *Was war Bielefeld? Eine ideengeschichtliche Nachfrage* (Göttingen, 2009)

Asche, Matthias & Stefan Gerber, 'Neuzeitliche Universitätsgeschichte in Deutschland: Entwicklungslinien und Forschungsfelder', *Archiv für Kulturgeschichte*, 90:1 (2008)

Ash, Mitchell G., 'Bachelor of What, Master of Whom? The Humboldt Myth and Transformations of Higher Education in Germany and the US', *European Journal of Education*, 41:2 (2006)

——, 'Humboldt the Undead: Multiple Uses of "Humboldt" and His "Death" in the "Bologna" Era', in *The Humboldtian Tradition: Origins and Legacies*, ed. by Peter Josephson, Thomas Karlsohn, & Johan Östling (Leiden and Boston, 2014)

——, 'Politicizing "Normal Science" in Nazi Germany', *H-Net Book Review* (2009) http://www.h-net.org/ (accessed 15 February 2016)

——, 'Scientific Changes in Germany 1933, 1945 and 1990: Towards a Comparison', *Minerva*, 37:4 (1999)

——, 'Verordnete Umbrüche, Konstruierte Kontinuitäten: Zur Entnazifizierung von Wissenschaftlern und Wissenschaften nach 1945', *Zeitschrift für Geschichtswissenschaft*, 43:10 (1995)

——, ed., *German Universities Past and Future: Crisis or Renewal?* (Providence, RI, 1997)

——, ed., *Mythos Humboldt: Vergangenheit und Zukunft der deutschen Universität* (Vienna, 1999)

Assmann, Aleida, *Arbeit am nationalen Gedächtnis: Eine kurze Geschichte der deutschen Bildungsidee* (Frankfurt am Main, 1993)

——, *Ist die Zeit aus den Fugen? Aufstieg und Fall des Zeitregimes der Moderne* (Munich, 2013)

Baeumler, Alfred, *Politik und Erziehung: Reden und Aufsätze* (Berlin, 1937)

Baier, Horst, ed., *Helmut Schelsky – ein Soziologe in der Bundesrepublik: Eine Gedächtnisschrift von Freunden, Kollegen und Schülern* (Stuttgart, 1986)

Barnett, Nicholas, '"RUSSIA WINS SPACE RACE": The British Press and the Sputnik Moment, 1957', *Media History*, 19:2 (2013)

Bartz, Olaf, 'Bundesrepublikanische Universitätsleitbilder: Blüte und Zerfall des Humboldtianismus', *die hochschule*, 2 (2005)

——, *Der Wissenschaftsrat: Entwicklungslinien der Wissenschaftspolitik in der Bundesrepublik Deutschland 1957–2007* (Stuttgart, 2007)

Bavaj, Riccardo, 'Intellectual History, Version 1.0', in *Docupedia-Zeitgeschichte*, http://docupedia.de/zg/Intellectual_History?oldid=106434 (accessed 15 February 2016)
Bayer, Karen, Frank Sparing, & Wolfgang Woelk, eds, *Universitäten und Hochschulen im Nationalsozialismus und in der frühen Nachkriegszeit* (Stuttgart, 2004)
Becker, Carl Heinrich, *Gedanken zur Hochschulreform* (Leipzig, 1919)
———, *Internationale Wissenschaft und nationale Bildung: Ausgewählte Schriften*, ed. by Guido Müller (Cologne, 1997)
———, *Vom Wesen der deutschen Universität* (Leipzig, 1925)
Becker, Thomas, ed., *Zwischen Diktatur und Neubeginn: Die Universität Bonn im 'Dritten Reich' und in der Nachkriegszeit* (Göttingen, 2008)
Beiser, Frederick C., *The German Historicist Tradition* (Oxford, 2011)
Benner, Dietrich, *Wilhelm von Humboldts Bildungstheorie: Eine problemgeschichtliche Studie zum Begründungszusammenhang neuzeitlicher Bildungsreform* (Weinheim and Munich, 2003)
Benner, Mats, *Kunskapsnation i kris? Politik, pengar och makt i svensk forskning* (Stockholm, 2009)
Berglar, Peter, *Wilhelm von Humboldt* (Reinbek, 1970)
Bexell, Göran, *Akademiska värden visar vägen* (Stockholm, 2011)
Bialas, Wolfgang & Anson Rabinbach, eds, *Nazi Germany and the Humanities* (Oxford, 2007)
Bichow, Stefan, *Die Universität Kiel in den 1960er Jahren: Ordnungen einer akademischen Institution in der Krise* (Frankfurt am Main, 2013)
'Bildung', corpus 'German', https://books.google.com/ngrams (accessed 15 February 2016)
'Bildung durch Wissenschaft', corpus 'German', https://books.google.com/ngrams (accessed 15 February 2016)
Bildung und Kultur: Personal an Hochschulen – Vorläufige Ergebnisse, Statistisches Bundesamt (Wiesbaden, 2015)
Bildungsforschung und Bildungspolitik: Reden zum 80. Geburtstag von Hellmut Becker (Berlin, 1993)
Birnbaum, Daniel & Sven-Olov Wallenstein, *Heideggers väg* (Stockholm, 1999)
Blackbourn, David, *History of Germany, 1780–1918: The Long Nineteenth Century* (Malden, 2003)
Blomqvist, Göran, *Elfenbenstorn eller statsskepp? Stat, universitet och akademisk frihet i vardag och vision från Agardh till Schück* (Lund, 1992)
Bloom, Allan, *The Closing of the American Mind: How Higher Education Has Failed Democracy and Impoverished the Souls of Today's Students* (New York, 1987)
Bollenbeck, Georg, *Bildung und Kultur: Glanz und Elend eines deutschen Deutungsmusters* (Frankfurt am Main, 1994)
Bollenbeck, Georg & Waltraud 'Wara' Wende, eds, *Der Bologna-Prozess und die Veränderung der Hochschullandschaft* (Heidelberg, 2007)
Borsche, Tilman, *Wilhelm von Humboldt* (Munich, 1990)

Bibliography

Bragesjö, Fredrik, *Bilda eller samverka? En studie av bakgrunden till universitetens tredje uppgift* (Göteborg, 2009)
Brandser, Gry Cathrin, *Humboldt Revisited: The Institutional Drama of Academic Identity* (Bergen, 2006)
Brandt, Reinhard, *Wozu noch Universitäten? Ein Essay* (Hamburg, 2011)
Brandt, Sebastian, 'Universität und Öffentlichkeit in der Expansions- und Reformphase des deutschen Hochschulwesens (1955-1967)', in *Universität, Wissenschaft und Öffentlichkeit in Westdeutschland: (1945 bis ca. 1970)*, ed. by Sebastian Brandt et al. (Stuttgart, 2014)
Brandt, Sebastian et al., eds, *Universität, Wissenschaft und Öffentlichkeit in Westdeutschland: (1945 bis ca. 1970)* (Stuttgart, 2014)
Broberg, Gunnar, 'Från jubileumshistoria till komparativ universitetshistoria', in *Nordiska universitetskulturer*, ed. by Sten Högnäs (Lund, 1998)
Brocke, Bernhard vom, 'Die Entstehung der deutschen Forschungsuniversität, ihre Blüte und Krise um 1900', in *Humboldt international: Der Export des deutschen Universitätsmodells im 19. und 20. Jahrhundert*, ed. by Rainer Christoph Schwinges (Basel, 2001)
——, 'Hochschul- und Wissenschaftspolitik in Preussen im deutschen Kaiserreich 1882-1907: Das "System Althoff"', in *Bildungspolitik in Preussen zur Zeit des Kaiserreichs*, ed. by Peter Baumgart (Stuttgart, 1980)
——, 'Die Kaiser-Wilhelm-Gesellschaft im Kaiserreich', in *Forschung im Spannungsfeld von Politik und Gesellschaft: Geschichte und Struktur der Kaiser-Wilhelm-/Max-Planck-Gesellschaft*, ed. by Rudolf Vierhaus & Bernhard vom Brocke (Stuttgart, 1990)
——, ed., *Wissenschaftsgeschichte und Wissenschaftspolitik im Industriezeitalter: Das 'System Althoff' in historischer Perspektive* (Hildesheim, 1991)
Broman, Thomas H., *The Transformation of German Academic Medicine, 1750-1820* (Cambridge, 1996)
Bruch, Rüdiger vom, 'A Slow Farewell to Humboldt? Stages in the History of German Universities, 1810-1945', in *German Universities Past and Future: Crisis or Renewal?*, ed. by Mitchell G. Ash (Providence, RI, 1997)
——, 'Abschied von Humboldt? Die deutsche Universität vor dem Ersten Weltkrieg', in *Die deutsche Universität im 20. Jahrhundert*, ed. by Karl Strobel (Vierow, 1994)
——, 'Die Gründung der Berliner Universität', in *Humboldt international: Der Export des deutschen Universitätsmodells im 19. und 20. Jahrhundert*, ed. by Rainer Christoph Schwinges (Basel, 2001)
——, 'Methoden und Schwerpunkte der neueren Universitätsgeschichtsforschung', in *Die Universität Greifswald und die deutsche Hochschullandschaft im 19. und 20. Jahrhundert*, ed. by Werner Buchholz (Stuttgart, 2004)
——, *Wissenschaft, Politik und öffentliche Meinung: Gelehrtenpolitik im Wilhelminischen Deutschland (1890-1914)* (Husum, 1980)
Budde, Gunilla-Friederike, *Frauen der Intelligenz: Akademikerinnen in der DDR 1945 bis 1975* (Göttingen, 2003)

Budde, Gunilla, Eckart Conze, & Cornelia Rauh, eds, *Bürgertum nach dem bürgerlichen Zeitalter: Leitbilder und Praxis seit 1945* (Göttingen, 2010)
Burke, Peter, *What Is the History of Knowledge?* (Cambridge, 2016)
Burtscheidt, Christine, *Humboldts falsche Erben: Eine Bilanz der deutschen Hochschulreform* (Frankfurt am Main, 2010)
Busch, Alexander, *Die Geschichte der Privatdozenten: Eine soziologische Studie zur grossbetrieblichen Entwicklung der deutschen Universitäten* (Stuttgart, 1959)
Bödeker, Hans Erich, 'Aufklärung über Aufklärung? Reinhart Kosellecks Interpretation der Aufklärung', in *Zwischen Sprache und Geschichte: Zum Werk Reinhart Kosellecks*, ed. by Carsten Dutt & Reinhard Laube (Göttingen, 2013)
Charle, Christophe, 'Patterns', in *A History of the University in Europe: Universities in the Nineteenth and Early Twentieth Centuries (1800–1945)*, ed. by Walter Rüegg (Cambridge, 2004)
Chou, Meng-Hsuan, Isaac Kamola & Tamson Pietsch, eds, *The Transnational Politics of Higher Education: Contesting the Global/Transforming the Local* (New York, 2016)
Clark, Christopher, *Iron Kingdom: The Rise and Downfall of Prussia, 1600–1947* (Cambridge, 2006)
Clark, Mark W., *Beyond Catastrophe: German Intellectuals and Cultural Renewal after World War II, 1945–1955* (Lanham, MD, 2006)
Clark, William, *Academic Charisma and the Origins of the Research University* (Chicago, 2006)
Cobb, James Dennis, *The Forgotten Reforms: Non-Prussian Universities 1797–1817* (Ann Arbor, 1984)
Collini, Stefan, *What Are Universities For?* (London, 2012)
———, *Speaking of Universities* (London, 2017)
Connelly, John, *Captive University: The Sovietization of East German, Czech and Polish Higher Education, 1945–1956* (Chapel Hill, NC, 2000)
Conrad, Sebastian, *Globalgeschichte: Eine Einführung* (Munich, 2013)
Cornelißen, Christoph, *Gerhard Ritter: Geschichtswissenschaft und Politik im 20. Jahrhundert* (Düsseldorf, 2001)
Dahlmann, Friedrich Christoph, *Die Politik, auf den Grund und das Maaß der gegebenen Zustände zurückgeführt* (Göttingen, 1835)
Dahrendorf, Ralf, *Arbeiterkinder an deutschen Universitäten* (Tübingen, 1965)
———, *Bildung ist Bürgerrecht: Plädoyer für eine aktive Bildungspolitik* (Hamburg, 1965)
———, *Gesellschaft und Demokratie in Deutschland* (Munich, 1965)
———, *Über Grenzen: Lebenserinnerungen* (Munich, 2002)
Dammann, Klaus & Dominik Ghonghadze, 'Helmut Schelskys sozialdemokratische Konversion und seine Einbindung in Leipziger/Königsberger Netzwerke', in *Helmut Schelsky – der politische Anti-Soziologe: Eine Neurezeption*, ed. by Alexander Gallus (Göttingen, 2013)

Bibliography

Daston, Lorraine & Glenn W. Most, 'History of Science and History of Philologies', *Isis*, 106:2 (2015)
Defrance, Corine, *Les Alliés occidentaux et les universités allemandes: 1945–1949* (Paris, 2000)
——, 'Die Westalliierten als Hochschulreformatoren (1945–1949): Ein Vergleich', in *Zwischen Idee und Zweckorientierung: Vorbilder und Motive von Hochschulreformen seit 1945*, ed. by Andreas Franzmann & Barbara Wolbring (Berlin, 2007)
Deiters, Heinrich, 'Wilhelm von Humboldt als Gründer der Universität Berlin', in Friedrich Herneck (ed.), *Forschen und Wirken: Festschrift zur 150-Jahr-Feier der Humboldt-Universität zu Berlin 1810–1960*, 3 vols (Berlin, 1960), vol. I
Derrida, Jacques, 'Mochlos, or The Conflict of the Faculties', in Jacques Derrida, *Eyes of the University: Right to Philosophy 2*, transl. by Jan Plug et al. (Stanford, CA, 2004)
——, *Die unbedingte Universität* (Frankfurt am Main, 2001)
Dhondt, Pieter, '"Humboldt" in Belgium: Rhetoric on the German University Model', in *The Humboldtian Tradition: Origins and Legacies*, ed. by Peter Josephson, Thomas Karlsohn & Johan Östling (Leiden and Boston, 2014)
——, 'University History Writing: More Than A History of Jubilees?', in *University Jubilees and University History Writing: A Challenging Relationship*, ed. by Pieter Dhondt (Leiden and Boston, 2015)
——, ed., *National, Nordic or European? Nineteenth-Century University Jubilees and Nordic Cooperation* (Leiden and Boston, 2011)
——, ed., *University Jubilees and University History Writing: A Challenging Relationship* (Leiden and Boston, 2015)
Dickson, Paul, *Sputnik: The Shock of the Century* (New York, 2001)
Diesterweg, Adolph, *Über das Verderben auf den deutschen Universitäten* (Essen, 1836)
Doering-Manteuffel, Anselm, *Wie westlich sind die Deutschen? Amerikanisierung und Westernisierung im 20. Jahrhundert* (Göttingen, 1999)
Droit, Emmanuel & Wilfried Rudloff, 'Vom deutsch-deutschen "Bildungswettlauf" zum internationalen "Bildungswettbewerb"', in *Geteilte Geschichte: Ost- und Westdeutschland 1970–2000*, ed. by Frank Bösch (Göttingen, 2015)
Droysen, Johann Gustav, *Grundriß der Historik* (Leipzig, 1868)
Dräger, Jörg & Ralph Müller-Eiselt, *Die digitale Bildungsrevolution: Der radikale Wandel des Lernens und wie wir ihn gestalten können* (Munich, 2015)
——, 'Humboldt gegen Orwell', *Die Zeit*, 2015, no. 39
Dutt, Carsten, 'Zweierlei Kompensation: Joachim Ritters Philosophie der Geisteswissenschaften gegen ihre Popularisatoren und Kritiker verteidigt', *Scientia Poetica*, 12 (2008)
Eberan, Barbro, *Vi är inte färdiga med Hitler på länge än* (Eslöv, 2002)
Echternkamp, Jörg, *Nach dem Krieg: Alltagsnot, Neuorientierung und die Last der Vergangenheit 1945–1949* (Zürich, 2003)

Eckardt, Philipp, *Der Bologna-Prozess: Entstehung, Strukturen und Ziele der europäischen Hochschulreformpolitik* (Norderstedt, 2005)
Eckel, Jan, *Geist der Zeit: Deutsche Geisteswissenschaften seit 1870* (Göttingen, 2008)
Edgerton, David, 'Science in the United Kingdom: A Case Study in the Nationalisation of Science', in *Science in the Twentieth Century*, ed. by John Krige & Dominique Pestre (Amsterdam, 1997)
'Education', *Encyclopædia Britannica: Britannica Academic*, http://academic.eb.com/EBchecked/topic/179408/education (accessed 15 February 2016)
Eichler, Martin, 'Die Wahrheit des Mythos Humboldt', *Historische Zeitschrift*, 294:1 (2012)
Eigen, Manfred et al., *Die Idee der Universität: Versuch einer Standortbestimmung* (Berlin, 1988)
Elkana, Yehuda & Hannes Klöpper, *Die Universität im 21. Jahrhundert: Für eine neue Einheit von Lehre, Forschung und Gesellschaft* (Hamburg, 2012)
Engelhardt, Ulrich, *'Bildungsbürgertum': Begriffs- und Dogmengeschichte eines Etiketts* (Stuttgart, 1986)
Ericksen, Robert P., *Complicity in the Holocaust: Churches and Universities in Nazi Germany* (New York, 2012)
Eriksson, Gunnar, *Västerlandets idéhistoria 1800–1950* (Stockholm, 1983)
Eskildsen, Kasper Risbjerg, 'Leopold Ranke's Archival Turn: Location and Evidence in Modern Historiography', *Modern Intellectual History*, 5:3 (2008)
Etzemüller, Thomas, 'Auf der Suche nach den "haltenden Mächten": Intellektuelle Wandlungen und Kontinuitäten in der westdeutschen Geschichtswissenschaft nach 1945', in *Die Rückkehr der deutschen Geschichtswissenschaft in die 'Ökumene der Historiker': Ein wissenschaftsgeschichtlicher Ansatz*, ed. by Ulrich Pfeil (Munich, 2008)
Fahlstedt, Frans Eugène, 'Universitet', *Nordisk familjebok*, vol. 30 (Stockholm, 1920)
Farías, Victor, *Heidegger et le nazisme* (Lagrasse, 1987)
Faye, Emmanuel, *Heidegger, l'introduction du nazisme dans la philosophie: Autour des séminaires inédits de 1933–1935* (Paris, 2005)
Felsch, Philipp, *Der lange Sommer der Theorie: Geschichte einer Revolte 1960–1990* (Munich, 2015)
Fichte, Johann Gottlieb, *Deduzierter Plan einer zu Berlin zu errichtenden höhern Lehranstalt, die in gehöriger Verbindung mit einer Akademie der Wissenschaften stehe* (Tübingen, 1817)
Fichter, Tilman P. & Siegward Lönnendonker, *Kleine Geschichte des SDS: Der Sozialistische Deutsche Studentenbund von Helmut Schmidt bis Rudi Dutschke* (Essen, 2007)
Fischer, Torben & Matthias N. Lorenz, eds, *Lexikon der 'Vergangenheitsbewältigung' in Deutschland: Debatten- und Diskursgeschichte des Nationalsozialismus nach 1945* (Bielefeld, 2007)
Fisher, Jaimey, *Disciplining Germany: Youth, Reeducation, and Reconstruction after the Second World War* (Detroit, 2007)

Bibliography

Flenner, Helmut, *Wilhelm von Humboldt und die Schwermut: Ein Beitrag zur Erkenntnis des Menschen Wilhelm von Humboldt* (Frankfurt am Main, 1953)

Flexner, Abraham, *Universities: American, German, English* (Oxford, 1930)

Flitner, Andreas, 'Humboldt, Wilhelm von', in *Deutsche biographische Enzyklopädie*, ed. by Rudolf Vierhaus, 2nd rev. and enl. edn, 10 vols (Munich, 2005–08), vol. V (2006)

——, ed., *Deutsches Geistesleben und Nationalsozialismus: Eine Vortragsreihe der Universität Tübingen* (Tübingen, 1965)

Forner, Sean A., *German Intellectuals and the Challenge of Democratic Renewal: Culture and Politics after 1945* (Cambridge, 2014)

Foucault, Michel, *Les mots et les choses: Une archéologie des sciences humaines* (Paris, 1966)

François, Etienne & Hagen Schulze, eds, *Deutsche Erinnerungsorte*, 3 vols (Munich, 2001)

Franzmann, Andreas & Barbara Wolbring, eds, *Zwischen Idee und Zweckorientierung: Vorbilder und Motive von Hochschulreformen seit 1945* (Berlin, 2007)

Freese, Rudolf, ed., *Wilhelm von Humboldt: Sein Leben und Wirken, dargestellt in Briefen, Tagebüchern und Dokumenten seiner Zeit* (Darmstadt, 1986)

Freytag-Loringhoven, Konstantin von, *Erziehung im Kollegienhaus: Reformbestrebungen an den deutschen Universitäten der amerikanischen Besatzungszone 1945–1960* (Stuttgart, 2012)

Friedman, Robert M., *Integration and Visibility: Historiographic Challenges to University History* (Oslo, 2000)

Frängsmyr, Tore, 'Universitet', *Nationalencyklopedin*, 20 vols (Höganäs, 1996), vol. XIX

Führ, Christoph, *The German Educational System since 1945: Outlines and Problems* (Bonn, 1997)

——, 'Zur deutschen Bildungsgeschichte seit 1945', in *Handbuch der deutschen Bildungsgeschichte: 1945 bis zur Gegenwart: Bundesrepublik Deutschland*, ed. by Christoph Führ & Carl-Ludwig Furck (Munich, 1998)

Föllmer, Moritz & Rüdiger Graf, eds, *Die 'Krise' der Weimarer Republik: Zur Kritik eines Deutungsmusters* (Frankfurt am Main, 2005)

Gadamer, Hans-Georg, 'The Idea of the University – Yesterday, Today, Tomorrow', in *Hans-Georg Gadamer on Education, Poetry, and History: Applied Hermeneutics*, ed. by Dieter Misgeld and Graeme Nicholson, transl. by Lawrence Schmidt and Monica Reuss (Albany, 1992)

——, 'Die Idee der Universität – gestern, heute, morgen', in Manfred Eigen et al., *Die Idee der Universität: Versuch einer Standortbestimmung* (Berlin, 1988)

Gall, Lothar, *Wilhelm von Humboldt: Ein Preuße in der Welt* (Berlin, 2011)

Gallus, Alexander, '"Intellectual History" mit Intellektuellen und ohne sie: Facetten neuerer geistesgeschichtlicher Forschung', *Historische Zeitschrift*, 288:1 (2009)

——, ed., *Helmut Schelsky – der politische Anti-Soziologe: Eine Neurezeption* (Göttingen, 2013)
Gallus, Alexander & Axel Schildt, eds, *Rückblickend in die Zukunft: Politische Öffentlichkeit und intellektuelle Positionen in Deutschland um 1950 und um 1930* (Göttingen, 2011)
Gebhardt, Bruno, *Wilhelm von Humboldt als Staatsmann*, 2 vols (Stuttgart, 1896–1899)
Geier, Manfred, *Die Brüder Humboldt* (Reinbek, 2009)
Geiger, Roger L., *Research and Relevant Knowledge: American Research Universities since World War II* (New Brunswick, NJ, 2004)
——, *To Advance Knowledge: The Growth of American Research Universities, 1900–1940* (New York, 1986)
Geppert, Alexander C. T. & Till Kössler, eds, *Obsession der Gegenwart: Zeit im 20. Jahrhundert* (Göttingen, 2015)
Geppert, Dominik & Jens Hacke, eds, *Streit um den Staat: Intellektuelle Debatten in der Bundesrepublik 1960–1980* (Göttingen, 2008)
Gerber, Stefan et al., 'Einleitung', in *Traditionen – Brüche – Wandlungen: Die Universität Jena 1850–1995*, ed. by Stefan Gerber et al. (Cologne, 2009)
Geulen, Christian, 'Plädoyer für eine Geschichte der Grundbegriffe des 20. Jahrhunderts', *Zeithistorische Forschungen/Studies in Contemporary History*, 7:1 (2010)
Gierow, Krister, *Lunds universitets historia: Utgiven av universitetet till dess 300-årsjubileum: 3. 1790–1867* (Lund, 1971)
Gieselbusch, Hermann et al., eds, *100 Jahre Rowohlt: Eine illustrierte Chronik* (Reinbek bei Hamburg, 2008)
Gilcher-Holtey, Ingrid, ed., *Eingreifende Denkerinnen: Weibliche Intellektuelle im 20. und 21. Jahrhundert* (Tübingen, 2015)
Glotz, Peter, *Im Kern verrottet? Fünf vor zwölf an Deutschlands Universitäten* (Stuttgart, 1996)
Goede, Arnt, *Adolf Rein und die 'Idee der politischen Universität'* (Hamburg, 2008)
Gordon, Peter E., 'Contextualism and Criticism in the History of Ideas', in *Rethinking Modern European Intellectual History*, ed. by Darrin M. McMahon & Samuel Moyn (Oxford, 2014)
——, 'What is Intellectual History? A Frankly Partisan Introduction to a Frequently Misunderstood Field' (2013), http://scholar.harvard.edu/files/pgordon/files/what_is_intell_history_pgordon_mar2012.pdf (accessed 15 February 2016)
Gordon, Peter E. & John P. McCormick, 'Introduction: Weimar Thought: Continuity and Crisis', in *Weimar Thought: A Contested Legacy*, ed. by Peter E. Gordon & John P. McCormick (Princeton, 2013)
Graf, Rüdiger, *Die Zukunft der Weimarer Republik: Krisen und Zukunftsaneignungen in Deutschland 1918 bis 1933* (Munich, 2008)
Grafton, Anthony, 'The History of Ideas: Precept and Practice, 1950–2000 and Beyond', *Journal of the History of Ideas*, 67:1 (2006)

Bibliography

Grau, Wilhelm, *Wilhelm von Humboldt und das Problem des Juden* (Hamburg, 1935)
Gray, Hanna Holborn, *Searching for Utopia: Universities and Their Histories* (Berkeley, 2012)
Greenberg, Udi, *The Weimar Century: German Émigrés and the Ideological Foundations of the Cold War* (Princeton, 2015)
Grondin, Jean, *Hans-Georg Gadamer: Eine Biographie* (Tübingen, 2013)
Grundmann, Herbert, 'Gebhardt, Bruno', *Neue Deutsche Biographie*, ed. by Historische Kommission bei der Bayerischen Akademie der Wissenschaften (Berlin, 1953–), vol. VI (1964)
Grüttner, Michael et al., eds, *Gebrochene Wissenschaftskulturen: Universität und Politik im 20. Jahrhundert* (Göttingen, 2010)
Gustavsson, Sverker, *Debatten om forskningen och samhället: En studie i några teoretiska inlägg under 1900-talet* (Stockholm, 1971)
Haase, Sven, *Berliner Universität und Nationalgedanke 1800–1848: Genese einer politischen Idee* (Stuttgart, 2012)
Habermas, Jürgen, 'Das chronische Leiden der Hochschulreform', *Merkur*, 3 (1957)
——, 'The Idea of the University: Learning Processes', transl. by John R. Blazek, *New German Critique*, 41 (1987)
——, 'Die Idee der Universität: Lernprozesse', in Manfred Eigen et al., *Die Idee der Universität: Versuch einer Standortbestimmung* (Berlin, 1988)
——, 'Die Liebe zur Freiheit', *Frankfurter Allgemeine Zeitung*, 18 June 2009
——, *Protestbewegung und Hochschulreform* (Frankfurt am Main, 1969)
——, 'Rationality out of Passion', in *On Liberty: The Dahrendorf Questions*, ed. by Timothy Garton Ash (Oxford, 2009)
——, *Strukturwandel der Öffentlichkeit: Untersuchungen zu einer Kategorie der bürgerlichen Gesellschaft* (Neuwied, 1962)
——, 'Vorwort', in Wolfgang Nitsch et al., *Hochschule in der Demokratie: Kritische Beiträge zur Erbschaft und Reform der deutschen Universität* (Berlin and Neuwied, 1965)
—— et al., *Student und Politik: Eine soziologische Untersuchung zum politischen Bewußtsein Frankfurter Studenten* (Neuwied am Rhein, 1961)
Hachtmann, Rüdiger, *Wissenschaftsmanagement im Dritten Reich: Die Geschichte der Generalverwaltung der Kaiser-Wilhelm-Gesellschaft*, 2 vols (Göttingen, 2007)
Hacke, Jens, 'Pathologie der Gesellschaft und liberale Vision: Ralf Dahrendorfs Erkundung der deutschen Demokratie', *Zeithistorische Forschungen/ Studies in Contemporary History*, 2 (2004)
——, *Philosophie der Bürgerlichkeit: Die liberalkonservative Begründung der Bundesrepublik* (Göttingen, 2006)
Hammerstein, Notker, *Antisemitismus und deutsche Universitäten 1871–1933* (Frankfurt am Main, 1995)

——, *Die Deutsche Forschungsgemeinschaft in der Weimarer Republik und im Dritten Reich: Wissenschaftspolitik in Republik und Diktatur 1920–1945* (Munich, 1999)
——, 'Epilogue: Universities and War in the Twentieth Century', in *A History of the University in Europe: Universities in the Nineteenth and Early Twentieth Centuries (1800–1945)*, ed. by Walter Rüegg (Cambridge, 2004)
——, 'Humboldt im Dritten Reich', in *Humboldt international: Der Export des deutschen Universitätsmodells im 19. und 20. Jahrhundert*, ed. by Rainer Christoph Schwinges (Basel, 2001)
——, 'National Socialism and the German Universities', *History of Universities*, 18:1 (2003)
Hansen, Reimer, 'Von der Friedrich-Wilhelms- zur Humboldt-Universität zu Berlin', in *Geschichte der Universität Unter den Linden: Sozialistisches Experiment und Erneuerung in der Demokratie – die Humboldt-Universität zu Berlin 1945–2010*, ed. by Heinz-Elmar Tenorth (Berlin, 2012)
Harnack, Adolf von, *Geschichte der Königlich preußischen Akademie der Wissenschaften zu Berlin*, 3 vols (Berlin, 1900), vol. I:II
Hartog, François, *Régimes d'historicité: Présentisme et expériences du temps* (Paris, 2003)
Haß, Ulrike & Nikolaus Müller-Schöll, eds, *Was ist eine Universität? Schlaglichter auf eine ruinierte Institution* (Bielefeld, 2008)
Hasselberg, Ylva, 'Reclaiming Norms: The Value of Normative Structures for the University as Workplace and Enterprise', in *The Humboldtian Tradition: Origins and Legacies*, ed. by Peter Josephson, Thomas Karlsohn & Johan Östling (Leiden and Boston, 2014)
Haupts, Leo, *Die Universität zu Köln im Übergang vom Nationalsozialismus zur Bundesrepublik* (Cologne, 2007)
Hausmann, Frank-Rutger, *Die Geisteswissenschaften im 'Dritten Reich'* (Frankfurt am Main, 2011)
Haym, Rudolf, *Wilhelm von Humboldt: Lebensbild und Charakteristik* (Berlin, 1856)
Heidegger, Martin, 'Die Selbstbehauptung der deutschen Universität', in Martin Heidegger, *Gesamtausgabe* (Frankfurt am Main, 1975–), Abt. I, vol. XVI: *Veröffentlichte Schriften 1910–1976: Reden und andere Zeugnisse eines Lebensweges: 1910–1976*, ed. by Hermann Heidegger (2000)
——, 'The Self-Assertion of the German University', transl. by Karsten Harries, *The Review of Metaphysics*, 38:3 (1985)
Heidegren, Carl-Göran, *Antropologi, samhällsteori och politik: Radikalkonservatism och kritisk teori: Gehlen – Schelsky – Habermas – Honneth – Joas* (Göteborg, 2002)
Heim, Susanne, Carola Sachse, & Mark Walker, eds, *The Kaiser Wilhelm Society under National Socialism* (Cambridge, 2009)
Heimbüchel, Bernd & Klaus Pabst, *Kölner Universitätsgeschichte: Das 19. und 20. Jahrhundert* (Cologne, 1988)
Heimpel, Hermann, *Liebeserklärung an die deutsche Universität: Festvortrag* (Regensburg, 1965)

——, *Probleme und Problematik der Hochschulreform* (Göttingen, 1956)
Heinemann, Manfred, ed., *Hochschuloffiziere und Wiederaufbau des Hochschulwesens in Deutschland 1945–1949: Die sowjetische Besatzungszone* (Berlin, 2000)
Herbert, Ulrich, *Geschichte Deutschlands im 20. Jahrhundert* (Munich, 2014)
Herkendell, Hans-Jörg, *Die Persönlichkeitsidee Wilhelm von Humboldts und das völkisch-politische Menschenbild* (Würzburg, 1938)
Hermand, Jost, *Culture in Dark Times: Nazi Fascism, Inner Emigration, and Exile* (New York, 2013)
Herneck, Friedrich, ed., *Forschen und Wirken: Festschrift zur 150-Jahr-Feier der Humboldt-Universität zu Berlin 1810–1960*, 3 vols (Berlin, 1960)
Herrmann, Ulrich, Markus Bok, & Günter Erdmann, 'Kommentare und Anmerkungen: Band IV', in Wilhelm von Humboldt, *Werke in fünf Bänden*, ed. by Andreas Flitner & Klaus Giel, 5 vols (Darmstadt, 1960–81), vol. V (1981)
Hertig, Hans Peter, *Universities, Rankings and the Dynamics of Global Higher Education* (London, 2016)
Herzog, Roman, 'Aufbruch in der Bildungspolitik', in *Aufbruch in der Bildungspolitik: Roman Herzogs Rede und 25 Antworten*, ed. by Michael Rutz (Munich, 1997)
Higher Education: Report of the Committee Appointed by the Prime Minister under the Chairmanship of Lord Robbins 1961–63 (London, 1963)
'History of European research universities', *Wikipedia*, https://en.wikipedia.org/wiki/History_of_European_research_universities (accessed 15 February 2016)
'History of Knowledge', presentation on its website https://www.zgw.ethz.ch/en/portrait.html (accessed 15 February 2016)
Hobsbawm, Eric J., *The Age of Revolution: Europe 1789–1848* (London, 1962)
Hochschule in der Demokratie: Denkschrift des Sozialistischen Deutschen Studentenbundes (Frankfurt am Main, 1965)
Hochschule in der Demokratie: Denkschrift des Sozialistischen Deutschen Studentenbundes zur Hochschulreform (Frankfurt am Main, 1961)
Hohendahl, Peter Uwe, 'Humboldt Revisited: Liberal Education, University Reform, and the Opposition to the Neoliberal University', *New German Critique*, 38:2 (2011)
Horkheimer, Max & Theodor W. Adorno, *Dialektik der Aufklärung: Philosophische Fragmente* (Amsterdam, 1947)
Horst, Johanna-Charlotte, ed., *Was ist Universität? Texte und Positionen zu einer Idee* (Zürich, 2010)
——, ed., *Was passiert? Stellungnahmen zur Lage der Universität* (Zürich, 2010)
Horst, Johanna-Charlotte et al., eds, *Bologna-Bestiarium* (Zürich, 2013)
Hossfeld, Uwe et al., eds, *Kämpferische Wissenschaft: Studien zur Universität Jena im Nationalsozialismus* (Cologne, 2003)
Howald, Ernst, *Wilhelm von Humboldt* (Zürich, 1944)

Howard, Thomas Albert, *Protestant Theology and the Making of the Modern German University* (Oxford, 2006)

Hoyer, Timo, *Nietzsche und die Pädagogik: Werk, Biografie und Rezeption* (Würzburg, 2002)

Humboldt, Wilhelm von, 'Der Königsberger und der Litauische Schulplan', in Wilhelm von Humboldt, *Werke in fünf Bänden*, ed. by Andreas Flitner & Klaus Giel, 5 vols (Darmstadt, 1960–81), vol. IV: *Schriften zur Politik und zum Bildungswesen* (1964)

——, *Gesammelte Schriften*, ed. by Albert Leitzmann & Bruno Gebhardt, 17 vols (Berlin, 1903–1936)

——, 'Gutachten über die Organisation der Ober-Examinations-Kommission', in Wilhelm von Humboldt, *Werke in fünf Bänden*, ed. by Andreas Flitner & Klaus Giel, 5 vols (Darmstadt, 1960–81), vol. IV: *Schriften zur Politik und zum Bildungswesen* (1964)

——, 'Ideen zu einem Versuch, die Grenzen der Wirksamkeit des Staates zu bestimmen', in Wilhelm von Humboldt, *Werke in fünf Bänden*, ed. by Andreas Flitner & Klaus Giel, 5 vols (Darmstadt, 1960–81), vol. I: *Schriften zur Anthropologie und Geschichte* (1960)

——, 'Om den inre och yttre organisationen av de högre vetenskapliga läroanstalterna i Berlin', transl. by Thomas Karlsohn, *Psykoanalytisk Tid/Skrift*, 26–27 (2009)

——, *Om gränserna för statens verksamhet*, transl. by Erik Carlquist (Umeå, 2012)

——, *Om språket*, transl. by Johan Redin (Stockholm, 2011)

——, 'Theorie der Bildung des Menschen: Bruchstücke', in Wilhelm von Humboldt, *Werke in fünf Bänden*, ed. by Andreas Flitner & Klaus Giel, 5 vols (Darmstadt, 1960–81), vol. I: *Schriften zur Anthropologie und Geschichte* (1960)

——, 'Über die innere und äussere Organisation der höheren wissenschaftlichen Anstalten in Berlin', in Wilhelm von Humboldt, *Werke in fünf Bänden*, ed. by Andreas Flitner & Klaus Giel, 5 vols (Darmstadt, 1960–81), vol. IV: *Schriften zur Politik und zum Bildungswesen* (1964)

——, 'University Reform in Germany, I: On the Spirit and the Organisational Framework of Intellectual Institutions in Berlin', trans. by Edward Shils, *Minerva*, 8:2 (1970)

——, *Werke in fünf Bänden*, ed. by Andreas Flitner & Klaus Giel, 5 vols (Darmstadt, 1960–81)

——, *Wilhelm von Humboldt: Gesammelte Werke*, ed. Carl Brandes, 7 vols (Berlin, 1841–1852)

'von Humboldt, Alexander', *Svensk uppslagsbok*, 2nd edn, 32 vols (Malmö, 1947–55), vol. XIII (1955)

'Humboldt, Friedrich Wilhelm Christian Karl Ferdinand', *Nordisk familjebok*, 38 vols (Stockholm, 1904–26), vol. XI (1909)

'Humboldt, Friedrich Wilhelm Heinrich Alexander', *Nordisk familjebok*, 38 vols (Stockholm, 1904–26), vol. XI (1909)

Bibliography

'Humboldt, Wilhelm von', *Nationalencyklopedin*, 20 vols (Höganäs, 1989–96), vol IX (1992)
'von Humboldt, Wilhelm', *Svensk uppslagsbok*, 2nd edn, 32 vols (Malmö, 1947–55), vol. XIII (1955)
'Humboldt', corpus 'German', https://books.google.com/ngrams (accessed 15 February 2016)
'Humboldtian model of higher education', *Wikipedia*, https://en.wikipedia.org/wiki/Humboldtian_model_of_higher_education (accessed 15 February 2016)
'Humboldtsches Bildungsideal', *Wikipedia*, https://de.wikipedia.org/wiki/Humboldtsches_Bildungsideal (accessed 15 February 2016)
Husén, Torsten, *Bokslut: Essäer om utbildning* (Stockholm, 2002)
Hübner, Ulrich, *Wilhelm von Humboldt und die Bildungspolitik: Eine Untersuchung zum Humboldt-Bild als Prolegomena zu einer Theorie der historischen Pädagogik* (Munich, 1983)
Hörisch, Jochen, *Die ungeliebte Universität: Rettet die Alma mater!* (Munich & Vienna, 2006)
Hörnig, Hannes, *Zu einigen Problemen im Hochschulwesen beim umfassenden Aufbau des Sozialismus in der DDR* (Berlin, 1965)
'Internationale Expertenkommission zur Evaluation der Exzellenzinitiative: Endbericht', https://www.bmbf.de/files/Endbericht_Internationale_Expertenkommission_Exzellenzinitiative.pdf (accessed 15 February 2016)
Jaeger, Werner, *Paideia: Die Formung des griechischen Menschen*, 3 vols (Berlin, 1934–1947)
Jahnke, Thomas & Wolfram Meyerhöfer, eds, *PISA & Co: Kritik eines Programms* (Hildesheim, 2007)
Jahrbuch für Universitätsgeschichte, 13 (2010)
Jalava, Marja, *The University in the Making of the Welfare State: The 1970s Degree Reform in Finland* (Frankfurt am Main, 2012)
——, 'When Humboldt Met Marx: The 1970s Leftist Student Movement and the Idea of the University in Finland', in *The Humboldtian Tradition: Origins and Legacies*, ed. by Peter Josephson, Thomas Karlsohn & Johan Östling (Leiden and Boston, 2014)
Jarausch, Konrad H., 'Demokratische Exzellenz? Ein transatlantisches Plädoyer für ein neues Leitbild deutscher Hochschulen', *Denkströme: Journal der Sächsischen Akademie der Wissenschaften*, 1 (2008)
——, 'The Humboldt Syndrome: West German Universities, 1945–1989', in *German Universities Past and Future: Crisis or Renewal?*, ed. by Mitchell G. Ash (Providence, RI, 1997)
——, *Students, Society, and Politics in Imperial Germany: The Rise of Academic Illiberalism* (Princeton, 1982)
——, 'Universität und Hochschule', in *Handbuch der deutschen Bildungsgeschichte: 1870–1918: Von der Reichsgründung bis zum Ende des Ersten Weltkriegs*, ed. by Christa Berg (Munich, 1991)

Jarausch, Konrad H., Matthias Middell, & Annette Vogt, eds, *Geschichte der Universität Unter den Linden: Sozialistisches Experiment und Erneuerung in der Demokratie – die Humboldt-Universität zu Berlin 1945–2010* (Berlin, 2012)

Jaspers, Karl, 'Erneuerung der Universität', *Die Wandlung*, 1 (1945/1946)

——, *Erneuerung der Universität: Reden und Schriften 1945/46*, ed. by Renato de Rosa (Heidelberg, 1986)

——, 'Europa der Gegenwart', in Karl Jaspers, *Erneuerung der Universität: Reden und Schriften 1945/46*, ed. by Renato de Rosa (Heidelberg, 1986)

——, *Die Idee der Universität* (Berlin, 1923)

——, *Die Idee der Universität* (Berlin and Heidelberg, 1946)

——, *Die Schuldfrage: Ein Beitrag zur deutschen Frage* (Zürich, 1946)

——, 'Vom lebendigen Geist der Universität', in Karl Jaspers & Fritz Ernst, *Vom lebendigen Geist der Universität und vom Studieren: Zwei Vorträge* (Heidelberg, 1946)

——, *Vom Ursprung und Ziel der Geschichte* (Munich, 1949)

Jaspers, Karl & Kurt Rossmann, *Die Idee der Universität: Für die gegenwärtige Situation entworfen* (Berlin, 1961)

Jay, Martin, 'Historical Explanation and the Event: Reflections on the Limits of Contextualization', *New Literary History*, 42:4 (2011)

Jeismann, Karl-Ernst, 'Geschichtsbewußtsein', in *Handbuch der Geschichtsdidaktik*, ed. by Klaus Bergmann, 2 vols (Düsseldorf, 1979), vol. I

Jessen, Ralph, *Akademische Elite und kommunistische Diktatur: Die ostdeutsche Hochschullehrerschaft in der Ulbricht-Ära* (Göttingen, 1999)

——, 'Zwischen Bildungspathos und Spezialistentum: Werthaltungen und Identitätskonstruktionen der Hochschullehrerschaft in West- und Ostdeutschland nach 1945', in *Eliten im Sozialismus: Beiträge zur Sozialgeschichte der DDR*, ed. by Peter Hübner (Cologne, Weimar and Vienna, 1999)

Jessop, Bob, Norman Fairclough, & Ruth Wodak, eds, *Education and the Knowledge-Based Economy in Europe* (Rotterdam, 2008)

Joas, Hans, *Die Sakralität der Person: Eine neue Genealogie der Menschenrechte* (Berlin, 2011)

Joas, Hans & Peter Vogt, eds, *Begriffene Geschichte: Beiträge zum Werk Reinhart Kosellecks* (Berlin, 2011)

John, Jürgen, '"Not deutscher Wissenschaft"? Hochschulwandel, Universitätsidee und akademischer Krisendiskurs in der Weimarer Republik', in *Gebrochene Wissenschaftskulturen: Universität und Politik im 20. Jahrhundert*, ed. by Michael Grüttner et al. (Göttingen, 2010)

Jonsson, Kjell, 'Bildning, utveckling och frihet: Om Wilhelm von Humboldt och *Om gränserna för statens verksamhet*', in Wilhelm von Humboldt, *Om gränserna för statens verksamhet* (Umeå, 2012)

Jordheim, Helge, 'Introduction: Multiple Times and the Work of Synchronization', *History and Theory*, 53:4 (2014)

——, *Läsningens vetenskap: Utkast till en ny filologi*, transl. by Sten Andersson (Gråbo, 2003)

Bibliography

Josephson, Peter, 'Böcker eller universitet? Om ett tema i tysk utbildningspolitisk debatt kring 1800', *Lychnos*, 2009
——, *Den akademiska frihetens gränser: Max Weber, Humboldtmodellen och den värdefria vetenskapen* (Uppsala, 2005)
——, 'The Publication Mill: The Beginnings of Publication History as an Academic Merit in German Universities, 1750–1810', in *The Humboldtian Tradition: Origins and Legacies*, ed. by Peter Josephson, Thomas Karlsohn & Johan Östling (Leiden and Boston, 2014)
——, 'Publicitetens politiska ekonomi: Introduktion av skriftställarskap som merit vid tyska universitet 1750–1810', *Lychnos*, 2014
Josephson, Peter, Thomas Karlsohn, & Johan Östling, 'The Humboldtian Tradition and Its Transformations', in *The Humboldtian Tradition: Origins and Legacies*, ed. by Peter Josephson, Thomas Karlsohn & Johan Östling (Leiden and Boston, 2014)
——, eds, *The Humboldtian Tradition: Origins and Legacies* (Leiden and Boston, 2014)
Junge, Marion, *Wilhelm von Humboldts akademischer Bildungsanspruch: Ein Beitrag zur Entideologisierung der klassischen deutschen Universitätsidee* (Hamburg, 1970)
Jureit, Ulrike, *Generationsforschung* (Göttingen, 2006)
Kadereit, Ralf, *Karl Jaspers und die Bundesrepublik Deutschland: Politische Gedanken eines Philosophen* (Paderborn, 1999)
Kaehler, Siegfried A., *Wilhelm von Humboldt und der Staat: Ein Beitrag zur Geschichte deutscher Lebensgestaltung um 1800* (Munich, 1927)
Kaiser, Tobias, 'Planungseuphorie und Hochschulreform in der deutschdeutschen Systemkonkurrenz', in *Gebrochene Wissenschaftskulturen: Universität und Politik im 20. Jahrhundert*, ed. by Michael Grüttner et al. (Göttingen, 2010)
Kaiserfeld, Thomas, 'Massuniversitetets forskningspolitik: Samverkan och innovation i slutet av 1960-talet', in *Universitetets gränser*, ed. by Peter Josephson & Thomas Karlsohn (Göteborg, forthcoming)
Kamenz, Uwe & Martin Wehrle, *Professor Untat: Was faul ist hinter den Hochschulkulissen* (Berlin, 2007)
Kant, Immanuel, *The Conflict of the Faculties*, trans. by Mary J. Gregor (Lincoln and London, 1992)
Kapczynski, Jennifer M., *The German Patient: Crisis and Recovery in Postwar Culture* (Ann Arbor, 2008)
Karlsohn, Thomas, 'On Humboldtian and Contemporary Notions of the Academic Lecture', in *The Humboldtian Tradition: Origins and Legacies*, ed. by Peter Josephson, Thomas Karlsohn & Johan Östling (Leiden and Boston, 2014)
——, *Originalitetens former: Essäer om bildning och universitet* (Göteborg, 2012)
Karpen, Ulrich, 'Peters, Hans Carl Maria Alfons', *Neue Deutsche Biographie* (Berlin, 1953–), vol. XX (2001)

Kaube, Jürgen, ed., *Die Illusion der Exzellenz: Lebenslügen der Wissenschaftspolitik* (Berlin, 2009)
Kawohl, Irmgard, *Wilhelm von Humboldt in der Kritik des 20. Jahrhunderts* (Ratingen, 1969)
Kelley, Donald R., *The Descent of Ideas: The History of Intellectual History* (Aldershot, 2002)
Kempf, Volker, *Wider die Wirklichkeitsverweigerung: Helmut Schelsky – Leben, Werk, Aktualität* (Munich, 2012)
Kerr, Clark, 'Remembering Flexner', in Abraham Flexner, *Universities: American, German, English* (London, 1968)
——, *The Uses of the University* (Cambridge, MA, 1963)
Kessel, Eberhard, *Wilhelm von Humboldt: Idee und Wirklichkeit* (Stuttgart, 1967)
Kettenacker, Lothar, 'Ernst Anrich und die Reichsuniversität Strassburg', in *Les 'Reichsuniversitäten' de Strasbourg et de Poznań et les résistances universitaires 1941–44*, ed. by Christian Baechler, François Igersheim & Pierre Racine (Strasbourg, 2005)
Kimmich, Dorothee & Alexander Thumfart, eds, *Universität ohne Zukunft?* (Frankfurt am Main, 2004)
Kirkbright, Suzanne, *Karl Jaspers: A Biography: Navigations in Truth* (New Haven, 2004)
Kittler, Friedrich A., *Aufschreibesysteme 1800/1900* (Munich, 1985)
Koch, Hans-Albrecht, *Die Universität: Geschichte einer europäischen Institution* (Darmstadt, 2008)
Kocka, Jürgen, 'Dahrendorf in Perspektive', *Soziologische Revue*, 27:2 (2004)
——, 'Ralf Dahrendorf in historischer Perspektive: Aus Anlass seines Todes am 17. Juni 2009', *Geschichte und Gesellschaft*, 35:2 (2009)
——, ed., *Wissenschaft und Wiedervereinigung: Bilanz und offene Fragen* (Berlin, 2010)
Kocka, Jürgen & Renate Mayntz, eds, *Wissenschaft und Wiedervereinigung: Disziplinen im Umbruch* (Berlin, 1998)
Kollmeier, Kathrin & Stefan-Ludwig Hoffmann, 'Zeitgeschichte der Begriffe? Perspektiven einer Historischen Semantik des 20. Jahrhunderts: Einleitung', *Zeithistorische Forschungen/Studies in Contemporary History*, 7:1 (2010)
Kolozs, Martin, ed., *Bildung ist ein Lebensprojekt: Im Gespräch mit Konrad Paul Liessmann* (Innsbruck, 2011)
Konrad, Franz-Michael, *Wilhelm von Humboldt* (Göttingen, 2010)
Kopetz, Hedwig, *Forschung und Lehre: Die Idee der Universität bei Humboldt, Jaspers, Schelsky und Mittelstrass* (Vienna, 2002)
Koselleck, Reinhart, 'Einleitung', in *Geschichtliche Grundbegriffe: Historisches Lexikon zur politisch-sozialen Sprache in Deutschland*, ed. by Otto Brunner, Werner Conze, & Reinhart Koselleck, 8 vols (Stuttgart, 1972–97), vol. I (1972)
——, 'Einleitung – Zur anthropologischen und semantischen Struktur der Bildung', in *Bildungsbürgertum im 19. Jahrhundert*, ed. by Werner

Conze and Jürgen Kocka (Stuttgart, 1985–), vol. II: *Bildungsgüter und Bildungswissen*, ed. by Reinhart Koselleck (1990)
——, 'Historia Magistra Vitae: Über die Auflösung des Topos im Horizont neuzeitlich bewegter Geschichte', in Reinhart Koselleck, *Vergangene Zukunft: Zur Semantik geschichtlicher Zeiten* (Frankfurt am Main, 1989)
——, *Kritik und Krise: Eine Studie zur Pathogenese der bürgerlichen Welt* (Munich, 1959)
Kowalczuk, Ilko-Sascha, *Geist im Dienste der Macht: Hochschulpolitik in der SBZ/DDR 1945 bis 1961* (Berlin, 2003)
Kraus, Elisabeth, ed., *Die Universität München im Dritten Reich: Aufsätze*, 2 vols (Munich, 2006–2008)
Kraus, Hans Ch., *Theodor Anton Heinrich Schmalz (1760–1831): Jurisprudenz, Universitätspolitik und Publizistik im Spannungsfeld von Revolution und Restauration* (Frankfurt am Main, 1999)
Krautkrämer, Ursula, *Staat und Erziehung: Begründung öffentlicher Erziehung bei Humboldt, Kant, Fichte, Hegel und Schleiermacher* (Munich, 1979)
Krautz, Jochen, *Ware Bildung: Schule und Universität unter dem Diktat der Ökonomie* (Kreuzlingen, 2007)
'Krise', corpus 'German', https://books.google.com/ngrams (accessed 15 February 2016)
Kristensen, Jens Erik, 'Gamle og nye ideer med et universitet', in *Ideer om et universitet: Det moderne universitets idehistorie fra 1800 til i dag*, ed. by Jens Erik Kristensen et al. (Århus, 2007)
Krohn, Claus-Dieter, 'Intellektuelle und Mandarine in Deutschland um 1930 und 1950', in *Rückblickend in die Zukunft: Politische Öffentlichkeit und intellektuelle Positionen in Deutschland um 1950 und um 1930*, ed. by Alexander Gallus & Axel Schildt (Göttingen, 2011)
Krüger, Gerhard, ed., *Die Humboldt-Universität gestern – heute – morgen: Zum einhundertfünfzigjährigen Bestehen der Humboldt-Universität zu Berlin und zum zweihundertfünfzigjährigen Bestehen der Charité* (Berlin, 1960)
Kubicki, Karol & Siegward Lönnendonker, eds, *Die Freie Universität Berlin 1948–2007: Von der Gründung bis zum Exzellenzwettbewerb* (Göttingen, 2008)
König, René, *Leben im Widerspruch: Versuch einer intellektuellen Autobiographie* (Munich, 1980)
——, *Vom Wesen der deutschen Universität* (Berlin, 1935)
Lambrecht, Wolfgang, 'Deutsch-deutsche Reformdebatten vor "Bologna": Die "Bildungskatastrophe" der 1960er-Jahre', *Zeithistorische Forschungen/Studies in Contemporary History*, 3 (2007)
Langewiesche, Dieter, 'Das deutsche Universitätsmodell und die Berliner Universität', in *Mittendrin: Eine Universität macht Geschichte*, ed. by Ilka Thom & Kirsten Weining (Berlin, 2010)
——, 'Humboldt als Leitbild? Die deutsche Universität in den Berliner Rektoratsreden seit dem 19. Jahrhundert', *Jahrbuch für Universitätsgeschichte*, 14 (2011)

——, 'Die "Humboldtsche Universität" als nationaler Mythos: Zum Selbstbild der deutschen Universitäten im Kaiserreich und in der Weimarer Republik', *Historische Zeitschrift*, 290:1 (2010)
Langholm, Sivert, *Helheten och delene: Hvordan skrive en 200 års historie for Universitetet i Oslo?* (Oslo, 1996)
——, 'Das "Humboldt-Modell" in Norwegen: Symbol, Begriff und Wirklichkeit', in *Humboldt international: Der Export des deutschen Universitätsmodells im 19. und 20. Jahrhundert*, ed. by Rainer Christoph Schwinges (Basel, 2001)
Lehmann, Hartmut & Otto Gerhard Oexle, eds, *Nationalsozialismus in den Kulturwissenschaften*, 2 vols (Göttingen, 2004)
'Lehrfreiheit', corpus 'German', https://books.google.com/ngrams (accessed 15 February 2016)
Leibfried, Stephan, ed., *Die Exzellenzinitiative: Zwischenbilanz und Perspektiven* (Frankfurt am Main, 2010)
Lenz, Max, *Geschichte der Königlichen Friedrich-Wilhelms-Universität zu Berlin*, 4 vols (Halle, 1910–1918)
Lepenies, Wolf, *The Seduction of Culture in German History* (Princeton, 2006)
'Lernfreiheit', corpus 'German', https://books.google.com/ngrams (accessed 15 February 2016)
Leroux, Robert, *Guillaume de Humboldt: La formation de sa pensée jusqu'en 1794* (Paris, 1932)
Levine, Emily, *Dreamland of Humanists: Warburg, Cassirer, Panofsky, and the Hamburg School* (Chicago, 2013)
Levine, Joseph M., 'Intellectual History as History', *Journal of the History of Ideas*, 66:2 (2005)
Levy, Daniel & Natan Sznaider, *Erinnerung im globalen Zeitalter: Der Holocaust* (Frankfurt am Main, 2007)
Lichtenstein, Ernst, 'Bildung', in *Historisches Wörterbuch der Philosophie*, ed. by Joachim Ritter, 13 vols (Basel and Stuttgart, 1971–2007), vol. I (1971)
Liedman, Sven-Eric, 'Institution and Ideas: Mandarins and Non-Mandarins in the German Academic Intelligentsia', *Comparative Studies in Society and History*, 28:1 (1986)
——, *Karl Marx: En biografi* (Stockholm, 2015)
——, 'Reply', *Comparative Studies in Society and History*, 28:1 (1986)
Liesner, Andrea & Ingrid Lohmann, eds, *Bachelor bolognese: Erfahrungen mit der neuen Studienstruktur* (Opladen, 2009)
Liessmann, Konrad Paul, *Geisterstunde: Die Praxis der Unbildung: Eine Streitschrift* (Vienna, 2014)
——, *Theorie der Unbildung: Die Irrtümer der Wissensgesellschaft* (Vienna, 2006)
Lilge, Frederic, *The Abuse of Learning: The Failure of the German University* (New York, 1948)
Lindberg, Bo, 'Akademisk frihet före moderniteten', *Lychnos*, 2014

Lindén, Claudia, 'It Takes a Real Man to Show True Femininity: Gender Transgression in Goethe's and Humboldt's Concept of *Bildung*', in *The Humboldtian Tradition: Origins and Legacies*, ed. by Peter Josephson, Thomas Karlsohn & Johan Östling (Leiden and Boston, 2014)

Lorenz, Chris, 'If You're So Smart, Why Are You under Surveillance? Universities, Neoliberalism, and New Public Management', *Critical Inquiry*, 38:3 (2012)

Lovejoy, Arthur O., *The Great Chain of Being: A Study of the History of an Idea* (Cambridge, MA, 1936)

Lundgreen, Peter, 'Mythos Humboldt Today: Teaching, Research, and Administration', in *German Universities Past and Future: Crisis or Renewal?*, ed. by Mitchell G. Ash (Providence, RI, 1997)

Lübbe, Herman, 'Die Idee einer Elite-Universität: Der Fall der Universität Bielefeld', in *Was war Bielefeld? Eine ideengeschichtliche Nachfrage*, ed. by Sonja Asal & Stephan Schlak (Göttingen, 2009)

Lyotard, Jean-François, *La condition postmoderne: Rapport sur le savoir* (Paris, 1979)

——, *The Postmodern Condition*, transl. by Geoff Bennington and Brian Massumi (Manchester, 1984)

Löning, Martin et al., eds, *'Wie gründet man Universitäten?': Helmut Schelskys Konzept und der gelungene Start der Universität Bielefeld* (Bielefeld, 2011)

Lönnendonker, Siegward, *Freie Universität Berlin: Gründung einer politischen Universität* (Berlin, 1988)

Lönnendonker, Siegward, Bernd Rabehl, & Jochen Staadt, *Die antiautoritäre Revolte: Der Sozialistische Deutsche Studentenbund nach der Trennung von der SPD: 1960–1967* (Opladen, 2002)

Löwith, Karl, *Meaning in History: The Theological Implications of the Philosophy of History* (Chicago, 1949)

Mandelkow, Karl Robert, *Goethe in Deutschland: Rezeptionsgeschichte eines Klassikers: 1773–1918* (Munich, 1980)

——, *Goethe in Deutschland: Rezeptionsgeschichte eines Klassikers: 1919–1982* (Munich, 1989)

Mannheim, Karl, 'Das Problem der Generationen', *Kölner Vierteljahreshefte für Soziologie*, 7:2 (1928)

Manovich, Lev, 'Trending: The Promises and the Challenges of Big Social Data', in *Debates in the Digital Humanities*, ed. by Matthew K. Gold (Minneapolis, 2012)

Markova, Hristina, *Exzellenz durch Wettbewerb und Autonomie? Deutungsmuster hochschulpolitischer Eliten am Beispiel der Exzellenzinitiative* (Konstanz, 2013)

Markschies, Christoph, *Was von Humboldt noch zu lernen ist: Aus Anlass des zweihundertjährigen Geburtstags der preussischen Reformuniversität* (Berlin, 2010)

Masschelein, Jan & Maarten Simons, *Jenseits der Exzellenz: Eine kleine Morphologie der Welt-Universität* (Zürich, 2010)

Masur, Gerhard & Hans Arens, 'Humboldt, Wilhelm von', *Neue Deutsche Biographie* (Berlin 1953–), vol. X (1974)
Maurer, Trude, *Kollegen – Kommilitonen – Kämpfer: Europäische Universitäten im Ersten Weltkrieg* (Stuttgart, 2006)
McClelland, Charles E., *The German Experience of Professionalization: Modern Learned Professions and Their Organizations from the Early Nineteenth Century to the Hitler Era* (Cambridge, 1991)
——, *State, Society, and University in Germany, 1700–1914* (Cambridge, 1980)
——, 'Die Universität am Ende ihres ersten Jahrhunderts – Mythos Humboldt?', in *Geschichte der Universität Unter den Linden: Gründung und Blütezeit der Universität zu Berlin 1810–1918*, ed. by Heinz-Elmar Tenorth (Berlin, 2012)
McMahon, Darrin M. & Samuel Moyn, eds, *Rethinking Modern European Intellectual History* (Oxford, 2014)
Meifort, Franziska, 'Liberalisierung der Gesellschaft durch Bildungsreform: Ralf Dahrendorf zwischen Wissenschaft und Öffentlichkeit in den 1960er Jahren', in *Universität, Wissenschaft und Öffentlichkeit in Westdeutschland: (1945 bis ca. 1970)*, ed. by Sebastian Brandt et al. (Stuttgart, 2014)
——, 'Der Wunsch nach Wirkung: Ralf Dahrendorf als intellektueller Grenzgänger zwischen Bundesrepublik und Großbritannien 1964–1984', *Geschichte in Wissenschaft und Unterricht*, 65:3/4 (2014)
Meinecke, Friedrich, *Die deutsche Katastrophe: Betrachtungen und Erinnerungen* (Zürich, 1946)
Menze, Clemens, *Die Bildungsreform Wilhelm von Humboldts* (Hannover, 1975)
Merton, Robert K., 'The Normative Structure of Science', in Robert K. Merton, *The Sociology of Science: Theoretical and Empirical Investigations* (Chicago, 1973)
Metzler, Gabriele, 'Am Ende aller Krisen? Politisches Denken und Handeln in der Bundesrepublik der sechziger Jahre', *Historische Zeitschrift*, 275:1 (2002)
Michel, Jean-Baptiste et al., 'Quantitative Analysis of Culture Using Millions of Digitized Books', *Science*, 331 (2011)
Middell, Matthias, 'Die Humboldt-Universität und die Hochschulpolitik der DDR, 1960–1985', in *Geschichte der Universität Unter den Linden: Sozialistisches Experiment und Erneuerung in der Demokratie – die Humboldt-Universität zu Berlin 1945–2010*, ed. by Konrad H. Jarausch, Matthias Middell & Annette Vogt (Berlin, 2012)
Mikat, Paul & Helmut Schelsky, *Grundzüge einer neuen Universität: Zur Planung einer Hochschulgründung in Ostwestfalen* (Gütersloh, 1966)
Mittelstraß, Jürgen, *Die unzeitgemäße Universität* (Frankfurt am Main, 1994)
Moberly, Walter, *The Crisis of the University* (London, 1949)
Moraw, Peter, 'Aspekte und Dimensionen älterer deutscher Universitätsgeschichte', in *Academia Gissensis: Beiträge zur älteren Gießener Universitätsgeschichte*, ed. by Peter Moraw & Volker Press (Marburg, 1982)

——, 'Universitäten, Gelehrte und Gelehrsamkeit in Deutschland vor und um 1800', in *Humboldt international: Der Export des deutschen Universitätsmodells im 19. und 20. Jahrhundert*, ed. by Rainer Christoph Schwinges (Basel, 2001)
Moses, A. Dirk, *German Intellectuals and the Nazi Past* (Cambridge, 2007)
——, 'Intellectual History in and of the Federal Republic of Germany', *Modern Intellectual History*, 9:3 (2012)
Moyn, Samuel, 'The First Historian of Human Rights', *The American Historical Review*, 116:1 (2011)
Moyn, Samuel & Andrew Sartori, eds, *Global Intellectual History* (New York, 2013)
Müller-Doohm, Stefan, *Jürgen Habermas: Eine Biographie* (Berlin, 2014)
Müller, Ernst, ed., *Gelegentliche Gedanken über Universitäten* (Leipzig, 1990)
Müller, Gerhard, *Ernst Krieck und die nationalsozialistische Wissenschaftsreform: Motive und Tendenzen einer Wissenschaftslehre und Hochschulreform im Dritten Reich* (Weinheim and Basel, 1978)
Müller, Gerhard, Klaus Ries, & Paul Ziche, eds, *Die Universität Jena: Tradition und Innovation um 1800* (Stuttgart, 2001)
Müller, Guido, *Weltpolitische Bildung und akademische Reform: C. H. Beckers Wissenschafts- und Hochschulpolitik 1908–1930* (Cologne, 1991)
Müller, Jan-Werner, 'European Intellectual History as Contemporary History', *Journal of Contemporary History*, 46:3 (2011)
Müller, Rainer A., 'Genese, Methoden und Tendenzen der allgemeinen deutschen Universitätsgeschichte: Zur Entwicklung einer historischen Spezialdisziplin', *Mitteilungen der Österreichischen Gesellschaft für Wissenschaftsgeschichte*, 20 (2000)
Münch, Richard, *Die akademische Elite: Zur sozialen Konstruktion wissenschaftlicher Exzellenz* (Frankfurt am Main, 2007)
——, *Akademischer Kapitalismus: Über die politische Ökonomie der Hochschulreform* (Frankfurt am Main, 2011)
——, *Globale Eliten, lokale Autoritäten: Bildung und Wissenschaft unter dem Regime von PISA, McKinsey & Co.* (Frankfurt am Main, 2009)
Münkler, Herfried, *Die Deutschen und ihre Mythen* (Berlin, 2009)
Mälzer, Moritz, '"Die große Chance, wie einstens die Berliner Universität so heute eine Modell-Universität zu schaffen": Die frühen 1960er Jahre als Universitätsgründerzeiten', *Jahrbuch für Universitätsgeschichte*, 13 (2010)
——, *Auf der Suche nach der neuen Universität: Die Entstehung der 'Reformuniversitäten' Konstanz und Bielefeld in den 1960er Jahren* (Göttingen, 2016)
Nagel, Anne C., *Hitlers Bildungsreformer: Das Reichsministerium für Wissenschaft, Erziehung und Volksbildung 1934–1945* (Frankfurt am Main, 2012)
Naimark, Norman M., *The Russians in Germany: A History of the Soviet Zone of Occupation, 1945–1949* (Cambridge, MA, 1995)
Neave, Guy, 'On Scholars, Hippopotami and von Humboldt: Higher Education in Europe in Transition', *Higher Education Policy*, 16:2 (2003)

Neuhaus, Rolf, ed., *Dokumente zur Hochschulreform 1945–1959* (Wiesbaden, 1961)
Nicolaysen, Rainer, *'Frei soll die Lehre sein und frei das Lernen': Zur Geschichte der Universität Hamburg* (Hamburg, 2008)
Nida-Rümelin, Julian, *Humanismus als Leitkultur: Ein Perspektivenwechsel* (Munich, 2006)
——, *Philosophie einer humanen Bildung* (Hamburg, 2013)
Niemeyer, Christian, *Nietzsche, die Jugend und die Pädagogik: Eine Einführung* (Weinheim and Munich, 2002)
Nipperdey, Thomas, *Deutsche Geschichte 1800–1866: Bürgerwelt und starker Staat* (Munich, 1983)
Nitsch, Wolfgang et al., *Hochschule in der Demokratie: Kritische Beiträge zur Erbschaft und Reform der deutschen Universität* (Berlin and Neuwied, 1965)
Nordin, Svante, *Filosofernas krig: Den europeiska filosofin under första världskriget* (Nora, 1998)
Nussbaum, Martha C., *Cultivating Humanity: A Classical Defense of Reform in Liberal Education* (Cambridge, MA, 1997)
——, *Not for Profit: Why Democracy Needs the Humanities* (Princeton, NJ, 2010)
Nybom, Thorsten, 'A Rule-Governed Community of Scholars: The Humboldt-Vision in the History of European University', in *University Dynamics and European University Integration*, ed. by Peter Maassen & Johan P. Olsen (Dordrecht, 2007)
——, 'Humboldts Vermächtnis: Betrachtungen zu Vergangenheit, Gegenwart und Zukunft des europäischen Hochschulwesens', in *Humboldts Zukunft: Das Projekt Reformuniversität*, ed. by Bernd Henningsen (Berlin, 2008)
——, 'The Persistent Use and Abuse of Wilhelm von Humboldt in History and Politics', in *Aurora Torealis: Studies in the History of Science and Ideas*, ed. by Marco Beretta, Karl Gradin & Svante Lindqvist (New York, 2008)
——, ed., *Universitet och samhälle: Om forskningspolitik och vetenskapens samhälleliga roll* (Stockholm, 1989)
Odén, Birgitta, *Forskarutbildningens förändringar 1890–1975: Historia, statskunskap, kulturgeografi, ekonomisk historia* (Lund, 1991)
Oertzen, Christine von, *Strategie Verständigung: Zur transnationalen Vernetzung von Akademikerinnen 1917–1955* (Göttingen, 2012)
Oertzen, Christine von, Maria Rentetzi, & Elizabeth Watkins Siegel, eds, *Beyond the Academy: Histories of Gender and Knowledge* (New York, 2013)
Olick, Jeffrey K., *In the House of the Hangman: The Agonies of German Defeat, 1943–1949* (Chicago, 2005)
Olsen, Niklas, *History in the Plural: An Introduction to the Work of Reinhart Koselleck* (New York, 2012)
Ortmeyer, Benjamin, *Eduard Spranger und die NS-Zeit* (Frankfurt am Main, 2008)

Bibliography

Osterhammel, Jürgen, *Die Verwandlung der Welt: Eine Geschichte des 19. Jahrhunderts* (Munich, 2009)
Ott, Hugo, *Martin Heidegger: Unterwegs zu seiner Biographie* (Frankfurt am Main, 1988)
Paletschek, Sylvia, 'Die deutsche Universität im und nach dem Krieg: Die Wiederentdeckung des Abendlandes', in *Der Zweite Weltkrieg und seine Folgen: Ereignisse – Auswirkungen – Reflexionen*, ed. by Bernd Martin (Freiburg and Berlin, 2006)
——, 'Die Erfindung der Humboldtschen Universität: Die Konstruktion der deutschen Universitätsidee in der ersten Hälfte des 20. Jahrhunderts', *Historische Anthropologie*, 10 (2002)
——, 'The Invention of Humboldt and the Impact of National Socialism: The German University Idea in the First Half of the Twentieth Century', in *Science in the Third Reich*, ed. by Margit Szöllösi-Janze (Oxford, 2001)
——, *Die permanente Erfindung einer Tradition: Die Universität Tübingen im Kaiserreich und in der Weimarer Republik* (Stuttgart, 2001)
——, 'Stand und Perspektiven der neueren Universitätsgeschichte', *N.T.M.*, 19:2 (2011)
——, 'Verbreitete sich ein "Humboldt'sches Modell" an den deutschen Universitäten im 19. Jahrhundert?', in *Humboldt international: Der Export des deutschen Universitätsmodells im 19. und 20. Jahrhundert*, ed. by Rainer Christoph Schwinges (Basel, 2001)
——, 'The Writing of University History and University Jubilees: German Examples', *Studium: Tijdschrift voor Wetenschaps- en Universiteitsgeschiedenis/Revue d'Histoire des Sciences et des Universités*, 5:3 (2012)
Pasternack, Peer, *Wissenschaft und Politik in der DDR: Rekonstruktion und Literaturbericht* (Wittenberg, 2010)
Paulsen, Friedrich, *Das deutsche Bildungswesen in seiner geschichtlichen Entwicklung* (Leipzig, 1906)
——, *Die deutschen Universitäten und das Universitätsstudium* (Berlin, 1902)
Paulus, Stefan, *Vorbild USA? Amerikanisierung von Universität und Wissenschaft in Westdeutschland 1945–1976* (Munich, 2010)
Payk, Marcus, *Der Geist der Demokratie: Intellektuelle Orientierungsversuche im Feuilleton der frühen Bundesrepublik: Karl Korn und Peter de Mendelsohn* (Munich, 2008)
Perreau-Saussine, Emile, 'Quentin Skinner in Context', *The Review of Politics*, 69:1 (2007)
Peters, Hans, *Zwischen Gestern und Morgen: Betrachtungen zur heutigen Kulturlage* (Berlin, 1946)
Philipps, Denise, *Acolytes of Nature: Defining Natural Science in Germany 1770–1850* (Chicago, 2012)
Phillips, David, *German Universities After the Surrender: British Occupation Policy and the Control of Higher Education* (Oxford, 1983)
——, *Pragmatismus und Idealismus: Das 'Blaue Gutachten' und die britische Hochschulpolitik in Deutschland 1948* (Cologne, Weimar and Vienna, 1995)

Picht, Georg, *Die deutsche Bildungskatastrophe: Analyse und Dokumentation* (Olten and Freiburg im Breisgau, 1964)
Pietsch, Tamson, *Empire of Scholars: Universities, Networks and the British Academic World 1850–1939* (Manchester, 2013)
Piper, Ernst, *Nacht über Europa: Kulturgeschichte des Ersten Weltkriegs* (Berlin, 2013)
Power, Michael, *The Audit Society: Rituals of Verification* (Oxford, 1997)
Pozzo, Riccardo, 'Kant's *Streit der Fakultäten* and Conditions at Königsberg', *History of Universities*, 16 (2000)
Prado, Plínio, *Das Prinzip Universität (als unbedingtes Recht auf Kritik)* (Zürich, 2010)
Prinz, Michael, 'Ralf Dahrendorfs "Gesellschaft und Demokratie" als epochenübergreifende Interpretation des Nationalsozialismus', in *Politische Zäsuren und gesellschaftlicher Wandel im 20. Jahrhundert: Regionale und vergleichende Perspektiven*, ed. by Michael Prinz & Matthias Frese (Paderborn, 1996)
Pulte, Helmut, 'Wissenschaft', in *Historisches Wörterbuch der Philosophie*, ed. by Joachim Ritter, Karlfried Gründer & Gottfried Gabriel, 13 vols (Basel, 1971–2007), vol. XII (2004)
Rantzau, Johann-Albrecht von, *Wilhelm von Humboldt: Der Weg seiner geistigen Entwicklung* (Munich, 1939)
Raulff, Ulrich, Helwig Schmidt-Glintzer, & Hellmut Th. Seemann, 'Einen Anfang machen: Warum wir eine Zeitschrift für Ideengeschichte gründen', *Zeitschrift für Ideengeschichte*, 1 (2007)
Rehberg, Karl-Siegbert, 'Vom soziologischen Neugründungs-Pragmatismus zur "Anti-Soziologie": Helmut Schelskys Position in der Nachkriegsgeschichte des Faches', in *Helmut Schelsky – der politische Anti-Soziologe: Eine Neurezeption*, ed. by Alexander Gallus (Göttingen, 2013)
Reinermann, Lothar, 'Richter, Werner', *Neue Deutsche Biographie* (Berlin, 1953–), vol. XXI (2003)
Remy, Steven P., *The Heidelberg Myth: The Nazification and Denazification of a German University* (Cambridge, 2002)
Richter, Melvin, *The History of Political and Social Concepts: A Critical Introduction* (New York, 1995)
Richter, Werner, *Re-Educating Germany* (Chicago, 1945)
——, *Die Zukunft der deutschen Universität* (Marburg, 1949)
Ridder-Symoens, Hilde de, ed., *A History of the University in Europe: Universities in Early Modern Europe (1500–1800)* (Cambridge, 1996)
Rider, Sharon, 'The Very Idea of Higher Education: Vocation of Man or Vocational Training?', in *The Humboldtian Tradition: Origins and Legacies*, ed. by Peter Josephson, Thomas Karlsohn, & Johan Östling (Leiden and Boston, 2014)
Rider, Sharon, Ylva Hasselberg, & Alexandra Waluszewski, eds, *Transformations in Research, Higher Education and the Academic Market: The Breakdown of Scientific Thought* (Dordrecht, 2013)

Ringarp, Johanna & Martin Rothland, 'Is the Grass Always Greener? The Effect of the PISA Results on Education Debates in Sweden and Germany', *European Educational Research Journal*, 9:3 (2010)

Ringer, Fritz K., *The Decline of the German Mandarins: The German Academic Community, 1890–1933* (Cambridge, MA, 1969)

——, 'Differences and Cross-National Similarities among Mandarins', *Comparative Studies in Society and History*, 28:1 (1986)

——, *Fields of Knowledge: French Academic Culture in Comparative Perspective, 1890–1920* (Cambridge, 1992)

——, '*Bildung* and Its Implications in the German Tradition, 1890–1933', in Fritz Ringer, *Toward a Social History of Knowledge: Collected Essays* (New York, 2000)

Ritter, Gerhard, 'Der deutsche Professor im Dritten Reich', *Die Gegenwart*, 1:1 (1945)

——, *Die Heidelberger Universität: Ein Stück deutscher Geschichte. Das Mittelalter (1386–1508)* (Heidelberg, 1936)

——, *Die Idee der Universität und das öffentliche Leben* (Freiburg im Breisgau, 1946)

——, *Stein: Eine politische Biographie* (Stuttgart, 1931)

Roberts, John, *Wilhelm von Humboldt and German Liberalism: A Reassessment* (Oakville, 2009)

Rohstock, Anne, 'Hemmschuh Humboldt oder Warum scheitert die Hochschulreform: Universitäre Neuordnungsversuche zwischen Sputnik-Schock und Bologna-Prozess, 1957–2009', *Zeitschrift für pädagogische Historiographie*, 2 (2009)

——, 'The History of Higher Education: Some Conceptual Remarks on the Future of a Research Field', in *Education Systems in Historical, Cultural, and Sociological Perspectives*, ed. by Daniel Tröhler & Ragnhild Barbu (Rotterdam, 2011)

——, '"Some Things Never Change": The (Re)Invention of Humboldt in Western Higher Education Systems', in *Theories of Bildung and Growth: Connections and Controversies between Continental European Educational Thinking and American Pragmatism*, ed. by Pauli Siljander & Arno Kivelä (Rotterdam, 2012)

——, *Von der 'Ordinarienuniversität' zur 'Revolutionszentrale'? Hochschulreform und Hochschulrevolte in Bayern und Hessen 1957–1976* (Munich, 2010)

——, 'Walter Rüegg (Hg.): Geschichte der Universität in Europa', *sehepunkte*, 12:1 (2012)

Rohwedder, Uwe, *Kalter Krieg und Hochschulreform: Der Verband Deutscher Studentenschaften in der frühen Bundesrepublik (1949–1969)* (Essen, 2012)

——, 'SDS-Hochschuldenkschrift und VDS-Neugründungsgutachten', in *Hochschulreformen früher und heute: Zwischen Autonomie und gesellschaftlichem Gestaltungsanspruch*, ed. by Rainer Pöppinghege & Dietmar Klenke (Cologne, 2011)

Rosa, Hartmut, *Beschleunigung: Die Veränderung der Zeitstrukturen in der Moderne* (Frankfurt am Main, 2005)
Roscher, Stephan, *Die Kaiser-Wilhelms-Universität Straßburg 1872–1902* (Frankfurt am Main, 2006)
Roth, Steffen, 'Fashionable Functions: A Google Ngram View of Trends in Functional Differentiation (1800–2000)', *International Journal of Technology and Human Interaction*, 10:2 (2014)
Rothblatt, Sheldon, *The Modern University and Its Discontents: The Fate of Newman's Legacies in Britain and America* (London, 1997)
——, *The Revolution of the Dons: Cambridge and Society in Victorian England* (London, 1968)
——, 'The Writing of University History at the End of Another Century', *Oxford Review of Education*, 23:2 (1997)
Rudloff, Wilfried, 'Ansatzpunkte und Hindernisse der Hochschulreform in der Bundesrepublik der sechziger Jahre: Studienreform und Gesamthochschule', *Jahrbuch für Universitätsgeschichte*, 8 (2005)
——, 'Der politische Gebrauchswert der Hochschulforschung: Zum Verhältnis von Hochschulforschung und Hochschulpolitik in den Jahren von Bildungsboom und Hochschulexpansion (1960 bis 1975)', in *Universität, Wissenschaft und Öffentlichkeit in Westdeutschland: (1945 bis ca. 1970)*, ed. by Sebastian Brandt et al. (Stuttgart, 2014)
Ruin, Hans, *Frihet, ändlighet, historicitet: Essäer om Heideggers filosofi* (Stockholm, 2013)
——, 'Philosophy, Freedom, and the Task of the University: Reflections on Humboldt's Legacy', in *The Humboldtian Tradition: Origins and Legacies*, ed. by Peter Josephson, Thomas Karlsohn & Johan Östling (Leiden and Boston, 2014)
Rupke, Nicolaas A., *Alexander von Humboldt: A Metabiography* (Chicago, 2008)
Rüegg, Walter, 'Der Mythos der Humboldtschen Universität', in *Universitas in theologia–theologia in universitate: Festschrift für Hans Heinrich Schmid*, ed. by Mathias Krieg & Martin Rose (Zürich, 1997)
——, 'Themes', in *A History of the University in Europe: Universities in the Nineteenth and Early Twentieth Centuries (1800–1945)*, ed. by Walter Rüegg (Cambridge, 2004)
——, ed., *A History of the University in Europe* (Cambridge 2003–2010), vol. III: *Universities in the Nineteenth and Early Twentieth Centuries (1800–1945)* (2004)
——, ed., *A History of the University in Europe* (Cambridge 2003–2010), vol. IV: *Universities since 1945* (Cambridge, 2011)
Rüegg, Walter & Jan Sadlak, 'Relations with Authority', in *A History of the University in Europe: Universities since 1945*, ed. by Walter Rüegg (Cambridge, 2011)
Sabrow, Martin, ed., *Erinnerungsorte der DDR* (Munich, 2009)
Safranski, Rüdiger, *Ein Meister aus Deutschland: Heidegger und seine Zeit* (Munich, 1994)

Bibliography

Salamun, Kurt, *Karl Jaspers* (Würzburg, 2006)
Sandmo, Erling, *Tid for historie: En bok om historiske spørsmål* (Oslo, 2015)
Saner, Hans, *Karl Jaspers: In Selbstzeugnissen und Bilddokumenten* (Reinbek bei Hamburg, 2005)
Sarasin, Philipp, 'Was ist Wissensgeschichte?', *Internationales Archiv für Sozialgeschichte der deutschen Literatur (IASL)*, 36:1 (2011)
Sauter, Christina M., *Wilhelm von Humboldt und die deutsche Aufklärung* (Berlin, 1989)
Schaffstein, Friedrich, *Wilhelm von Humboldt: Ein Lebensbild* (Frankfurt am Main, 1952)
Schalenberg, Marc, *Humboldt auf Reisen? Die Rezeption des 'deutschen Universitätsmodells' in den französischen und britischen Reformdiskursen (1810–1870)* (Basel, 2002)
Scheler, Max, *Die Wissensformen und die Gesellschaft* (Leipzig, 1926)
Schelling, Friedrich von, *Vorlesungen über die Methode des akademischen Studiums* (Tübingen, 1803)
Schelsky, Helmut, *Abschied von der Hochschulpolitik oder die Universität im Fadenkreuz des Versagens* (Bielefeld, 1969)
——, *Einsamkeit und Freiheit: Idee und Gestalt der deutschen Universität und ihrer Reformen* (Reinbek bei Hamburg, 1963)
——, *Einsamkeit und Freiheit: Idee und Gestalt der deutschen Universität und ihrer Reformen* (Düsseldorf, 1971)
——, *Einsamkeit und Freiheit: Zur sozialen Idee der deutschen Universität* (Münster, 1960)
——, *Rückblicke eines 'Anti-Soziologen'* (Opladen, 1981)
Schildt, Axel, 'Im Kern gesund? Die deutschen Hochschulen 1945', in *Vertuschte Vergangenheit: Der Fall Schwerte und die NS-Vergangenheit der deutschen Hochschulen*, ed. by Helmut König, Wolfgang Kuhlmann & Klaus Schwabe (Munich, 1997)
——, *Moderne Zeiten: Freizeit, Massenmedien und 'Zeitgeist' in der Bundesrepublik der 50er Jahre* (Hamburg, 1995)
——, *Zwischen Abendland und Amerika: Studien zur westdeutschen Ideenlandschaft der 50er Jahre* (Munich, 1999)
Schildt, Axel & Detlef Siegfried, *Deutsche Kulturgeschichte: Die Bundesrepublik – 1945 bis zur Gegenwart* (Munich, 2009)
Schildt, Axel, Detlef Siegfried, & Karl Christian Lammers, eds, *Dynamische Zeiten: Die 60er Jahre in den beiden deutschen Gesellschaften* (Hamburg, 2000)
Schiller, Friedrich, 'The Nature and Value of Universal History: An Inaugural Lecture [1789]', *History and Theory*, 11:3 (1972)
Schivelbusch, Wolfgang, *Vor dem Vorhang: Das geistige Berlin 1945–1948* (Munich, 1995)
Schleiermacher, Friedrich, *Gelegentliche Gedanken über Universitäten in deutschem Sinn* (Berlin, 1808)
Schlerath, Bernfried, ed., *Wilhelm von Humboldt: Vortragszyklus zum 150. Todestag* (Berlin, 1986)

Schlesier, Gustav, *Erinnerungen an Wilhelm von Humboldt*, 3 vols (Stuttgart, 1843–1845)
Schlüter, Andreas & Peter Strohschneider, eds, *Bildung? Bildung! 26 Thesen zur Bildung als Herausforderung im 21. Jahrhundert* (Berlin, 2009)
Schmoll, Heike, *Lob der Elite: Warum wir sie brauchen* (Munich, 2008)
Schneider, Barbara, *Die Höhere Schule im Nationalsozialismus* (Cologne, 2000)
Scholz, Christian & Volker Stein, eds, *Bologna-Schwarzbuch* (Bonn, 2009)
Schraut, Alban, *Biographische Studien zu Eduard Spranger* (Bad Heilbrunn, 2007)
Schröder, Kurt, '150 Jahre Humboldt-Universität zu Berlin', in *Forschen und Wirken: Festschrift zur 150-Jahr-Feier der Humboldt-Universität zu Berlin 1810–1960*, ed. by Friedrich Herneck, 3 vols (Berlin, 1960), vol. I
Schubring, Gert, 'Spezialschulmodell versus Universitätsmodell: Die Institutionalisierung von Forschung', in *'Einsamkeit und Freiheit' neu besichtigt: Universitätsreformen und Disziplinenbildung in Preussen als Modell für Wissenschaftspolitik im Europa des 19. Jahrhunderts*, ed. by Gert Schubring (Stuttgart, 1991)
Schultheis, Franz et al., eds, *Humboldts Albtraum: Der Bologna-Prozess und seine Folgen* (Konstanz, 2008)
Schultz, Werner, 'Wilhelm von Humboldt und der Faustische Mensch', *Jahrbuch der Goethe-Gesellschaft*, 16 (1930)
Schulz, Tobias, *'Sozialistische Wissenschaft': Die Berliner Humboldt-Universität (1960–1975)* (Cologne, Weimar and Vienna, 2010)
Schwabe, Klaus, 'Change and Continuity in German Historiography from 1933 into the Early 1950s: Gerhard Ritter (1888–1967)', in *Paths of Continuity: Central European Historiography from the 1930s to the 1950s*, ed. by Hartmut Lehmann & James van Horn Melton (Cambridge, 1994)
Schwartz, Christina, 'Erfindet sich die Hochschule neu? Selbstbilder und Zukunftsvorstellungen in den westdeutschen Rektoratsreden 1945–1950', in *Zwischen Idee und Zweckorientierung: Vorbilder und Motive von Hochschulreformen seit 1945*, ed. by Andreas Franzmann & Barbara Wolbring (Berlin, 2007)
Schwinges, Rainer Christoph, ed., *Humboldt international: Der Export des deutschen Universitätsmodells im 19. und 20. Jahrhundert* (Basel, 2001)
Schäfer, Gerhard, 'Der Nationalsozialismus und die soziologischen Akteure der Nachkriegszeit: Am Beispiel Helmut Schelskys und Ralf Dahrendorfs', in *Soziologie und Nationalsozialismus: Positionen, Debatten, Perspektiven*, ed. by Michaela Christ & Maja Suderland (Berlin, 2014)
Schöttler, Peter, 'Die historische "Westforschung" zwischen "Abwehrkampf" und territorialer Offensive', in *Geschichtsschreibung als Legitimationswissenschaft 1918–1945*, ed. by Peter Schöttler (Frankfurt am Main, 1999)
——, ed., *Geschichtsschreibung als Legitimationswissenschaft: 1918–1945* (Frankfurt am Main, 1997)
Scurla, Herbert, *Wilhelm von Humboldt: Werden und Wirken* (Berlin, 1970)
Segerstedt, Torgny T., *Den akademiska friheten 1809–1832* (Uppsala, 1976)

Bibliography

———, *Den akademiska friheten under frihetstiden: En sammanställning* (Uppsala, 1971)
———, *Den akademiska friheten under gustaviansk tid* (Uppsala, 1974)
———, *Hotet mot den högre utbildningen* (Stockholm, 1974)
———, *Studentrevolt: Vetenskap och framtid* (Stockholm, 1968)
Shils, Edward & John Roberts, 'The Diffusion of European Models Outside Europe', in *A History of the University in Europe: Universities in the Nineteenth and Early Twentieth Centuries (1800–1945)*, ed. by Walter Rüegg (Cambridge, 2004)
Skinner, Quentin, 'Meaning and Understanding in the History of Ideas', *History and Theory*, 8:1 (1969)
Sluga, Hans, *Heidegger's Crisis: Philosophy and Politics in Nazi Germany* (Cambridge, MA, 1993)
Speich Chassé, Daniel & David Gugerli, 'Wissensgeschichte: Eine Standortbestimmung', *Traverse: Zeitschrift für Geschichte*, 1 (2012)
Spiewak, Martin, 'Falsches Vorbild', *Die Zeit*, 2009, no. 26
Spix, Boris, *Abschied vom Elfenbeinturm? Politisches Verhalten Studierender 1957–1967: Berlin und Nordrhein-Westfalen im Vergleich* (Essen, 2008)
Spranger, Eduard, *Der gegenwärtige Stand der Geisteswissenschaften und die Schule* (Leipzig, 1925)
———, *Wandlungen im Wesen der Universität seit 100 Jahren* (Leipzig, 1913)
———, 'Das Wesen der deutschen Universität', in *Das akademische Deutschland*, ed. by Michael Doeberl et al., 4 vols (Berlin, 1930–31), vol. III (1930)
———, *Wilhelm von Humboldt und die Humanitätsidee* (Berlin, 1909)
———, *Wilhelm von Humboldt und die Humanitätsidee* (Berlin, 1936)
———, *Wilhelm von Humboldt und die Reform des Bildungswesens* (Berlin, 1910)
———, ed., *Fichte, Schleiermacher, Steffens über das Wesen der Universität* (Leipzig, 1910)
Sprenger, Gerhard & Peter Weingart, 'Zentrum für interdisziplinäre Forschung', in *Reformuniversität Bielefeld 1969–1994: Zwischen Defensive und Innovation*, ed. by Peter Lundgreen (Bielefeld, 1994)
Steffens, Heinrich, *Ueber die Idee von Universitäten* (Berlin, 1809)
Sternberger, Dolf, 'Nachbemerkung', in Karl Jaspers & Fritz Ernst, *Vom lebendigen Geist der Universität und vom Studieren: Zwei Vorträge* (Heidelberg, 1946)
Stifter, Christian H., *Zwischen geistiger Erneuerung und Restauration: US-amerikanische Planungen zur Entnazifizierung und demokratischen Neuorientierung österreichischer Wissenschaft 1941–1955* (Vienna, 2014)
Strömholm, Stig, *Resonerande katalog: Minnen 1958–2003* (Stockholm, 2014)
Sundqvist, Bo, *Svenska universitet – lärdomsborgar eller politiska instrument?* (Hedemora, 2011)
Sweet, Paul R., *Wilhelm von Humboldt: A Biography: 1767–1808* (Columbus, OH, 1978)

———, *Wilhelm von Humboldt: A Biography: 1808–1835* (Columbus, OH, 1980)

Szöllösi-Janze, Margit, '"Der Geist des Wettbewerbs ist aus der Flasche": Der Exzellenzwettbewerb zwischen den deutschen Universitäten in historischer Perspektive', *Jahrbuch für Universitätsgeschichte*, 14 (2011)

Söllner, Alfons, 'Mehr Universität wagen! Helmut Schelsky und die Hochschulpolitik der 1960er Jahre', in *Helmut Schelsky – der politische Anti-Soziologe: Eine Neurezeption*, ed. by Alexander Gallus (Göttingen, 2013)

Tejerina, Fernando, ed., *The University: An Illustrated History* (New York, 2011)

Tenorth, Heinz-Elmar, 'Eine Universität zu Berlin – Vorgeschichte und Einrichtung', in *Geschichte der Universität Unter den Linden: Gründung und Blütezeit der Universität zu Berlin 1810–1918*, ed. by Heinz-Elmar Tenorth (Berlin, 2012)

———, 'Genese der Disziplinen – Die Konstitution der Universität', in *Geschichte der Universität Unter den Linden: Genese der Disziplinen: Die Konstitution der Universität*, ed. by Heinz-Elmar Tenorth (Berlin, 2010)

———, 'Geschichte der Universität zu Berlin, 1810–2010: Zur Einleitung', in *Geschichte der Universität Unter den Linden: Gründung und Blütezeit der Universität zu Berlin 1810–1918*, ed. by Heinz-Elmar Tenorth (Berlin, 2012)

———, 'Verfassung und Ordnung der Universität', in *Geschichte der Universität Unter den Linden: Gründung und Blütezeit der Universität zu Berlin 1810–1918*, ed. by Heinz-Elmar Tenorth (Berlin, 2012)

———, 'Wilhelm von Humboldts (1776–1835) Universitätskonzept und die Reform in Berlin – eine Tradition jenseits des Mythos', *Zeitschrift für Germanistik*, N.F. 20:1 (2010)

———, 'Wilhelm von Humboldt, ein Philosoph als Bildungspolitiker: Zuschreibungen, historische Praxis, fortdauernde Herausforderung', *Zeitschrift für Religions- und Geistesgeschichte*, 69:2 (2017)

———, ed., *Geschichte der Universität Unter den Linden: Genese der Disziplinen: Die Konstitution der Universität* (Berlin, 2010)

———, ed., *Geschichte der Universität Unter den Linden: Gründung und Blütezeit der Universität zu Berlin 1810–1918* (Berlin, 2012)

———, ed., *Geschichte der Universität Unter den Linden: Selbstbehauptung einer Vision* (Berlin, 2010)

———, ed., *Geschichte der Universität Unter den Linden: Transformation der Wissensordnung* (Berlin, 2010)

Tenorth, Heinz-Elmar & Michael Grüttner, eds, *Geschichte der Universität Unter den Linden: Die Berliner Universität zwischen den Weltkriegen 1918–1945* (Berlin, 2012)

Tent, James F., *Mission on the Rhine: Reeducation and Denazification in American-occupied Germany* (Chicago, 1982)

Teß, Werner, 'Professoren – Der Lehrkörper und seine Praxis zwischen Wissenschaft, Politik und Gesellschaft', in *Geschichte der Universität*

Unter den Linden: Gründung und Blütezeit der Universität zu Berlin 1810–1918, ed. by Heinz-Elmar Tenorth (Berlin, 2012)
Thue, Fredrik W. & Kim G. Helsvig, *Universitetet i Oslo 1945–1975: Den store transformasjonen* (Oslo, 2011)
Titze, Hartmut, 'Hochschulen', in *Handbuch der deutschen Bildungsgeschichte: 1918–1945: Die Weimarer Republik und die nationalsozialistische Diktatur*, ed. by Dieter Langewiesche & Heinz-Elmar Tenorth (Munich, 1989)
Todorov, Tzvetan, 'Literary Genres', in *The Fantastic: A Structural Approach to a Literary Genre*, trans. by Richard Howard (Ithaca, NY, 1975)
Trawny, Peter, *Heidegger und der Mythos der jüdischen Weltverschwörung* (Frankfurt am Main, 2015)
Truscot, Bruce, *Red Brick University* (Harmondsworth, 1951)
Tully, James, ed., *Meaning and Context: Quentin Skinner and His Critics* (Cambridge, 1988)
Turner, George, *Universitäten in der Konkurrenz: Möglichkeiten und Grenzen von Wettbewerb im Hochschulbereich* (Stuttgart, 1986)
——, *Von der Universität zur university: Sackgassen und Umwege der Hochschulpolitik seit 1945* (Berlin, 2013)
Turner, James, *Philology: The Forgotten Origins of the Modern Humanities* (Princeton, 2014)
Turner, Roy Steven, 'Humboldt in North America? Reflections on the Research University and Its Historians', in *Humboldt international: Der Export des deutschen Universitätsmodells im 19. und 20. Jahrhundert*, ed. by Rainer Christoph Schwinges (Basel, 2001)
——, 'The Prussian Universities and the Research Imperative, 1806–1848' (unpublished doctoral dissertation, Princeton University, 1972)
——, 'University Reforms and Professorial Scholarship in Germany 1760–1806', in *The University in Society: Europe, Scotland, and the United States from the 16th to the 20th Century*, ed. by Lawrence Stone (Princeton, 1974)
'University', *Wikipedia*, https://en.wikipedia.org/wiki/University (accessed 15 February 2016)
'Universität', *Brockhaus*, vol. 28 (Leipzig and Mannheim, 2006)
Vierhaus, Rudolf, 'Bildung', in *Geschichtliche Grundbegriffe: Historisches Lexikon zur politisch-sozialen Sprache in Deutschland*, ed. by Otto Brunner, Werner Conze, & Reinhart Koselleck, 8 vols (Stuttgart, 1972–1997), vol. I (1972)
——, 'Die Brüder Humboldt', in *Deutsche Erinnerungsorte*, ed. by Etienne François & Hagen Schulze (Munich, 2001–), vol. III (2001)
Vollhardt, Friedrich, ed., *Hölderlin in der Moderne: Kolloquium für Dieter Henrich zum 85. Geburtstag* (Berlin, 2014)
Vossler, Karl, *Forschung und Bildung an der Universität* (Munich, 1946)
Völker, Daniela, *Das Buch für die Massen: Taschenbücher und ihre Verlage* (Marburg, 2014)

Wæhrens, Anne, *Erindringspolitik til forhandling: EU og erindringen om Holocaust, 1989–2009* (Copenhagen, 2013)

Weber, Max, *Wissenschaft als Beruf* (Munich and Leipzig, 1919)

Wehler, Hans-Ulrich, *Deutsche Gesellschaftsgeschichte: Vom Feudalismus des Alten Reiches bis zur Defensiven Modernisierung der Reformära 1700–1815* (Munich, 1987)

Wehrs, Nikolai, 'Auf der Suche nach einem "Pronunciamento": Helmut Schelsky im Hegemonialkampf der "Reflexionseliten" in den 1970er Jahren', in *Helmut Schelsky – der politische Anti-Soziologe: Eine Neurezeption*, ed. by Alexander Gallus (Göttingen, 2013)

——, *Protest der Professoren: Der 'Bund Freiheit der Wissenschaft' in den 1970er Jahren* (Göttingen, 2014)

Weibull, Jörgen, *Lunds universitets historia: Utgiven av universitetet till dess 300-årsjubileum: 4. 1868–1968* (Lund, 1968)

Weinberger, Ota & Werner Krawietz, eds, *Helmut Schelsky als Soziologe und politischer Denker: Grazer Gedächtnisschrift zum Andenken an den am 24. Februar 1984 verstorbenen Gelehrten* (Stuttgart, 1985)

Weingart, Peter, 'Humboldt im Ranking', in *Bildung? Bildung! 26 Thesen zur Bildung als Herausforderung im 21. Jahrhundert*, ed. by Andreas Schlüter & Peter Strohschneider (Berlin, 2009)

Weinrich, Max, *Hitler's Professors: The Part of Scholarship in Germany's Crimes against the Jewish People* (New York, 1946)

Weisbrod, Bernd, 'Dem wandelbaren Geist: Akademisches Ideal und wissenschaftliche Transformation in der Nachkriegszeit', in *Akademische Vergangenheitspolitik: Beiträge zur Wissenschaftskultur der Nachkriegszeit*, ed. by Bernd Weisbrod (Göttingen, 2002)

——, ed., *Akademische Vergangenheitspolitik: Beiträge zur Wissenschaftskultur der Nachkriegszeit* (Göttingen, 2002)

Weischedel, Wilhelm, ed., *Idee und Wirklichkeit einer Universität: Dokumente zur Geschichte der Friedrich-Wilhelms-Universität zu Berlin* (Berlin, 1960)

Wellmon, Chad, *Organizing Enlightenment: Information Overload and the Invention of the Modern Research University* (Baltimore, 2015)

Wende, Erich, *C. H. Becker: Mensch und Politiker: Ein biographischer Beitrag zur Kulturgeschichte der Weimarer Republik* (Stuttgart, 1959)

Werner, Anja, *The Transatlantic World of Higher Education: Americans at German Universities, 1776–1914* (Oxford, 2013)

Wiener, Martin J., *English Culture and the Decline of the Industrial Spirit, 1850–1980* (Cambridge, 1981)

'Wilhelm von Humboldt', corpus 'German', https://books.google.com/ngrams (accessed 15 February 2016)

Wilke, Jürgen, ed., *Mediengeschichte der Bundesrepublik Deutschland* (Cologne, 1999)

Wimmer, Andreas & Nina Glick Schiller, 'Methodological Nationalism and Beyond: Nation-State Building, Migration and the Social Sciences', *Global Networks*, 4:2 (2002)

Wittrock, Björn, 'The Modern University: The Three Transformations', in *The European and American University since 1800: Historical and Sociological Essays*, ed. by Sheldon Rothblatt & Björn Wittrock (Cambridge, 1993)

Wobbe, Theresa, 'Für eine Historische Semantik des 19. und 20. Jahrhunderts: Kommentar zu Christian Geulen', *Zeithistorische Forschungen/Studies in Contemporary History*, 7:1 (2010)

Wolbring, Barbara, *Trümmerfeld der bürgerlichen Welt: Universität in den gesellschaftlichen Reformdiskursen der westlichen Besatzungszonen (1945–1949)* (Göttingen, 2014)

Wolfrum, Edgar, *Die geglückte Demokratie: Geschichte der Bundesrepublik Deutschland von ihren Anfängen bis zur Gegenwart* (Stuttgart, 2006)

Wright, Susan, 'Humboldt, Humbug! Contemporary Mobilisations of "Humboldt" as a Discourse to Support the Corporatisation and Marketisation of Universities and Disparage Alternatives', in *The Humboldtian Tradition: Origins and Legacies*, ed. by Peter Josephson, Thomas Karlsohn & Johan Östling (Leiden and Boston, 2014)

Wöhrle, Patrick, *Zur Aktualität von Helmut Schelsky: Einleitung in sein Werk* (Wiesbaden, 2015)

Zakaria, Fareed, *In Defense of A Liberal Education* (New York, 2015)

Zauner, Stefan, *Erziehung und Kulturmission: Frankreichs Bildungspolitik in Deutschland 1945–1949* (Munich, 1994)

Ziolkowski, Theodore, *German Romanticism and Its Institutions* (Princeton, 1990)

Östling, Johan, 'Bolognaprocessen ett ramverk att fylla', *Svenska Dagbladet*, 16 May 2007

——, 'Bortom konventionens gränser: Universitetshistoria som idé- och kunskapshistoria', in *Universitetets gränser*, ed. by Peter Josephson & Thomas Karlsohn (Göteborg, forthcoming)

——, 'The Humboldtian Tradition: The German University Transformed, 1800–1945', in *University Jubilees and University History at the Beginning of the 21st Century*, ed. by Pieter Dhondt (Leiden and Boston, 2015)

——, 'Humboldts idé: Bildning och universitet i det moderna Tyskland', in *Humaniora i kunskapssamhället: En nordisk debattbok*, ed. by Jesper Eckhart Larsen & Martin Wiklund (Malmö, 2012)

——, 'The Regeneration of the University: Karl Jaspers and the Humboldtian Tradition in the Wake of the Second World War', in *The Humboldtian Tradition: Origins and Legacies*, ed. by Peter Josephson, Thomas Karlsohn & Johan Östling (Leiden and Boston, 2014)

——, 'Rezension zu: Wolbring, Barbara: *Trümmerfeld der bürgerlichen Welt. Universität in den gesellschaftlichen Reformdiskursen der westlichen Besatzungszonen (1945–1949)*', in *H-Soz-Kult*, http://www.hsozkult.de/publicationreview/id/rezbuecher-21761 (11 March 2014) (accessed 15 February 2016)

——, 'Richard Münch: Marknadsekonomin har koloniserat universitetet', *Respons*, no. 1 (2012)

——, 'The Swansong of the Mandarins: Humboldt's Idea of the University in Early Post-War Germany', *Modern Intellectual History*, 13:2 (2016)
——, 'Tyska historiker i Tredje riket: Historiografi som självprövning', *Historielärarnas förenings årsskrift* (2010)
——, 'Tysklands väg mot moderniteten: Hans-Ulrich Wehler och *Sonderwegtesen*', in *I historiens skruvstäd: Berättelser om Europas 1900-tal*, ed. by Lennart Berntson & Svante Nordin (Stockholm, 2008)
——, 'Universiteten hämmas av krav på effektivitet', *Svenska Dagbladet*, 17 October 2011
——, 'Universitetets historia: Humboldttraditionen som akademiskt historiemedvetande', in *Historiens hemvist*, ed. by Hans Ruin, 3 vols (Göteborg, 2016), vol. 2: *Etik, politik och historikerns ansvar*, ed. by Patricia Lorenzoni & Ulla Manns
——, 'Universitetets moderna tid', in *Tiden: Symposier på Krapperups borg nr 10*, ed. by Kim Salomon (Göteborg, 2017)
——, 'Universitetshistoria: Friska vindar över gammalt fält', *Respons*, 2015, no. 2
——, 'Vad är ett universitet? Svar på en mycket tysk fråga', in *Tänka vidare: Forskning, finansiering, framtid: RJ:s årsbok 2015/2016*, ed. by Jenny Björkman & Björn Fjæstad (Göteborg, 2015)
——, 'Vad är kunskapshistoria?', *Historisk tidskrift*, 135:1 (2015)
——, 'What Is a University? Answers to a very German question', in *Thinking Ahead: Research, Funding and the Future: RJ Yearbook 2015/2016*, ed. by Jenny Björkman & Björn Fjæstad (Göteborg, 2015).

Index

Note: A page number in italics refers to an illustration. An 'n.' after a page reference indicates the number of a note on that page. Scholarly works can be found under the authors' names.

Aarhus (university) 65n.37
Abendland ('Occident') rhetoric 94, 121, 123
Åbo Akademi University 65n.37
academic freedom xiii, 9, 24, 29, 41–43, 47, 61–62, 79, 81, 83, 93, 98, 104, 109–10, 113, 116, 117, 122, 125, 131, 135, 144, 155, 167, 179, 189, 195, 222, 224, 227n.35, 234
see also Lehrfreiheit; Lernfreiheit
Adorno, Theodor W. 17n.36, 84–85, 181n.98, 200, 218, 241
'Theorie der Halbbildung' (1959) 17n.36, 218
Althoff, Friedrich 50–51, 71
Americanisation 135, 146, 202–03
see also United States
Anderson, Robert D. 134
Anrich, Ernst 196
anti-experimentalism 173–74
Armitage, David 14–15, 62, 88, 239, 245
Aron, Raymond 171
Asche, Matthias 3
Ash, Mitchell G. 11, 45, 91, 92n.17, 222–23, 230, 237–38
Assmann, Aleida 241–42
Athens (university) 31n.19, 226
Auerstedt 27
Auschwitz trials 200

Baeumler, Alfred 63, 64n.35
Bartz, Olaf 13, 146–47
Bauer, Karl Heinrich 103

Becker, Carl Heinrich 17, 66, 70–71, 72, 81, 82, 105, 117, 130, 157–59, 189, 192, 196, 211
Gedanken zur Hochschulreform (1919) 70–71
Vom Wesen der deutschen Universität (1925) 70
Becker, Hellmut 145, 175
Belgium, Humboldt's impact in 225
Berlin (university) xii–xiii, xivn.3, 9–10, 11, 22, 24, 27–31, 35, 43–47, 51, 58–60, 62, 64, 65n.37, 75, 76, 86, 93, 109, 117, 122, 136, 151, 152–57, 162, 164–65, 172, 176, 185–89, 191–93, 193, 195, 208, 219, 226–28, 240, 243
see also Freie Universität (Berlin)
Bielefeld (university) 167–68
see also Helmut Schelsky; 'theoretical university'
Bildung xiii, 20, 29–31, 36–41, 53, 55, 59, 61, 64, 65n.37, 69–72, 81, 82, 84, 94, 95–97, 106, 108, 115, 119–20, 122, 126, 129–31, 133, 136, 138–39, 143n.4, 144, 151–52, 154, 156–62, 164–66, 171, 175–79, 181–82, 185–92, 198, 205–06, 208–09, 215, 218, 219–20, 223–24, 227, 231–32, 234, 245, 247
see also Humanität; New Humanism; world citizenship

Bildung durch Wissenschaft 154, 165, 176, 179, 234
Bildungsbürgertum 36, 231–32
'Blaues Gutachten' 89, 132–33
Boeckh, August 35
Böll, Heinrich 199
Bollenbeck, Georg 231–32
Bologna (university) *xviii*
Bologna process 17n.36, 22, 206, 212–44 *passim*
Bonn (university) 29, 46, 70, 90, 118, 226
Brandi, Karl 92n.17
Brandser, Gry Cathrin 49n.54, 229
Brandt, Reinhard 219
Breslau (university) 29, 85
Broberg, Gunnar 2n.3
'the brown university' 73n.53
vom Bruch, Rüdiger 11, 28n.12, 45, 57, 83
Brussels (university) 31, 226
Bund Freiheit der Wissenschaft 168

California Master Plan for Higher Education 203
Cambridge School 6
Christiania (university) see Oslo (university)
Clark, William 24–25, 240n.53
Coing, Helmut 85, 143
collège 25–26
 see also French university system
Collège de France 25
Collini, Stefan 245
Cologne (university) 65, 86, 130
Colomb, Marie-Elisabeth 31
commercialisation of knowledge 205, 212, 216, 218
Communism 4, 85, 93, 156, 179, 195, 202
 see also Marxism; SDS; Socialism; West Germany vs GDR
concepts of knowledge 8, 16, 20, 79, 148, 233
Confessing Church 111
Cornelißen, Christoph 117
crisis awareness 68, 94, 137, 141, 145, 208, 212, 234–35
CUDOS principles 249n.71
culture of history 238, 243, 244n.63
Curtius, Ernst Robert 98

von Dacheröden, Karoline 32
Dahrendorf, Ralf 149, 170–79, 198, 200, 205
Bildung ist Bürgerrecht (1965) 170–71, 174–78
Gesellschaft und Demokratie in Deutschland (1965) 170–74, 178–79
 see also forty-fivers (generation)
Deiters, Heinrich 194
democratisation 68–69, 87, 89, 105, 121–41 *passim*, 167, 181, 184, 201
 see also denazification; *Vergangenheitsbewältigung*
denazification 87, 90–91, 111
 see also democratisation; *Vergangenheitsbewältigung*
Derrida, Jacques 243
Deutsche Forschungsgemeinschaft 67, 213
Deutsche Physik 72
Dhondt, Pieter 225
Dilthey, Wilhelm 173
Dräger, Jörg 220
Droysen, Johann Gustav 46n.47

Eckel, Jan 74, 92n.17
Edding, Friedrich 175
Eichmann trial 199
Eigen, Manfred 208
Einheit der Wissenschaften 20, 165, 183
Einheit von Forschung und Lehre 20, 160, 164, 172, 176, 178, 182, 191, 192, 233
Einsamkeit und Freiheit 114, 154–57, 160, 165, 169, 173, 179, 182, 185, 191, 192, 233
Einstein, Albert xii
Eliade, Mircea 151
Elias, Norbert 230
Elkana, Yehuda 220
Erhard, Ludwig 141
Erlangen (university) 91
Eriksson, Gunnar 228n.36
Etzemüller, Thomas 92
European Research Council (ERC) 212
 see also Bologna process; internationalisation of universities

Index

European Union 211
Exzellenzinitiative 213–15

Fichte, Johann Gottlieb 16, 26, 29, 30, 32, 35, 45, 47, 58, 70, 78n.63, 80, 106, 112, 119, 131, 148, 153, 162, 164, 185, 190
Finland 204–5n.155
Flenner, Helmut 62
Flexner, Abraham 49n.54, 228
Universities (1930) 49n.54
Forschungsgemeinschaft deutsches Ahnenerbe 74
forty-fivers (generation) 197–98
see also Ralf Dahrendorf; Jürgen Habermas
Foucault, Michel 16, 239
Fraenkel, Ernst 132n.130
France, Humboldt's impact in 48
Frankfurt am Main (university) 50, 76, 86
Frankfurt an der Oder (university) 31
Frankfurt School 180–81, 191
Frankfurter Allgemeine Zeitung 195, 215n.17
Frauenhofer-Gesellschaft 91
Frederick William III, King of Prussia 31, 34
Freie Universität (Berlin) 93, 180, 193, 195
see also Berlin (university)
French Revolution 25, 35, 194
French university system 25, 28, 47, 226
see also collège
Freiburg im Breisgau (university) 77, 111
Freyer, Hans 148, 162
von Friedeburg, Ludwig 181n.99, 198n.143
Friedrich Wilhelm III *see* Frederick William III
Friedrich-Wilhelms-Universität zu Berlin *see* Berlin (university)
Führerprinzip 74
see also Gleichschaltung; Nazi university policy
Fulbright Program 204

Gadamer, Hans-Georg 92, 151, 208–10, 225

Gebhardt, Bruno 36n.25, 40n.33, 55–56, 60
Wilhelm von Humboldt als Staatsmann (1896–1899) 55
Gehlen, Arnold 148, 154, 162
Geistesgeschichte 4, 5n.8
Geisteswissenschaft 53, 58, 67, 127
Georg-August-Universität *see* Göttingen (university)
Gerber, Stefan 3
Gerhardt, Uta *see* SDS
Gleichschaltung 98
see also Führerprinzip; Nazi university policy
Glotz, Peter 211
Godesberg programme 180
von Goethe, Johann Wolfgang 29, 33, 37, 64, 103, 123, 136
Gordon, Peter E. 5–7, 245
Gothenburg (university) 65n.37
Göttingen (university) 11, 26, 28, 31, 34, 46, 59, 86, 92n.17, 152, 226, 227n.33
Grau, Wilhelm 63
Great Britain xvi, 89, 135, 143, 175, 184, 185, 204
Humboldt's impact in 48
Greifswald (university) 85, 117, 193, 243
Großforschung 56
Gugerli, David 7
Gundolf, Friedrich 105n.57
Gustavsson, Sverker 229n.39

Haber, Fritz 67
Habermas, Jürgen 171, 181, 184, 191, 198, 208–10, 225, 239
'Die Idee der Universität' (1988) 208–10
Protestbewegung und Hochschulreform (1969) 198
see also forty-fivers (generation)
Halle (university) 12, 26, 28, 46, 59, 85, 152, 226, 227n.33
Hamburg (university) 65n.37, 70, 76–77
Hamm-Brücher, Hildegard 175
von Hardenberg, Karl August 27
von Harnack, Adolf 11, 40n.33, 53, 56–57, 59–62, 67, 82
Hartog, François 240–42
Haß, Ulrike 216
von Hayek, Friedrich August 171

Heer, Friedrich 90n.13
Hegel, Georg Wilhelm Friedrich 35, 106, 173
Heidegger, Martin 77–79, 81, 82, 125n.117
Heidelberg (university) 70, 76, 88, 90, 99, 103, 105n.57, 111, 208
Heimpel, Hermann 196
Heisenberg, Werner xii
Hennis, Wilhelm 198n.43
von Herder, Johann Gottfried 32, 37–38
Herkendell, Hans-Jörg 63
Herzog, Roman 210
Hillgruber, Andreas 198n.43
historical consciousness 238–39
history in ideas 15
history of ideas 5–6, 14
history of knowledge 7–8, 14, 15–18
history of science 4, 228n.36
Hobbes, Thomas 148, 162
Hobsbawm, Eric J. 239
Hochschule in der Demokratie (1961; 1965) see SDS
Hochschulrahmengesetz 211
Hoffmann, Werner 198n.43
Hohe Schule der NSDAP 74
Hohendahl, Peter Uwe 137
Holborn, Hajo 132n.130
Hölderlin, Friedrich 29, 64, 85
Holocaust 244n.63
Hong Kong University of Science and Technology *xviii*
Hörisch, Jochen 217–18
  Die ungeliebte Universität (2006) 217–18
Horkheimer, Max 181n.99, 200, 241
Hörnig, Johannes (Hannes) 201–02
Howald, Ernst 63
Hufeland, Christoph Wilhelm 35
human rights 117, 121, 246
Humanität 37, 161
  see also *Bildung*; humanism; New Humanism
humanism 69–70, 101, 106, 121, 131, 133
  see also *Bildung*; *Humanität*; New Humanism
von Humboldt, Alexander xivn.3, 31, 34n.21, 35, 64, 93, 226n.32, 235
von Humboldt, Alexander Georg 31

von Humboldt, Wilhelm *passim*
  'Der Königsberger und der Litauische Schulplan' (1809) 39, 155n.34
  'Ideen zu einem Versuch, die Grenzen der Wirksamkeit des Staates zu bestimmen' (1792) 42, 113
  'Über die innere und äussere Organisation der höheren wissenschaftlichen Anstalten in Berlin' (1809/1810) 39–41, 55–57, 108
Humboldt myth 45, 224, 237
Humboldt-Universität zu Berlin see Berlin (university)
Humboldt University see Berlin (university)
Husén, Torsten 228
Husserl, Edmund 78n.63

Imboden, Dieter 213
im Kern gesund 71n.48, 105, 127, 132, 182, 191, 196, 219
imago Dei 37
infotainment 218
Ingolstadt (university) see Munich (university)
institutes of technology 53
  see also vocational education
Institut für Bildungsforschung 145
Institut für Sozialforschung see Frankfurt School
intellectual history 5–8, 13–15
internationalisation of universities 27, 204, 210–11, 230
  see also Bologna process; European Research Council (ERC)
Italy 134

Jaeger, Werner 69
Jalava, Marja 204–5n.155
Jarausch, Konrad H. 52, 96, 136–37
Jaspers, Karl 71–72, 82, 98–110, 100, 116, 118, 123–27, 133, 137, 138, 181, 197, 205, 208, 241
  'Die Erneuerung der Universität' (1945/1946) 103–05, 123
  Die Idee der Universität (1923) 71–72
  Die Idee der Universität (1946) 102–03, 108–10, 124

Index

Die Idee der Universität (1961; with Kurt Rossmann) 196–97
Jena (university) 28, 29, 85, 164, 193, 243
Jessen, Ralph 96
Joas, Hans 246–47
Johns Hopkins University 48, 49n.54
Jordheim, Helge 242
'jubilee syndrome' 2, 243
Jugendbewegung 148

Kaehler, Siegfried A. 62
Kaiser-Wilhelm-Gesellschaft 56–57, 91
Kant, Immanuel 16, 26, 29, 38, 47, 72, 103, 106, 109, 246
Der Streit der Fakultäten (1798) 26
Kawohl, Irmgard 59
Kennedy, John F. 201
Kerr, Clark 49n.54, 177, 203
The Uses of the University (1963) 203–04
Kiev (university) 31n.19
Killy, Walther 144
Klöpper, Hannes 220
Kluge, Alexander 184
knowledge actors 17–19, 148, 199, 232
Koch, Robert xii
König, René 79–82, 153
Königsberg (university) 85, 148
Konstanz (university) 170, 210
Koselleck, Reinhart 20, 200n.147, 239, 242
Kraus, Hans Ch. 28n.12
Krieck, Ernst 76–77, 79, 81
Krieger, Leonard 132n.130
Kulturträger 18

Landshut (university) *see* Munich (university)
Langewiesche, Dieter 45, 62, 96, 224
Langholm, Sivert 2
left-wing radicalism *see* SDS
Lehrfreiheit xiii, 9, 20, 42, 154, 234
see also academic freedom; *Lernfreiheit*
Leipzig (university) 28, 85, 92, 148, 193, 243
Leipzig School 148

Lenz, Max 27n.11, 59, 164n.62
Geschichte der Königlichen Friedrich-Wilhelms-Universität zu Berlin (1910–1918) 27n.11, 59
Lepenies, Wolf 208, 230–31
Lernfreiheit xiii, 9, 20, 42, 154, 159, 162, 178, 179, 187, 234
see also academic freedom; *Lehrfreiheit*
Leroux, Robert 63
Levine, Emily J. 65n.37
liberal arts 248
liberalism 46, 58, 63, 171
Liedman, Sven-Eric 54–55, 229n.39
Liessmann, Konrad Paul 17n.36, 218
Lilge, Frederic 131–32
The Abuse of Learning (1948) 131
Lisbon Strategy 211
London (university) 31n.19
London School of Economics 170
Lovejoy, Arthur O. 6, 14
Löwith, Karl 151, 241
Lübbe, Hermann 198n.143
Lübke, Heinrich 141
Ludwig-Maximilians-Universität *see* Munich (university)
Luhmann, Niklas 209
Lundgreen, Peter 15
Lyotard, Jean-François 243

McClelland, Charles E. 44–45, 60
Macmillan, Harold 204
Madrid (university) 31n.19
Mainz (university) 87, 213
Manchester (university) 31n.19
mandarins 18, 53–55, 60, 67–69, 75–76, 82, 88, 97–98, 123–27, 136–38, 199, 201, 225, 232, 237, 238
Mann, Thomas 84, 122, 171
Mannheim, Karl 68, 155
Marburg (university) 86, 118
'Marburger Hochschulgespräche' 89
Marcuse, Herbert 184, 191
Markschies, Christoph 108, 219
Was von Humboldt noch zu lernen ist (2010) 219
Marquard, Odo 198n.143
Marx, Karl xii, 170

Marxism 32, 179
  see also Communism; SDS;
  Socialism; Social Democracy
mass university 69, 106, 115, 138,
  147, 189, 221, 230, 240, 247
Max-Planck-Gesellschaft 91
media forms of knowledge 16–17, 235
Meinecke, Friedrich 68, 138, 171,
  241
  Die deutsche Katastrophe (1946)
  138
Meifort, Franziska 171n.72
von Melle, Werner 65n.37
Merton, Robert K. 249n.71
Michels, Robert 61
Mikat, Paul 167
Mill, John Stuart 42n.39
Mitscherlich, Alexander 151
Mittelstraß, Jürgen 210, 225
Moberly, Walter 134–35
  The Crisis of the University
  (1949) 134–35
modernisation 175, 205, 231
modernity 94, 171, 230, 240,
  242–44
Mommsen, Theodor xii
Moraw, Peter 83
Moses, A. Dirk 197, 198n.143
Mößbauer, Rudolf 143
Mosse, George L. 132n.130
Moyn, Samuel 117
Müller, Johannes 35
Müller-Eiselt, Ralph 220
Müller-Schöll, Nikolaus 216
multiversity 177, 203
Münch, Richard 215n.18
Munich (university) 46, 91, 118,
  129, 142, 226
Münster (university) 50, 149, 150, 168
Mythos Humboldt see Humboldt
  myth

Napoleon I, Emperor of the French
  25, 28, 43, 113, 185, 240
Napoleonic Wars 25, 27, 47, 68, 85,
  226
national cause 53, 58, 74, 77, 81,
  90, 103, 231
National Socialism 18, 54, 63, 64,
  67, 68, 72–83, 75, 84–87, 90,
  91, 93, 94, 97–101, 103–05,
  107–08, 110–11, 113,
  115–16, 118, 123–25,
  129–32, 137–38, 140, 148,
  155, 156, 168, 180,
  196n.139, 197–98, 199, 200,
  236, 239
Naturwissenschaft (natural science)
  40n.34, 52–53, 56, 67
Nazi Germany *see* National
  Socialism
Nazi university policy 72–80
  see also Führerprinzip;
  Gleichschaltung; National
  Socialism
Nazism *see* National Socialism
Neue Zürcher Zeitung 215n.17
Neumann, Eduard 195
Neumann, Franz 132n.130
New Humanism 10, 36, 46, 47, 58,
  60, 61, 64, 68, 69, 70, 72,
  77, 82, 96, 102, 126, 133,
  155, 161, 165, 166, 186,
  187, 188, 191, 196n.139,
  231, 239
  see also Bildung; humanism;
  Humanität
New Public Management (NPM) 211
Newman, John Henry 29n.15,
  248n.70
Nida-Rümelin, Julian 219
Nietzsche, Friedrich 61, 72, 106,
  246
Nitsch, Wolfgang *see* SDS
Nobel Prize xii, 143, 201, 207
Norway 135, 226
  Humboldt's impact in 225
Novalis (Georg Philipp Friedrich von
  Hardenberg) 29
Nybom, Thorsten 29n.15, 229n.39

OECD (Organisation for Economic
  Co-operation and
  Development) 205, 211, 222
Oehler, Christoph 181n.99
von Oertzen, Peter 198n.143
Offe, Claus *see* SDS
Oppenheimer, J. Robert 151
Ostforschung 74
Oxbridge model 204
Oxford (university) 29n.15, *128*

paideia 37
Paletschek, Sylvia 4, 11, 45, 56, 60,
  68–69, 82, 95, 147, 164n.62,
  224, 237

Index

Paulsen, Friedrich 59
Paulus, Stefan 146, 203
Peers, Edgar Allison 134n.135
Pestalozzi, Johann Heinrich 38
Peters, Hans 129–31
Philipps, Denise 40n.34
Picht, Georg 144–45, 175
   Die deutsche Bildungskatastrophe (1964) 144–45, 175
PISA (Programme for International Student Assessment) 212
Planck, Max xii
Plessner, Helmuth 171
Popper, Karl 171
Preuß, Ulrich K. *see* SDS

von Ranke, Leopold 35
von Rantzau, Johann-Albrecht 63
regime of historicity 240–42
Reichsinstitut für Geschichte des neuen Deutschlands 74
Rein, Adolf 76–77
Reiser, Marius 213
research imperative 44, 60, 167, 240
Richter, Werner 98, 117–27, 129, 131–32, 135, 138
   Re-Educating Germany (1945) 121
   Die Zukunft der deutschen Universität (1948) 118–21
Ringer, Fritz K. 18, 53–54, 67, 230
   The Decline of the German Mandarins (1969) 18, 53–55, 67–68
Ritter, Carl 35
Ritter, Joachim 161
Ritter, Gerhard 98, 110–17, 123–27
   Die Idee der Universität und das öffentliche Leben (1946) 111–17
Robbins, Lionel 204
   The Robbins Report (1963) 204
Rohstock, Anne 13, 141, 143, 146, 205
'the romantic university' 29
Rosenberg, Alfred 74
Rosenberg, Hans 132n.130, 184
Rossmann, Kurt 196
Rothblatt, Sheldon 3
Rüegg, Walter 11, 45, 133
Rupke, Nicolaas A. 34n.21

Saarbrücken (university) 87
Sarasin, Philipp 7–8

von Savigny, Friedrich Carl 35
Schaffstein, Friedrich 63
Schalenberg, Marc 45, 48
Scheler, Max 17, 69, 72, 81–82, 159–60, 189, 192
   Die Wissensformen und die Gesellschaft (1926) 69
von Schelling, Friedrich 16, 29, 30, 119, 153, 164–65, 185
Schelsky, Helmut 17, 30, 148–70, 163, 172, 178–79, 185–86, 189–92, 197, 200, 203–06, 221, 225, 237
   Einsamkeit und Freiheit (1960) 150, 161
   Einsamkeit und Freiheit (1963) 150–67, 169, 179, 185, 192, 197, 203, 205, 221
   Einsamkeit und Freiheit (1971) 168
   see also Bielefeld (university); 'theoretical university'
Schildt, Axel 94, 127
von Schiller, Friedrich 16, 29, 32, 38, 144, 153, 164
Schlegel, August Wilhelm 29, 32
Schlegel, Caroline 29
Schleiermacher, Friedrich 16, 26, 29–31, 35, 45, 47, 58, 106, 110, 112, 119, 153, 185–86, 190, 192, 219
   Gelegentliche Gedanken über Universitäten in deutschem Sinn (1808) 30–31
Schmid, Carlo 123, 141
Schmidt, Helmut 179
Schmoll, Heike 215n.17
school (as opposed to university) 40, 158
Schröder, Kurt 194
Schultz, Werner 63
Schwartz, Christina 96, 127, 129
SDS (Sozialistische Deutsche Studentenbund) 179–92
   see also Marxism; Socialism; Social Democracy
secularisation 121
Segerstedt, Torgny T. 227n.35, 227–28
serial contextualism 14–15
Skinner, Quentin 6, 15, 245
Snow, C. P. 67

Social Democracy 141, 149, 168, 179, 180, 205, 211, 219
see also Marxism; SDS; Socialism
social history 4
Socialism 181, 190, 192–94, 200, 202, 205
see also Communism; Marxism; SDS; Social Democracy
sociology 133, 150, 215n.18
Sonderweg thesis 132n.130, 171, 200, 230
SPD (Sozialdemokratische Partei Deutschlands) 179
Speich Chassé, Daniel 7
Der Spiegel 215n.17
Spiegel affair 200
Spiewak, Martin 220
Spranger, Eduard 11, 38n.29, 56–60, 62, 64, 69, 70n.46, 76, 80–82, 85, 164n.62, 225
Wilhelm von Humboldt und die Humanitätsidee (1909) 57
Sputnik effect 141
Steffens, Heinrich 30, 45, 58
Stein, Erwin 130–31
vom und zum Stein, Karl 27
Stern, Fritz 132n.130
Sternberger, Dolf 87, 101
Strasbourg (university) 50
Strömholm, Stig 229n.39
Stroux, Johannes 92–93
studium generale 133
Süddeutsche Zeitung 215n.17
Sweden, Humboldt's impact in 225–28
Switzerland, Humboldt's impact in 225

Tellenbach, Gerd 96
Tenorth, Heinz-Elmar 16n.34, 28n.11, 44–45, 164n.62
'theoretical university' 162, 192
see also Bielefeld (university); Helmut Schelsky
Third Reich *see* National Socialism
Todorov, Tzvetan 17
Tönnies, Ferdinand 68
transtemporal history 14–15
Troeltsch, Ernst 68, 247
Truscot, Bruce [pseud. for Edgar Allison Peers] 134
Tübingen (university) 56, 86, 170

Turner, Roy Steven 44

United States 89, 98, 118, 121, 122, 124, 131, 143, 175, 202, 203
Humboldt's impact in 48–49, 229
see also Americanisation
universitas litterarum 120
Universität zu Berlin *see* Berlin (university)
University of Berlin *see* Berlin (university)
University of California 177, 203

Veit, Dorothea 29
Vergangenheitsbewältigung 4, 91
see also democratisation; denazification
Virchow, Rudolf 52
vocational education 65n.37, 69, 71, 112, 120, 130, 144, 152, 186, 190, 212, 240
see also institutes of technology
völkisch 63, 74
Vossler, Karl 124n.116, 129–30

Warburg, Aby 65n.37
Weber, Alfred 155
Weber, Max 51, 61–62, 68, 99, 234
Wehrs, Nikolai 13, 146
Weischedel, Wilhelm 194–96
Die Welt 215n.17
Weltz, Friedrich 181n.99
West Germany vs GDR 193–95, 201–02, 222
Windelband, Wilhelm 99
Wissenschaft 40, 52, 177
Wissenschaftsrat 143, 145, 146, 176, 211, 213
Wittrock, Björn 9, 43, 229n.39, 239–40
Wolbring, Barbara 13, 93, 95, 102, 138
Wolfrum, Edgar 140n.1
women in universities 69, 115, 184
world citizenship 160, 166
Wright, Susan 222

Die Zeit 144, 215n.17, 220
Zentrum für interdisziplinäre Forschung 167
Zentrum Geschichte des Wissens (Zürich) 7–8